# Americans
## and
## Their Guns

# Americans
# and

## History Advisory Committee

# Their Guns

## The National Rifle Association Story
## through nearly a century
## of service to the nation

Compiled by JAMES B. TREFETHEN

Edited by JAMES E. SERVEN

STACKPOLE BOOKS

*Published by*

STACKPOLE COMPANY
Cameron and Kelker Streets
Harrisburg, Pa. 17105

Library of Congress Catalog Card Number: 67-12925
Printed in U.S.A.

# Dedicated

To those American citizens
who came before
and won freedom,
those now here
who fight to preserve it,
and to those yet to come
who will perpetuate it.

# Contents

# Introduction

The history of the National Rifle Association reveals the response of patriotic citizens to a national need; it reflects essentially the rise, growth, and problems of the United States during the past century. Within the span of the NRA's lifetime the nation has changed from a relatively new country with sprawling frontiers to a highly urbanized and well-populated world power. Against this changing background, the gun as an instrument in shaping our destinies has had a vital role throughout, and is today as important as when our country was wrested from foreign rule years ago.

The changing needs of nearly a century have been faithfully recognized in shaping major policies of the NRA. In the realm of national defense, it has initiated or sponsored some of the basic military training programs. This may have given the impression that the NRA is a semi-military organization. That is far from the truth. Military leaders provided much of the leadership of NRA during the years after the Civil War and at many intervals since. This, however, has been primarily because they represented the most capable, informed, and dedicated Americans then available.

As the Association's mission and goals have expanded into broader fields, its leadership has broadened to include eminent judges, lawyers, doctors, members of law enforcement agencies, and many others in civilian life. A continued active participation by men in the military services and by those connected with the law merely reflects their knowledge of the national needs and their firm support of NRA objectives.

Services of the NRA in the interest of public welfare rival its activities for national defense. With our population increasing and our cities spreading out into the countryside, the need for firearms safety training in both field and home has become apparent. The NRA is the largest national organization of any description engaged in servicing this need. NRA assistance in the fields of hunting and game conservation has helped to make hunting safer and to promote the preservation of game.

One of the Association's activities which is sometimes challenged is

competitive shooting. What good does it do, critics ask, to punch holes in a piece of paper with lead bullets? Actually, much good comes from local, national, and international competition. Competitive shooting accomplishes much more than proving one man or one woman has a steadier hand, a clearer eye, and greater general skill in handling a gun than his or her competitors. It provides the training ground wherein better safety methods are learned, more efficient guns and ammunition are tested and developed. Thousands of boys, girls, men and women are taught the basic principles of good sportsmanship; they learn to handle a gun properly for wholesome recreational activities—and for protecting themselves, their dear ones, and their country should the need arise. Many of our nation's great past Presidents have praised this NRA contribution to the national welfare.

In our history books, we pay tribute to the man with the gun. He won the American Revolution and the War of 1812. He defended democracy in 1917-18. He fought the greatest global war in history in 1941-45. The American with a gun has been a great stabilizing influence in maintaining a balance of world power. Between wars, the National Rifle Association has been the primary guardian of this American rifleman tradition which becomes so vital in time of war. The NRA has stood firm in the face of unjust criticism. It has stood firm in the face of persistent misunderstanding which at times has exceeded belief. Contrary to the assertions of some, the National Rifle Association has recognized changes in American living and the desirability for corresponding changes in the use and control of firearms. It has merely sought to hold new controls to a sane and workable basis that will warrant public respect and observance.

The founding fathers of our nation realized the importance of the gun in our form of society and provided a clear-cut right to unfettered ownership of private firearms by the law-abiding. Down the years the National Rifle Association of America has shown an undeviating determination to defend this right of the American citizen—a determination tempered with reason, but rock-fast in principle. It is a principle that has been good for the nation.

# Response to a National Need

1

When considering anniversaries of events that have led to outstanding national service, November 17 is a day worthy of remembrance. On this day in 1871 a charter was granted by the State of New York. Its language was not sensational but its purpose has remained vital to this day. The charter authorized efforts "to promote rifle practice, and for this purpose to provide a suitable range or ranges in the vicinity of New York, and a suitable place for the meetings of the association in the city itself, and to promote the introduction of a system of aiming drill and target firing among the National Guard of New York and the militia of other states." The charter was granted to the National Rifle Association.

Of the several objectives stated above, the last was especially important. Defense-conscious Americans were then giving serious second thoughts to the lessons taught during the War of Independence, the War of 1812, the Mexican War, the War between the States, and more recently the Franco-Prussian War. Positive steps to improve the defense efficiency of the United States were overdue.

The initial undertakings of the newly-formed National Rifle Association will be better understood if we review briefly the background of events which had demonstrated a clear need for an organization of this nature.

Records for the century prior to 1871 provide lessons which

expose both the strength and the weaknesses of our society in that period. These records are crystal clear for those who might care to look deep enough but, as in the evaluation of many national events, the true significance of old lessons learned has a way of fading into obscurity with the mists of time. There were many hard lessons which had come from the crucible of wars.

During the War of Independence (the American Revolution) 2000 citizen-soldiers at Bunker Hill had shown to the world that they could stand up to a trained force of 2500 redcoats which included five of the crack foot regiments of the British Army, among them the famed Welsh Fusiliers, the King's own regiment. A few days earlier the members of that stalwart American force had been farmers, mechanics, shipwrights, lawyers, students and teachers, shopkeepers and blacksmiths. The example shown by these citizen-soldiers hardened the resolution throughout the colonies and converted what might have been an abortive rebellion into a full-scale war for independence.

The example shown by citizen-soldiers at Bunker Hill hardened the resolution throughout the colonies and converted what might have been an abortive revolution into a full-scale war for independence.

Not the least of the attributes of the typical American citizen of those days, from the standpoint of his potential military usefulness, was his intimate familiarity with firearms. In every household, rich or poor, country or town, a gun of some kind stood in a convenient corner or hung on pegs over the fireplace, and it was not merely an ornament; it represented both protection and food.

Threading his way through the warp and woof of history at this time was a tall man dressed in buckskin or fringed homespun and carrying a long gun. His weapon was a flintlock like all other small arms of the day, but its resemblance to the military musket or civilian fowling piece stopped right there. From the muzzle of its long barrel to its deep crescent butt plate, it bespoke of expert craftsmanship and loving care. Its lines were slender and graceful, its wood of the finest cherry, curly maple, or figured walnut that had been burnished by hand-rubbing to a warm glow. Its most radical departure from other arms, however, was less obvious to the eye. This lay in the shallow spiral grooves that its maker had cut into the bore to impart a spinning motion to the ball. The spherical ball itself varied from gun to gun, but it usually was between .40 and .50 caliber.

Both the man and his weapon had been around for some time. The man was a more restless offshoot of the same stock that produced the citizen-soldiers who met the British at Bunker Hill and who rallied to George Washington's colors all along the coastal plain in the opening days of the war. Where the citizens of the seaboard were only influenced by the frontier, the rifleman was an integral part of it. Living in scattered farms and settlements along the Appalachian Mountains from Pennsylvania to Georgia, threatened constantly by hostile Indians, he was as tough as the elements of nature could make him. While familiarity with firearms was characteristic of nearly all Americans, an intimate knowledge of weapons was an indispensable part of life on the frontier.

The rifleman became a national figure when, in July, 1775, Captain Dan Morgan arrived at Dorchester Heights with ninety-six Virginia riflemen to help bolster Washington's siege of Boston, having covered the distance in twenty-one days. To the Yankee militiamen, few of whom had ever seen a rifle, these southerners must have seemed like supermen. At sixty yards, where the well-directed smoothbore musket might or might not hit a target the size of a man's body, the rifle could put a ball within a six-inch circle. The rifleman could hit a man regularly at ranges of between 125 and 150 yards and, shooting from a rest, he might risk shots out to 300 yards with some hope of a hit. The rifleman of the American Revolution looked and acted the part of a man on whom legends would be built, and inevitably they were.

Because of the aura of romanticism that surrounds him, it is difficult to place the frontier rifleman in proper historical perspective; to over-emphasize his role would reflect on the memory of many less romantic

12

The Rogers Rangers were typical of the hardy colonial fighting men.

men who fought and died for American independence. *Freedom from Great Britain was not won by supermen using superweapons; it was won by ordinary citizens whose will to fight for liberty was backed by an intimate knowledge of firearms gained through the use of personal weapons.*

The same factors have been a bulwark in defending our liberty in every war since that time. The assorted weapons used by the men at Bunker Hill and in many other engagements of the Revolutionary War were, by contemporary military standards, often inferior to those employed by the British. What counted was that the men behind the weapons knew the capabilities and limitations of their arms and applied what they had, whether smoothbore or rifle, with maximum effect. Only men who knew firearms and knew them well could have stood their ground against the superior forces usually thrown against them.

The experiences of the Revolutionary War consolidated several traditions into American policy as soon as independence was assured. One of these was reliance for defense upon the citizen-soldier, which by then already was a tradition dating from earliest colonial times.

Just fifteen years before the Battle of Bunker Hill, a young militia colonel named George Washington, commanding Virginian citizen-soldiers, had held French bayonets and Huron scalping knives away from Gen. Edward Braddock's British regulars at the Battle of the Monongahela and had converted an almost certain massacre into an orderly retreat. In the same war, Major Robert Rogers and his Rangers from the backwoods farms and coastal settlements of New England had made an "impossible" march through the wilderness of Maine to wipe out a French strongpoint at St. Francis and to turn the flank at Quebec.

These feats of arms, which would have been a credit to any professional military unit, were accomplished by Americans who had made the abrupt transition from civilian to military life largely by sticking cockades in their hats, picking up muskets or rifles, and mustering on the village green. The opening battles of the Revolutionary War established the citizen-soldier as the mainstay of the defense system for the new nation in time of war. It has remained that way to the present. It was to assure the existence of a large force of armed citizens capable of springing to the defense of the nation on short notice that the founding fathers of the United States adopted the second amendment to the Constitution:

**A well-regulated militia being necessary for the security of a free state, the right of the people to keep and bear arms shall not be infringed.**

Between the close of the Revolutionary War and the War of 1812, only minor changes had taken place in military tactics and equipment. The way of life of the average eastern citizen in the early 1800s was little softer than that of his father's day. But some important changes had taken place in America between the two wars. After the Revolutionary War, the frontier, which had molded and shaped the citizen-soldier of 1776, had moved swiftly westward. Where in 1776 it had lain just beyond the slopes of the Appalachians, by 1812 it rested on the banks of the Mississippi.

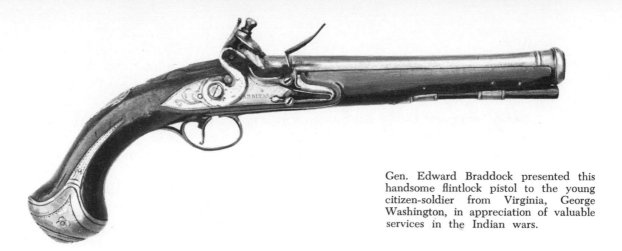

Gen. Edward Braddock presented this handsome flintlock pistol to the young citizen-soldier from Virginia, George Washington, in appreciation of valuable services in the Indian wars.

The older and larger towns had doubled and trebled in population, and new towns had sprung up where formerly there had been trackless forest. The Industrial Revolution, whose early influences were becoming apparent, was beginning to replace the self-sufficient jack-of-all-trades with classes of specialists, whose talents and training did not adapt them to military life.

Hunting and shooting remained popular sports, particularly in the rural communities, but the proportion of American citizens, especially those in the east, who knew how to handle firearms with skill was much lower than it had been in earlier times. The near-universal familiarity and association with personal weapons that had characterized the colonial citizen was being lost. Moreover, many of the European immigrants who were flocking to American shores came from countries where the possession and use of firearms by the public was actively discouraged.

The Bladensburg and other military disasters of the War of 1812 should have been the cause for a major over-

The battle for New Orleans provided a brilliant example of American courage and marksmanship. When the smoke cleared, over 2000 British soldiers lay dead; American losses were 71.

hauling of the militia training system. The apparent reasons they were not are three:

First, in none of the great professional armies of the world was there any formalized training in aimed fire; everything was based upon massed firepower delivered by squads, companies, and regiments. Under the European manual of arms, a soldier was rated as a shooter on the precision with which he could load, raise his piece, and pull the trigger on command. Whether or not, as an individual marksman, he could hit a barn door at fifty paces was considered a matter of small moment; with from ten to several hundred muskets sending a hail of lead balls in the direction of the enemy, the law of averages would assure that some would find their marks. Green part-time soldiers could never hope to match rock-firm battle discipline like that of the full-time professionals serving under Napoleon and Wellington. By trying to impose European professional standards upon inexperienced militia units commanded by friends and neighbors of little or no experience themselves, contemporary military philosophy unintentionally de-emphasized the two strong features of the American marksman—his ability to shoot accurately and his almost innate feeling for terrain.

15

Second, out of the successes of American arms during the Revolutionary War, there had grown a general complacency concerning the quality of American marksmanship. Many of the ranking officers of the War of 1812 had been junior officers or had served in the line in the Revolution. There is every indication that they failed to notice the gradual deterioration of general public knowledge of firearms. The prevailing attitude appeared to be that you might have to teach an American to march in step and to shoot by the numbers, but no one had to teach an American how to use his gun.

Third, and perhaps most important as an influence on the thinking of military leaders after the War of 1812, was the spectacular note of victory on which hostilities ended. On January 8, 1815, on the Plains of Chalmette by the banks of the Mississippi east of New Orleans, a force of nearly 10,000 British regulars commanded by Major General Sir Edward Pakenham was met by General Andrew Jackson and a motley force of about 5000, including some regulars, militiamen from Kentucky and Tennessee, backwoods riflemen, sailors, Negroes, Creole planters, and a contingent of pirates under Jean Lafitte. When the smoke of battle had cleared, more than 2000 British soldiers, including Pakenham himself, were dead; American losses totaled 71.

The battle for New Orleans, although it had been fought, unknown to the combatants of either side, two weeks after the Treaty of Ghent had ended the war, was a victory of the old style, and it was much easier for unobjective historians and patriotic orators to remember than the bitter defeats that had characterized much of the earlier War of 1812 land action. The fact that the superior individual marksmanship of Jackson's sharpshooting frontiersmen and southern planters was no longer typical of that of Americans in general went unnoticed.

As a result of all of these factors, the object lessons of the War of 1812 remained generally unrecognized and, after hostilities had ceased, the military training program reverted virtually to where it had been in 1810. Its one significant contribution to battle tactics was to consolidate the place of the rifleman in the plan of battle, although the smoothbore flintlock remained the standard infantry weapon. Long after 1815, however, the rifleman was considered to be a supplement to the troops of the line rather than an integral part of the line itself.

After the War of 1812, the militia seemed to put more emphasis on marching and drill than realistic training or maneuvers under simulated

Flintlock muskets patterned after the French 1763 model were long the standard arm of United States military forces.

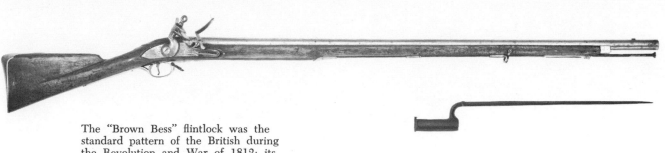

The "Brown Bess" flintlock was the
standard pattern of the British during
the Revolution and War of 1812; its
pinned forestock without bands also
served as a pattern for some flintlocks
made in the colonies.

battle conditions. Their practice almost never extended to the point of
marching into the country and maneuvering in mud and rain. If the
weather turned bad, drill in the larger cities was conducted indoors and
in the smaller towns postponed entirely. A more serious failing was that
the drill rarely extended to the point of actually discharging the well-
polished muskets, except for an infrequent ceremonial volley fired with
blank loads on occasions of special note. Some militiamen served for years
without once firing their weapons.

The United States was not openly involved in the Texas War of Independence, and the costliest conflict of the period, the Mexican War, was fought
largely by regulars and volunteers, most of whom were incorporated into
regular army units. The volunteers of 1845 to 1848 were predominantly
adventuresome youngsters who adapted readily to military life, and many,
like the Texas Rangers, came from those portions of the country where
familiarity with firearms was most common. There was little of the feverish
urgency and social pressures that would characterize the recruitment of
volunteers in the approaching Civil War, and the quality of the average
recruit in the Mexican War was relatively high. The victories of American
forces at Palo Alto, Buena Vista, Molino del Rey, Chapultepec, and
elsewhere, like the earlier victories at Fallen Timbers, Tippecanoe, and
San Jacinto, consolidated the complacency of Americans on the superiority
of their marksmen and the invincibility of their soldiers. In the meantime,
the unbloodied militia regiments of the East continued their monthly stint
at close-order drill with unfired muskets and with renewed confidence that
they represented the finest troops in the world.

This situation prevailed at a time when enormous strides were being
made in the improvement of firearms. For more than a century inventors
had struggled with the problems of producing a reliable breechloader, a
practical repeating firearm, and a system of rapid loading that would be
adaptable to rifles.

The first real breakthrough in practical firearms design since the invention of the flintlock came in 1807 when the Reverend Alexander John
Forsyth, a Scotsman, patented a new system for priming firearms by the
use of small charges of fulminate distributed to the touchhole. The fulminate, usually put up in pills, pellets, tubes, discs, or tape, discharged upon
impact caused by the falling hammer. Forsyth's discovery opened new

17

horizons for inventors everywhere, and from that point on the flintlock, which had remained supreme for two centuries, was doomed.

Extending Forsyth's invention a step further, Joshua Shaw, a British immigrant to America, developed the percussion cap in 1814, his first being a refillable iron cap that slipped over a nipple leading to the powder charge. A few years later production of fulminate caps contained in soft disposable copper cups sealed with paper had been firmly established, and percussion caps of this character remained the standard up to the general introduction of self-contained cartridges.

This single invention in the field of ignition opened up dozens of new avenues of exploration for the inventors of the day. It made possible the development of the revolver by Samuel Colt in 1835, the Sharps rifle in 1848, and dozens of other radically new systems that had been impossible or impractical in the flintlock era.

Another highly important development was the invention around 1840 by Capt. C. E. Minié of the French Army of a conical bullet designed for use in muzzle-loading muskets. The new conical bullet, like the old round musket ball, fitted loosely into the bore for easy loading, but its concave base expanded to a snug fit in the bore as soon as the firearm was discharged. Its conical shape permitted the use of heavier bullets without corresponding increase in the size of the bore, and it was much more accurate, especially in high winds, than the spherical ball. Moreover, it worked as easily in rifles as it did in smoothbores, and with this invention the military rifle really came into its own. Captain Minié's discovery coincided fortunately with great technological strides that were being made in manufacturing and metallurgy.

The first serious attempt to produce a standard U. S. military rifle had been undertaken with the half-stock models of 1803 and 1814 at Harpers Ferry. A full-stock model of 1817 was produced by several arms contractors, and the Hall breech-loading flintlock rifle of 1819 came off workbenches at Harpers Ferry. Production of these arms was limited to relatively small quantities. A very good percussion rifle, known variously as the Model

Ignition by detonating powder, developed by the Reverend Alexander Forsyth, revolutionized gunmaking. Shown here is a rifle fitted with one of his odd "scent-bottle" firing mechanisms.

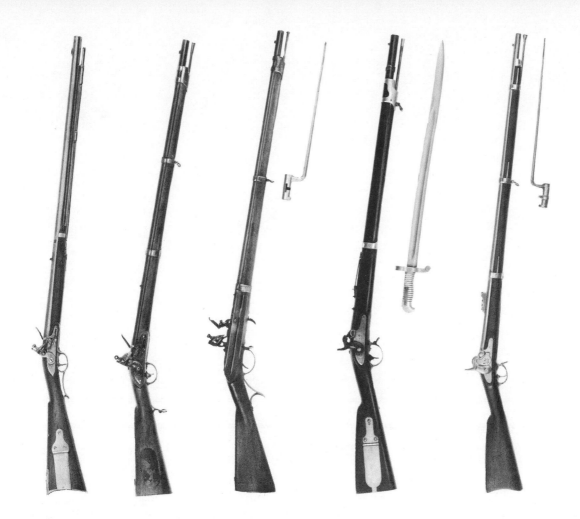

*From left:* (1) First standard model of a U. S. military rifle was a half-stock flintlock made at Harpers Ferry. (2) This Model 1817 flintlock was known as "The Common Rifle." (3) Hall's radically new breech-loading flintlock rifle of 1819. (4) The Model 1841, first military caplock rifle, was sometimes called the "Mississippi." (5) The Springfield Model 1855 rifle with Maynard tapclock mechanism.

1841, the "Mississippi Rifle," or the "Yager," was produced at Harpers Ferry, at Springfield, and by several arms contractors. But it was not until 1856 that the rifle was fully recognized in military service.

In 1856, the United States Army adopted as its official arm the Model 1855 Springfield muzzle-loading rifle, a .58 caliber percussion arm adapted to the use of the long, hollow-based Minié bullet, and the government armories turning out small arms were tooled up to produce the new weapon. Production, however, still was geared to peacetime conditions. Only a few rifled muskets found their way into the hands of the militia, who for the most part continued to drill with the old smoothbore guns.

In addition to being deficient in modern weapons, the militia regiments were still being schooled in tactics that were not much different from those the British had used at Bunker Hill. Such was the military training program in the state militia units on the eve of the bloodiest war in which the United States was to be engaged!

19

2

# A Critical Decade in American

The opening guns of the Civil War shattered more than the calm of a pleasant spring; they shattered the complacency of generals and politicians who, until that time, had equated military strength largely with the quantitative manpower and materiel that could be brought to bear against the enemy. Before 1850 that theorem may have held true, and if the War Between the States had been fought entirely with smooth-bore muskets, it probably would have ended quickly and decisively in an overwhelming victory for the North. Due largely to the Reverend Forsyth, Joshua Shaw, Captain Minié, and other inventive and mechanical geniuses who had flourished between 1800 and 1860, the day had passed when massed armies could stand toe to toe in the open and slug it out with musket volleys and bayonets. So subtly and so quietly that few military leaders had noticed the change, the inventors had rewritten the rules of war.

The first inkling that all was not as it should have been in the existing infantry training came in July, 1861, when Gen. Irvin McDowell marched southward from Washington with 32,500 untried ninety-day Union volunteers to drive Gen. G. T. Beauregard's equally untested Confederate force of 23,000 from its positions around Manassas Junction. The Union Army was made up of the cream of the militia regiments of the northeastern states, each swelled to maximum strength by last-minute enlistments, most of which had been sparked by true patriotic fervor. They marched toward battle, Zouaves and all, in their natty regimental uniforms behind waving flags and beating drums.

In all of the army only McDowell appears to have had any misgivings about the outcome of the approaching battle. He had pleaded vainly for time in which to whip his raw levies into a disciplined fighting force before launching an attack. Many of his men had never had a rifle in their hands before being issued their new Harpers Ferry and Springfield rifled muskets in Washington a few weeks before. But McDowell had been over-ruled by overconfident politicians who had drunk too deeply of the propaganda flood being poured out by the northern press, especially Horace

# History

Although the major weapons of the war were rifles and cannon, small arms such as this Model 1860 Colt Army pistol often came into action.

Greeley's New York *Tribune* with its heady war cry: "On to Richmond!" And the ninety-day enlistments of McDowell's volunteers were fast running out.

Like Bunker Hill, First Manassas was a battle that made a war. The politicians, fire-eating abolitionists, and cheering sightseers who had journeyed close to the front in a holiday mood to watch the volunteers drive open the doors to Richmond, suddenly found themselves on July 21 incredulously swelling the route of McDowell's broken army as it streamed back toward Washington. Richmond lay less than a hundred miles away, but the road leading to it would remain closed for nearly four more years, and before it was opened its right-of-way would be paved with blood.

The surprising strength demonstrated by the Confederacy throughout the war did not lie in manpower, industrial strength, or material wealth; in all of these it was much poorer than the North. But it did possess less obvious advantages that permitted it to hold out against seemingly insuperable odds for four long years, even though after Antietam the end could not have remained long in doubt. Part of its advantage lay in a more efficient political structure in relation to the military; Jefferson Davis, a product of West Point himself, had his problems with cabinet members and politicians, but they were nothing compared to the tangled skein of political woes that Lincoln was forced to unravel before he could free the northern armies for effective action. The Confederate high command, except for battle casualties, remained stable throughout the war. In the North the fantastically complicated political machinations in the war effort, until the ascendancy of Ulysses S. Grant, chewed up and spit out generals so rapidly that field officers often had to think twice before they could name their commanding general.

A second and equally important factor that favored the Confederacy was the greater adaptability of the average southern soldier to the changing complexion of the war. Although there were frontiersmen, hunters, and target shooters in the northern armies who could shoot and shoot well and recruits in the Confederate armies who could not have told a sling swivel

from a bayonet lug, the proportionate number of marksmen in the southern forces was much higher than in those of the North. Rifle matches, for the most part a waning form of recreation in the northeastern states, remained highly popular in much of the South, especially in the small mountain towns and villages from Virginia south to Georgia. Squirrel, turkey, and deer hunting with rifles, sports that honed the eye and sharpened the skill of the sniper and skirmisher, were more popular and more prevalent south of the Mason and Dixon Line than in the northern states east of the prairies. The agrarian economy of the South, which produced a higher percentage of shooters, also created an average citizen, like the citizen-soldier of the Revolutionary War, who was better conditioned physically to hiking, foraging, and camping than did the more urbanized and industrialized economy of the North.

Training in individual marksmanship among the hundreds of thousands of recruits, volunteers, and draftees who flocked to the colors on both sides throughout the War Between the States appears to have been all but non-existent. Occasionally some officer, more perceptive than most, would order his unit out into the fields to shoot a few rounds at an improvised target, but most were issued too little ammunition to indulge in this luxury; many units were not issued rifles until just before preparing to head for the front. Neither side could have foreseen, when the guns at Fort Sumter began to roar, the staggering demands that the coming war would create both in manpower and materiel. It strained the resources of the hard-pressed training officers merely to equip their new regiments and to instill in the men something resembling military discipline before the War Department ordered the half-trained units into action. Replacements often were sent into battle with only fundamental information on how to load, prime, and fire their rifles, and at Shiloh raw troops were thrown into the line without even this basic instruction! General George G. Meade, after the battle of Gettysburg, complained bitterly to his regimental commanders that hundreds of soldiers had failed to fire their rifles in the engagement. His observation was confirmed by ordnance men who examined rifles salvaged from the battlefield. Several thousand were found to contain unfired cartridges, and some contained several rounds jammed one atop the other in the barrels. In the excitement and confusion of battle, untrained soldiers either

This Model 1861 Springfield rifled musket is typical of the arms issued to Union soldiers.

had failed to prime their pieces or had neglected to tear the paper cartridges before loading. In other instances, the rifles were found to have been loaded with the cartridge inserted backward with the bullet against the breech. With the muzzle-loading rifle, such errors were enough to put the piece out of action since, to clear the barrel, the charge had to be drawn with a worm screw or the gun disassembled and the breech plug unscrewed.

Although the battles of the Civil War were bloody enough by any standards, there is little doubt that, if both sides had taken the time to train their recruits in marksmanship and the proper handling of firearms, the resultant initial slaughter, under existing tactics, would have paled even the grim casualty lists of Antietam and Gettysburg. On the other hand, heavier casualties at the outset might have hastened the end of the conflict and reduced the total number of those who were to give their lives or suffer serious wounds in four hard years of protracted fighting, not to mention the tremendous property damage inflicted over those years.

Oddly enough it was among the amateur officers, rather than the professionals, that the light first appears to have dawned that the rifle had made radical changes in the face of war and among whom the first attempts were made to alter tactics to fit the new arm. One of the first of these was Hiram Berdan, a stocky, balding mechanical engineer, inventor, and target shooter from New York. In match shooting circles, he was regarded as the best shot in his state. In response to President Lincoln's second call for volunteers on May 3, 1861, Berdan wrote to the Secretary of War proposing that a special force be organized consisting of companies of selected marksmen recruited from among the state volunteers, the unit to be equipped with the most reliable rifle of the day. This unusual proposal, which was endorsed by Gen. Winfield Scott, was accepted by Secretary of War Simon Cameron on June 15, 1861, and Berdan was offered a commission as a colonel to organize the group.

Berdan's standards of marksmanship were high, and the 1800 men who finally were selected as members of Berdan's Sharpshooters, as the two regiments were called, were the best shots the Union Army could produce.

The Sharpshooters rendezvoused at Weehawken, New Jersey, in August, and a number of the recruits reported for duty carrying their favorite guns, some of which were heavy

23

Confederate soldiers were armed with a variety of weapons, but English Enfields of this general pattern were in best supply.

percussion muzzle-loading target rifles weighing from fifteen to thirty pounds and equipped with long-tubed telescopic sights. Colonel Berdan's personal weapon was of this type, mounted with a ten-power scope. On the range the Colonel took pride in demonstrating his ability with this cumbersome rifle, which permitted him on many occasions to place five shots in a ten-inch ring at 600 yards.

Berdan's Sharpshooters arrived in Washington on September 24, 1861, and they ran immediately into the stone wall of reactionary thinking that characterized much of the high command of the North in the early days of the war. Berdan had raised his regiment with the understanding that they would be armed with the Sharps breech-loading rifle, a reliable and highly practical arm for men who would do much of their shooting from a prone position or from positions in trees, since it could be loaded and fired with a minimum of movement. But Gen. Winfield Scott, whose men had done great execution in the Mexican War with smoothbores and muzzle-loading rifles, insisted that breechloaders were new-fangled gadgets of unproven value as military arms. In this he was backed solidly by Assistant Secretary of War Thomas Scott and by autocratic Chief of Ordnance, Gen. James Wolfe Ripley,

who felt that the most practical infantry weapon was the smoothbore musket loaded with the buck-and-ball! The majority of these officials insisted that the standard-issue Springfield rifle was the best and most reliable infantry arm, and Berdan's persistent demands that his men receive Sharps rifles were refused. Field generals, looking over the unique organization with its distinctive uniform of green coat, blue trousers, black cap, and natural calfskin knapsacks and watching its members shoot, could see more possibilities in its use. They suggested that the special force be broken down into small units and distributed as snipers among the line regiments, back where they had started.

Berdan resisted all of these proposals, and the crusty walrus-mustached colonel soon became one of the least popular officers in the Army of the Potomac; it was only through the personal intercession of President Lincoln that his Sharpshooters finally received anything better than the standard Springfield.

In those days of enormous demand and short supply, promises, even those made by Presidents, were more easily made than fulfilled. When the shipment of rifles for the Sharpshooters arrived, it consisted, not of the coveted Sharps, but of 1000 Colt repeating rifles. The new Colt military rifle

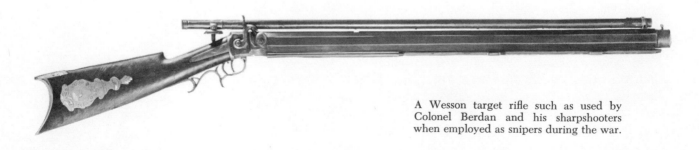

A Wesson target rifle such as used by Colonel Berdan and his sharpshooters when employed as snipers during the war.

Colonel Berdan, of the Berdan Sharp-shooters, practicing at a target at Weehawken, New Jersey.

was an accurate arm, and it had the advantage of being a repeating firearm, but it lacked the reliability of the single-shot Sharps because of a disconcerting tendency to discharge accidentally all of the five chambers in its revolving cylinder at once. Although the Sharpshooters eventually were issued the rifle of their choice, they carried the Colts and their personal target rifles in the Battle of Big Bethel on March 27, 1862, the first engagement of the war in which repeating rifles were used by a unit of combat troops.

At Yorktown, a few days later on April 5, Berdan's men successfully silenced Confederate cannon by picking off the gun crews at distances of one-quarter of a mile, and from that point on their reputation on both sides was assured. Before the war was over, they took a prominent part in sixty-five recognized engagements fought by the Army of the Potomac.

On the third day of Gettysburg, a force of 100 Sharpshooters reconnoitering under the personal command of Colonel Berdan collided in the woods at Pitzer's Run on the west slope of Seminary Ridge with Gen. James Longstreet's corps, which had moved to flank the Union left. On contact with the enemy, Berdan ordered his men to advance firing, throwing the advancing southerners into confusion while the Sharpshooters' support, a force of 200 riflemen from the Third Maine Regiment, moved up. The little band of 300 men delayed Longstreet's advance for several hours before it retired with ammunition exhausted and in danger of being surrounded. It was only a short time later that Union forces dispatched by Gen. Gouverneur Warren gained the critical summit of Little Round Top with only minutes to spare, with Gen. John B. Hood's tough Texas Brigade already thundering up the lower slope. Most authorities regard the race for Little Round Top,

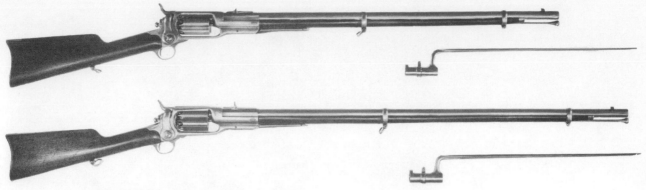

Although the Colt five-shot repeating rifles had some advantages, they were prone to multiple discharge and lacked the reliability Colonel Berdan had demanded in rifles for his sharpshooters.

which anchored the entire Union line, as the turning point of the Battle of Gettysburg, and the gallant but otherwise minor action at Pitzer's Run by Berdan's Sharpshooters may well have turned the tide for the North. Berdan's Sharpshooters, like the riflemen of the Revolutionary War and War of 1812, were, from the standpoint of military philosophy, simply ahead of their time.

As the war progressed, however, both men and generals began to learn about rifles and accurate fire. Both sides made increasing use of snipers and skirmishers. Men who had been in the lines for months had learned to aim simply by shooting at the enemy. The raw recruits of the early battles had become hardened veterans undisturbed by the whine of a passing Minié ball, and the presence of such men had a steadying influence on the raw replacements moved into the lines. Troops in the static positions learned to dig in; attacking infantry learned to use available cover and to maintain wider intervals between men. Companies more frequently advanced in rushes while flanking units covered their movement with fire. The simultaneous volley gradually gave way to file fire, in which men in the ranks shot one after another in order to maintain a steady pressure while they advanced or retreated. Charges by massed units still took place but much less frequently than in the early battles and only after the enemy positions had been thoroughly worked over by artillery. At the sieges of Vicksburg and Petersburg, the war bogged down for weeks on end with both sides fighting from trench systems.

This was the type of war that improved artillery and the rifle had created —a dirty, muddy impersonal war in which a man challenged death if he raised his head above the rim of his rifle pit. To the men at Petersburg, filthy, vermin-ridden, shoddy and standing knee-deep in mud, the early battles—with their gay uniforms, their clean fluttering flags and spirited charges across green fields—must have seemed a century ago and a world away.

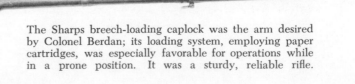

The Sharps breech-loading caplock was the arm desired by Colonel Berdan; its loading system, employing paper cartridges, was especially favorable for operations while in a prone position. It was a sturdy, reliable rifle.

But memories are short, especially of things that men prefer to forget. As soon as the war was over, America did what it had done after every other major conflict. The mighty armies stacked arms and marched home to the cheers and tears of wives and friends, and the reunited nation settled down to the task of picking up the broken threads. The standing army almost overnight faded rapidly back to a point close to its prewar strength and marched west to ride herd on the Comanches, Sioux, Apaches, and Cheyennes, who were reacting violently to the white invasion of their hunting grounds. Except for a few garrisons of regulars at coastal forts and border outposts, the major responsibility for the land defenses of the nation reverted in the East to the state militia units, now more closely linked to the Army as units of the National Guard and armed with Springfield rifles instead of smoothbore muskets.

A sharpshooter of the Union Army using a heavy match rifle with telescope sight. Sketch by Winslow Homer.

In their early postwar years the National Guard regiments, their ranks strongly laced with veterans of the recent war, were efficient fighting organizations, but as the veterans dropped out they were made up increasingly of youngsters with only an inkling of the rigors of war; the quality of the units suffered proportionately. The tendency of the new officers was to emphasize marching drill and the practice of formations that would show off their units to best advantage in parades and ceremonies. In short, the National Guard would have rated high on spit and polish and were experts in keeping step, but would have been all but useless if they had been called upon to repel an invasion by seasoned European troops.

Just as this deterioration of military efficiency was becoming apparent to men who still remembered Gettysburg, Antietam, and Vicksburg as though they had happened yesterday, Napoleon III of France made the serious error of trying to impose his will upon Prussia. When his demands

The German Dreyse needle gun, a rifle that played an important part in the quick rout of French forces in the Franco-Prussian War.

were refused, he sent a declaration of war against Prussia to Count Bismarck, the Chancellor of the North German Federation, on July 19, 1870, and the Franco-Prussian War was on.

Up until that point, the French Army had been considered the strongest in Europe. Its units could run through the manual of arms with the precision of clockwork, and a fleck of dust on a polished boot was enough to gig a private for a week. In Paris and most of the rest of the world's capitals, it was expected that this well-drilled body of professionals would sweep through Prussia and its allied principalities with ease.

The German soldier lacked the color of the French, although he was no slouch at close-order drill, but he had important military assets of his own. Where the French were armed with muzzle-loading rifled muskets similar to the contemporary United States Springfield, most of the German infantrymen were equipped with needle guns—breech-loading, bolt-action, single-shot rifles of relatively small caliber, firing self-contained cartridges in which the primer cap was buried in the powder charge and activated by a long needlelike firing pin. Under Bismarck's organization of allied German armies, no unit was sent to a forward position until all of its men had been thoroughly schooled in marksmanship and fully equipped for war.

As soon as Napoleon confidently launched his first attack, he realized that he had run headfirst into a buzz saw. His proud legions were cut to ribbons by German marksmen who could shoot five aimed shots a minute at ranges far beyond the capabilities of the French muzzle-loader. Instead of France invading Germany, France almost immediately found herself overrun with Germans and with disaster piling upon disaster. At Sedan, the Germans easily defeated the last major segment of the French Army and forced the capitulation of 84,000 troops, 4000 officers, and 40 generals, including Napoleon III himself. By January 19, 1871, six months after the declaration of war, they had invested Paris; the only serious opposition by the French in the entire war came from armed civilians during the siege of the capital.

The manner in which the German armies had overrun France demonstrated new concepts in warfare. In America military leaders began to take a more critical look at the training program of our part-time soldiers in the National

28

Guard. Our training methods were so similar to those of France's routed army that there was cause for grave concern. France had at least made some attempt to teach its professionals to shoot; in America many members of the National Guard served out their enlistments without once firing their rifles. Even soldiers in the regular army received no formal schooling in marksmanship. In the West, soldiers newly arrived from the East learned to shoot primarily by hunting or in informal target practice around the posts. Some post commanders set up crude ranges on which the enlisted men were encouraged to practice shooting before being sent into battle against the Indians, but even in these scattered instances there were no overall standards for ranges, for scoring, or for training.

That was the way things were down the years in our military establishments from the 1770s to the beginning of the 1870s. Against this background, dedicated men with military experience and other patriotic citizens realized that serious weaknesses existed in our defense capabilities and that the United States could be dangerously imperilled by the fast-rushing course of foreign ambitions for world power. In the interest of our overall military strength, these men were convinced there was a vital national need for an organization devoted to the promotion of marksmanship and rifle practice. A group of concerned Americans took positive action to satisfy this national need by founding the National Rifle Association.

Well-trained German riflemen, armed with breech-loading needle guns, blazed a quick trail.

Col. William C. Church, NRA president (1873-1875), whose enthusiasm and influence were major factors in bringing the Association to life.

3

Two men who played vital roles in shouldering the organizational groundwork for the National Rifle Association were Col. William Conant Church and Capt. George Wood Wingate. In civilian life these two men had little in common except relative youth. Neither, in spite of his military title, was a professional soldier, although both had seen action in the Civil War. Church was a member of a socially prominent family and at thirty-five was considered the "boy wonder" of American journalism; Wingate was a struggling thirty-one-year-old New York lawyer only approaching the threshold of success.

Colonel Church had been born in Boston in 1836 of a generally literary family and had gravitated naturally into a career in journalism. In 1860, he became acting publisher of the *New York Sun*, then the largest daily newspaper in the United States. Because of disagreements which arose with the owners of the *Sun*, he elected to serve out the remaining months of his contract as European correspondent. During this roving assignment, he had an excellent opportunity to observe military training methods in France, Germany, and Great Britain.

The outbreak of the Civil War found Church operating as a free-lance war correspondent covering activities of the Army of the Potomac. No rear-echelon reporter, he was wounded at Fair Oaks while gathering material on the Peninsula Campaign. In 1862, he accepted a commission as Captain of Volunteers on the staff of Gen. Silas Casey.

During the early years of the war, prominent citizens of the Northern states had become alarmed over what they considered a disloyal and subversive press. They determined to sponsor the establishment of a newspaper for servicemen, national in scope, "to diffuse knowledge and stimulate a broad national patriotism." To guide this enterprise, which was launched on June 18, 1863, they selected young Capt. William C. Church, who resigned his commission to accept the assignment. The first edition of the *United States Army and Navy Journal and Gazette of the Regular*

# Men

# Go to Work

Gen. George Wingate, one of the founders and NRA president (1886-1902).

*and Volunteer Services* appeared on August 29, 1863. Under Church's guidance, the paper prospered from the start and soon became a running encyclopedia of contemporary military affairs. By the end of the war Church was known by name or personally to practically every officer and enlisted man in the Union Army and Navy. Although his military career had been short, he was brevetted at the end of the war to the rank of lieutenant colonel.

In nearly every issue of his newspaper up to 1871, Church published articles on rifles and editorials decrying the lack of marksmanship training in America's volunteer militia units. Most of these editorials compared American training methods, usually unfavorably, with those he had seen in Europe. After watching a parade of the New York National Guard, he commented on the precision with which the troops ran through their manual of arms, far better than the British Volunteers, he said, who had impressed him as sloppy marchers. Then, deftly pricking this balloon, he observed that every member of the British Volunteers was expected to be able to place bullets on a six-foot target at 1000 yards; and he wondered, editorially, how many of the well-drilled New Yorkers could do the same! This, and a running barrage of similar editorials, helped point out the need for organizing a National Rifle Association.

One who was deeply impressed by Church's editorials was George W. Wingate, a captain in the Twenty-second Regiment, New York National Guard, and, like Church, a veteran of the Army of the Potomac. Since boyhood, Wingate had taken a keen interest in shooting, both as a hunter and as a target shooter, and he had been appalled by the poor marksmanship of the average American soldier that he had seen in battle. As a conscientious officer, he felt that his duties included preparing his unit for possible combat rather than merely making an impression on the parade ground. But when he began to search for published material that might help teach his men to shoot, he discovered that neither the War Department nor any other logical sources could provide anything of value.

# ARMY NAVY
# AND
# JOURNAL.

GAZETTE OF THE
REGULAR

AND VOLUNTEER
FORCES.

VOLUME IX.—NUMBER 5.
WHOLE NUMBER 421.

NEW YORK, SATURDAY, SEPTEMBER 16, 1871.

SIX DOLLARS PER YEAR.
SINGLE COPIES, FIFTEEN CENTS.

Masthead of *Army and Navy Journal*, edited by Colonel Church, and a vehicle
through which much support for the National Rifle Association was gained.

Among those whom he contacted was Colonel Church. In the course of their discussion, Church suggested that Wingate prepare a manual on target practice for publication by the *Army and Navy Journal*. The result was Wingate's *Manual of Rifle Practice*, which appeared serially in six installments in the *Journal* in late 1870 and early 1871 and in expanded booklet form in 1872; it was the first full treatise on rifle practice published in the United States.

While doing the research for his manual, Wingate wrote to the War Ministry of Great Britain, which, in addition to sending him the official British service handbooks, referred him to the National Rifle Association of Great Britain. He gave this information to Colonel Church, who conducted additional research of his own.

The British Association had been founded in 1859, when Napoleon III had begun to expand his armed forces and to hint at a possible attack on France's traditional enemy across the English Channel. In the face of this threat, the British War Ministry had organized a Volunteer Force of citizen-soldiers similar to the volunteer militia units of our various states. With hostile armies eyeing English shores from less than twenty miles away, the lack of combat readiness of these militia men was much more apparent than that of their counterparts in America. If the Volunteers were to be of any use in repelling an invasion they had first to learn to shoot. Under the urgency of the threat of imminent invasion, close-order drill and precision in marching assumed secondary importance to

skill in marksmanship. Costly lessons learned in the American Revolution and the War of 1812 had not been forgotten in Great Britain.

In July and August, 1859, a number of high-ranking officers of the new Volunteer Force attended the School of Musketry at Hythe. Comparing notes, they decided that a national organization, with affiliated clubs throughout the islands, should be formed to provide facilities for target practice among the Volunteers. They then organized themselves into a committee with the purpose of founding such an organization. Almost simultaneously, the London Rifle Brigade, the largest unit of the Volunteer Force, had formed another committee to develop an annual "rifle meeting," or match, open to members of the Brigade. A joint meeting of the leaders of these two groups incorporated both proposals into a single plan, with the proposed rifle match of the London Volunteers expanded to a national competition open to any member of the Volunteer Force.

Out of this meeting came the National Rifle Association of Great Britain, formally established on November 16, 1859 "for the encouragement of Volunteer Rifle Corps and the promotion of rifle shooting throughout Great Britain." Part of its program consisted of regular competition under standardized rules, with the winners of regimental matches competing annually in a national match. As an incentive to participate the Association offered prizes, cups, and other trophies to the winners in the various classes.

To assist this new organization, the British War Office placed at its disposal 1000

Long Enfield rifles, which were issued on a loan basis for one month before each match. The 1853 Enfield, comparable to our Model 1855 Springfield and used by many Americans in the Civil War, had proven effective at ranges over 600 yards, although it had been supplanted as the regular British Infantry arm by the more accurate Whitworth. To provide suitable facilities for the national championship matches, the British National Rifle Association next built a rifle range with firing lines out to 1000 yards from the targets at Wimbledon Common in Surrey. On July 2, 1860, the Wimbledon Rifle Range was formally opened by Queen Victoria, who scored a pinwheel bullseye at 600 yards—by pulling a lanyard attached to the trigger of a fixed and carefully presighted Whitworth rifle!

By 1870, as a result of the efforts of its National Rifle Association, Great Britain, with almost no tradition for skill with the rifle, had thousands of marksmen who could score on the 1000-yard target with monotonous regularity. In the United States, traditionally "a nation of riflemen," there were few shooters who would not have considered the three-foot-square bullseye at this range an impossible mark. Even the best American marksmen considered 600 yards the maximum range for practical rifle work. By contrast, until 1871, all competitors in British Volunteer matches were required to shoot standing or kneeling at all distances out to 600 yards, and many ran up high scores using regulation fixed military sights.

The success of the National Rifle Association of Great Britain created a sharp increase in rifle practice throughout the Empire. By 1870, the United States was one of the few, and certainly the largest of the English-speaking nations, where soldiers and militiamen were not being trained formally in marks-

manship. No ammunition was allocated for rifle practice in the United States Army. This was in sharp contrast to the situation in the British and Canadian armies. Whenever any ten or more enlisted men asked permission to practice on the range, the officer was required by regulation to accompany them and supervise their practice. The government supplied almost unlimited amounts of practice ammunition to all units of the Army and the Volunteers.

It was a comparison between the smartly-uniformed New York National Guardsmen and the straight-shooting, but mediocre-marching British Volunteers that had inspired Colonel Church's acid editorial comment. But many other American army and militia officers recognized the need for improving the marksmanship of their men, and Wingate's *Manual of Rifle Practice* helped fill a recognized need. Church's running barrage of editorials pricked the conscience of many officers, and Wingate's manual received immediate acceptance and its author national recognition as the leading authority on military marksmanship.

Wingate's manual and Church's editorials also appeared at an ideal time in which to capture public interest. In 1870, Napoleon III was still rattling the saber in Europe but, discouraged by the British show of strength, had turned his eyes eastward. On July 19, 1870, France had sent a declaration of war against Prussia to Count Bismarck, Chancellor of the North German Federation. As has been mentioned earlier, the ensuing Franco-Prussian War had been quickly ended with the surprising defeat of France by Prussian riflemen.

The ease with which the German armies overran France jolted military leaders around the world. In America, many officers of militia regiments, burned by Church's acid edi-

Officer's Model of the British Long Enfield rifle, used on the range at Wimbledon.

torials, began to look more critically at their part-time soldiers briskly and proudly running through the manual of arms in armories and on parade grounds throughout the country with rifles that they had never fired. The comparison between Napoleon's ill-fated legions and American militiamen was inescapable. Although Wingate's manual was shrugged off by some professional military men as the work of an amateur, his *Manual of Rifle Practice* received prompt acceptance by most leaders of the organized militia and enjoyed a brisk and widespread sale.

Wingate's training technique was novel in that it emphasized a long course of aiming drill with unloaded weapons preparatory to actual firing. This emphasis on dry firing was arrived at for a sound reason. In the larger cities, especially in New York City, the militia regiments had no place to shoot. The traditional parade grounds of colonial times had been large enough to be used for actual shooting with short-range smoothbore muskets, but those that remained were now surrounded by residential and business developments, and many had disappeared entirely. The surrounding countryside was a patchwork of villages and farms whose owners objected to having armed troops marching and shooting on their lands. Many of the units that used Wingate's manual had to content themselves with dry firing in their armories. But the effectiveness and soundness of the training prescribed was proven when they finally had a chance to fire their weapons at targets. Once they had an opportunity to shoot on a rifle range, most of the men so trained found that they could do reasonably well with their first shots, even though they had never fired a rifle before.

But to round out the training of these citizen troops, facilities had to be provided so that they could engage in actual shooting. The National Rifle Association of Great Britain had managed to provide such facilities close to London under even more difficult problems of urbanization. Why could not a similar organization accomplish the same thing near New York City or any other large metropolitan center in America? Capitalizing on the interest in rifle practice that his editorials and the publication of Wingate's manual had stimulated, Church, on August 12, 1871, wrote in the *Army and Navy Journal:*

> An association should be organized in this city to promote and encourage rifle shooting on a scientific basis. The National Guard is today too slow in getting about this reform. Private enterprise must take up the matter and push it into life. We would suggest that a meeting of those favorable to such a project be called, and should be only too happy to hear from representatives of the different commands of the First and Second Divisions relative to this subject. The subject already has been presented to several enterprising officers and ex-officers of the National Guard, and they have been found enthusiastic in the matter. It only requires hearty cooperation and an actual start to make the organization successful.
>
> Let us have our rifle practice association, also a Wimbledon on American principles.

Thus the great national need was brought to public attention and the blueprint was drawn for an American "National Rifle Association." All that remained was to put effective plans in motion.

Once a promising plan had been formulated to improve the training of America's citizen-soldiers, developments piled swiftly one upon another. On August 19, 1871, one week after the release of his editorial, Colonel Church invited all officers of the New York National Guard who were in-

Pulling a string attached to the trigger, Queen Victoria fired the first shot at a meeting of the National Rifle Association of Great Britain on Wimbledon Common, July 2, 1860.

terested in forming an association to improve marksmanship of state troops to meet informally at his office at 192 Broadway, on the first Monday in September. Including Church, fifteen men, almost all of them officers of the First and Second Divisions of the New York National Guard from New York City and Brooklyn, crowded into the editorial office of the *Army and Navy Journal*.

Colonel Church opened the meeting by reading letters from civic leaders and military officers endorsing his proposal and offering their encouragement and support. Included among this correspondence was a letter of congratulations from Governor John T. Hoffman offering the full cooperation of his office in any movement designed to increase the efficiency of the state's National Guard. Church's editorials also had been widely endorsed by newspapers in New York City, Albany, and other metropolitan centers.

With this encouragement, the meeting got down to cases. Col. Frederick E. Mason of the Thirteenth Infantry was elected chairman of a ten-man Committee on Organization whose members included Maj. Gen. John B. Woodward, Brigadier Generals Augustus Funk and Thomas S. Dakin, Colonels Church, Harry Rockafellar and Henry G. Shaw, Maj. George Moore Smith, Captains Bird W. Spencer and George W. Wingate, and Adjutant William J. Harding. The discussion that followed these committee assignments centered on the possibility of establishing a rifle range, which would be essential to the proposed organization. Several of those present had visited ranges in Canada and Great Britain or had studied the British National Rifle Association and were well informed on suitable ranges, targets, and rifles. These men were organized under Colonel Church as a committee to draw up rules for the proposed range and to obtain any further information on target shooting that they could find.

"It is plain," Church wrote in another

An old label typical of that found on powder cans in the muzzle-loading era.

editorial in the *Journal* of September 9, 1871, "that it needs only united effort, and a little energetic action to secure the establishment of our American Wimbledon. . . . We hear from both Connecticut and Maryland that the subject of rifle practice is arousing great attention among their National Guards. The success of the movement in New York will undoubtedly incite other states to similar action, and by another season, thousands of National Guards all over the country will be competing before the target."

On the following Monday, September 12, the Committee on Organization met again in the offices of the *Army and Navy Journal*. This entire meeting was devoted to the reading, section by section, by Colonel Church, of the tentative constitution and bylaws. These documents, with a few verbal amendments, were adopted by the full committee.

The original Bylaws specified a directorate of fifteen members. Annual dues were $2.00 with an admission fee of $3.00 for each new member. A special rate was given to military units who joined *en masse*. Range rules were established, and among them, on the lighter side, that "No betting shall be allowed on the grounds of the Association."

A Certificate of Incorporation was drawn up by the Committee on Organization, as required by the state of New York. On November 17, 1871, the certificate was approved and the charter issued by the Secretary of State of New York. The National Rifle Association, long in conception and overdue in operation, was now ready to proceed with its mission.

Prior to the Civil War, General Burnside was engaged in the manufacture of a breech-loading carbine of his own invention.

Important

a

Maj. Gen. Ambrose E. Burnside was invited by the Committee on Organization to become the Association's first president. General Burnside, who then lived in New York City, was a logical choice for this office. Many of the National Guard officers among the founders of the National Rifle Association had served under him during the recent war. Colonel Church knew him well.

Burnside had emerged from the war as a national hero. While modern historians are inclined to remember only his two major defeats, his contemporaries knew the big, handsome Hoosier with the distinctive whiskers as a gallant and brave soldier and as a modest, forthright, and impeccably honest man.

He had graduated from West Point in 1847 but had retired from the Army in 1853 to manufacture a breech-loading carbine of his own invention in Bristol, Rhode Island. His familiarity with firearms and interest in their development was perhaps a secondary reason for selecting him as the first president of the National Rifle Association.

Burnside attained national prominence early in the Civil War when, as a colonel, he led Rhode Island's Volunteers to the defense of Washington in response to Lincoln's first call. At First Manassas, he commanded a brigade of New England troops and distinguished himself in leading an assault on enemy batteries. After the war Burnside was elected governor of Rhode Island and later a member of the U. S. Senate.

Except for the prestige of his name, which was a major asset in itself, General Burnside's contribution to the program of the National Rifle Association was largely in the Association's formative stages. He appeared

36

# 4

# People Give

# Helping Hand

as one of the thirty-six incorporators of the NRA before William J. Bell, a notary public in New York City, to be sworn and to sign the Certificate of Incorporation. He also attended the meeting of the incorporators on November 24, 1871, seven days after the certificate was approved and the charter issued by the Secretary of State of New York on November 17. General Burnside also helped obtain key legislation that the organization needed for its survival, and his prestige probably helped attract other military men of high rank to its membership rolls.

Burnside became president of the Association on November 24, 1871. On the same day, Colonel Church was elected vice-president, Capt. Wingate secretary, Frederick M. Peck corresponding secretary, and Maj. Gen. John B. Woodward, Commanding General of the Second Division, New York National Guard, was elected treasurer. Burnside served only until July 22, 1872, just long enough to see the new organization smoothly launched. He resigned when the press of personal affairs made it impossible for him to take an active part in the Association's direction, but he remained a member for many years.

The original Board of Directors and officers of the National Rifle Association, for the greater part, were serious, dedicated, and hard-working men, and the Board or Executive Committee met at least once a month throughout the last months of 1871 and all of 1872. These meetings usually took place in the offices of the *Army and Navy Journal* or in the officers' rooms of various divisional or regimental armories. Since General Burnside found it impossible to attend the meetings of the Board, Colonel Church, as vice-president, presided at nearly all. At the special meeting called on

July 22, 1872, to consider Burnside's resignation, the Board of Directors elected Colonel Church to fill the vacated office and Maj. Gen. Alexander Shaler as vice-president. The members of the first Board of Directors, in addition to Burnside, Church, Woodward, Wingate, Peck, Shaw, Funk, Mason, Smith, and Harding from the Committee on Organization and the original panel of officers, included Joshua M. Varian, Alfred W. Craven, Anthony W. Dimock, and John Powell, Jr. Shaler replaced Burnside on the Board after the latter's resignation.

The guiding force behind the organization in its founding years unquestionably was William Conant Church. If the founding members of the National Rifle Association had been forced to search for a man to get their program moving, they could never have found a better qualified leader. He possessed the necessary contacts in the State Legislature, in Congress, and among the military services to cut swiftly through the heaviest red tape, and he could get a "good press" for any important matter merely by contacting his newspaper friends as well as through the pages of his own publication. In spite of the brilliant career behind him, Church at the time of the founding of the NRA had scarcely passed his thirty-fifth birthday.

George Wingate was the agent who carried out many of Church's ideas, and in later years his contributions to the continuing existence of the National Rifle Association were to prove vital. Wingate was born in New York City on July 1, 1840, and received his education in the city's public schools. On graduation, he worked in the building of Brooklyn's elevated railway, apparently working his way up to a supervisory position. Soon after the outbreak of the war, he enlisted in New York's Twenty-second Regiment and saw action in the campaigns in Pennsylvania and northern Virginia. Later he

became the regimental historian. At the end of the war, with the rank of captain, Wingate retained his affiliation with the Twenty-second and studied law. He was admitted to the bar in New York State shortly before the founding of the National Rifle Association. Unlike Church, Wingate had a lifelong interest in target shooting.

Much of the work of the new organization fell on Wingate's shoulders, as secretary of the National Rifle Association, and he devoted himself unstintingly to its program and advancement. His office, next door to Church's, was in Room 7, 194 Broadway, New York City. This was the first official address of the National Rifle Association. Throughout the early history of the Association until well after the turn of the century, George W. Wingate was never far in the background.

Another key figure in the early organization was Maj. Gen. Alexander Shaler, who succeeded Church as vice-president in July, 1872, when Church became president of the NRA.

Shaler was forty-four at the time of the founding of the National Rifle Association and was born in Haddam, Connecticut, in 1827. At eighteen, he enlisted as a private in the Seventh Regiment but soon became a commissioned officer. He attained the rank of major on December 13, 1860 and, with the outbreak of war, was transferred to the newly organized Sixty-fifth Regiment of New York Volunteers with the rank of lieutenant colonel. Shaler served with distinction at Manassas, in the Peninsula Campaign, and in nearly all of the major battles of the Army of the Potomac until 1863. In that year, he was transferred to the Department of the Ohio under General Burnside. Returning east in 1864 to fight under General Grant, he was captured in the Battle of the Wilderness, released in an exchange of prisoners, and finished the war as a major general in command of the Seventh Corps in the Southwest.

At the end of the Civil War, Shaler continued his association with local National Guard organizations and became commanding general of the First Division in 1867, a post that he held until retirement in 1886. Shaler was a man of great prestige and considerable political power, since he was president of the New York Fire Department, originally organized as a coordinating body for the numerous volunteer fire-fighting companies unaffiliated with any political party. In 1870 he became City Fire Commissioner and held that position until 1873.

At the time of the first meetings, the future of the National Rifle Association hinged largely upon its ability to produce a rifle range on which its program could be carried out. In the beginning its total assets were only $485, mostly in pledges for life memberships made by the first members themselves. Since these funds were inadequate to buy the needed land, the only recourse was to follow the lead of the British National Rifle Association and seek public funds. Such a request was appropriate since the Association, as originally conceived, was almost exclusively geared to the program of the New York State National Guard.

On February 7, 1872, the Board of Directors met at the headquarters of the First Division and formed themselves into a committee to draft a proposed bill that would provide the needed state assistance without endangering the private non-political status of the Association. The result was "An Act to Establish a Rifle Range and Promote Skill in Marksmanship." Under the terms of this bill, the state was asked to appropriate $25,000 for the purchase of land on the condition that the National Rifle Association would raise $5000 and assume its ownership, development, maintenance, and manage-

Gen. A. E. Burnside, NRA president (1871-1872).

ment. The state also was obligated to contribute prizes to stimulate competition among the members of the National Guard. Further, the bill authorized, but did not require, the supervisors of the cities of New York and Brooklyn to appropriate $5000 each to help defray expenses.

Among Church's many personal friends was a young New York attorney, David W. Judd, who had just been elected to the State Assembly from Richmond County. Church, accompanied by Wingate, who also knew the assemblyman, called upon Judd to explain the nature and importance of the bill and asked him to serve as its sponsor. Judd agreed and, after making a few minor changes to improve its clarity, carried the bill with him to Albany. With the bill in the legislative hopper, Church immediately went to work to build support for it, publicizing it in the pages of his *Journal* and encouraging his military friends and acquaintances to write letters in its support. General Burnside, as president of the Association, wrote many letters to friends in the Assembly and obtained a letter of endorsement for the bill from Gen. Joseph Hooker, who had succeeded him as Commander of the Army of the Potomac. Generals Shaler and Woodward used their own not inconsiderable influence. As a result of this concerted effort, the bill passed the lower house by an overwhelming 84-19 vote.

Just before adjournment, with the help of Senator James O'Brien, the bill was squeezed through the State Senate. Thus the Judd Bill was approved and the National Rifle Association was given the monetary support necessary to launch its program.

With their range now approaching reality, the founders of the National Rifle Association went to work on the project with renewed energy. General Shaler used his influence at City Hall to obtain the authorized appropriations from the supervisors of New York City and Brooklyn. A Range Committee, which had been organized within the Board of Directors under Colonel Church as chairman in December, 1871, in anticipation of the enactment of the law, began advertising for appropriate land and canvassing real estate agents.

Col. Harry Rockafellar, soon before the passage of the Judd Bill, was called to Great Britain on personal business, and he was named a committee of one to contact the National Rifle Association of Great Britain for suggestions that might be useful in the American organization. Wingate, in 1872, visited Canada in company with John A. Church, a prominent engineer and a member of the editorial staff of the *Engineering and Mining Journal*. John A. Church (not to be confused with Col. William C. Church) had been engaged by the Association as a super-

vising engineer to lay out the range. On his return to the United States, Rockafellar reported that he had found the British "reticent" and failed to provide any useful information. In view of the warm reception accorded Americans shortly after this time, Rockafellar appears to have made only a token effort to gain the facts. Wingate and Church, however, were shown every possible courtesy by the Canadians and returned to New York with many valuable suggestions on the layout, organization, and management of rifle ranges. At the suggestion of the Canadians, Wingate wrote to the engineering firm of Hugh McCullock and Co., Ltd., of London for further information on the plans and engineering features of the Wimbledon Range.

The search of the Range Committee for suitable land had been limited from the start to New Jersey, Staten Island, and Long Island, but the enactment of the Judd law, which brought the state of New York into the program, ruled out New Jersey even though flat land ideally suited for use as a rifle range was being offered for sale there at low prices. Staten Island was eliminated as a possibility because it was less accessible at that time than Long Island. On Long Island the major stumbling block was land prices. At Little Neck the owners were asking $1000 an acre, at Pearsall's Corner $500, at Westerly $300, near Flushing $325, and at Mineola $215 an acre. The accessible lands were too expensive and those priced within reason could not easily be reached under the existing transportation system.

Just as matters seemed to be reaching an impasse, Colonel Church learned that Her-

Crowds of enthusiastic spectators were anticipated at the Long Island range when all was ready for the first formal matches.

mann C. Poppenhusen, president of the Central and North Side Railroad of Long Island, which was then building a line the length of the island, had acquired a seventy-acre farm adjoining the right of way. He was willing to sell it at low cost to any group that might stimulate travel into that still little-developed part of the island. His price was $375 an acre, where neighboring landowners were asking at least $500. An inspection of the site in July by the Range Committee and John A. Church showed the land known as Creed's Farm to be admirably adapted to the proposed use as a rifle range. It was almost perfectly level, with an even slope of only 1 foot in 150 feet. It was readily accessible, being only a half-hour's run from the slip of New York's Thirty-fourth Street Ferry and was situated twelve miles from Hunter's Point. In late July, the contract for the purchase was approved (as required by the Judd law) by the Adjutant General and the commanding officers of the First and Second Divisions, all of whom were members of the NRA. The land was deeded to the National Rifle Association for the price of $26,250.

The passage of the Judd Act and the acquisition of land for its rifle range turned the National Rifle Association from a small, if purposeful, society into an action organization with a functioning program. Its changing status was reflected in rapid growth and expansion in its first year of existence. In January, 1872, it had fewer than one hundred members and little more than $1000 in assets. The treasurer's report at its annual meeting of January 15, 1873, at the Seventh Regiment Armory, its first full-scale annual meeting, showed a gross income for the calendar year 1872 of $37,234.75. Nearly all of the officers of the local National Guard divisions had become members, and a number of companies of the Seventh, Twenty-second, and Twenty-third Regiments had joined *en masse*. Included among its twenty-five Life Members were

Gen. Alexander Shaler, one of the founders of the NRA, a man of great influence, NRA president (1875-1877).

such dignitaries as Gen. Franz Sigel, Gen. H. G. Sharp, Gen. Samuel W. Johnson, and Gen. E. L. Molineux. At the time of the meeting, the development of the range at Creed's Farm was already under way, and the property was estimated to be worth more than $42,000. In addition, during the previous year, the Association had raised more than $6000 in donations from individuals and firms that were interested in stimulating traffic on the new railway. Many other organizations, individuals, and business firms had donated valuable prizes to be used in future rifle matches. During the same twelve months it had spent $32,295.71, leaving a cash balance in its treasury of $4938.34, a good beginning for an organization that was still less than fifteen months old!

The National Rifle Association now had a desirable chunk of real estate, a few thousand dollars in the bank, and a very ambitious program. Much hard work remained to be done. First on the program was the development of that Long Island real estate which was to become famous as Creedmoor, our first suitable range for national and international rifle matches.

41

# 5

# Creedmoor-

A member of the first NRA Range Committee, which selected the Long Island property, was Colonel Henry G. Shaw, a member of the Board of Directors, editor of the New York *Sun*, and a much-traveled man with a gift for words. As the Range Committee stepped from the special railroad train that Poppenhusen had put at its disposal, the members surveyed the brushy fields with the morning mists sifting across them. "Just like the moors of southern England," Shaw observed. "Perhaps we should call it Creed's Moor, rather than the Creed Farm." And so Creedmoor, one of the most famous names in shooting history, became the official name of the range before the first spade of earth had been moved to develop it.

The Creed farm in 1872 was an unprepossessing bit of real estate. The last of the Creeds, who had worked its sandy Long Island soils since Colonial times, had moved on after selling their land to the Central Railroad. Little is known of the Creeds except that they had been farmers and they had probably been more than willing to sell. The soil of their isolated homestead, never rich, was about worn out, and the buildings threatened to collapse every time a northeaster roared down past Montauk Point. By the time their seventy acres passed into the hands of the National Rifle Association little trace of the Creeds remained except their name, which was retained in the deed to describe the farm only because it possessed no other distinguishing characteristics. Yet, before the decade was over, it was a name that would ring in shooting circles around the world.

When the National Rifle Association acquired the property in late July, 1872, the Creed farm was an almost unrelieved tangle of weeds and scrubby brush clothing land as flat as a tabletop. Neither lakes, streams, nor hills lent it beauty. Scrub oaks, pitch pines, gray birches, and greenbriers were invading its abandoned garden plots and pastures, defined only by tumbled walls and broken fences. Scraggly lilacs and a few shade trees marked the sites of its former buildings, which had been

# Attainment of
# a Primary Goal

One of the first Creedmoor badges, made by Tiffany & Co. and presented by Maj. Gen. Alexander Shaler.

converted into firewood by the railroad workers. Along the southern boundary, the railroad construction work had created an unsightly jumble of litter, stacks of ties, and mounds of ballast. In spite of its rough appearance, however, it was exactly the sort of tract the Association had been seeking.

From the standpoint of the National Rifle Association, the property was near-ideal. It was more suitable in many ways than most of the Canadian ranges that Wingate and John A. Church had inspected and even better situated than the world-famous Wimbledon Range in England. Wimbledon and most of the Canadian ranges were built on rolling land with undesirable humps and hollows that made necessary the use of platforms and elevated ramps on the firing lines. The shape, size, and orientation of the Creed property were almost perfect, lying as it did in a 1200-yard-long narrow oblong that ran almost due north and south. With the firing lines running across the 570-foot breadth facing the butts at its northern end, shooters would never have to fire into the sun. The east-west orientation of the Wimbledon Range made morning shooting difficult on sunny days.

Although that part of Queens County near the Creed farm was sparsely settled, there were scattered farms and villages near enough to cause concern for safety. A public road skirted the north boundary. With the completion of the railroad, the development of nearby lands was certain to follow. At Wimbledon the British were plagued by complaints from neighboring farmers when occasional stray shots whizzed over backyards. Since Creedmoor lacked any natural backstop, an artificial barrier was needed before it could be used. Again Hermann C. Poppenhusen and his railroad company came to the aid of the National Rifle Association. When John

Church approached the railroad president to obtain an estimate of the cost of hauling fill dirt to the site, Poppenhusen replied that the company was about to cut through a hill two miles away and had been looking for a place to dump the spoil. If the National Rifle Association could use the material for building an embankment they were welcome to it at the cost of hauling and incidental expenses.

The Association, in August, 1872, signed a contract for the construction of the embankment with the understanding that the railroad company would complete it by late September, in time for an opening match. A series of problems arose almost as soon as the contract was signed, however, and the timetable had to be set back almost a year. First, difficulty with its roadbed near the proposed cut forced the railroad to postpone the start of excavation. The first carload of fill did not reach Creedmoor until October. This alone killed any chance of opening the range in 1872. To make matters worse, the winter of 1872-73 was unusually severe and work often had to be halted for weeks. The officers and members of the Association, watching this snail's-pace progress, gave up talk of a spring opening and began to plan for an opening match sometime in the next summer.

Only one small patch of silver lined the dark cloud that the delays cast over the eager young organization. Plans for the range called for an embankment twenty-five feet high across the entire north boundary; because of a shortage of funds, however, the NRA had decided to leave a gap and to build only two sections, one 300 and the other 150 feet long, and to fill the 120-foot gap between them at a later date. Because its contract contained a penalty clause, the railroad company offered to extend the embankment across the entire back boundary at an additional cost of only $500 over the $4000 that

it had asked to build the split structure. The cost of the entire project, including two small embankments for proposed Running Man and pool ranges was far below the expected cost.

Before the railroad company started work on the embankment at Creedmoor, the task of clearing the range began. To assist in this work, the Association asked help of Maj. Gen. Henry L. Abbot, who commanded a detachment of Army engineers stationed at Willett's Point, Long Island, a few miles north of Creedmoor. Not only did Abbot supply skilled manpower and construction equipment at minimum cost, but he provided invaluable technical advice. Abbot, a graduate of the Military Academy in the class of 1854, had entered the Civil War as a first lieutenant and emerged with the brevetted rank of major general for gallantry in action. As recognition for his services, he was voted an honorary member of the Board of Directors at the annual meeting in January, 1873.

Far from resenting their involuntary part in the construction of the Creedmoor Range, Abbot's men became so interested in the project that they built a smaller range of their own at their base where they practiced regularly and held formal matches under the NRA rules. They were the first Regular Army troops to hold matches under standardized rules. These engineers participated in the Creedmoor matches, formed a rifle club that was among the first associated with the NRA, and supplied paid volunteers who served as markers at most of the early NRA matches.

As soon as construction had started the Association wrote to England to order 50 targets, with necessary accessories, like those used at Wimbledon. No American manufacturer then produced such equipment.

The targets of that period were entirely different from those in use today. The basic target was a thick slab of iron, 6 feet high by 2 feet wide weighing more than 400

# DIAGRAM OF TARGETS

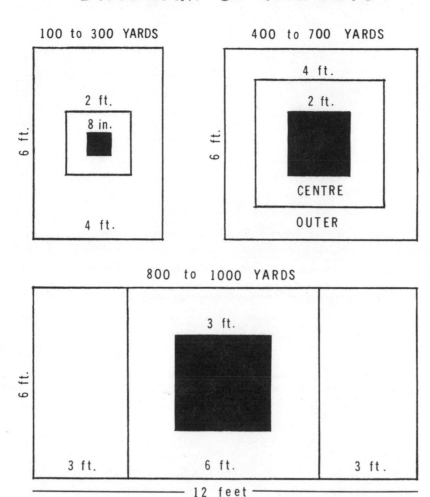

The first targets used at Creedmoor were of this style and dimensions.

pounds. Several of these slabs could be bolted together in combinations to increase the width of the target area at various ranges. Bolted to the face of the target were "centers" of tempered steel, which rang like bells when struck by bullets. The target was divided in squares or rectangles rather than the concentric circles of modern targets. At ranges of from 100 to 300 yards, the bullseye was a black 8-inch square on a white 24-inch square "inner," or center. Any shot falling outside the center but in a rectangle 6 feet high and 4 feet broad was scored as an "outer." At ranges of from 400 out to 700 yards, the bullseye was 2 feet square, the center 4 feet square and the outer 6 feet square. For long-range shooting, at 800 yards and beyond, the target was 12 feet wide by 6 feet high, the inner 6 feet square, and the bullseye 3 feet square. At these longer ranges outers could be scored only by placing bullets on either of the two wing slabs

45

that flanked the inner.

Under the scoring system, a bullseye counted 4, an inner 3, and an outer 2 points. In the long-range matches, beyond 700 yards, a shot that missed the inner by several feet to right or left would still score 2 points; but if the shooter was over or below the center by as little as half an inch it counted as a miss. This was a logical application of target shooting to military reality. Since most long-range combat rifle shooting was expected to be against troops in formation or against enemy gun batteries, a rifleman could miss the individual soldier at whom he was aiming and still score against another in the group, provided he gauged elevation properly. But if he shot high or low, the shot would pass harmlessly over the heads of the enemy or into the earth at their feet.

In addition to targets, the National Rifle Association obtained from England marking equipment like that developed at Wimbledon. The British, in their early matches, had used flags of various colors to signal the score from the butts to the firing line. In 1863, however, they had discarded this crude system in favor of a disc system developed by the Swiss.

Instead of flags, discs mounted on long poles were used to signal hits. They were a vast improvement, since the disc could show the exact position of the hit on the target. A white disc indicated a bullseye, red a center, and black an outer. Erasing the marks of previous hits on the painted iron targets presented problems that had been overcome by the British. Originally the marker had to climb out of his shelter and paint out the bullet splashes, a system that exposed him to danger. Long-handled brushes had been tried but these proved to be awkward. Then some genius at Wimbledon conceived the idea of combining the disc and the brush, mounting the latter on the back of the disc.

During shooting, the marking poles rested on racks in the butts with the brush hanging in paint of the appropriate color. When the marker raised the disc to indicate the position of a hit, the paint-laden brush automatically erased the bullet mark. This sort of equipment was used at Creedmoor until the iron target was replaced with fabric.

The adoption by the National Rifle Association of targets and scoring procedures already in use by the National Rifle Association of Great Britain and its subsidiaries throughout the British Empire standardized target shooting throughout the English-speaking world. Before that time there were no standards against which American marksmen could measure their skill, even against other Americans, unless they shot shoulder-to-shoulder.

Informal shooting matches were being held all over the country but, for each match, rules were made on the spot. Distances were paced off and the usual target was a cross painted on a plank. The common method of scoring was by "string length," the aggregate distance of all shots from a common center, but there was no standardization of the number of shots that might be fired. When the National Rifle Association adopted the British system, the performance of American shooters could be measured against that of Scot Highlanders or of Sikh warriors guarding the Khyber Pass.

The plans for the Creedmoor range—patterned after Wimbledon by John A. Church with help from Capt. William A. Prince of the Department of Ordnance, United States Army—called for twenty individual ranges, nearly all of which could be used for shooting at distances up to 1000 yards. Nine were built on the Scoble, or sunken-pit system, and eleven on the side-hill system. In the former, the markers were protected by a trench or connected pits shielded from the splash of bullets against the iron targets

46

Creedmoor turned from a weed-covered farm to a colorful, flag-draped range where men in sporty shooting jackets and soldiers in dress uniform mingled with top-hatted civilians and their ladies.

by trap doors of heavy planks. In the latter, the markers were housed above ground in shelters protected by an earthen embankment. The Americans, like the British, found that the side-hill system had disadvantages and soon discarded it in favor of the Scoble system.

The first shots on the Creedmoor range were fired on April 25, 1873, by NRA secretary George W. Wingate, while Gen. John B. Woodward, the treasurer, marked the shots with his hat. At that time, in spite of the efforts of the railroad, which was running seven carloads of fill a day into the embankment, the range was far from complete. Heavy rains in mid-January had caused a landslide over the entire face of the dirt fill, flooding the drains and burying the service roads with tons of mud. Several of the butts had been filled or damaged, and some of the 500-yard targets, each consisting of three heavy iron slabs, had been knocked down or forced out of position.

It cost $2000 to repair the damage, and the additional expense made it necessary to delay installation of the Running Man and pool ranges that the Association hoped to have operating at its inaugural meet. The pool match was a popular money-making device developed at Wimbledon. In this match, shooters paid a stipulated fee to shoot at a 4-inch bullseye at 200 yards. Anyone who scored in the black collected a percentage of the gross receipts and the Association kept the rest.

In the spring of 1873 Wingate travelled to great Britain on professional business. While there he availed himself of the chance to study British shooting methods and range procedure. Contacting the British National Rifle Association, he was given a conducted tour of Wimbledon by Capt. Charles Costin, executive officer of the range, and Capt. E. H. St. John Mildmay, secretary of the British Association. Wingate was shown every courtesy and provided with much useful information based on the long experience of the English. His reception was in marked contrast to the "reticence" that Colonel Rockafellar had reported a year before. Wingate made excellent use of this information on his return to New York where he found the NRA preparing to open Creedmoor with a one-day inaugural meet in June.

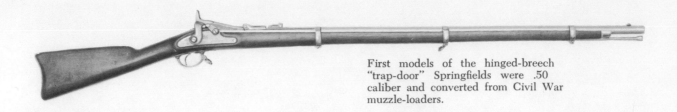

First models of the hinged-breech "trap-door" Springfields were .50 caliber and converted from Civil War muzzle-loaders.

On the day before the inaugural meet, heavy rains swept Long Island, leaving the unsodded range a sea of mud and the markers' pit filled with muck and water. The day of the meet, however, dawned bright and clear, a foreshadowing of better things to come. Enough water had drained off or had been bailed from the pits during the night to make the range usable before the first units of the National Guard detrained at the temporary station at Creedmoor. By 10 A.M. the muddy terrain of the unfinished installation was gayly decorated with the massed colors of the regiments and by orderly lines of tents behind a bunting-draped speakers' platform. Hundreds of soldiers in dress uniform mingled with top-hatted civilians and their ladies.

The dedication ceremonies were brief. The brass band of the Army engineers from Willett's Point played a few patriotic numbers. Colonel Church, as president of the National Rifle Association, introduced Adjutant General John F. Rathbun, Commissary General Kilburn Knox of New York State and General Joseph R. Hawley, the former governor of Connecticut and a target-shooting enthusiast himself. Nathaniel Niles, Speaker of the New Jersey State Assembly, congratulated the National Rifle Association on its contribution to national defense. The British National Rifle Association extended its encouragements to its American counterpart through the naval attaché of the British Embassy. A delegation of Canada's best marksmen were on hand to appraise the performance of the Americans with a view toward future international competition.

With these formalities out of the way, the opening gun boomed, and the shooters trooped to the 200-yard firing line to christen Creedmoor properly with gunpowder and lead.

There were four separate matches in the dedicatory meet at Creedmoor on June 21. The first was an individual competition open to any member of the National Guard with each competitor shooting five rounds in a standing position at the 200-yard target.

The second competition, another individual match, was shot at the same range and under the same rules, except that the shooters were allowed to use "any rifle." By definition under the range regulations, "any rifle" matches were limited to weapons weighing less than ten pounds with a minimum trigger pull of three pounds and not equipped with set triggers or telescopic sights.

The third match was the feature event, the regimental team competition. Participating were teams of twelve from eight regiments of the First Division from New York City; five regiments from Brooklyn's Second Division; the Nineteenth Regiment from Newburg and the Fourth and Ninth Regiments and Second Battalion of New Jersey's National Guard. The Regular Army was represented by two teams, one from General Abbot's engineer detachment and the second of troopers from the Sixth U. S. Cavalry, who had come from Governor's Island to show the part-time soldiers how to shoot.

The shooting in the regimental competition started at 200 yards, with contestants in the standing position. After all had fired five shots, the contestants moved to the 500-yard line where they were permitted to fire from any position. Under the rules, anyone who failed to score eight points at the 200-yard distance was ineligible to shoot at the longer range. The cavalrymen were full of confidence as many of the competing guardsmen were eliminated, but when it came time for the regulars to shoot, the red flag, signalling a miss, was raised as often as a marking disc. At the end of the 200-yard phase, the cavalry team had been reduced by eliminations to four men. And when the four survivors dropped back with the other teams to the 500-yard line, they squinted in disbelief at the tiny fleck of black on the stamp-sized white target. Not one of them had ever thought of shooting at so small a mark at such a long range. As the first cavalryman stepped up to shoot, Wingate, who was on the line as a member of the Range Committee, noticed that the man had not elevated the rear sight of his breech-loading Springfield. None of the cavalrymen had been instructed in this simple procedure. Even after Wingate showed them how to adjust their sights, two of the men missed all five of their shots at 500 yards. The cavalrymen finished with a score of 83. And these were first-line combat troops, and presumably better shots than the average since they had been selected to represent the Army in the match!

By contrast, the team of engineers, who were not combat troops at all, scored 161 to take second place. The Twenty-second Regiment, New York National Guard, which Wingate had subjected to heavy doses of "aiming and position drill," was the walk-away winner, with a score of 263. The Ninth

New Jersey, which had had no training at all and which was still armed with muzzle-loading Springfields, shot almost as well as the Sixth U. S. Cavalry team.

The fourth and final event of the day was sponsored by Gen. William G. Ward as an incentive to National Guardsmen to gain skill in rapid fire with their new breechloaders. Open to all comers shooting any military rifle, the match was shot at 100 yards from a standing position. On the command of "Fire," each competitor shot as many times as possible within one minute at a 2 by 6 foot slab, loading from a standard belt cartridge box. The greatest number of hits anywhere on the slab determined the winner. The results provided an excellent comparison of rates of fire of the military rifles of the day.

Two men from the Army Engineers using Springfield breechloaders, the standard weapon of the United States Army, scored four and two hits respectively. Four members of the National Guard shooting Remington breechloaders averaged ten hits each. The match, however, was won by a man from the Twenty-second New York shooting a Ward-Burton. This was a single-shot breech-loading rifle and probably one of the first bolt-action cartridge models manufactured in the United States. A relatively small number were produced at Springfield Armory from 1871.

The inaugural Creedmoor meet, in addition

Remington .50 caliber "rolling block" breechloaders were the most prominent military rifles in the early days of the Creedmoor range.

Ward-Burton bolt-action Army rifle.

to providing scores against which future improvement could be measured, was a perfect proving ground for theories that had been advanced by Colonel Church and George Wingate. The teams finished almost in the exact order of the time they had spent in aiming drill, although few had actually fired their pieces. Shooters of the Twenty-second Regiment, which had practiced most religiously, made almost a clean sweep of the match. In addition to the team prize of $50, its members walked away with seven of the twelve individual prizes offered, including a gold-mounted Model 1866 Winchester rifle valued at $100.

The NRA inaugural matches at Creedmoor were apparently gratifying to all involved, and probably few others than the Canadian visitors knew how bad most of the shooting had been. Only the Twenty-second New York team had shown enough skill to put it in a class with any low-ranking Canadian or British rifle team. The surprising thing was that the winning scores were as good as they were and that the affair went as smoothly as it did.

This inaugural meet at Creedmoor on June 21 was a "special" event, and the first full-scale annual meet was not held until October. Subsequent to the June matches, Creedmoor was used almost daily by units of the National Guard or by groups of Association members. During August and September, more than 5000 men practiced on the range, and on every weekend the available space was filled with tents and wagons of encamped military units.

In contrast with the inexperience that characterized much of the June competition, the first annual meet was conducted with precision and a degree of professionalism that would have brought admiration from the range officers at Wimbledon. And if ever the value of practice was demonstrated, it was abundantly evident in comparing the scores of the shooters in October with their poor performance in June. Only a few units had been unable to practice at Creedmoor, and the majority conducted themselves with the discipline of veterans.

The first "Annual Matches" of the National Rifle Association were held on October 8, 1873, and consisted of twelve separate events. The opening match was a 200-yard event open to any member of the Association using any military rifle, the contestants shooting in the standing position, and each firing five rounds. This was the "Judd Match," shot in honor of David W. Judd for his services in securing the enabling act that had made Creedmoor possible. The Judd Match became the standard opening event of all of the annual meetings at Creedmoor. In 1873, it was won by W. Robertson of the Seventy-ninth Regiment.

The second event was another individual match open to any shooter using any rifle of less than ten pounds weight. Set triggers and telescopic sights were banned for all prize events at Creedmoor. Otherwise the "Sportsman's Match" was shot under rules identical to those applying in the Judd Match. The first prize in this event was a Metford rifle with case and accessories donated by Schuyler, Hartley and Graham, the importers of

50

The famous Regimental Trophy presented by the proprietors of the *Army & Navy Journal.*

500 yards from any position. The first prize was a handsome silver cup, donated to the National Rifle Association by Colonel William C. Church on behalf of the *Army and Navy Journal.* Under his terms the cup was to become the property of any military unit whose rifle team won it three times. The cup was won, as expected, by the Twenty-second Regiment. This was the only event of the day in which a team from the Regular Army shot against the National Guardsmen.

The sixth, or "All-Comer's Match," was shot at 500 yards and 600 yards from any position with approved "any rifles." This was an individual match in which the prize was an F. Wesson combination rifle with case and accessories.

The eighth, or "Gatling Match," was another match open to teams of twelve from any regiment or battalion of the National Guard of New York, with each competitor shooting seven rounds at 500 yards. The first prize and the most valuable one offered in any event was a Gatling gun, complete with carriage, valued at $3000.

The ninth match was open only to teams of the New Jersey National Guard, with each man firing five rounds at the 200-yard and at the 400-yard distances. It was apparent that the New Jersey guardsmen had not neglected their practice. In the June opening, the team of the Fourth New Jersey Regiment had scored a pathetic 35 of a possible 480. Only one of its members had qualified to shoot at 500 yards and his total score for the longer range had consisted of a lone bullseye and four clean misses. In the October match, the New Jersey team scored a respectable 179.

The tenth event, known as the "Railroad Match," offered nine prizes provided by Hermann C. Poppenhusen on behalf of the Central Railroad of Long Island. It consisted of seven rounds at 500 yards.

The eleventh competition of the day was the first long-range match held at Creedmoor

the Creedmoor targets.

In the third and fourth competitions regimental twelve-man teams in each of the two New York National Guard divisions competed against one another. Each man fired five shots standing at 200 yards and five shots from any position at 500 yards with the Remington rifle.

The fifth competition was the *Army and Navy Journal* Match open to teams of twelve from any organized unit of the Armed Forces with each competitor firing seven shots at under the direct auspices of the NRA. Sponsored by the Association, it was open to all comers with any rifle, with seven rounds being shot at 800 and 1000 yards by each competitor. With a possible score of 56, the match was won by J. Adam of the Canadian Volunteers, who used a Metford rifle, then the favorite target arm of the British and Canadians. American shooters trailed the Canadians badly with scores of 41 and 39 in taking the second and third positions. Most of the Americans in this match used the Remington rifle, although there were Metfords, Winchesters, Sharps, Ward-Burtons, Ballards, and a scattering of other makes.

The twelfth and final match of the meet was a press match, open only to employees of newspapers and periodicals. Each entrant was required to shoot five rounds at 400 and 500 yards. Of the ten entrants in this match, Gen. J. R. Hawley, the former governor of Connecticut, who also was publisher of the Hartford *Courant,* won easily with a score of 36 of a possible 40, overshadowing most of the younger military officers who had competed in the earlier matches.

The seventh match of the day had been the most important event, and the one of the most interest to the spectators; this was the State Match, in which teams of twelve representing the various regiments competed against one another for the championship of the New York State National Guard. The

winning team was to become custodian for the next year of a magnificent trophy donated by the state of New York. As a prize for the highest individual score E. Remington & Sons contributed a fine gold-and-silver-mounted rifle.

The State Match, again, was dominated by the Twenty-second Regiment. In the match that had opened the range in June in which the same teams had competed under practically identical conditions, the team of the Twenty-second Regiment had scored 263. In this match it scored 280. The improvement of seventeen points by the winning team, however, was insignificant compared with the improved scores made by most of the other regimental teams. The Twelfth New York, which had felt so uncertain of its skill when Creedmoor opened that it had not entered a team, placed second in October with a solid 235. The Seventy-ninth, whose team had placed ninth in the opening match with a score of 85, placed third in the annual match with 252; the Ninth, which had placed eighteenth in June with a score of 42, placed fourth in October with 225. Most of the other teams that had had an opportunity to practice at Creedmoor showed equally spectacular improvement. Thus, the immediate mission of the National Rifle Association was showing good progress much earlier and much more impressively than even the most optimistic of its founders had thought possible.

Although the 1873 annual matches set the general pattern for those that followed in subsequent years, they were not the only matches that were held at Creedmoor in the

A Gatling Gun was one of the most valuable prizes offered during the early matches at Creedmoor.

first year of its operation. The proprietors of *Turf, Field and Farm,* a popular sportsman's magazine of the day, had donated to the Association a challenge badge to be shot for once a month by members of the National Rifle Association.

Nearly all of the participants in the *Turf, Field and Farm* Matches were members of the Amateur Rifle Club, an organization devoted to long-range shooting. It had been formed within the National Rifle Association and was the first club to be affiliated with it. Organized in October, 1872 by George W. Wingate, who became its first president, and Judge Henry A. Gildersleeve, who was its first vice-president, it was made up entirely of members of the NRA. By October, 1873, its program had become geared to non-military target shooting. The formation of the Amateur Rifle Club, therefore, was the first slight deviation in the NRA program away from purely military shooting.

The Amateur Rifle Club was, in every sense of the word, a well-organized shooting club. George Wingate, its president, had drafted the regulations for local and state clubs that desired affiliation with the National Rifle As-

Silver trophy presented by the State of New York to the Regiment whose team made the highest score in the State Match.

sociation, and the club followed these rules to the letter. Because of this it provided a perfect pattern for any similar club that might be planned elsewhere. This club contained the most enthusiastic marksmen in the ranks of the Association, and before another year had passed, it would make shooting history.

By the end of 1873 Wingate's office was being bombarded with letters from many other states asking how they might enter the NRA program or become associated with it. The acceptance by officers and officials of the National Guard of principles advanced by the NRA had already become widespread. A bill had been drafted for introduction in the New York State Assembly calling for the appointment of an inspector of rifle practice to promote rifle training throughout the state militia organization. The Regular Forces, the Army in particular, had begun to look with a critical eye at their own training methods and were taking steps to adopt systems developed at Creedmoor. At Creedmoor the National Rifle Association had generated an enthusiastic response to its drive for improved American marksmanship.

# 6

The Elcho Shield, symbolic of the rifle championship of the British Isles.

# The

# Spectacular

# 1874 International Match

It came as a surprise to no one that, when the Irish Rifle Team won the Elcho Shield in 1873, they were eager to challenge the world. The Elcho Shield, symbolic of the rifle championship of the British Isles, had originated in 1862 in a challenge to English riflemen published in a Scottish newspaper by a group of Highlander Volunteers. It offered 200 pounds sterling to any team of eight English Volunteers who could beat the Scots in a rifle match consisting of fifteen rounds fired by each man at each of the 800-, 900-, and 1000-yard targets. To perpetuate this match as an annual event, Lord Elcho, the tenth Earl of Wemyss and March, one of the founders of the British National Rifle Association, commissioned silversmiths in England to produce an appropriate trophy. The result was a massive silver shield that was to be awarded each year to the winner of a match between Scotland and England. Ireland had not been included since that country at the time was considered in a state of rebellion against the Crown, and there was neither inclination nor desire by the British to encourage its marksmen.

By 1865, however, the Irish, largely through the efforts of Capt. Arthur Blennerhasset Leech, had been permitted to enter a team in the Elcho Shield Match. Each year they had placed second to the English, but in 1873 the Irish eight produced the highest score ever made in the match, an 1195 that topped the English by 20 points and beat the Scots by a resounding 67. Whiskey flowed like water in the pubs of Ireland that night. The coveted trophy was paraded through the streets of Dublin on a gun carriage in a tumultuous procession which ended in a victory celebration that began at city hall and spread all over Ireland.

In a thoroughly exultant mood, the Irish looked around for new marksmen to conquer, and finding none on their side of the Atlantic whom

at Creedmoor

they thought were worthy of their mettle, they looked across the seas to the United States. They had no idea whether America had long-range shooting teams, but it seemed logical that it should. Every Irishman knew, through letters from Erin's native sons in the New World, that the United States was a country of Indian fighters and buffalo hunters!

America did have superb marksmen, and many of them. However, most were "practical" short-range shooters who could kill a running deer or knock an Indian warrior off his horse if within 100 yards. There were very few, however, even among the buffalo hunters, who could have placed a bullet in a six-foot-square target a half-mile away. American rifles and American marksmanship had not been geared to that kind of shooting.

In November, 1873, a letter signed by then-Major Arthur Blennerhasset Leech on behalf of the Irish Rifle Association appeared in New York's *Herald.* It was an open challenge to any team of Americans to meet the Irish team in America in 1874 in a match under the general rules of the Elcho Shield Match, the Americans to use American-made rifles.

The challenge caused a stir in the ranks of the National Rifle Association. The first reaction was resentment that the letter had not been sent directly to the Association. But the Irish had intended no slight; they were merely unaware of the existence of the American shooting organization. In view of the irregular challenge, the Directors of the National Rifle Association decided to ignore it. The Amateur Rifle Club, however, was less constrained, and it wrote to Major Leech accepting his challenge.

Although both the Irish and the Americans were then unaware of the fact, this, in the fall of 1873, was like a small-town sandlot baseball club picking up a challenge from the World Series champions. The Irish Rifle Association had several thousand members, most of whom had been practicing for years and many of whom had engaged in international competition. The mainstay of the Irish team was John Rigby, one of the best shots in the British Empire and one of the finest gunsmiths in the world. The standard-grade Rigby match rifle was one of the most accurate rifles made and those used by the Irish team were the best Rigby's gun works could produce. The Rigby was a muzzle-loader of .45 caliber, and it had won or placed high in each of the annual gunmakers' trials in Great Britain since 1864.

By contrast, the Amateur Rifle Club boasted a total membership of 67, only a few of whom had competed in formal matches at distances beyond 500 yards and at least half of whom had not attained proficiency at that range. All matches held by the Club in 1873 had been at

500 yards or less. In the first annual competition of the National Rifle Association on October 8, only the Sharpshooters' Match had approximated the conditions of the Elcho Shield Match, and this had been won by a Canadian. The American who had taken second place had shot a Rigby rifle. In the 1000-yard phase of this match, more than half of the 231 rounds fired by 33 competing shooters had resulted in clean misses and only 12 had been in the black. Moreover, several of the best shots in the Club favored Metfords and other British rifles, which under the terms of the proposed match would be barred from competition. No American rifle then made approached the Rigby or the Metford for long-range work. If the challenge had required the Americans to meet the Irish in 1873 or early 1874, the certain result would have been a runaway victory for the Irish.

Although the National Rifle Association had given the Irish challenge no official recognition, its involvement was more than indirect. Every member of the Amateur Rifle Club was a member of the NRA; the secretary and one of the founders of the Association was a founder and president of the Club, whose membership and officers contained most of the members of the Executive Committee of the NRA. Another reason why the Association had not picked up the gauntlet hurled out blindly by the Irish Rifle Association had been that its own program was then geared rigidly to military shooting. With the honor of the nation at stake, however, the NRA threw its full support behind the Amateur Rifle Club.

At its second annual meeting on January 13, 1874, the Association voted to place Creedmoor at the disposal of the Amateur Rifle Club, and much of the discussion centered around the approaching international match. At this meeting, Wingate declined nomination as secretary and was replaced by Lt. Henry Fulton and moved to the Executive Committee. He was presented with an embossed copy of a resolution expressing the appreciation of the Association for his contribution to its "permanency and future success." Wingate had just been promoted from captain to a full colonel and had been assigned to duty in the office of the Inspector General of the State National Guard. In April, 1874, he became the first General Inspector of Rifle Practice for the State of New York under the Act for the Promotion of Rifle Practice in the National Guard, which was passed on April 25.

As soon as the Americans accepted the Irish challenge, correspondence between the two organizations began in an effort to arrange details. The agreed date was September 26, four days before the regular annual matches of the National Rifle Association.

With the end of winter, Creedmoor became a scene of feverish activity. The grounds were disced and seeded to grass to control wild carrots and other weeds that had bothered shooters in the previous year. Carpenters rushed to finish the buildings and to fence the range to discourage trespassers and stray livestock. A new telegraph system connected the butts and the firing lines. The embankment, which again had slipped and settled during the winter, was resodded, and a ten-foot-high bulletproof fence had to be built along the full length of its crest. In some places, settling had reduced the height to less than twenty feet.

The Irish had accidentally picked the right newspaper through which to challenge the Americans. James Gordon Bennett, Jr., the publisher of the *Herald,* could be counted on to give the match full publicity. Bennett had just obtained control of the newspaper on the death of his father in 1872. The *Herald* was one of the most widely read and most frequently quoted publications in the world. It was the first American daily to publish a London edition, and the Irish probably selected it as the medium for their challenge because it was the only American newspaper known to them.

In contrast to his recluse-like father, young Bennett was an internationally famous sportsman, philanthropist, and financier. Bennett had become one of the first Life Members of the National Rifle Association, joining in 1873. At the time the Irish challenge appeared in the *Herald,* he was engaged in the enterprise that would bring his paper the greatest scoop of the Nineteenth Century, the dispatch of Henry M. Stanley to Africa to seek out Dr. Livingstone.

The Irish challenge stirred both the printer's ink and the sporting blood in Bennett's veins, and he immediately

SILVER TROPHY
Designed and manufactured by the GORHAM COMPANY, No. 1 Bond St., New York, N. Y., and presented by JAMES GORDON BENNETT, Esq., for the highest score in the "Bennett Match."

began to build publicity for the match through his newspaper at home and abroad. Because of the huge influx of Irish immigrants into New York at this time, the approaching match was a journalistic natural. It also had political overtones, since the Irish were using the match in an effort to dramatize injustices of British rule.

When the challenge was published, the Americans were as well prepared to shoot for the championship of the English-speaking world as the average city office worker would be to scale Mount Everest. Since winter made use of Creedmoor impossible, they had less than six months in which to whip together a creditable team. They also faced the problem of suitable rifles. The terms of the challenge limited the American shooters to arms of American make. It had also been arranged through correspondence that the match would be a proving ground to compare the merits of the breechloader with those of the muzzleloader.

Few European authorities on firearms at that time felt that the movable breechblock lent itself to accuracy. All rifles used in long-range competition in Great Britain loaded from the muzzle. This was the midpoint of a transition period leading toward general acceptance of the breechloader. For a number of years the "blowoff" pit was a standard accessory at Creedmoor, as it was at all European ranges. Shooters with muzzle-loading rifles were required to prime their pieces and snap the caps with the rifles pointed into the pit to assure that the weapons were unloaded before they left the line.

The members of the Amateur Rifle Club began to practice as soon as spring permitted reopening of the Creedmoor range. The Directors of the National Rifle Association had reserved each Wednesday and Saturday for use of the Club, and each week, whenever weather permitted, its members were on the firing lines earnestly practicing at the distant targets. Some of the shooters had never even seen a 1000-yard target before that spring. At 800 yards the shooting was fairly good, but that at greater ranges was no better than indifferent. The Remingtons and Sharps rifles that most of the members used had no windage adjustments. L. L. Hepburn, a mem-

ber of the Club who also was foreman of the mechanical department of E. Remington & Sons, always carried a small hammer with him on the range. Hepburn would test the wind, tap the front sight with his hammer, and hold dead on. But such crude adjustments, even if all of the American shooters had possessed Hepburn's mechanical genius, could scarcely match the precise windage adjustments built into the sights on the Rigby rifles.

Soon after the impending international match was announced, E. Remington & Sons and the Sharps Rifle Manufacturing Company offered to build special long-range rifles for the American team. Not only did these companies agree to make the rifles without charge, but they also advanced the stake of $500 that the American team had to post as a sign of good faith. Philo Remington assigned Hepburn to the task of designing a long-range target rifle around the rolling block action. The management of the Sharps Company put its own best craftsmen to work under its general superintendent, G. W. Yale. Its match rifle was designed around the hunting model that buffalo hunters and Indian fighters considered the best in the world. Both rifles were chambered for the

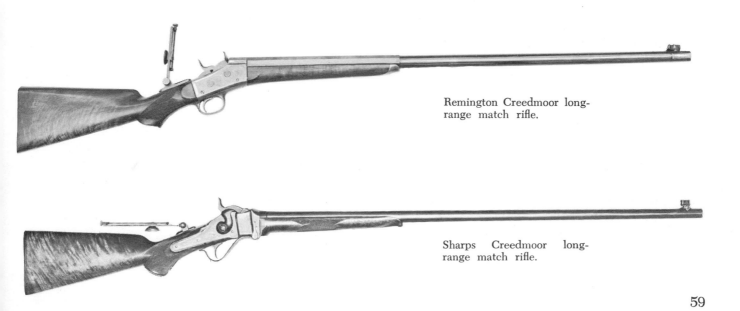

Remington Creedmoor long-range match rifle.

Sharps Creedmoor long-range match rifle.

G. W. Yale      T. S. Dakin      John Bodine

L. L. Hepburn      Henry Fulton      H. A. Gildersleeve

Members of the 1874 U. S. rifle team for the great International Match with Ireland at Creedmoor.

.44-90 cartridge. In contemporary commercial loads, bullet weights for the .44-90 then ran between 300 and 370 grains. To give improved performance at long range, this was stepped up to 500 grains of slightly hardened lead.

The rifles of both manufacturers were magnificent specimens of the gunmakers' art. After the international match, Remington made the Creedmoor model available as a standard item. Those comparable to the ones used by the American team retailed for $100 in an age when a house could be built for $2000. Each rifle weighed nine and a half pounds and had a thirty-four-inch barrel. The stock and slender forearm were of selected walnut. A semipistol grip and a decided drop to the comb, the line of which ran parallel with the bore, gave the butt-stock an odd "bent-up" appearance. This was to adapt the rifle to the "feet-forward" reclining position favored by many long-range shooters at that time. The rifles were equipped with vernier rear peep sights mounted on the tangs and excellent globe front sights with spirit levels to correct cant. The Remington rolling block and Sharps falling mortise block were rivals as the strongest and most reliable actions then made, and both companies dedicated themselves to turning out the finest target weapons their skilled craftsmen could produce.

To select the best shooters within its ranks, the Amateur Rifle Club initiated a series of matches beginning in May, 1874. The top-scoring twelve were to constitute the team, six or eight of whom would be shooting members with the others serving as alternates. It had not been determined whether the match would be between teams of six or eight. The Irish reserved the right to choose, after their arrival in America, the size of the competing teams; teams of six and eight had shot in various matches for the Elcho Shield.

Following the first elimination match in May, additional competitions were held in June, July, and August, the last only seven weeks before the upcoming international match. With the end of the series of elimination matches, the six who had made the highest scores were selected to form the American team with Colonel Wingate as captain. Under the agreement, the captains of the respective teams functioned as managers and coaches and did not themselves participate in the shooting.

The team was made up of Lt. Henry Fulton, G. W. Yale, Col. John Bodine, Lt. Col. Gildersleeve, L. L. Hepburn, and Gen. T. S. Dakin. This was doubtless the strongest team that America could have then produced to compete under the Elcho Shield rules. The betting odds around New York, however, still favored the Irish heavily, and not only because of intense national pride among the Irish immigrants. Anyone who read the scores that the Irish were making in practice on their range at Dollymount—and the *Herald* published them regularly—could only assume that the Americans were hopelessly outclassed.

The Irish team, with Major Leech as captain, arrived in New York on September 15 with a glittering entourage of high society. The party numbered twenty-six and included Lord Mayor and Lady Massarene of Dublin and Alderman Manning and his daughter, and for the next two weeks the Windsor Hotel where they stayed was the social center of New York City. The Irish had elected to confine the match to six men on each team, and Leech had selected John Rigby, James Wilson, Dr. J. B. Hamilton, J. K. Millner, Edmund Johnson and Capt. Philip Walker as his

Members of the 1874 Irish rifle team. Front Row, from left: Dr. J. B. Hamilton, Capt. P. Walker, J. K. Millner, Edmund Johnson, James Wilson. Standing, from left: Maj. Arthur B. Leech, John Rigby.

first string. They arrived in time to permit Rigby and several other members to attend the Remington Diamond Badge Match of September 17 and to size up the American competition. The Irish came away not overly impressed, although Fulton won the match with a 77 out of a possible 84, the highest ever made in that competition. Rigby reported to Leech that Fulton would be the man to watch in the coming event but that most of the other shooters fell far short of championship material.

If the newspapers were looking for a grudge match, they were badly disappointed. The two teams practiced together on September 22 in a spirit of friendly rivalry. After their first day, they were calling one another by his first name and congratulating one another on his shooting. On the twenty-fourth, the practice became a dress rehearsal for the big event, and Fulton surprised everyone by chalking up the highest score ever made under Elcho Shield rules. The Americans left the range greatly encouraged by their prospects, although they were still weak at the 1000-yard distance.

In the summer of 1874, the big International Rifle Match had no major competition as a news event, for the American economy was in the doldrums of a depression. As a result, the newspapers were filled with news of the impending event, and the gilt-edged camp following of the Irish team made the match a major social affair.

The big day finally arrived, and on that hot, dry morning of September 26, 1874, the regular and special trains of the Central Railroad were filled to capacity with the cream of New York society mingling with denim-clad Irish laborers who had come to watch the lads from the Old Country clobber the Yankees. Clouds of dust hung heavily over the unpaved roads leading to Creedmoor as streams of cyclists and horse-drawn vehicles converged on Creedmoor. By 10 A.M. the crowd numbered 6000 and it was still growing. John Klein, the proprietor of the newly-opened Century Hotel across from the railroad depot, beamed as he watched the influx. Only soft drinks were served at the refreshment stands on the range. The hotel was the only place in miles which, as Klein's banners proclaimed, "has always on hand refreshments of all kinds, together with a large assortment of ALES, WINES, LIQUORS and the Finest Brands of CIGARS."

By 11 A.M. the crowd had swelled to nearly 8000 and as the opening gun boomed to signal the opening of the match, they pressed against the ropes behind the 800-yard line where the members of the two teams were making last-minute adjustments of their sights or scrubbing the bores of their long rifles. Batteries of long-barreled spotting scopes on tripods stood behind the firing line or protruded from the forefront of the crowd. A roar of applause swelled from the crowd as Major Leech, Colonel Wingate, and General Shaler, who served as umpire, strode to the center of the line. The two heavily whiskered captains shook hands and tossed a coin for the choice of targets while the respective teams grouped on either side. To the spectators, the Irish, in smart tweed shooting outfits and pith helmets or deerstalker caps, looked more like shooters than the Americans. In their ordinary business suits and slouch hats or toppers, the Americans might have been a delegation of hardware salesmen.

The Irish won the toss, and Capt. Philip Walker of the Irish team went up

62

to the firing line. Assuming a prone position, he drew a bead on the flyspeck of a bullseye that showed against the tiny white oblong that was target 16. The crowd was silent as Walker took long and careful aim. Like all of the Irish, Walker was bothered greatly by the heat. Only Dr. J. B. Hamilton, who had been an Army surgeon in India, where he had won the colonial rifle championship, had experienced such temperatures. And the cool climate of the Emerald Isle never produced heat waves that set the target to dancing. Walker's first try was a clean miss. The American rooters cheered, but Colonel Wingate quickly reprimanded them for their poor manners.

Shooters on each team alternated by pairs, and Dr. Hamilton, a handsome man with blond muttonchop whiskers, followed Walker. Hamilton was right at home in the tropical heat, and he made a bullseye on his first try.

The spectators became almost as intrigued by the positions assumed by the shooters as with the shooting itself. Fulton lay on his back with his feet toward the target, supporting the rifle barrel in the V formed by his crossed legs. He held the butt against his shoulder with his left hand, which was passed behind his head. J. K. Millner, a twenty-year-old Dublin wool merchant and the youngest man in the match, used a similar style but

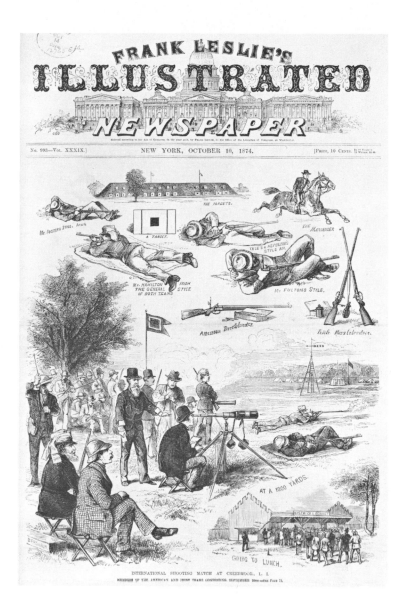

FRANK LESLIE'S ILLUSTRATED NEWSPAPER

No. 993—Vol. XXXIX.] NEW YORK, OCTOBER 10, 1874. [PRICE, 10 CENTS.

INTERNATIONAL SHOOTING MATCH AT CREEDMOOR, L. I.
MEMBERS OF THE AMERICAN AND IRISH TEAMS CONTESTING. SEPTEMBER 26TH.—SEE PAGE 71.

held the muzzle between the toes of his crossed boots. One of his teammates used his left hand to support his head while he lay on his back, controlling the rifle entirely with his right hand and his toes. Yale and Hepburn lay on their sides, supporting the rifles on their thighs. Awkward as these positions seemed, they were extremely steady. The shooters who used them outshot those using the conventional prone position throughout the match.

As the match progressed, tension mounted not only on the range but in New York, London, and

Dublin. The *Herald* and rival newspapers telegraphed shot-by-shot scores to New York City where they were posted on public bulletin boards and relayed to Great Britain by cable. Around each bulletin board crowds followed the progress of the match with intent interest.

At the end of the 800-yard stage, the score stood at 326 to 317, the Americans leading. The Americans were doing far better than anyone had expected, and the next train to Creedmoor was crammed with more spectators. It was noon by the time the first stage of the match was ended, and the two teams and dignitaries from both countries adjourned to a large tent to dine. Both sides appeared supremely confident.

The Irish knew that they could outshoot the Americans at the longer ranges; the Americans had exceeded their own expectations at 800 yards, and they were beginning to catch the first faint whiff of victory. As a result, the luncheon was a gay occasion, free of tension and doubts. Major Leech toasted his hosts and presented them with a handsome silver tankard and was toasted in turn by the Americans. This magnificent token of international friendship became known as the Leech Cup, one of the oldest and most coveted of shooting trophies.

Soon after one o'clock a gun signalled the start of the second stage of the match, and the two teams filed out to the 900-yard line followed by their large and excited gallery. Young Millner opened for the Irish. He lay on his back, took careful aim, and fired. Seconds later, there drifted back to the spectators the sharp "ping" of a solid hit. With a little experience, shooters on the iron targets were able to tell from the sound the value of their shot even before the marker went up. But none

followed Millner's shot. He had made a perfect bullseye—but on the adjacent target! For the record, it was a miss.

To even matters, with misfortune for the Americans, General Dakin's fourth shot, following a clean bullseye, hit the dirt halfway to the target. He had drawn a squib load, and most of his powder had blown out unburned with the bullet! The teams at this point were so close that either shot could have been decisive. At the end of the 900-yard round, the score was 636 to 629, with the Americans still clinging to a slim lead.

The police herded the crowd behind the 1000-yard firing line for the final and crucial phase of the match. Even the members of the American team held scant hope that they could beat the Irish at that range, but they now had reason to hope that they might hold their own. Their hopes rose even higher when Walker, who led off for the Irish, missed on his first try.

To the surprise of everyone, the Americans shot better at 1000 yards than they had at 900. Rigby and Wilson of the Irish team were shooting superbly, piling bullseye on bullseye with only a scattering of centers. But the Americans were matching them almost shot for shot. Midway through the final phase of the match, the crowd began to pay special attention to Henry Fulton. His unorthodox shooting position already had attracted their notice, but now, with almost monotonous regularity, the white disc rose over the distant bullseye every time he pulled the trigger.

Fulton at twenty-eight was the youngest man on the American team. A civil engineer from Brooklyn, he had been wounded in action in the Civil War, had put in a tour of duty against the Indians in the West, and had prospected for gold in

Colorado. Fulton's method of loading his breech-loading Remington was as unorthodox as his style. After each shot, like all other shooters in the match, he cleaned his rifle. Then he inserted a primed empty case in the chamber, poured a measured amount of powder down the bore, and seated the bullet through the muzzle with a ramrod. Although they made no complaints during the match, the Irish noted Fulton's loading method. Soon after they returned to Ireland, the National Rifle Association of Great Britain passed a resolution requiring that all shooters using breechloaders m u s t l o a d through the breech.

Fulton was one of those competitors who operate best when the heat is on. In the formal practice with the Irish two days earlier, he had run up the highest score ever

The Arthur B. Leech Cup, destined to be the object of many exciting matches down the years.

made under Elcho Shield rules; yet his scores in the earlier NRA and Amateur Rifle Club matches had been far from spectacular. On the day of the big match, however, he was in rare form. He opened with a bullseye. Then after a center that strayed from the black by the breadth of an eyelash, he proceeded to run up ten consecutive 4's. A bullseye counted 4; a center 3, and an outer 2. The Irish groaned almost as loudly as the Americans when his final three shots, two of which almost touched the black, were centers. His personal score of 171 out of a possible 180 was higher than any ever made in the Elcho Shield matches.

Even steadier under pressure than Fulton, however, was Col. John Bodine; and Wingate had arranged the order of his shooters to be

certain that the tall gray-haired infantryman would be the last to fire. Fulton and Bodine were paired, and as they stalked to the firing line, the score stood 931 to 913 in favor of the Irish, who, as expected, had performed best at 1000 yards. In spite of Fulton's fine strings of bullseyes, several of the Irish, who had now finished shooting, had done nearly as well. Rigby and Wilson between them had run up 110 points at the longest range, and all of the Americans except Fulton had trailed their Irish counterparts at this range by one to several points. Fulton and Bodine together had six shots in which to score eighteen points to tie the score or nineteen points to win, and a single miss by either might lose the match.

Fulton was beginning to feel the pressure. He scored a center that ended his string of bullseyes. Then Bodine, whose shooting on the 1000-yard target to this point had been good but not spectacular, put a shot into the black. Fulton's next shot landed in the upper left-hand corner of the center, but Bodine had hit his stride; his next shot was another bullseye. Fulton then ended his string with another center. With one shot to end the match, the Americans trailed by one point, and even John Bodine felt the weight that suddenly rested on his shoulders. Before proceeding, he decided to wash the dust from his mouth. A friend handed him a bottle of ginger beer. Standing behind the firing line in full view of the crowd, he tugged at the cork. Suddenly there was a report like a pistol shot, followed by a tinkle of glass. The sun-heated beverage, innocent of ice, had

65

The Soldier of Marathon Trophy, originally given in 1875 as first prize in the Interstate Military Match, is one of the oldest trophies in current competition.

exploded. Broken glass had sliced deeply in the tall colonel's right hand, and he stood in momentary shock watching the blood drip from his fingers. Doctor Hamilton of the Irish team rushed over to examine the wound, and recommended that the wound be given prompt medical attention. Major Leech generously offered to postpone the final shot of the match until Bodine had recovered.

Bodine, however, wrapping a handkerchief around his hand, waved back his well-wishers and assumed his shooting position. Waiting until the wind and light were exactly right, with blood dripping from the white handerchief, he finally squeezed off the shot. The crowd held its collective breath as the heavy bullet made its long subsonic way down the range. There was a long pause, and then the sharp, unmistakable sound of a hit drifted back to the crowd, and the white marker went up over the bullseye! Bodine had made a perfect shot, and America had won the match 934 to 931.

The American victory set off a wave of excitement that began in the front ranks of the spectators and spread by telegraph over much of the world. Bodine, bloody but beaming like a schoolboy, was carried on the shoulders of his cheering admirers to accept a medal from the hand of Lady Massarene. Even the Irish

were not too disheartened by the results, since they felt they would have won if Millner had not shot on the wrong target.

As a test between the muzzle-loading and the breech-loading systems, the match had proved nothing, thanks to Fulton's unusual loading technique. The Irish conceded some advantage to the breech-loaders, since they could be cleaned more thoroughly of powder fouling between shots, but the comparative scores had been too close to be decisive.

The Americans had much of which to be proud. In less than one year they had jumped from the sandlots into the big league of rifle shooting, and they had more than held their own against the finest shooters in the world. Small wonder that Colonel Church, the retiring president of the National Rifle Association, was still in an exultant mood when he addressed the annual meeting on January 12, 1875:

> That ultimate success would attend our efforts, was never for a moment doubted; that this success has been so soon achieved, I confess has surprised me. How brilliant that achievement has been, the facts . . . will tell you. We have not only successfully inaugurated rifle practice in this country, but in connection with one of our subsidiary organizations, the Amateur Rifle Club, we have established for the National Rifle Association a record so brilliant that the name of Creedmoor has become a synonym the world over . . . for the highest skill in marksmanship yet attained.

After this address, Church declined to become a candidate for another term as president and was succeeded in that post by General Shaler. Gen. John B. Woodward became vice-president, and Gen. Martin T. McMahon, a prominent New York lawyer, was re-elected treasurer, having succeeded Woodward in this post in 1874. Judge Henry Gildersleeve was elected secretary.

In 1874, the offices of the Association had been moved to 93 Nassau Street in New York City, and it was here that plans were soon being discussed for a return match at Ireland's Dollymount Range in 1875.

# International Matches Under NRA Direction Firmly Establish Americans as World Champions

## 7

The dramatic victory of the American team over the Irish immediately stimulated shooting competition throughout the Western Hemisphere. National organizations similar to the NRA were being organized in Latin America, and a number of clubs patterned on the Association's "Suggestions in Regard to the Organization of Local Rifle Associations" were forming in Connecticut, Massachusetts, New Jersey, and California.

Because of the closeness of the scores in the 1874 International Match, a return match was almost inevitable. Major Leech, who attended the meeting of the NRA Board of Directors on October 6, formally presented the challenge after accepting a special medal struck in his honor. Before the Irish sailed, plans for the return match in Ireland had already been roughed out, and the NRA had appointed a committee to work out the details.

The date of the return match finally was set at June 29, 1875. Wingate found that he would be unable to leave the United States at this time, and the captaincy of the American team fell to Colonel Gildersleeve, the secretary of the NRA and vice-president of the Amateur Rifle Club. Gildersleeve was a prominent New York attorney and a veteran of the Civil War. He had served with distinction in the Georgia and Carolina campaigns with the rank of captain and major and had been brevetted to the rank of lieutenant colonel on leaving active duty. He later became president of the National Rifle Association, and soon after 1875 was appointed a judge of the New York Court of General Sessions. He served on the bench of the Supreme Court of New York from 1891 until his retirement in 1904. Gildersleeve retained his place as an active member of the team, which except for the replacement of Hepburn by R. C. Coleman, was the same as that for 1874. L. M. Ballard and Capt. L. C. Bruce accompanied the team to Ireland as reserves. With Col. C. B. Mitchell as referee and John H.

IRELAND.—THE INTERNATIONAL RIFLE-MATCH BETWEEN THE AMERICAN AND IRISH TEAMS AT DOLLYMOUNT, NEAR DUBLIN.

Bird as manager, the Americans sailed from New York City on June 5 aboard the S.S. *City of Chester*.

If the American welcome of the Irish had been warm and cordial, the reception given the American team in Ireland can only be described as overwhelming. Cheering crowds greeted their ship when it docked at Queenstown (Cobh). As the carriages entered the outskirts of Dublin, the crowd unharnessed the horses and pulled the carriages to the hotel by hand. This was only the beginning. The Americans found themselves almost inundated in a flood of invitations—to tours, luncheons, dinners, and banquets, including a sumptuous dress affair at Trinity College. In spite of this social whirl, they managed to get out on the range to practice every day that weather permitted.

The Dollymount Range, operated by the Dublin Sporting Club, was located on North Bull, a broad, sandy, wind-swept island separated from the mainland at the village of Dollymount by a tidal gut on the northern shore of Dublin Bay, whose waters formed the backdrop for the line of targets. In preparation for the match, the Irish had constructed a palisade fence in the form of a horseshoe behind the shooting lines. Within the several acres enclosed there were grandstands for the dignitaries and refreshment stands, latrines, and other facilities for spectators. Admission into the enclosure, which surrounded the elevated shooting platforms that the uneven terrain made necessary, was a shilling a head.

On the day of the match, the teams arrived on the range shortly after nine o'clock. A gusty wind was kicking up sand across the range. The overcast was so heavy that the Hill of Howth, which on a clear day was a checkerboard of brown and green, was scarcely visible across the bay. By eleven, however, conditions had improved. The murky haze had dissipated and the gusty wind had subsided to a steady breeze.

The arrangements for the spectators were handled very professionally. Huge spotting telescopes could be rented and great billboard-size dummy targets, on which the shots would be marked as they were made, stood behind the firing lines. White, red, and black paper discs pasted on these false targets would keep the spectators informed of the progress of the match. A miniature target to use in plotting his score stood at the elbow of each shooter on a tripod beside a tele-scope. The planning was perfect, except for one slight detail: All of this careful preparation had been made in the expectation of a crowd numbering, perhaps, 6000. Shortly after noon more than 30,000 hot, hungry, and short-tempered Irishmen had crowded onto the range, and the road from Dollymount to Dublin was filled with more!

The shooting began a little after eleven o'clock, with the spectators' enclosure only start-ing to fill. At 800 yards, both sides appeared to be in rare form. As the *Irish Times* stated it: "Bullseyes became common hits." At the end of the 800-yard phase, the score stood at 338 to 337 in favor of Ireland.

As the teams fell back to the 900-yard range, the Irish were confident that they could widen their narrow lead at the longer ranges. But this year they found themselves shooting against a more experienced and thor-oughly conditioned American team. Part of the success also may have been attributable to a system that Wingate had devel-oped while captain of the team the year before. Wingate called it "team shooting." No sighting shots were permitted in the Elcho Shield matches, but each member of the American team arrived on the range with all rifles zeroed in for identical points of impact. After the first man had shot, his teammates used

his first shot as a reference against which to correct their sights for the prevailing conditions of wind and distance. In the cross wind at Dollymount, the Ameri-cans usually got "on target" much more rapidly than their Irish rivals, each of whom was forced to dope the wind for himself.

As the 900-yard shooting began, the crowd was be-coming so thick that the lower end of North Bull seemed about to break off and sink into the bay. The fence went down under the press of the crowds and the refreshment stands, overwhelmed, were stripped

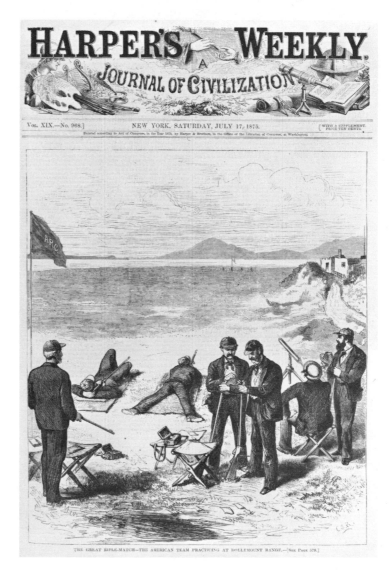

HARPER'S WEEKLY.
JOURNAL OF CIVILIZATION

Vol. XIX.—No. 968.]        NEW YORK, SATURDAY, JULY 17, 1875.        [WITH A SUPPLEMENT. PRICE TEN CENTS.
Entered according to Act of Congress, in the Year 1875, by Harper & Brothers, in the Office of the Librarian of Congress, at Washington.

THE GREAT RIFLE-MATCH—THE AMERICAN TEAM PRACTICING AT DOLLYMOUNT RANGE.—[See Page 578.]

of food and drink. Hunger and thirst added to the irritation of thousands who had paid hard-earned shillings to stare at the backs of the early-comers' necks. Occasionally the police had to herd the unruly crowd from in front of the targets, and at times groups of Irishmen threatened to overrun the entire range.

In spite of the turmoil, the Americans forged steadily ahead throughout the 900-yard phase. Gildersleeve made seven consecutive bullseyes before scoring a pair of centers, and finished his fifteen shots with a good score of 56. John Bodine, who had to let the pressure build up before he really started to shoot, now had a full head of steam. With a noisy crowd all but surrounding his shooting platform, he ran off fourteen consecutive bullseyes, finishing his string with a center that gave him fifty-nine of a possible sixty points. Bodine had not won the nickname of "Old Reliable" for nothing! Pollock, for the Irish, duplicated Bodine's score with only a single hit out of the black. But none of the other members of his team approached him, although most shot better than they had at Creedmoor. They ended the phase with an aggregate of 327, ten points higher than their score at the same point in 1874. The Americans, however, had built up a lead of twelve points.

The spectators now were booing and

The Wimbledon Trophy presented by riflemen of Great Britain to be awarded annually to the champion long-distance rifleman of the United States.

hooting their own team and cheering the Americans, and, as the 1000-yard shooting started, the Irish team fell apart at the seams. Only Wilson shot well, ending with a score of 55, and Millner, steadying down after a demoralizing performance at 900 yards, managed to score 41. But the Americans were unbeatable. Every member of the team except Fulton scored more than 50 points each, with three making 52. At 5:45, Bodine, sighting down along a narrow lane

The victorious United States International Rifle Team of 1875, armed with Sharps and Remington rifles. Front row, from left: L. M. Ballard, A. V. Canfield, Col. H. A. Gildersleeve, R. C. Coleman. Seated: George W. Yale, Col. John Bodine, Gen. T. S. Dakin. Standing: Capt. L. C. Bruce, Maj. Henry Fulton.

that had been cut by the police through a forest of humanity, prepared to fire the final shot. The corridor through the milling crowd was so narrow that he could see only the one target. It was a clean bullseye. The Americans won by 968 to 929, a solid margin of 39 points!

The American victory had been as fairly won as it was decisive. The Irish team and most of the Irish people accepted the fact with good grace. As soon as they reached Dublin, the American team was nearly mobbed by well-wishers. And that night, they had scarcely had time to shake the sands of Dollymount from their boots before the round of entertainment began again with a banquet in their honor given by the Lord Mayor at the Mansion House.

While they were in the British Isles, the Americans decided to try to carry the Elcho Shield to the United States, and they applied to the National Rifle Association of Great Britain for permission to compete in the Elcho Shield Match. If they had succeeded, it would have clinched their already well-founded claim to the championship of the English-speaking world.

The original terms under which the Elcho Shield had been donated, however, restricted the competition to teams representing Scotland and England; Ireland had been admitted only under a special dispensation from the donor. The National Rifle Association of Great

Capt. Henry Fulton was the first winner of the Wimbledon Cup.

Britain stuck rigidly to those terms. Colonel Gildersleeve, politely but firmly rebuffed, then challenged the teams of England and Scotland to shoot against the Americans without risking the loss of the British trophy. The governing council of the British association went into another long huddle and decided that it could not legally sanction a match of this kind.

In an effort to spread salve on injured feelings that their adherence to the rules might have caused, the British presented the National Rifle Association of America with a fine silver trophy to be awarded each year to the champion long-distance rifleman of the United States. The members of the American team competed among themselves for the cup at Wimbledon, with each firing thirty shots at 1000

71

# DIAGRAM OF TARGETS

## IN USE UPON THE RANGE AT CREEDMOOR, L. I.

ADOPTED BY THE NATIONAL RIFLE ASSOCIATION.

### 1875.

**THIRD CLASS TARGET, 4 x 6 FEET.**
All distances up to and including 300 yards.

**SECOND CLASS TARGET, 6 x 6 FEET.**
All distances over 300 to and including 600 yards.

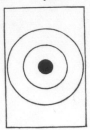 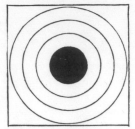

Bull's-eye, circular, 8 in. in diameter.
Centre, " 26 " "
Inner, " 46 " "
Outer, square, 4 feet x 6 feet.

Bull's-eye, circular, 22 in. in diameter
Centre, " 38 " "
Inner, " 54 " "
Outer, " 70 " "

**FIRST CLASS TARGET, 6 x 12 FEET.**
All distances over 600 yards.

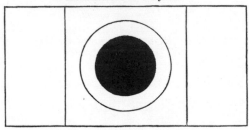

Bull's-eye, circular, 36 inches in diameter.
Centre, " 54 . " "
Inner, square, 6 feet x 6 feet.
Outer, " 6 feet x 12 feet.

A change in targets to a circular form was made by the National Rifle Associations of Great Britain and America in 1875.

---

ton also won the Rifle St. Leger, a special individual match at Wimbledon, with a perfect score. The performance of the Americans in these and other matches left no doubt that they would have walked away with the Elcho Shield, if they had been permitted to compete for it, even if it had been defended by the best shots in all of the British Isles.

The victorious Americans returned home to receive the enthusiastic plaudits of their countrymen. The National Rifle Association was now riding high. Everything that it had undertaken had succeeded beyond the dreams of its most optimistic founding members. The organization was growing rapidly. Life Members were being added to its rolls at the rate of nearly fifty a year. Clubs and state associations dedicated to rifle practice were being formed all over America, and many were affiliating themselves with the NRA.

Creedmoor, now fenced, improved, and neatly landscaped, had become a model of the ideal rifle range, rivaling famed Wimbledon as the most modern and best equipped in the world. The original seventy acres had been increased to ninety-five under a ten-year lease from Hermann C. Poppenhusen, providing much-needed additional space for tents and public facilities. The added twenty-five acres also

yards. This was the famous Wimbledon Trophy, which remains a most coveted award in American rifle competition.

The first winner of this handsome silver tankard, which was presented by Princess Louise on behalf of the National Rifle Association of Great Britain, was won by Capt. Henry Fulton, who scored 133 out of a possible 150. In 1874, the British had just adopted the circular target as standard, with each bullseye counting five instead of four points as it had on the old iron rectangular targets. Ful-

72

# FRANK LESLIE'S ILLUSTRATED NEWSPAPER

Entered according to the Act of Congress, in the year 1875, by Frank Leslie, in the Office of the Librarian of Congress, at Washington.

No. 1,040—Vol. XL.]     NEW YORK, SEPTEMBER 4, 1875.     [PRICE 10 CENTS. $4 00 YEARLY. 13 WEEKS, $1 00.

THE "CITY OF BERLIN" PASSING SANDY HOOK.

THE SALUTES FROM FORTS HAMILTON AND WADSWORTH AND THE STEAMERS.

CHASING THE "CITY OF BERLIN."

THE MEMBERS OF THE AMERICAN TEAM LEAVING THE "CITY OF BERLIN."

THE RECEPTION OF THE TEAM ON BOARD THE "N. K. HOPKINS."

THE ARRIVAL OF THE "HOPKINS" AT THE BATTERY, WITH THE AMERICAN TEAM AND THEIR FRIENDS—THE SALUTE AND THE FIREWORKS.

NEW YORK CITY.—ARRIVAL AND RECEPTION OF THE AMERICAN RIFLE TEAM—VICTORS OF DOLLYMOUNT—AUGUST 21st.—SEE PAGE 447.

A gala reception awaited the victorious American rifle team on its return from the Matches at Dollymount, Ireland, and was front-page news in New York's newspapers.

provided adequate room for the Running Deer range, valued at $1500, which the Winchester Repeating Arms Company had donated to the Association. As 1875 came to a close, the NRA showed a record of solid accomplishment.

The year 1876 marked the centennial of American independence. It was to be observed by massive public festivities, fairs, and fireworks throughout the land. To the officers and directors of the NRA it offered an opportunity to stage a rifle match that would dwarf anything the world had seen. The original suggestion was offered by Judge Gildersleeve at a meeting of the Board of Directors on November 9, 1875. His motion provided that the Association send a general invitation to all nations to participate in a match to determine the long-range shooting championship of the world. The resolution named specifically England, Ireland, Scotland, France, Germany, Austria, the Dominion of Canada, the South American countries and "all other countries having rifle associations or clubs." It passed unanimously.

To tie the matches more closely with the national observance, the Association next asked permission of the National Centennial Commission for authority to use its name in promoting the matches in international circles. No difficulty was encountered from this source. The president of the Commission was Gen. Joseph R. Hawley, an enthusiastic target shooter himself, an Honorary Director of the NRA and an active member of the Association since its earliest days.

Following the lead of the British, the National Rifle Association had adopted the circular target in 1875, and it undertook considerable research in an effort to develop a practical substitute for the unwieldly iron slab. The British and the Canadians had already abandoned iron in favor of canvas panels. Many of the original iron slabs at Creedmoor had been cracked by continual use, and replacements were expensive.

Although the pattern of the new targets was changed from a rectangular to a circular format, the outside dimensions for the three distance classes remained the same. The third-class target, used for distances up to and including 300 yards, remained 4 feet broad by 6 feet high with a circular bullseye 8 inches in diameter. Concentric rings 26 and 46 inches in diameter marked the "center" and "inner." Any hit outside the inner was scored as an "outer." The second-class target, 6 by 6 feet square, used at distances greater than 300 yards out to 600 yards, had concentric center, inner, and outer rings of 38, 54, and 70 inches around a 22-inch bullseye. The first-class target, used at all distances beyond 600 yards, like that of the third class, showed the transition toward a pure circular format. The rectangular 12-by-6-feet dimension was retained to mark the outer, and the inner was still 6 feet square. The bullseye, however, was a 36-inch black disc enclosed in a circular center 54 inches in diameter. The respective values of bullseye, center, inner, and outer at all ranges were 5, 4, 3, and 2. The possible score for each shot, therefore, was increased by one point, but the chances of making a perfect score were reduced by about one-third by the proportionate decrease in the area of the bullseye.

The British had been using canvas targets for more than a year, although the

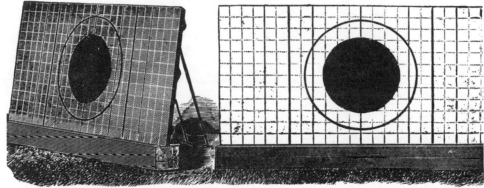
change had caused some grumbling among the more conservative members of the British National Rifle Association. The Americans also managed to find strenuous objections to every material except iron, although they tested many systems. Most of these objections appear to have been smoke screens for the real reason. The fact is that the shooters, accustomed to hearing the soul-satisfying "splat" or "ping" of a bullet hitting iron, felt that shooting had lost some of its thrill when they had to punch silent holes in cloth.

All of the target experimentation ended when the Association located a reliable domestic source of iron slabs costing only $25 each. The time-tested iron target with a more modern face received a new lease on life and the old-timers at Creedmoor breathed a collective sigh of relief.

The National Rifle Association of Great Britain, experiencing trouble with the Irish and Scots, declined the invitation to the 1876 matches, but teams from Scotland, Ireland, Canada, and Australia straggled into New York throughout August and early September. They were greeted with a great outpouring of hospitality.

During this pleasant interlude before the big match, the various members of the visiting teams practiced at Creedmoor whenever weather and their social commitments permitted. They were also given ample opportunity to inspect the magnificent Grand Centennial Trophy that the National Rifle Association had commissioned from Tiffany's at a cost of $1500. It was a full-sized replica of an ancient Roman legionary standard executed in silver, gold, and bronze, bearing on its silver banner the legend: "In the name of the United States of America to the Riflemen of the World." Below the beautifully sculptured crowning eagle, which clutches in its claws a wreath of palm leaves, was a plaque bearing the single word PALMA, the Latin word for palm tree, which was used in the days of the Romans to signify victory or the ultimate in excellence. Although the trophy

was known initially as the Grand Centennial Trophy, it became known in 1878 as the "Palma Trophy" and is known by that name to the present day.

A short-range event opened the American Centennial Rifle Matches of 1876 at Creedmoor on the morning of September 12. Only a few members of the long-range teams participated, however, and the Scots kept to their hotel, resting up for the big event. Public interest in the short-range match was slight, but the mid-range match, which was held on the afternoon of the first day, was another matter. Many members of the long-range teams entered, and the match had the aspects of a trial run for the long-range event. Exceptionally clear weather with only a light wind favored the shooters,

The exciting International Match of 1876 at Creedmoor —shooting at 1000 yards. Sketched by the famous artist A. B. Frost.

and individual scores were high. All in all, the results of the mid-range competition did little to shake the confidence of the American team, although some of the strongest shooters of the foreign teams had not entered the mid-range match.

The big match started soon after 10 A.M. on September 13 as a sea of humanity poured through the Creedmoor gates from the railroad depot and swirled past the dozens of bunting-draped tents just inside the entrance. There were mess tents, shelters for the individual teams, and a special tent for the display of the trophies; dozens of National Guard units had camped under canvas on the grounds.

Weather conditions for the long-range match were nearly perfect, and the distant row of targets stood out sharply in the sunlight. The wind was light. The shooting was superb. The eight men selected to represent the United States were Gen. T. S. Dakin, W. B. Farwell, L. Weber, Henry Fulton, Judge Gildersleeve, John Bodine, Ransom Rathbone, and Isaac L. Allen. When the last shot had been fired it was found that the scores stood: America, 3126; Ireland, 3104; Scotland, 3063; Australia, 3062; and Canada, 2935.

The results of the match caused considerable newspaper comment and some controversy. Although for the record the Irish still swore by their Rigbys and the Scots, Canadians, and Australians stood by their Metfords,

The Centennial Trophy, quickly known as the Palma Trophy, was won first by the United States in 1876. Down the years, the Palma Match has been one of the most exciting of International contests.

nearly every member of each of the foreign teams placed an order for a Remington or Sharps Creedmoor match rifle before leaving for home.

In 1876 the National Rifle Association obtained an amendment to its charter whereby the words "of America" were added to the official name which thus became "National Rifle Association of America." This prevented any international confusion between the American association and the National Rifle Association of Great Britain.

It was to smooth the ruffled feelings in Great Britain caused by the nature of the 1876 challenge that the NRA challenge of 1877 was very diplomatically worded. As a result, the British agreed to organize an Imperial team whose members would be drawn from the three principal rifle associations in the British Isles.

The Imperial team was received in New York

Judge N. P. Stanton, NRA president (1877-1880).

with great courtesy and hospitality. But it was all serious business on the Creedmoor firing line, where on September 13 and 14, 1877, the American hosts outscored their guests from overseas by a very decisive 3334 to 3242. The members of the winning United States team were Leslie C. Bruce, C. E. Blydenburgh, L. Weber, I. L. Allen, H. S. Jewell, Frank Hyde, W. H. Jackson, and Gen. T. S. Dakin.

The overwhelming victory of the American team jolted the National Rifle Association of Great Britain, which had believed firmly that America would be hard-pressed to organize a team that could stand against the best in the British Isles. On his return to England, C. Lennox Peel, the adjutant of the British team, submitted a long and detailed report on American shooting methods and range procedure, indirectly recommending adoption of some methods originated by Wingate.

The 1877 victory of the American team was so devastating that it almost entirely discouraged foreign competition. When the National Rifle Association issued its annual challenge to the world in May, 1878, not a single foreign team picked up the gauntlet. As a result, the International Palma Trophy Match of 1878 was shot without foreign competition before a small crowd of spectators, most of whom were members of the National Rifle Association. The scene was in sharp contrast to that of previous years when thousands of non-shooting spectators had swamped the facilities at Creedmoor.

The 1878 team was more representative of American marksmanship than any that had been organized before. Where earlier teams had been dominated by members of the Amateur Rifle Club of New York City, only one Creedmoor veteran made the team in 1878. This was Ransom Rathbone. The team captain was W. H. Jackson of Boston. J. S. Sumner, J. F. Brown, and W. Gerrish, like Jackson, had learned long-range shooting at Walnut Hill in Massachusetts; H. T. Rockwell was a Virginian; and C. E. Dwight hailed from West Virginia. H. F. Clark was a native of Poughkeepsie, New York.

There were sweeping changes, too, in the armament used by the shooters. This was the first long-range match of importance in which the Remington and Sharps sidehammer Creedmoor target rifles were not used by American shooters. Dwight used a Maynard, but all the other shooters, including Rathbone, shot the Sharps-Borchardt concealed-hammer rifles.

A squall that swirled around the range at Creedmoor on the second day of the 1878 match was almost prophetic of an equally unwanted storm that was beginning to threaten the National Rifle Association itself.

Sharps-Borchardt concealed hammer long-range match rifle.

# The American Marksmanship Program Falters

During the first few years after its launching, the National Rifle Association sailed over calm seas without once sighting reef, shoal, or hint of foul weather. Its first real storm struck from an unexpected quarter.

On October 27, 1877, the *Army and Navy Journal* published an editorial critical of the current NRA program. Although the editorial was unsigned, it could have come from only one pen, that of Col. William C. Church, the founder and first active president of the Association. Although he had been the dominant figure in the NRA in its formative years, Church had not continued his active participation in the affairs of the NRA since relinquishing its presidency. Both the editorial and the two-column follow-up, which appeared in his next issue,

were in marked contrast to the earlier praise that Colonel Church and the *Journal* had been accustomed to give to the NRA. In Church's mind, the existing National Rifle Association was representative only of the state of New York, although its officers and directors had striven, with some success, to expand its program to encompass all formal rifle shooting in America.

There was evidence that Church looked with displeasure on what he considered to be an overemphasis of long-range shooting at the expense of "practical" military exercise. Church himself was not a shooter but a spokesman for the military. He found it difficult to imagine soldiers in wartime contorting themselves into the popular match-shooting positions of the day to shoot at an enemy. The Soldier's Match, which was introduced as a regular event at Creedmoor in 1877, was more to his liking. This event consisted of team shooting by squads of eight soldiers under the command of an officer; on command each squad fired five rounds per man by file within two minutes and followed this with five volleys. All shooting was done in the standing position at the 200-yard target. It was a colorful, crowd-pleasing event, but to many it seemed like a step backward in the developing of military marksmanship.

Church and other critics of match shooting overlooked the value that already had accrued to military training from the long-range matches. Not only had the match rifle inspired a search for more accurate military firearms, but the international matches had given more impetus to military training in marksmanship than anything else could ever have given it. Creedmoor rules had become standards for marksmanship training throughout America, and ranges patterned after Creedmoor were being built all over the country, many in New York State alone. More than 90 per cent of the shooting at Creedmoor and the other ranges was by state militiamen training or competing with standard military arms.

In reply to this criticism of its program, the NRA was not without friends. *Turf, Field and Farm* sprang editorially to the defense, and Charles Hallock, the crusading editor of *Forest and Stream Weekly,* also took up the cudgel.

This first squall blew itself out quickly, however; Church retained his status as an Honorary Director and the *Army and Navy Journal* Match continued to be a regular feature of the annual matches. All that remained of the dispute was a slightly perceptible coolness in the relationship between Church and the other founding members.

While Col. William C. Church had missed the mark on many points, he had hit home on others. One of these was the undisputable weighting of the management and membership of the organization in favor of New Yorkers, and a top-heavy representation of Creedmoor shooters on the international team. In the early days there had been ample justification for both situations, but they had become less valid every day.

An early result of Church's criticism was action designed to broaden the base of the organization and to give it a true national character. At a meeting of the Board of Directors on January 2, 1878, a resolution was passed making the General Commanding the Army, the commanders of the various Army Departments, the Superintendent of West Point, the Chief of Ordnance of the United States, the adjutants general of the several states and territories, and the presidents of all affiliated state rifle associa-

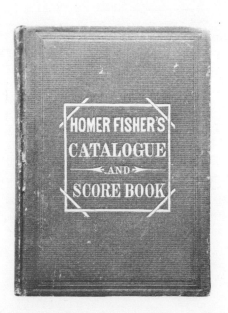 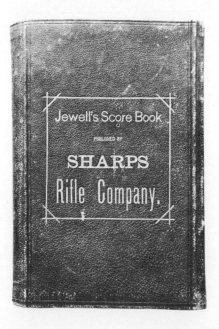

Special score books, containing the scoring forms along with shooting data and advertisements, were popular with the Creedmoor shooters.

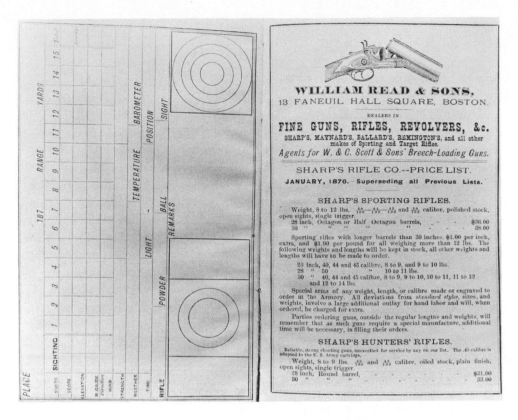

Typical pages of score books published in the Creedmoor era.

tions all honorary directors ex officio of the NRA. These individuals were "allowed a voice in all matters relating to the association, but will only be entitled to vote upon general rules of the association in relation to rifle practice, and all rules governing international and inter-state rifle matches."

To consolidate further its position in the field of national shooting affairs the National Rifle Association on May 25, 1878, called a "Convention of Riflemen" at Creedmoor. In that it was the first time that the NRA had gathered representatives of its affiliated organizations in a single meeting, this was the first real annual convention of the Association. Represented at this meeting were the Amateur Rifle Club, the New Jersey Rifle Association, the Massachusetts Rifle Association, the Maryland Rifle Club, the Columbia Rifle Club of the

District of Columbia, and the Stock Exchange Rifle Club. The Stock Exchange Rifle Club, one of the earliest affiliated with the NRA, was a small but distinguished shooting club comprised entirely of Wall Street brokers and bankers. George W. Wingate was elected president of the convention with NRA secretary Schermerhorn and W. H. Jackson as secretaries.

It was resolved to hold future annual conventions for the purpose of making recommendations to the National Rifle Association, and was voted that future international matches would continue to be held in New York, with the NRA providing facilities for shooters living outside New York to compete for places on the American team.

The idea of an international rifle match with standard infantry weapons had been discussed since 1876. The refusal of the NRA to offer the Palma Trophy for such a match had been one of the things that had caused Church's displeasure. After the moves of the Association to embrace all military interests in the United States, the proposal was renewed. While still adamant about changing the rules for the Palma Trophy Match, the NRA voted, on August 6, 1878, to hold a separate international military match in conjunction with its fall meeting with a special trophy to be offered to the winner.

The adjutant general of Massachusetts, the commander in chief of the militia of Connecticut, the generals commanding the U. S. Military Divisions of the Atlantic and of Louisiana and Texas, as well as spokesmen for the Canadian Army in Montreal and Nova Scotia all endorsed the proposal and stated that they would be willing to send teams to compete in such a match.

A letter from Maj. Gen. Winfield Scott Hancock, who commanded the Division of the Atlantic, was of especial interest. It stated: "The efforts of your association to introduce rifle shooting among our people merits and has always received the support and approval, not only of myself, but of the officers of the Army in general." Moreover, General Hancock reported, "Judge Henry Hilton of New York City, at my suggestion, has agreed to present a trophy valued at not less than $1,000 as a first prize of the International Rifle Match."

Hancock was one of the most prominent men in American public life; he had become a national hero by holding Gettysburg until Meade's arrival and in commanding the critical left wing of the Union Army throughout the ensuing battle. His endorsement of the program of the NRA gave the Association a major boost; two years later he became its president.

The first International Military Match for the magnificent Hilton Trophy, a massive silver shield executed by Tiffany's, was held on September 17, 1878. This was open to teams of eight from state militia organizations, from the various departments of the Regular Army, and to teams from the armed forces of any foreign country. The teams were required to shoot in uniform with their standard-issue military rifles. No teams from outside the United States competed in the first International Military Rifle Match, and the event was won easily by the Creedmoor-

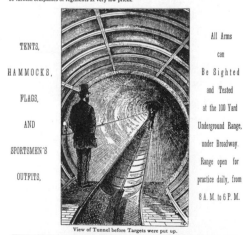
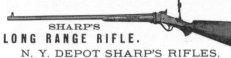

Advertisement of a famous supply house that catered to Creedmoor shooters. Their indoor range was called "Creedmoor Jr.," and was under New York's famous Broadway.

82

trained shooters of the New York National Guard with a score of 1044. The team of the Department of Missouri of the United States Army scored only 803 points. The Regulars also showed up badly in the individual match for the military championship of the United States, which was held on the same day.

Although competitive shooting between military units enjoyed a new spurt of enthusiasm, international match shooting languished. Because the NRA was unable to reach an understanding with the National Rifle Association of Great Britain, the Palma Trophy gathered dust throughout 1879. The fall matches of 1879 were dominated by short-range military events that lacked the public appeal of the international matches of earlier years. The bright spot was the expanded interest of the United States Army in the International Military Rifle Match. In spite of its drubbing at the hands of the New York National Guard team in 1878, the Army stubbornly returned in 1879 to enter teams from the Divisions of the Atlantic, Pacific, and Missouri in the competition for the Hilton Shield. The Army showed a great improvement in its performance over the preceding year. The New York National Guard twelve chalked up a score of 1043 points, but the team from the Division of the Atlantic made an even 1000 points, only 39 more than that of the third-place Division of the Pacific.

The following year when Judge Henry A. Gildersleeve succeeded Judge Stanton as president of the NRA, one of his first official acts was to extend invitations to the three commanders of the Military Divisions of the United States—Irvin McDowell, Phil Sheridan, and Winfield S. Hancock—to organize teams of Army riflemen to compete in the matches of 1880.

The Hilton Trophy, presented in 1878 by the Honorable Henry Hilton of New York.

Secondly, the old wheelhorse of American long-range rifle shooting determined to do something to break the stalemate in the field of international competitions.

In April, 1880, changes in the rules governing the conduct of the International Long-range Rifle Match for the Palma Trophy were adopted by the NRA. The changes eliminated controversial separate invitations to Ireland and Scotland. Mean-

83

Col. Henry A. Gildersleeve, NRA president (1880-1881).

while, however, the NRA had received an invitation from the secretary of the Irish Rifle Association, suggesting that a friendly match (with no involvement of the Palma Trophy) might stimulate waning public interest in long-range shooting.

The proposal was promptly accepted by the NRA and invitations were sent to all affiliated clubs to supply their best shooters as candidates for the American team. After some minor controversy in the selection of its members, the United States team reached Ireland, June 13. All the Americans except W. Milton Farrow, who stuck with his Ballard, used Sharps match rifles of the Borchardt concealed-hammer type.

Pitted against them was a formidable team of Irish shooters five of whom were armed with the new Rigby breech-loading match rifle, which Bodine reported resembled the American Remington-Hepburn rifle. The five Rigbys were the only finished rifles of their kind in existence, and the craftsmen of the Rigby Gun Works had labored to turn them out especially for this match. Major S. S.

Young of the Irish team used a Metford. The Rigby-armed members were Lt. Col. Fenton, J. Russell Joynt, Joshua K. Millner, and the gunmaking cousins, William and John Rigby. Although Major Leech was still nominally in charge as the team captain, Bodine later reported that John Rigby, who was grimly out to prove the superiority of his new breechloader, was the real leader of the Irish team.

The match, which was held on June 29, 1880, proceeded smoothly and without hitch except for a single incident. At midpoint in the 900-yard phase, some misguided Irish booster fired the gorse thickets to windward of the butts, ostensibly with a view toward interfering with the shooting of the American team. Actually the strategy backfired since the smoke did not become troublesome until the Irish resumed their shooting, and John Rigby later claimed that it cost him four points.

The shooting was superb on both sides. It was a fight almost to the last shot, and both teams exceeded anything that had ever been done at Dollymount before. For the Americans, of eighteen separate individual scores at the various distances, only four showed fewer than 70 points out of a possible 75. When it was over, the Americans had won the match with a total score of 1280 to 1202.

The defeat was a bitter one for John Rigby, although he accepted it in good grace and contented himself with making the best of a bad situation. Rigby had hoped for an Irish victory to boost his flagging gun business by being able to attribute a win to the new Rigby breechloader. The reputation of the Rigby Gun Works had been based on the dying muzzle-loader and on beautifully made duelling pistols. A contemporary reporter observed after the match that the demand for duelling pistols appeared to be "dropping off somewhat in recent years."

If the American team had returned to the United States after the customary post-match banquets and tours, there would have been no problem, except for some hard feelings against Bodine on the part of the Massachusetts Rifle Association for his failure to select Jackson as a member of the active team. Colonel Bodine had eliminated Jackson at the last minute because the ace marksman of the Bay State had not shot up to his usual standards in the prematch trials. Since the team had won handily, no one could take serious exception to Bodine's management of its affairs.

The majority of the team, however, did not return immediately to the United States. Nearly a year earlier, Frank Hyde, a prominent American long-range shooter and an agent for Sharps Rifle Company, had visited England and had been in close contact with Sir Henry St. John Halford. The former captain of the British international team had been spoiling for a return match with the Americans ever since his defeat two years before, but he had been foiled by restrictions imposed by the

NRA on the competition for the Palma Trophy. Hyde, acting entirely without authority from or knowledge of the NRA, agreed to organize an American team to compete against the British in 1880.

The first inkling the National Rifle Association of America had of Hyde's move was a letter of June 17, 1880, written by Sir Henry Halford to Gildersleeve. Halford stated that, "Mr. Frank Hyde has arranged to form a team at my instigation to compete at Wimbledon," and asked the blessings of the American NRA on the proposed match. Gildersleeve and the Directors of the NRA were understandably furious about the suggestion and flatly refused to have anything to do with the contest.

Hyde had brought a few shooters with him, but he was counting on recruiting the remainder of his team from the American team in Ireland. He started his sales pitch as soon as the team reached Dollymount, playing on the theme that six of the Americans had journeyed across the Atlantic simply to watch the others shoot. The argument was especially attractive to a proud man like Jackson, who was smarting under his failure to make a position on

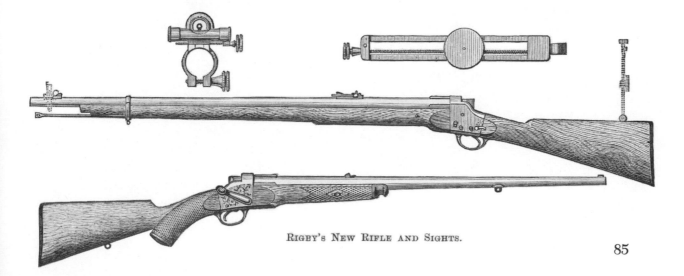

RIGBY'S NEW RIFLE AND SIGHTS.

85

Martini-Henry rifle, popular in the British Isles, was presented to George Wingate by Arthur B. Leech.

the active six. Separated from the restraining hand of the NRA by the full breadth of the Atlantic, Dr. Scott, Jackson, and most of the remainder of the reserve signed up with Hyde; others of the United States team declined to have anything to do with the affair and sailed for home as soon as the Irish-American match was concluded.

The self-appointed American group soon found that the English had been doing a lot of homework since they had received their new Martini-Henry rifles. The result was a disastrous defeat, the first suffered by an American team at the hands of the British. The final score was 1647 to 1568. Although the American team had no official sanction, the British, quite naturally, played the event up as a major international victory. *Forest and Stream*, which had become the unofficial public spokesman for the NRA, heaped a blast of brimstone on the originators of the match in a blistering editorial.

It seemed that these years in the life of the National Rifle Association were destined to be touched in one way or another by an unwanted share of controversy. Even one of the manifestations of the newfound interest of the Army in individual marksmanship had unfortunate overtones. Wingate's manual, which had entered its sixth printing, was the only official handbook on individual and team shooting available in the United States up to 1879. It had become the textbook of all National Guard or state militia organizations in the United States. In 1877, the book had been reviewed by a board appointed by the Chief of Ordnance of the United States with a view toward using it in training army marksmen. The board found that parts of the book were not applicable to use by Regulars, since it had been written entirely for use by National Guard troops. It recommended that an entirely new manual be prepared. In view of this, Col. T. T. S. Laidley, Commander of the Watertown Arsenal, was asked to prepare a system of rifle practice for use by the Regular Army.

Laidley was no rifleman, so he was forced to fall back upon the writings of other authorities, who were very few in number. The result was that, when Laidley's *Instructions in Rifle Firing* appeared in 1879 under the auspices of the War Department, much of it was an almost verbatim copy of Wingate's manual. As a result, W. C. and F. P. Church as publishers and Wingate as author brought suit against W. R. Pelton, the agent for Lippincott & Sons, the publishers of Laidley's book. On February 6, 1880, Judge Blanchford of the United States Circuit Court issued a permanent injunction against the further sale and distribution of *Instructions in Rifle Firing*.

In the meantime, however, since it was not aware of the action of the Chief of Ordnance, the Army Equipment Board, headed by Gen. Nelson A. Miles, also in 1879, had initiated a similar project and had assigned the writing to Lt. Edward S. Farrow. In this case, too, the author made liberal use of Wingate's manual but obtained permission from the author and publishers to avoid charges of plagiarism. Farrow's book, however, was rejected by the Chief of Ordnance, and a heavily revised version of Laidley's was accepted. In 1883, a further revision of the work was made by Capt. S. E. Blunt, who drew heavily on Wingate, as did Lt. H. K. Gilman of the United States Marine Corps in drawing up the Navy manual of 1885.

Although the National Rifle Association was not directly involved in these affairs, the activity did indicate several things. It was a tacit admission by the Army that the NRA-sponsored National Guard marksmanship training program was far superior to anything that then existed in the Regular Services; secondly, it indicated that the Regular Army had determined to overcome its deficiencies in that respect.

Metford match rifling and bullet after firing.

The Army proved the second point in 1880 when it sent to Creedmoor the strongest rifle teams that it had ever put in the field to that time. The New York National Guard, still armed with the old .50 caliber Remington breechloader, took one look at the practice scores the Regulars had made with their new Springfields and decided they wanted no part in the International Military Match of 1880. The Regulars ran roughshod over every team thrown against them. In the match for the Hilton Shield, teams from the Military Divisions of Missouri, the Atlantic, and the Pacific plowed under those from the New Jersey and Connecticut National Guard. The respective scores for the three teams of Regulars were: 1023, 1014, and 1004, while the guardsmen of New Jersey scored 969 and those of Connecticut 959.

Ill winds continued to blow. Having won the Hilton Shield, the Army then abruptly decided to send no further teams to matches sponsored by the

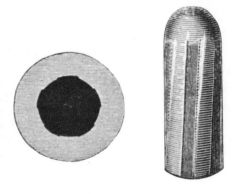

The Henry rifling and elongated bullet.

National Rifle Association. The Hilton Trophy later was sent back to the NRA, and all subsequent Army matches for a number of years were held at Army posts throughout the United States, primarily at Forts Niagara and Leavenworth.

The withdrawal of the Army teams was a hard blow to the National Rifle Association, but it was only a love tap compared to the crushing haymaker that Governor Alonzo B. Cornell of New York had suddenly unleashed against it. Alonzo B. Cornell entered the governor's mansion in Albany on January 1, 1880, after winning the election on a promise of economy in government. The event was to prove costly for the National Rifle Association.

Until 1880, a succession of state governors, beginning with John T. Hoffman and John A. Dix, had given the NRA every encouragement in strengthening the program of the State National Guard and in developing a non-military reserve of trained marksmen.

Soon after Cornell became governor, Gen. George W. Wingate, the vice-president of the NRA, who had just resigned as general inspector of rifle practice of New York State, found himself in Albany on business and decided to pay a courtesy call on Gen. Frederick Townsend, Cornell's newly appointed adjutant general. Ever since the earliest days of the NRA it had been the custom for the governor or his adjutant general to present to the winning team the Soldier of Marathon Trophy, which the state itself had contributed as a stimulus to interstate competition among the various National Guard organizations. Wingate planned to ask the new governor to follow this custom and also to present the Hilton Shield in the customary post-match ceremony.

General Wingate found Townsend in a state of depression. The Governor, he told Wingate, was entirely hostile in his attitude toward the National Guard and was already sharpening his knife to make the first cut. The Adjutant General invited Wingate to visit Cornell with him to see if he could persuade the Governor to change his mind.

Wingate, a skilled attorney, was a persuasive speaker, but Cornell would hear none of his arguments. Instead he launched into a diatribe, one that marks him as one of the worst prophets in American political life. "There will be no war in my time or in the time of my children," he told Wingate. "The only need for a National Guard is to show itself in parades and ceremonies. I see no reason for them to learn to shoot if their only function will be to march a little through the streets. Rifle practice for these men is a waste of money, and I shall not countenance in my presence anything as foolish as a discussion of the rifle shooting at Creedmoor."

Wingate, taken completely aback, tried the logical approach. "But, Governor, if we are going to have soldiers armed with

Remington "rolling block" .50-70 rifle, long the standard arm of the New York National Guard.

weapons, it seems a matter of common sense to teach them to use those weapons."

"Then," roared the Governor, "we should take their rifles away from them and sell them to benefit the Treasury. It would be more practical and far less expensive to arm them with clubs which require no instruction in their use. Good day, Sir!"

When Cornell made his inevitable cuts in the budget of the National Guard he used a broadaxe rather than a knife. The procedure of transporting teams from distant National Guard units to the matches at Creedmoor at state expense was summarily abolished. The issue of tents and other state-owned materiel for use by the NRA at Creedmoor was withdrawn. Moreover, the new state regulations required that those national guardsmen traveling to Creedmoor go there as formal military units rather than as individuals or in informal groups. There they were required to spend more time drilling and marching than they were in shooting, and ammunition allotments were cut to the bone.

Wingate, in his 1907 "Recollections of the National Rifle Association," deals more gently with Townsend than the Adjutant General seems to deserve. If Townsend was not the originator of the drastic, shortsighted instructions that ensued he was at least Cornell's willing tool. In his annual report to the Governor in January, 1881, Townsend suggested, among other things, that, "I would recommend the immediate abrogation of the orders whereby prizes and decorations are furnished at the expense of the State, for the time, even the cessation of all rifle practice by the guard until the force shall have

# MANUAL

FOR

# RIFLE PRACTICE.

INCLUDING SUGGESTIONS FOR PRACTICE AT LONG RANGE AND FOR THE FORMATION AND MANAGEMENT OF RIFLE ASSOCIATIONS.

BY

## GEN. GEO. W. WINGATE,

GENERAL INSPECTOR OF RIFLE PRACTICE, N. G. S. N. Y.

*SEVENTH REVISED EDITION.*

Go—bid the soldiers shoot.—HAMLET, *Act V, Scene 2.*

NEW YORK:
W. C. & F. P. CHURCH,
ARMY AND NAVY JOURNAL, 240 BROADWAY,
1879.

been reduced to within twelve thousand officers and enlisted men, and the State shall have provided the proper camping sites, with butts thereon for the drill and discipline of its troops in all that pertains to the duties of the soldier."

This report shook the National Rifle Association to its core. In other words, military training in New York State was to revert to its spit-and-polish status before the days of the NRA when marksmanship was considered secondary to fancy close-order drill.

The effect of these orders was to destroy almost entirely the program of the National Rifle Association as it had existed to that time. The abrupt withdrawal of the Army and the sudden shift of state support now threatened the very existence of the Association.

# 9

# End

# of an Era—

By 1881 the National Rifle Association faced a difficult future. Much of its financial support stemmed directly or indirectly from the state of New York, and Governor Cornell had knocked this prop out from under it. The organization had reached a point where drastic measures were required if it was to survive.

Its first move was to seek a nationally known figure, who, like General Burnside in its first year, would provide firm support and at least token leadership to guide the Association toward renewed national prestige. On January 20, 1881, the Executive Committee met in special session and voted to ask General Hancock to serve as president, appointing vice-president George W. Wingate as a delegation of one to visit the recent Presidential candidate and solicit his support. Of all the leading public figures in the United States, Hancock had demonstrated the strongest sympathy for the program of the NRA, not only by obtaining the Hilton Shield Trophy but through expressions of personal interest and support. Hancock accepted readily with the understanding that his military and political duties would make it difficult for him to play a very active role in the affairs of the organization. With the promise from Wingate that he, as vice-president, would handle the routine duties of the presidency, General Hancock became the president of the NRA.

With this encouragement, the Association early in 1881 moved its offices from the cramped third floor walk-up quarters at 37 Park Row to a roomier ground floor location at 75 Nassau Street and started to rebuild its program.

The withdrawal of strong financial help from the state, however, proved a difficult obstacle, although in 1881 the NRA did receive $3000 under its contract with the state of New York for the use of Creedmoor by the National Guard. This was enough to keep it operating in the black but not enough to expand its already reduced schedule of matches. The September meeting at Creedmoor was little more than a shadow of its former self. Events that had seen up to 300 individual entries in earlier years had fewer than 50 in 1881.

The high point of the otherwise lackluster tournament of 1881 was the introduction of the Skirmishers' Match. Like

Gen. Winfield S. Hancock, NRA president
(1881-1882).

# Goodbye to Creedmoor

the Soldiers' Match, this attempted to carry to the rifle range a practical exercise in battlefield marksmanship. But unlike the older event, which perpetuated the obsolescent volley and file fire of the War between the States, the Skirmishers' Match was a step forward in infantry training. As in the Soldiers' Match, the men, in uniform and armed with standard service weapons, were arranged in squads, each forming a single rank. All commands were given by bugle. At the initial command, the first man in each squad advanced to the 600-yard firing line and fired one shot before charging at the run toward the target. At the sound of the bugle, he was required to stop and, within twenty seconds, fire his second round, proceeding in this way until he had fired five shots and reached the 200-yard line. Then at the sound of "Recall the Skirmishers," he retreated at double time, stopping on command to fire at the target until he reached his starting point, where he shot his tenth and final round.

The first Skirmishers' Match at Creedmoor was won by Pvt. John Cavanaugh of the Army engineers from Willett's Point, the only representa-

Gen. E. L. Molineux, NRA president (1882-1883).

tives of the federal forces on the field. Their team walked away with the *Army and Navy Journal* Cup and several other trophies that had gone consistently to New York guardsmen in previous matches. On September 29, General Hancock sent Cavanaugh's first-prize gold Travers Medal to General Abbot, asking him to present the trophy to the soldier in an appropriate ceremony. In his letter to Abbot, the president of the NRA stated: "The object of the National Rifle Association is to increase the military strength of the country by making skill in the use of arms as prevalent as it was in the days of the Revolution."

As another step toward rebuilding its strength, the NRA in 1881 reopened negotiations with the National Rifle Association of Great Britain on the long-proposed British-American military rifle competition. A proposal, advanced by the British, was that a team of twelve

American National Guardsmen would shoot against a squad representing the Volunteer Service of Great Britain, using standard military rifles. The British first proposed that the match be held at Wimbledon in July, 1882, after the Americans declined an invitation to send a team of long-range match shooters to England for a "friendly competition." In October, the NRA tentatively accepted the new invitation, and Capt. Edmund St. John Mildmay wrote to General Hancock that the British welcomed the opportunity to resume competition with the Americans.

Negotiations with the British concerning terms were placed in the hands of a committee under the chairmanship of General Wingate. On November 11, this committee sent out notices to all state National Guard and militia organizations informing them of the impending match and asking them to pick their best marksmen as candidates for the team.

After numerous communications concerning technicalities, terms, and location, it was agreed that the match would be held at Creedmoor. The tacit understanding was that a return match would be held the following year at Wimbledon.

On March 15, 1882, Wingate's committee issued its first call for candidates in a general circular, following it on May 1 with letters to the adjutants general of all states and territories. The letters were signed by George J. Seabury, Secretary, and Gen. Edward L. Molineux, who had succeeded General Hancock as president of the NRA in January, 1882. On May 13, the Associa-

Match rifles used by United States team:
*From top:* (1) Remington-Hepburn military
match rifle. (2) Remington-Hepburn long-range
match rifle. (3) Sharps-Borchardt long-range
match rifle. (4) Winchester's Hotchkiss bolt
action repeating rifle.

tion issued, through the national press, an open letter "To the National Guard and the Public," asking for public contributions to help the National Rifle Association finance the forthcoming international match.

On May 25 another committee was assigned to select a rifle that would meet all requirements specified by the terms of the match. It first applied to the Ordnance Department of the United States Army for help in obtaining a government rifle that would equal those available to the British.

The response of the state militia organizations was generally favorable, and most with range facilities meeting the standards of the National Rifle Association held preliminary trials throughout the spring of 1882. After checking the results of these matches, the steering committee of the NRA selected the forty-seven best marksmen to compete in shoulder-to-shoulder competition at Creedmoor on August 15-18. Fourteen men were picked to comprise the team and its reserve, but two additional men were added later. The team promptly elected Col. John Bodine its captain. Most of the finalists, as expected, came from the ranks of the experienced New York National Guard regiments. The American team began serious practice on August 26, the day the British team, captained by Sir Henry Halford, sailed from England.

During the prematch practice an aura of defeatism permeated American shooting circles. It contrasted sharply with the great confidence that had preceded the Irish-American matches of a decade before. There were valid reasons for pessimism, but none that had not applied also to the American team in 1874. The thing that concerned most of the Americans, however, was the comparative manpower of the American National Guard and the British Volunteer Force. The latter boasted 500,000 men to slightly more than 50,000 Guardsmen. The Volunteer Force was also a tightly organized unit and a subsidiary of the Regular Army; the National Guard at that time was an aggregation of independent military organizations whose actions were only slightly coordinated with one another or with those of the regular forces. The British emphasis on training its volunteers in long-range marksmanship was well known; only a few National Guardsmen outside the Northeast had been trained to shoot beyond 600 yards.

There was also pessimism about the quality of American military rifles in comparison to those of the British. The committee appointed by the NRA to select a rifle had made little progress, and after the team had been picked, Bodine decided to permit his shooters to use their own favorite rifles. Nine selected the .44 Remington-Hepburn, two used the .45 Sharps-Borchardt, and one selected the Hotchkiss repeating rifle manufactured by Winchester. The latter, although used in this instance as a single-shot, was said to be the first repeating rifle used in a major competition in America.

The gloom that permeated the American camp was not relieved by the appearance of the British in their natty regimental dress uniforms. Sir Henry Halford, handsome and white-haired, was a born administrator who knew how to squeeze every ounce of effort from his team. His brisk military efficiency contrasted sharply with the loose, rather bumbling control that Bodine exerted over the Americans. Although the aging Bodine took a back seat to few as a shooter, he had little talent as an administrator. He made little or no effort to coach his men in long-range shooting, a field in which he excelled. In practice with the British, this deficiency of the Americans was apparent to all.

Although the Americans had bowed to the British demands that the rifles all have laterally fixed rear sights, most of the Americans "shot over the bar," a common practice in American military events at that time. In this process the slide of the rear sight was reversed to form a solid bar, the rear face of which was scribed with spaced vertical lines against which the front sight was aligned to adjust for windage. This had been accepted by the British in prematch negotiations, but Sir Henry took rather violent exception to some of the front sights used on the American rifles. The British barleycorn front sight formed a tapered outline when seen from the shooting position. Many of the American sights were of the post variety. But since it was too late to make any change, the British finally agreed to accept the American sight design.

The British, however, had little cause to criticize the design of American arms, since their own pieces were scarcely of government issue. Most had been customized by Gibbs, the famous British gunmaker, to obtain maximum accuracy and to combine Farquharson and Deeley actions with Metford barrels. The British also used specially loaded ammunition, which they brought with them, while the Americans loaded their own cases on the range, each using loads based on his individual taste. Bodine was quite horrified on the day of the match to find some of his men using "Bracket Powder," a smokeless powder mixed with black powder, in the belief that it prevented fouling of the bores. This mixed loading of the cartridges did little to improve the consistency of the American scores.

The British team did not compete in the various matches of the fall meeting at Creedmoor which preceded the international match on September 12, 1882, although individual members shot in some matches open to foreigners. The effect of the renewed effort of the NRA was apparent in this 21-event tournament, however, both in public interest and in the representation of out-of-state teams. Michigan and Maine both competed for the first time in the Hilton Trophy Match, and the United States Army Division of the Atlantic, apparently through the influence of General Hancock, also entered a team. This match was won by the National Guard of Pennsylvania.

Another significant event at the fall meeting was the inauguration of the *Army and Navy Journal* Revolver Match, initiated by Col. William C. Church, whose differences with the organization appear to have been settled. Church donated a $200 double-barreled Webley shotgun as a prize for this match, which was open to all members of the armed forces. It

British breech-loading match rifles and their highly developed adjustable target sights.

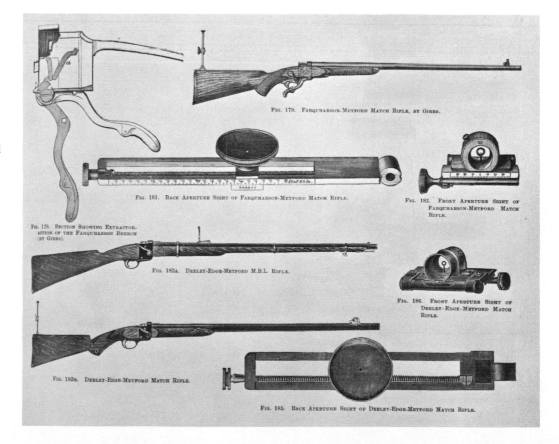

FIG. 179. FARQUHARSON-METFORD MATCH RIFLE, BY GIBBS.

FIG. 181. BACK APERTURE SIGHT OF FARQUHARSON-METFORD MATCH RIFLE.

FIG. 182. FRONT APERTURE SIGHT OF FARQUHARSON-METFORD MATCH RIFLE.

FIG. 178. SECTION SHOWING EXTRACTOR-ACTION OF THE FARQUHARSON BREECH (BY GIBBS).

FIG. 183A. DEELEY-EDGE-METFORD M.B.L. RIFLE.

FIG. 186. FRONT APERTURE SIGHT OF DEELEY-EDGE-METFORD MATCH RIFLE.

FIG. 183B. DEELEY-EDGE-METFORD MATCH RIFLE.

FIG. 185. BACK APERTURE SIGHT OF DEELEY-EDGE-METFORD MATCH RIFLE.

was the first featured event involving the handgun held by the NRA. Under the terms of this match each shooter fired six shots at thirty-five yards from a standard military revolver at the "tramp" target, a disappearing-man target that had been used in informal shooting at Creedmoor since its opening. The match was won by Pvt. John Cavanaugh, the Army engineer from Willett's Point who had won the first Skirmishers' Match in 1881.

The big international match was held on September 15 and 16, and from the first the poorly coached and motley-armed Americans were hopelessly outclassed. After a slim initial lead of seven points at the end of the third round of the 200-yard phase, the Americans began to trail, and the British steadily widened their lead throughout the match. The British had practiced intensively in the offhand position as soon as they learned that they would have to use that position in the match. In shooting over the three longest distances, nearly all of the British shooters selected the back position, while only a few of the American marksmen employed it—an almost exact reversal of the situation in the previous British-American competitions. When the last shot had been fired, the British had rolled up an overwhelming lead of 170 points, winning the match by a score of 1975 to 1805 out of a possible 2530.

The defeat of the American team was a surprise to no one, but the extent of the British victory came as a shock. The National Rifle Association immediately began to lay plans for the return match at Wimbledon, drawing solace from the belief that the defeat would jar America's shooters and military leaders from their lethargy. Even before the British team

sailed for home, general agreement was reached on the terms for another British-American match on July 20 and 21, 1883.

At a special meeting on October 3, the Board of Directors discussed ways of organizing the strongest and best equipped American team and financing its trip to England. The Association had interested itself in pressing constantly for improved military arms no less than for improved training methods. This crushing defeat by the British dramatized the relatively poor quality of the available American army rifles as well as the need for marksmanship training at the longer distances.

Meanwhile, the Subcommittee on the Selection of a Rifle, under the chairmanship of Col. H. G. Litchfield, had received splendid cooperation from the management of E. Remington & Sons. As soon as they had been approached the famous gunmakers assigned their best craftsmen to design a new model based on the time-tested Hepburn patent to meet all of the specifications agreed to by the two national organizations. The new Remington Long-Range Military Rifle was of .44 caliber but chambered to accept a .45 caliber cartridge case for greater powder capacity behind the 550-grain bullet. The barrel was improved by deepening the grooves and narrowing the lands. Bodine and Thomas J. Dolan of the 1882 team spent several weeks at the Remington factory experimenting to determine its most reliable load.

At the same time, however, J. H. Brown, a member of the Board of Directors of the NRA, had developed another rifle with a falling block action and a half-concealed

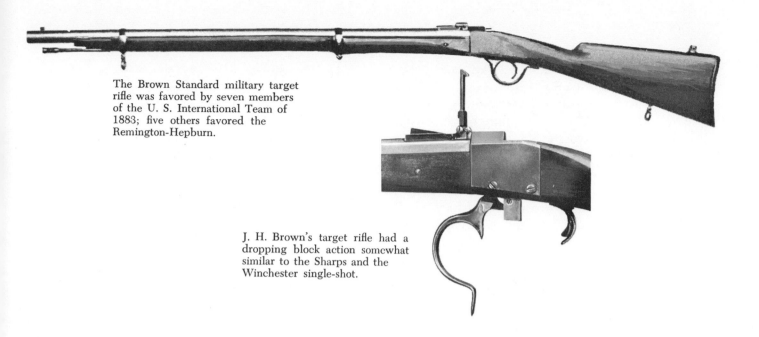

The Brown Standard military target rifle was favored by seven members of the U. S. International Team of 1883; five others favored the Remington-Hepburn.

J. H. Brown's target rifle had a dropping block action somewhat similar to the Sharps and the Winchester single-shot.

hammer. The Brown Standard Rifle was of .45 caliber with an 8-groove bore, chambered for a Winchester case using a 550-grain bullet. Colonel Litchfield was enthusiastic about the Brown and made a glowing report advocating its adoption after he and W. Milton Farrow tested it. In this test, Brown shot one group of ten shots from the back position at 200 yards that he could cover with his watch.

When the Subcommittee on the Selection of a Rifle found itself unable to decide between the Brown and the Remington, the matter was thrown into the lap of the Board of Directors. By June 6, 1883, with the sailing date of the team approaching rapidly, no firm decision had been reached. The upshot was that the respective members of the team were permitted to choose between the two rifles. Of those who comprised the first string, seven were partial to the Brown Standard while five preferred the Remington.

Meanwhile competitions had been conducted by National Guard organizations across America to select contenders for the team. The team finally selected in a series of elimination matches held at Creedmoor was somewhat more representative of the United States than that of 1882, and only five members of the earlier team won places in 1883.

For a while it had appeared that the National Rifle Association would be unable to raise the $5000 needed to finance the travel of the team. But at the last minute its old benefactor, James Gordon Bennett, wrote a check for $2500, placing the fund over its goal by $1500.

As soon as the American team arrived in England it immediately ran into its old thorn of contention—the wind-gauge rear sight. Both the Brown and the Remington were equipped with screw-activated windage adjust-

97

ments like those used on the latest-model Spring-field rifles. Sir Henry Halford protested that the sights were impractical for military use, although they then received rough daily use in garrisons on the American frontier. He tried to obtain a ruling that the screw mechanism be disengaged, stating that the British concession referred only to rear slides activated by hand pressure. The Council of the British NRA, however, overruled Sir Henry, but it refused to permit the Americans to compete in the regular matches at Wimbledon until they had disengaged the screw mechanism of their sights.

The second British-American Military Match was held on July 20 and 21, 1883. The opening day was cold and blustery with gusts of rain sweeping the range, and, although such weather favored the British, the Americans maintained a slight lead at every distance throughout the first three phases, ending the 600-yard shooting in the afternoon of the twentieth with a score of 1424 to 1400 for the British. The results surprised the Americans as much as it did their hosts.

On the second day, it appeared that the weather was about to clear. When the British shooters led off, the sun appeared from behind the clouds, and American hopes began to soar. If fair weather prevailed they had a good chance of holding their lead. The break in the cloud cover, however, was only a lull before the storm, one of the worst in the memory of the oldest Wimbledon shooters. The rain came down in sheets that at times hid the targets completely. Gale-force winds drove it straight into the faces of the marksmen. As the men stretched out in puddles on the shooting ramps and fought to align their sights on the half-visible targets, crews of British Volunteers struggled behind them to keep the tents from blowing away.

None of the American shooters had ever experienced such conditions, and their scores suffered badly. The British, more accustomed to foul-weather shooting, whittled down the American lead and then pulled ahead. The rain squalls persisted on and off, reaching a peak as the 1000-yard phase began. Although the Americans continued to battle down to the last shot, shooting with determination and skill against heavy odds, the final score found them trailing by forty-five points, the British winning the match by a score of 1951 to 1906.

For an underdog team with everything against them, this defeat was a victory of sorts, for even the British conceded that, given more favorable weather conditions, the scores might well have been reversed.

Along with this revived interest in international matches there was a growing interest

Cartridges of this style were the ones usually fired on the Creedmoor range.

98

in target shooting at moderate ranges. Creedmoor, where primary attention was given to long-range and military shooting, left much to be desired for many shooters who enjoyed precision shooting at the shorter ranges. The Massachusetts Rifle Association's Walnut Hill Range soon became a Mecca for those who liked to shoot at the favorite 200-yard range, where fast target marking provided more shooting in a half day. This led to some diminishing of attendance at Creedmoor and also to the evolution of new targets.

The increasing activities at ranges like Walnut Hill and the excellent showing of the American team at Wimbledon acted on the National Rifle Association like a shot of adrenalin, although it was about the last drop in the vial. The following Creedmoor program of 1884 was one of the strongest in years, and at the fall meeting of September 9 through 13, the prize list soared over $7000, of which $1800 was in cash. There were more than 1500 entries in the nineteen matches, among which was a new "General Sheridan Skirmishers' Match," similar to the Travers Match but open to teams of six men rather than individuals. The match was won by a team from the Fourth Artillery of the United States Army, while a team from the Division of the Atlantic picked up the Hilton Shield from the Michigan National Guard, which had won the trophy in 1883. This same match was marked by a change in policy relative to prizes. In previous years the organization had issued cups and medals for second and third place in all the matches. In 1884, it began to issue a preponderance of cash prizes.

Gen. Ulysses S. Grant had become president of the NRA in April, 1883, at the urging of a committee headed by General Wingate. This committee had been appointed at a meeting of the Board of Directors on January 9 to request General Grant's acceptance in an effort to bolster the program of the NRA.

Gen. Ulysses S. Grant, NRA president (1883-1884).

Grant at the time was working on his memoirs in New York City and at Mount McGregor near Saratoga, physically ill and somewhat mentally soured by his ventures from 1869 through 1874 into a political world that was completely foreign to his temperament and training.

The war hero and former President of the United States received the delegation from the NRA politely but with reservations. As a soldier he was entirely in sympathy with its program, but he made clear his inability to play a very active part in its affairs. He finally accepted, as General Hancock had done, with the understanding that the position would involve no time-consuming formal duties. Grant maintained a close interest in the affairs of the NRA, but poor health prevented active participation. He was succeeded in the presidency the following year by Gen. Philip H. Sheridan, the Commander-in-Chief of the United States Army, in honor of whom the Sheridan Skirmishers' Match had been named.

Throughout the administrations of Han-

The National Rifle Association
OF AMERICA.
Office, Room 406, Temple Court, 5 & 7 Beekman St., N. Y.

PROGRAMME
—OF—

MATCHES AT CREEDMOOR

Commencing September 1st,

1891.

For Long Island Railroad Time Table see inside page. Should any change be made, notices
will be posted at Creedmoor.

Stages run continuously between
Queens Station and the Range.

BROUN, GREEN & ADAMS, STATIONERS, 40 BEAVER STREET.

The 1891 matches signalled an end to Creedmoor's prominence on the American shooting scene.

cock, Grant, and Sheridan, the actual direction of the program of the National Rifle Association fell on the broad shoulders of George W. Wingate. In a very real sense, the National Rifle Association was reaching a point where its very survival might well depend upon the survival of the tall lawyer whose career had been so closely interwoven with its own. In January, 1886, Wingate, his once long beard now close-cropped and iron gray, became the tenth president of the NRA.

This was a period of severe economic crisis for the nation as well as for the NRA. The economy of the United States was still reeling under the impact of the Panic of 1884 and beset by labor problems that climaxed in the

Haymarket Riot in Chicago in 1886. The Association, beset by financial problems, moved into progressively smaller headquarters between 1883 and 1886—102 Williams Street, 31 Chandler Street, and finally to 5 Beekman Street.

In spite of these difficulties it tried to hold another International rifle match at Creedmoor and on October 24, 1884, invited the National Rifle Association of Great Britain to send a team to America in 1885. Britain also was in the depths of a depression, however, and the Sudanese Rebellion, which had begun with the Massacre at Khartoum, had placed the Empire on a war footing. Late in March, 1885, the British advised that "in view of the very unsettled state of affairs at home and abroad, the National Rifle Association do not think they would be justified in accepting the challenge of the National Rifle Association of the United States of America. . . ."

With the doors closed to another International match that might have revived public interest in its program, the National Rifle Association struggled to maintain its program at Creedmoor. It operated against serious odds. The Long Island railroad was facing bankruptcy, and rail service had been severely cut. Merchants and manufacturers who had been lavish in donating prizes in prosperous years dropped their support. The recruitment of Life Members fell to a trickle and many annual members dropped from the rolls.

Faced with these problems the NRA fought for survival. Since earliest days, it had been customary for the officers of the Association to finance the annual matches at Creedmoor through personal notes, which always had been repaid from state appropriations. Since the administration of Governor Cornell, however, this procedure had involved the risk of serious financial loss to the officers of the NRA, and matters showed little sign of im-

100

provement. Disgusted with the lack of appreciation for what had been accomplished for the benefit of the National Guard, and to eliminate the financial burdens, the Association finally voted in January, 1890, to deed Creedmoor to the state of New York with the understanding that the Association would be permitted to hold its customary matches on the range and to issue its marksmanship qualification medals to members of the National Guard.

A crowning blow to the old organization was the elevation of Capt. B. M. Whitlock to position of Inspector General of Rifle Practice with the rank of brigadier general by New York's Governor Roswell P. Flower in January, 1892. Whitlock's first official act was to withdraw recognition by the state of the marksmanship badges issued by the NRA. He also adopted a new policy of free use of Creedmoor by state troops, which had the effect of eliminating the entrance fees that the NRA had charged to help finance the Creedmoor program. Deliberately or unintentionally he also ordered various units of the state National Guard to practice on the range at times customarily occupied by the matches of the National Rifle Association.

A short time before, the New York *Graphic* had done a masterful job in summarizing the accomplishments of the NRA to that time, stating:

> It should not be forgotten that to the National Rifle Association belongs the credit for elevating the use of the rifle to the dignity of the present service; of directing popular attention to its importance as a part of the national military training; of stimulating American patriotism through the international matches; and finally causing a revolution in army target-practice, which, based on flintlock and smoothbore principles, had become an obsolete exercise. A few years since, the War Department, thus reminded, introduced the

Gen. Philip H. Sheridan, NRA president (1885-1886).

> needed reforms and, seconded by Generals Sherman, Sheridan, and Hancock in their respective commands, availed itself of the benefits of Creedmoor. . . .

On June 16, 1892, the Board of Directors of the Association met to discuss the very serious problems faced by the Association and voted to place its records in storage and to enter into negotiations with the New Jersey State Rifle Association to see if the NRA matches could be transferred from Creedmoor to the new Sea Girt Range of that state organization. After reelecting the existing panel of officers—Wingate as president; Gen. John B. Woodward as vice-president; and Capt. John S. Shepherd as secretary—the meeting adjourned without further business. It was the next to the last formal meeting of the Board of Directors during the Nineteenth Century.

This was the end of an era. The National Rifle Association of America would never again be largely dependent on any one state; it would become national in fact as well as in name, or it would cease to exist.

# Interim Leadership in New Jersey

The Krag-Jorgensen .30 caliber rifle was the first magazine rifle put in general use by the U. S. Army.

General George W. Wingate, who had been a major force in guiding the destiny of the National Rifle Association since its inception, must have felt the loss of Creedmoor as a crushing defeat. The organization that he had helped to create seemed to be fighting a losing battle, a victim of economic depression, political apathy, and changing times. But Creedmoor and the NRA had succeeded far beyond his realization. By 1890, Creedmoor, by contemporary standards, was already antiquated, and it had served its purpose far better than Wingate realized.

A major achievement of the National Rifle Association to that time was in altering basic military attitudes toward the rifle. Before 1871, infantry tactics were based largely on the concentration of fire, aimed or unaimed, by massed troops, against a general target. Individual skill in shooting, although universally considered a useful attribute in a recruit, was rarely thought of as a skill that could be taught or improved. Only a few commanders on the western frontier seemed to realize that individually aimed fire had any place on the battlefield except on the skirmish line. Except for some improvised installations set up by a few local commanders, no facilities for formal rifle practice had existed on any Army post in America.

After its early drubbings at the hands of Creedmoor-trained citizen-soldiers, the Army abruptly awakened and initiated training in marksmanship for combat troops. By 1890, it was holding regular rifle matches at

10

# Sea Girt

# Replaces Creedmoor

all levels of command and had elevated skill in rifle shooting to an important requirement of the foot soldier. The militia organizations of the various states had started comparable training programs.

The role of the National Rifle Association in initiating these reforms is clear. As late as 1890, the basic Army and Navy training manuals on marksmanship were only modifications of Wingate's *Manual of Rifle Practice.* Until 1885, the Army used targets identical to those that were standardized under rules laid down by the NRA. The Army also had appointed inspectors of rifle practice through all levels of command down to the regiment patterned after the system first established in the New York National Guard at the instigation of the National Rifle Association.

The competitions at Creedmoor had also spurred the development of more accurate and more efficient infantry weapons. The poor showing of Regulars armed with standard-issue Springfields against National Guardsmen equipped with more modern weapons had resulted in the adoption of rifles of progressively flatter trajectories, smaller bores, longer ranges, and better sights. In 1872, many first-line Army regiments were still armed with relics from the Civil War. By 1890, the Army Ordnance Department was conducting experiments with small-caliber repeating rifles that led to the adoption in 1892 of the .30 caliber Krag-Jorgensen, the first magazine rifle in general use by the United States Army.

Although the Creedmoor Range had been lost to the NRA, its name was firmly established in the lexicon of shooting sports. During the late 1800s it was seized upon by dozens of advertising copy writers. "Creedmoor" implied the highest standards or the best of its kind. The best-grade rifles produced by Remington, Sharps, Marlin, and other gun manufacturers were their "Creedmoor" models. One manufacturer produced a "Creedmoor parlor gun," and a thriving indoor tunnel-gallery range in New York City was called "Creedmoor Junior."

Although its program continued to move forward under the momentum of earlier successes, the National Rifle Association as an organization became relatively dormant for eight years after 1892. The major contributing factors that led to this dormancy were three. A succession of pacifist-inclined and economy-minded governors in New York State, beginning with Governor Cornell, provided a poor political climate for the promotion of rifle practice. General economic depression cut heavily into the Association's financial support and made progressive action next to impossible. Finally, there had been a general loss of public interest in long-range shooting as a spectator sport.

During the early days of Creedmoor, the great international rifle matches had captured the imagination of the American public. Led by James Gordon Bennett's *New York Herald,* the newspapers of the 1870s had vied with one another in giving space to the most minute details of the more important rifle matches. Crowds had thronged the field at Creedmoor to watch Bodine, Gildersleeve, and Dakin practice for their contests with the Irish and English. In 1875, long-range shooting had little competition from other spectator sports. But by

DR. W. F. CARVER

1890 it was competing for public interest with horse racing, baseball, football, track, rowing, yacht racing, and dozens of other sports. It was even competing with other forms of shooting that provided more action for the spectator.

Stripped of the color, suspense, and national patriotism that attended the previous international matches, long-range rifle shooting became a dull spectator sport in contrast to some other forms such as trapshooting, in which the spectator could more closely identify himself with the shooter. The fall of a flying pigeon, the breaking of a glass target ball, or the shattering of a clay pigeon following the crack of a shotgun had an immediate visual impact that was lacking in the invisible plunk of a bullet against a far distant target. Trapshooting clubs often spiced their programs with intermission performances by exhibition shooters like Doc Carver, Adam H. Bogardus, and Ira Paine, whose incredible feats with shotguns and rifles at thrown

104

CAPTAIN A. H. BOGARDUS

CHEVALIER IRA PAINE

Three talented American shooters who combined their shooting skill with crowd-pleasing showmanship.

targets attracted throngs of non-shooting spectators. Competitive shotgunning enjoyed major economic and geographic advantages over long-range rifle shooting. A satisfactory trap range could be set up within hours on a few acres of open land. A rifle range on the Creedmoor pattern required a large tract of land, costly installations, and elaborate safety measures.

Aside from those shooting activities which had special spectator appeal, short-range target shooting had developed into a popular sport during the last half of the Nineteenth Century. Indoor and outdoor rifle and pistol ranges were available in many communities. New York City in 1890 had at least ten commercial shooting galleries or shooting parks with facilities for shooting at from 50 feet to 200 yards. Many of the long-range marksmen of the National Rifle Association practiced at these inexpensive facilities, and there

were hundreds of short-range shooters for every man who had ever fired at a 1000-yard target.

Little effort had been made by the National Rifle Association to bring these short-range shooters under its wing; it had remained primarily an association of long-range rifle shooters throughout the 1800s. In the meantime, public interest in long-range shooting was declining, while recreational shooting with rifles, shotguns and pistols was enjoying widespread growth.

The latent strength of the National Rifle Association of America during the few years of its relative eclipse was dispersed among many relatively small but enthusiastic groups of riflemen organized in local clubs and state associations throughout the nation. They had been organized under rules established by the NRA. Their members shot on ranges patterned after Creedmoor with Creedmoor rifles at Creedmoor targets and under Creedmoor rules. The original concept of the National Rifle Asso-

ciation had been of a truly national organization of such clubs, all affiliated under its own single standard. In actuality, the NRA had had difficulty in extending its direct control over many clubs outside New York State, although it had done everything within its power to effect such a union. But communication and transportation facilities had not developed far enough to make close liaison possible and few others than New Jersey, the District of Columbia, and Massachusetts had much contact with the parent organization.

Some of the state organizations had developed programs and ranges that rivaled those of the NRA. Among the earliest was the Massachusetts Rifle Association. Founded by Col. Horace T. Rockwell in 1875, it had opened its Walnut Hill Range on the outskirts of Boston in November, 1876. In 1889 the Massachusetts Volunteer Militia sent a Walnut Hill-trained rifle team to Wimbledon, and it won every match it could enter under the rules of the National Rifle Association of Great Britain. By 1890, Walnut Hill had become almost as well known as Creedmoor.

When the National Rifle Association deeded Creedmoor to the state of New York, nearly every state in the Union had a state rifle association. Of these, the one with the closest ties to the NRA was the New Jersey State Rifle Association, which had been founded on March 11, 1878. The founders were a group of Creedmoor-trained marksmen from the New Jersey National Guard, including Col. W. H. DeHart and Maj. Henry Fulton, a member of the first American international rifle team. The New Jersey organization had obtained an immediate appropriation from the State Legislature to build a state rifle range. Until that time, under an agreement with the National Rifle Association, the New Jersey National Guard had practiced regularly at Creedmoor. New Jersey teams competed in nearly every match held on the Creedmoor range. It also obtained the appointment of inspectors of rifle practice within the National Guard similar to those in New York. Part of the New Jersey association's initial success came from the sympathetic influence of then-Governor George Brinton McClellan, who as a former commanding general of the Army, a veteran of the Civil War, and a former Presidential candidate, carried a great deal of influence.

Brinton Range, named in honor of the Governor, who dedicated it in August, 1878, was on the edge of the salt meadows of Newark Bay between Elizabeth and Elizabethport. Its location was at once its greatest strength and weakness. Like all major ranges of the day, Brinton was patterned closely after Creedmoor, but its greater area permitted shooting out to 1200 yards. It was readily accessible by rail from New York City as well as the major population centers of northern New Jersey.

Unlike Creedmoor and Walnut Hill, however, Brinton was laid out on water-logged soil. The grounds were subject to

Walnut Hill Range in Massachusetts, *showing from left:* shooting house, range keeper's cottage, stable, and 500-yard firing point.

flooding at high tide, and shooters often found themselves separated from the targets by open water. Shooting ramps dredged from the marsh had to be used to bring the firing lines to a level with the targets, which were elevated behind sod bulwarks built to protect the markers. Hip boots were standard accessories for the markers and range officers. The quality of the drinking-water supply was atrocious.

But an even greater hazard at Brinton was the infamous Jersey mosquito. A reporter from a New York weekly who covered the dedication observed that the attendance included Governor McClellan, dozens of other dignitaries, hundreds of prominent shooters, and "several million mosquitoes." In summer the bloodthirsty insects swarmed so densely that it was often difficult for one to concentrate on his target. The "Brinton flinch," in which a shooter paused in midaim to slap at neck or forehead, was a standard joke in the New Jersey National Guard. Because of these deficiencies, Brinton never attained much prominence as a range.

During its early years, the New Jersey State Rifle Association was oriented even more toward purely military shooting than the New York-based NRA. It was also much more restrictive in its membership qualifications. Only members of the New Jersey National Guard could join, and the annual dues of ten dollars restricted membership largely to officers. Until its reorganization in 1891, the Association was, in fact, a relatively small society of high-ranking officers in the State National Guard.

As the changing political climate in New York forced a wedge between the state administration and the National Rifle Association, New Jersey gradually found itself squeezed out of the Creedmoor program. At the same time, relations between the New Jersey state administration and the New Jersey State Rifle Association improved with each succeeding governor. While the National Rifle Association was reaching an impasse in its relations with successive inspectors general of rifle practice in New York, Brig. Gen. Bird W. Spencer, inspector general of rifle practice of New Jersey and a founder of the NRA, became president of the state organization across the Hudson. In 1891, Spencer was succeeded in the presidency by the New Jersey Governor Leon Abbott—a far cry

SHOOTING HOUSE.      RANGE KEEPER'S HOUSE.      STABLE. (SHOOTING HOUSE PRIOR TO 1891)      500 YD. FIRING

from the situation in New York where the NRA was fighting the state administration for its life.

With this strong political backing, and with the gates of Creedmoor fast closing, the New Jersey State Rifle Association began searching for a new range to replace soggy Brinton, which had been all but abandoned after a few years of use. In 1889 it obtained an appropriation to build a range on a 148-acre tract at the New Jersey State Camp near Sea Girt, in the state's beach resort country. The site was readily accessible by rail from Trenton and the northern cities and was less than sixty miles from New York City.

In contrast to Brinton, the new range was perfectly drained and as level as a tabletop. Two driven wells, 700 feet deep, provided high-grade drinking water. Picturesque sand dunes, with gaps giving broad vistas of the Atlantic Ocean formed a backdrop for the 22 targets. The shore of Squan Lake formed its southern boundary while the northern boundary was defined by a road leading to the Stockton Mansion. This was a large frame building which later became a community center for the range and was renamed the Beach House. Permanent mess halls and officers' quarters, and ample space for the A-tents of the enlisted men permitted large numbers of troops to camp without crowding.

The targets—ten short-range, ten midrange, and two 1000-yard—were of the new regulation Army canvas type with elliptical rings. The only minor inconvenience was the layout of the 1000-yard ranges, which cut diagonally across the firing lines of the short- and midrange targets. There were other shortcomings that would show up later, but, all in all, Sea Girt in 1891 was the last word in rifle ranges and one of the most modern and best equipped in the world.

The inaugural rifle matches at Sea Girt were held on September 1 through 4, 1889, under the auspices of the Department of Rifle Practice of the New Jersey National Guard. Although impressive enough by normal standards, with nearly 1000 competitors on the field, the attendance was somewhat disappointing. General Spencer, as executive officer of the Sea Girt Range, had invited the adjutants general of all states to send teams to compete in an interstate military team match. Acceptances, formal or informal, were received from Massachusetts, Connecticut, New York, Pennsylvania, Delaware, Maryland, the District of Columbia, and the Division of the Atlantic of the United States Army. On the day of the opening match, however, only teams from New York, Delaware, and the District of Columbia appeared.

The New Jersey State Rifle Association assumed management of the rifle matches at Sea Girt in 1891, holding its fall meeting of that year on August 24 through 29. The first annual event was not a success in terms of attendance; only the District of Columbia sent representatives to compete in the interstate matches. The New York National Guard, after tentatively accepting the invitation to enter a team, withdrew because its members were still armed with the obsolete .50 caliber State Model Remington that General Townsend and later inspectors general of rifle practice had insisted on retaining. Nearly all other state militia organizations, including New Jersey's, had by then adopted the latest .45 caliber Springfields and Remingtons.

The Travers and Sheridan skirmishers' matches that had been held earlier at Creedmoor had captured the imagination of General Spencer and other officers of

Early days on the range at Sea Girt.

the New Jersey State Rifle Association. The skirmishers' run soon became to Sea Girt what long-range rifle shooting had been to Creedmoor. The Jerseymen excelled in this active form of shooting and developed it to a high state of refinement. The interstate matches that had been initiated in 1889 included skirmish runs as a supplement to stationary shooting at the 200- and 500-yard targets. As practiced in the early days at Sea Girt the skirmishers' matches were colorful as well as invaluable for training men in the latest battle tactics in dispersed formation.

In the typical skirmishers' match at Sea Girt the men lined up on the 600-yard line with unloaded rifles and twenty rounds in their cartridge boxes. General Spencer, a tall, erect man with a walrus mustache, dressed in dress uniform and cavalry boots and mounted on a bay horse, rode behind the line with a mounted bugler at his side. At the command "Fire!" the men popped loads into the breeches of their Springfields and Remingtons, dropped to prone, kneeling, or back positions and fired one shot each. Then they rose and raced through the black-powder smoke toward the target. A few seconds later, the notes from the bugle checked their advance, and again they dropped to shooting positions, continuing in this fashion until they had reached the 200-yard firing line. After firing their tenth rounds, they turned at the sound of "Retreat," with arms shouldered, pausing at the sound of the bugle to shoot back at the target until they had reached their starting point. The course was a test of a man's physical stamina as well as his marksmanship.

With the transfer of the National Rifle Association matches to Sea Girt in 1892, the New Jersey State Rifle Association, for all practical purposes, temporarily assumed the functions of the NRA.

For the New Jersey State Rifle Associa-

combined matches were held on September 5-10, 1892, with teams from Pennsylvania, New York, and New Jersey on the field. The next year saw the entry of teams from the District of Columbia, one of which won the Hilton Trophy, while Dr. S. I. Scott, a former member of the international team, took the Wimbledon Cup back to Washington, D. C.

These annual matches attracted relatively modest crowds and only a few teams, but they served to spread the reputation of Sea Girt and the New Jersey State Rifle Association throughout the shooting world. As a result, in 1894 thirteen teams representing the states of New York, Maine, Georgia, Pennsylvania, Connecticut, Massachusetts, and the Territory of Alaska entered the competition on September 3 through 8. This was the first time that a territorial team had competed.

Encouraged by its success and the growing interest of America's marksmen, the New Jersey State Rifle Association increased its efforts to expand the Sea Girt program. Although its membership was still restricted to members of the New Jersey National Guard, it had dropped the annual dues in 1892 from $10 to a more realistic $2, permitting more enlisted men

tion, the custodianship of such historic events as the Wimbledon Cup, Hilton Trophy, and Interstate Military Team Matches was a major boost. It conducted the matches, along with its own, under rules that had been laid down by the National Rifle Association. The result, with emphasis on skirmishing in the New Jersey matches, was a well-balanced medley of long-range, short-range, and skirmishers' events at each annual meeting. The first

Mitglieder des San Francisco Turn-Vereins.

A good time was had by all at the old-time *schuetzenfest*, where sport and refreshment were equally enjoyed.

to join. In 1895, it made its first effort to attract civilian shooters. Two events that year represented a departure from military rifle shooting. One was the Revolver Match, comparable to the *Army and Navy Journal* Military Revolver Match that had been held for a few years at Creedmoor a decade earlier. The second was a *schuetzen* match, the state association's first venture in the field of civilian shooting.

In contrast to the purely military skirmishers' run, the *schuetzen* match had almost no military application. It was a stylized form of shooting with customized small-caliber rifles, equipped with pronged butt plates, hand rests, elaborate sights, and heavy barrels. Shooting was usually from the standing position at targets, out to 200 yards. Although a number of other targets were used at many *schuetzen* matches, including a wooden eagle that must be systematically dismembered and which exploded when hit in the final target area, the standard 200-yard target consisted of 24 concentric rings spaced ¾ inch apart around a 1½-inch bullseye, the central 12 inches being black to provide an aiming point. For shorter distances this target was reduced to scale.

The *schuetzen* match was one of the oldest forms of organized shooting in the United States. It had been introduced around the midcentury by Swiss and German immigrants in the Middle West. By 1890 *schuetzen* clubs, or *schuetzenbunds*, were found in almost every American community where there were more than a few citizens of Teutonic ancestry. The North American Schuetzen Bund, the oldest shooting organization in America, was organized in 1865 and conducted an annual national *schuetzenfest*, attended by shooters from all over America. The *schuetzenfest* combined a massive Bavarian-style picnic with the more serious business of

DRINKING CUP. RIFLEMAN OF THE ZURICH SHOOTING CLUB, 1616

Du Pont copied the figure from an old Swiss drinking cup for their decoration on cans of Schuetzen smokeless powder.

punching holes in targets. The winner of the national match was crowned *koenig,* or king, to toasts drunk in gallons of foaming beer. Although dominated by German shooters, the national and local *schuetzenbunds* rarely restricted their membership to shooters of Teutonic ancestry. W. Milton Farrow, Frank Hyde, and other prominent non-Germanic marksmen were regular devotees of the *schuetzenfest* and attained the coveted title of "king."

In addition to five *schuetzen* matches, the twenty-four competitions in 1900 included six separate competitions involving handguns, including one featuring the new Colt autoloading pistol.

Other innovations made their appearance at Sea Girt, too, and the year 1895 saw the reintroduction of the President's Match for the Military Rifle Championship of the United States which had last been shot at Creedmoor in 1891. This individual championship had been instituted in the NRA matches of 1878. It was patterned after an event for British Volunteers called the Queen's Match, which the National Rifle Association of Great Britain had initiated in 1860.

In 1884, the name of the American Military Rifle Championship Match had been changed to the President's Match, although the name then lacked the significance that its counterpart enjoyed in Great Britain. In 1904, President Theodore Roosevelt gave substance to the name by starting the custom of writing a congratulatory letter to the winner.

Repeating firearms and smokeless powder appeared together on the range at Sea Girt for the first time in 1896. The New Jersey teams arrived with newly issued Krag-Jorgensens to compete against a team of Georgia Volunteers armed with lever-action Model 1895 Winchesters chambered for the new .30 caliber Government cartridge. The initial sally of the Georgians into interstate competition was a signal success. They carried away the Hilton Trophy on their first attempt.

Georgia marksmen also dominated the matches in September, 1897 and in 1899; because of the Spanish-American War, no matches were held in 1898. In 1897, Winchester-armed teams from the Georgia Volunteers almost swept the field, even though the competition from teams of New York,

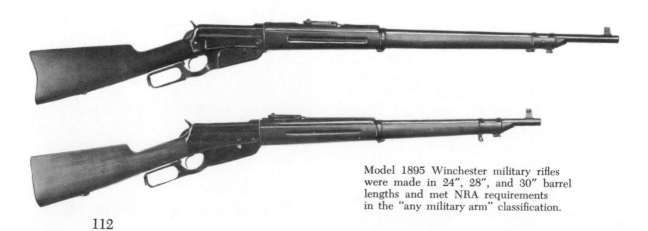

Model 1895 Winchester military rifles were made in 24", 28", and 30" barrel lengths and met NRA requirements in the "any military arm" classification.

At Sea Girt in 1899 rifles officially used by the Navy and Marines were the old single-shot .45-70 Springfield and new Lee caliber .236 magazine rifles *(top)*. The Naval Reserve used the same rifles plus a .45 caliber Lee single-shot rifle with a high cocking spur *(bottom)*. The Army used the .30 caliber Krag-Jorgensen.

the District of Columbia, and New Jersey was bolstered by a team of Regulars from the Army's Thirteenth Infantry.

Georgia did not send a team to Sea Girt in 1900, but other state representation that year was gratifying enough, and, for the first time in years, the Department of the East of the United States Army again decided to match its skill with the non-professional soldiers of the National Guard. The Regulars fared badly; all of the state teams—the District of Columbia, New York, Massachusetts, and New Jersey—scored more than 1000 points in the Hilton Trophy Match, while the Army finished a poor fifth with a score of 772.

The turn of the century was a major turning point in the affairs of the National Rifle Association. With increasing national prosperity and improvements both in communications and transportation, the Sea Girt Matches were rapidly assuming a national character far beyond the scope of any state organization. In 1900, the Palma Centennial Trophy, which had been gathering dust since the 1870s, was polished up and brought back into play. Although no foreign team appeared, a team selected from the winners of the regular matches shot a token match symbolizing the return of the international trophy to active status.

The supervision of an international rifle match, however, required the attention of a truly national organization. Although it had assumed national responsibilities in sponsoring the President's, Hilton Shield, and Palma Trophy matches, the New Jersey State Rifle Association was handicapped in its dealings with the national shooting associations of Great Britain and other nations since it could speak officially for only one state. The United States Revolver Association, on the other hand, although scarcely six months old, had already competed in an international match with France on June 10, 1900 and was negotiating with pistol associations in other nations for future competitions.

The success of the Sea Girt program had had two effects: It had revived a generally waning interest in long-range rifle shooting and had led to a renewed demand for an active national organization of riflemen to coordinate and expand the shooting programs in the armed services and among interested civilians.

As early as 1893, the New York *Sun* had published an editorial applauding the continuation of the National Rifle Association matches under sponsorship of the New Jersey Association and calling for a broader representation of the states and federal services in the matches. Even more positive encouragement came from the editorials of Arthur Corbin Gould in *Shooting and Fishing*, a sportsman's journal that had been originally published as *The Rifle* in 1885. Gould was a Bostonian and a member of long standing of the Massachusetts Rifle Association. A student of ballistics and an authority on military marksmanship, he had written two books on rifles and was widely respected as a spokesman for shooting interests.

After moving his offices to New York City in 1894, Gould attended all of the matches at Sea Girt and took a close personal interest in the affairs of the New Jersey State Rifle Association. Although he applauded the success of the Sea Girt matches and was impressed with their management, he was disturbed, as were others, by the lack of direction and coordination that then existed at the national level. Early in 1899, Gould ran a series of articles and editorials calling public attention to this deficiency and urging action to correct it. One of those who paid particular heed was Lt. Albert S. Jones of the New Jersey National Guard, the secretary of the New Jersey State Rifle Association. Inspired by Gould's editorials, Jones began corresponding with the officers of other state and local shooting organizations in the United States, asking their views on supporting a national society that would represent all of the nation's riflemen. The response was almost universally favorable. Among those who endorsed Jones's proposal was Theodore Roosevelt, then governor of New York State.

With this support, Jones, on July 1, 1900, mailed a printed form letter to the officers of every shooting association and National Guard organization in the nation, using lists supplied by Gould. The circular urged each to be present or to send representatives to a convention of riflemen at Sea Girt on the following September 5 to discuss the formation of a "League of American Riflemen."

A substantial number of organizations accepted the invitation. At the convention, however, Jones had scarcely finished stating the purpose of the meeting before Gen. George W. Wingate rose and asked to be heard. The need for an active organization, as proposed by Mr. Gould and Lieutenant Jones, he said, was more than apparent. But the organization that these gentlemen proposed already existed. It had been established nearly thirty years before. Its matches had been held almost continuously since that time, and were nationally and internationally known and recognized. Its constitution and bylaws were already written, and it had traditions that no new organization could hope to acquire. In view of these facts, should the delegates not first try to breathe new life back into the old organization? Wingate's proposal was accepted and, with this approval, he returned to New York City to begin the task of reviving the dormant NRA.

As president of the Association, Wingate began by writing to all surviving Life Members. He asked those who could to attend a meeting at his offices at 20 Nassau Street on December 5 and for those who could not come in person to provide him with proxies that would let him reactivate the National Rifle Association of America.

Gen. Bird W. Spencer, NRA
president (1902-1907).

On December 20, 1900, the first meeting of the Board of Directors of
the National Rifle Association since 1892 was held in New York City. At
this meeting they elected Maj. Gen. Wesley Merritt of the United States
Army as honorary president and Brig. Gen. Bird W. Spencer as president.
They revised the Bylaws to increase the number of vice-presidents to three
and elected Brig. Gen. John S. Saunders, Adjutant General of Maryland;
Brig. Gen. George H. Harris, Commanding Officer of the National Guard
of the District of Columbia; and Col. James W. Rice of the Illinois National
Guard to fill the posts. Lieutenant Jones became secretary and Nathan
Spering, president of the Philadelphia Rifle Association, treasurer. Wingate,
although accepting an appointment to the Board of Directors, declined
office, feeling that the new officers were quite capable of moving the program ahead at maximum speed.

Among other things, the Board of Directors decided: "That the National
Rifle Association of America hold an international rifle shooting competition in the month of September . . . and that the Centennial Trophy
'Palma,' emblematic of the World's Championship . . . be again put up
for competition. . . ."

The old Bylaws were taken apart, reviewed and reassembled to bring
them in line with contemporary conditions. The size of the Board of
Directors was increased and the ex officio membership was expanded to
include the Secretary of War and all general officers of the United States
Army, including the Chief of Ordnance and the Adjutant General of the
United States. These actions, in later years, were to become a major
problem to the organization.

But the National Rifle Association now came out from its period of in-
activity with new life and renewed vigor. From this point on the Association was to grow rapidly in stature; close in the offing was congressional
recognition of its patriotic purpose and important services.

The Members Trophy, placed in competition by the NRA in 1901, is a large sterling silver pitcher. A miniature is given to each winner.

11

# International Matches Renewed

Ambitious plans in the first year of NRA reactivation reflected the vigor of the new management. The Spanish-American War had set a new generation in the saddle. An immediate membership drive was started. The officers organized a summer shooting program that was then the most varied ever held in America.

On May 19, 1901, they mailed large numbers of circulars announcing preliminary competitions for the eight places on the American team that would defend the Palma Trophy in late August, and invitations to compete for this trophy were sent to nations around the world. A resolution adopted by the New Jersey State Rifle Association gave the NRA use of the range at Sea Girt for practice by aspirants to the team on every Saturday between May 25 and July 15. The New Jersey association also extended all privileges of the clubhouse to members of the NRA and its affiliates.

Except for specifications of rifles, the terms of the new Palma Match were comparable to the old. All team candidates were required to shoot with the .30 caliber Government rifle. The format of the old Class I Creedmoor 12-by-6-foot target with its 36-inch bullseye, 54-inch four ring on a 6-foot-square inner, was revived; the controversial official Army target with elliptical markings had been used by the armed services since 1885 and in all NRA competitions since 1891. The circular NRA Class II and Class III targets were also reinstated for use in the Interstate Military Team Match and similar midrange events.

A wider scope was added to the summer matches, which opened on August 30, 1901, when the United States Revolver Association agreed to combine its second annual matches with those of the NRA and the New Jersey State Rifle Association. The USRA had held its first matches the year before at Conlin's Shooting Gallery in New York City. On June 16, 1900, its leading marksmen had shot against the French, winning by a margin of twenty-one points. This was a telegraphic match, the French shooting in Paris, the Americans at Greenville, New Jersey. The results

# Congress Honors NRA

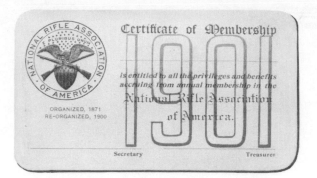

Membership card of 1901, showing the earlier form of the NRA seal, with E. Pluribus Unum motto.

were exchanged by cablegram. The telegraphic match was not new. It had been used as early as the 1880s in competitions between shooters in various parts of America, but this was its first known application in international shooting.

Although, until that time, the National Rifle Association had shown but minor interest in the handgun, formal pistol competition in America had started at Creedmoor under its auspices. In the absence of any official pistol shooters' organization, the NRA also had been arbiter in one of the most heated controversies in American shooting sports—a rivalry between W. W. Bennett and Ira Paine for the pistol championship of the United States in 1886 and 1887.

The highlight of the matches in 1901, of course, was the defense of the Palma Trophy in the Centennial Match. Until 1900, when a representative of *Shooting and Fishing Magazine* discovered it in a military museum in Washington, D. C., the Palma had been out of action and all but forgotten for nearly twenty years.

The American team, captained by General Spencer and with Maj. C. H. Laucheimer, USMC, serving as adjutant, entered the field under heavy handicaps. The various National Guard organizations of the respective states were then in the process of phasing out the .45 caliber Springfield, and, of the teams at Sea Girt, only New York, the District of Columbia, New Jersey, Ohio, and Maryland had received the new magazine service rifle. Most had acquired their new rifles so recently that they had not attained proficiency in their use. The Canadian Volunteer Service, on the other hand, had been fully equipped with the .303 Lee-Enfield for at least two years. The Canadians also had continued to shoot regularly over the longer distances, while, since 1892, the emphasis in America had been on distances of 600 yards or less.

In prematch trials, only members of the New Jersey and District of Columbia National Guard shot well enough to win places on the team. They had been among the first militia organizations armed with the Krag-Jorgensen rifle, and both had many men who had shot at the longer distances. The Columbia Rifle Club, an NRA affiliate made up of members of the National Guard of the District of Columbia, had always produced strong rifle teams in the interstate matches at Creedmoor and Sea Girt. Its Benning Range, on the banks of the Anacostia River, was patterned after Creedmoor and permitted shooting out to and beyond 1000 yards.

The eight-man Palma Team included Henry H. Leizear of the District of Columbia. Leizear, at that time, was one of the best long-range shots in the world, and he had made several near-possible

118

Remington-Lee bolt-action
magazine rifle.

scores under terms of the Elcho Shield Match. In the regular matches of the NRA that preceded the international competition, he won the President's Match to become the military rifle champion of the United States. But if the marksmen from New Jersey and the District of Columbia had not neglected long-range shooting, neither had the shooters from our neighbor to the north. Canada won the Palma Trophy with a score of 1522 to 1494.

Eleven teams, including one made up of visiting Canadians, competed for the Hilton Trophy in 1901. Although the Army did not send a team to Sea Girt that year, a team of United States Marines represented the federal services. This was the first time that any branch of the regular services other than the Army shot against National Guardsmen in an NRA match. One of the Marine riflemen was a young lieutenant, Thomas Holcomb, Jr., who, after a distinguished record in two World Wars, became the first Marine to wear four stars as Commandant of the Corps.

The entry of the Canadians in the Hilton Trophy Match permitted the Americans to gain some satisfaction after their loss of the Palma Match. The District of Columbia won the event, New York placed second, and Canada placed third. Teams representing Pennsylvania, the Marine Corps, Massachusetts, Maine, Maryland, Rhode Island, and Ohio finished the match in that order.

An all-comers long-range rifle match, open to foreigners as well as Americans, was another international feature of the matches of 1901. Each entry shot ten shots each at 800, 900, and 1000 yards on two consecutive days. Frank Hyde, who had done his early shooting at Creedmoor with muzzle-loading rifles, won this match with a Remington-Lee bolt-action rifle, beating J. C. Sellers of Ireland, who used a Mannlicher, by three points.

Although the loss of the Palma Trophy to the Canadians was a bitter disappointment to the newly reactivated National Rifle Association, the defeat probably did more to stimulate national interest in marksmanship than a decisive victory would have done. With the quick victory of American arms over Spain in the recent war fresh in the mind and with Roughrider Theodore Roosevelt in the White House, America had achieved a new national image. A self-complacency bordering on smugness over American skill with weapons was apparent in the press and in statements of public officials. The defeat at Sea Girt pricked the national ego, brought

119

about a more realistic self-appraisal, and stimulated a search for corrective measures. It started a determined effort to bring back the symbolic Palma Trophy to American soil.

The United States, in September, 1902, through the National Rifle Association, sent a team of riflemen to Canada to retrieve the Palma Trophy. It was the most representative team organized in the United States for an international match to that time. The finalists were the top-scoring members of the various teams represented at the annual NRA matches at Sea Girt in 1902. These men had shot against one another in a series of matches on September 8 to determine the eight strongest marksmen.

The match was held on Saturday, September 13, at Rockcliffe, the home range of the Canadian Association just outside Ottawa. The shooting began in rain, and cloudy skies prevailed throughout the match, conditions that favored the team from Great Britain, which had responded also to the Canadian invitation.

Most of the Americans shot Krag-Jorgensens, but two, Graham and Casey, used experimental models of a new rifle made at the Springfield Armory under a patent held by Paul von Mauser of Germany. This was the debut of a rifle that, with improvements and refinements, would dominate American military shooting competition for many years. Then known as the "Improved Springfield" rifle, it was a .30 caliber magazine rifle that was soon to become the Model 1903 Springfield. Although the Federal Armory at Springfield, Massachusetts, has produced dozens of models ranging from muzzle-loading muskets to automatic weapons, the Model 1903 remains *the* Springfield to millions of American war veterans and sportsmen. The prototypes used in this match fired a 220-grain bullet at a muzzle velocity of 2300 foot-seconds.

The Krag-Jorgensen, although a strong and reliable weapon, remained the official rifle of the United States Army only a little longer than ten years, thanks in large measure to the NRA skirmishers' matches at Sea Girt. These matches, and experiences in the recent war with Spain, had disclosed unsuspected deficiencies in the Krag as a battlefield weapon. The worst of these was its awkward loading system. Since the shooter was forced to load the lateral five-shot magazine with single cartridges, its sustained rate of fire was little greater than that of the single-shot models it had replaced. Many other nations were already using clip-loaded infantry rifles in comparison with which the Krag fared badly. By 1900,

The Springfield Model 1903 rifle, a time-tested weapon on rifle range and on battlefield.

120

Testing a Springfield rifle on one of the bench-rest blocks at Sea Girt.

the Ordnance Department had begun experiments with various rifles using rimless cartridges and these led to the adoption of the Model 1903. Those used in 1902 by Graham and Casey were among the first rifles of this design issued to American troops.

In the opening phase of the 1902 shooting at Rockcliffe, the American team made a strong bid for supremacy, and they finished the 800-yard phase with a lead of 22 points over the British and 42 over the Canadians. But the British won the match with a score of 1459 to 1447 for the United States and 1373 for Canada. Lieutenant Holcomb of the American team made a personal score of 194 points, the highest individual mark of the three teams, but not enough to offset the generally higher averages of the British riflemen. All in all, the spirit of true sportsmanship and international good will shown here was perhaps the most important result.

In this match the back position still had many proponents, and several Americans and one Canadian used it. All of the British shot in the prone position. In America, the back position had become popularly known as the "Texas position," although it had originated in Europe and had been popularized in the United States by eastern shooters at Creedmoor. In assuming it, the marksman lay on his back with his feet toward the target, supporting the rifle barrel with his left knee while grasping the butt with his left hand, which was passed behind his head. He pressed the trigger with his right thumb, absorbing the recoil with the sling, which was looped over the bent right knee. But now the days of the back position were

121

The caption "Uncle Sam beats all creation" accompanied this cartoon in *Harper's Weekly* in 1875.

numbered, and it died out rapidly with the advent of the Model 1903 Springfield with its shorter barrel.

As a result of the Palma Trophy Match of 1902, the NRA found itself in a rather frustrated position. Its team had beaten the Canadians far worse than the Canadians had beaten the American team in winning the Palma Trophy in 1901. But the trophy, carried in triumph to London by Lieutenant Colonel the Honorable R. F. Fremantle and his British marksmen, was now farther from home than before.

In its own post-mortem of the Palma Match of 1902, the British National Rifle Association conceded the narrowness of its own victory, crediting it largely to the superiority of the British in judging the shifting wind. Oddly enough, this was the result of lessons learned from the

Americans, who had won the earlier international matches through a more advanced system of wind doping.

As winners of the Palma Trophy, the National Rifle Association of Great Britain immediately announced plans to defend it in an international competition, which would be held at Bisley in the summer of 1903. The National Rifle Association of America, delighted to have the chance to bring the Palma Trophy back to the United States, was among the first to accept. Canada, Australia, Natal, Norway, France, Russia, and Switzerland also accepted, and the national shooting organizations of Germany, Austria, and several other nations of Central Europe expressed official interest.

The National Rifle Association of America made every effort to build its strongest possible team of American shooters. On May 18, 19, and 20, it held a series of matches at Sea Girt among the sixty-seven top marksmen of the United States. The twelve winners would be the team and its reserve. Three veterans of the Palma Team of 1902—Holcomb of the Marine Corp, Casey of New York, and Cook of the District of Columbia—won positions on the team of 1903. The other members of the first string were Sgt. J. H. Keough of Massachusetts; Cpl. W. B. Short, Lt. E. A. Wells, and Sgt. G. B. Doyle of New York; and Cpl. C. B. Winder of Ohio. With Col. Leslie C. Bruce, a veteran of the international matches of 1876 and 1877, as Captain, the team sailed for Liverpool on June 13.

The team was equipped with Improved Krag-Jorgensen Government rifles in the last model of the Krag issued before its abandonment in favor of the Model 1903 Springfield. Those carried by the American team had been fitted by Harry Pope, America's great barrel-maker, with special gain-twist barrels made by the Stevens Arms Company. In contrast with the standard issue barrel with its four grooves, the Stevens-Pope barrel had eight grooves. Although of a design, among several others, that the Ordnance Department of the United States Army then was considering for adoption, the barrels had not been approved for official use. In a further effort to standardize the equipment of the team, the Americans carried with them 10,000 rounds of ammunition specially loaded for their use by the Union Metallic Cartridge Company.

The British proved to be ideal hosts. They extended every courtesy to the visiting teams, opening the full facilities of the superb Bisley Range to unrestricted use. By order of King Edward himself the foreign teams were quartered at the Royal Review at Aldershot, the famous British military station adjoining the range.

Like Creedmoor, Wimbledon, the paragon of the Nineteenth-Century rifle ranges, had been made obsolescent by changing times. Both had been squeezed in by suburban development with re-

THE PALMA TROPHY—SCENES AT ROCKCLIFFE RANGES.

In 1902 Uncle Sam did not look so pleased with the results of the International Palma Match.

sultant hazards to public safety. As a result, the National Rifle Association of Great Britain in 1889 had abandoned their famous old Wimbledon range. It had found safer shooting grounds in the village of Bisley at the edge of the military station at Aldershot. Bisley was opened formally on July 12, 1890. With fifty long-range targets, ninety midrange targets, and thirty-three miscellaneous targets for shorter distances, including Running Man, Running Deer, and pistol ranges, it was, in 1903, the largest and most modern range in the world. Its one drawback was its lack of easy access. Although it lay as close to London as Wimbledon, it could be reached only by a circuitous rail journey. On the morning of the Palma Trophy Match, there were scarcely 1000 spectators on the field. The London *Telegraph* speculated that if the match had been shot at Wimbledon, it would have attracted no fewer than 100,000.

But what the gallery lacked in numbers it made up for in high society. It included the Duke of Cambridge, the aging president of the National Rifle Association of Great Britain, uniformed generals, admirals, and top-hatted nobility. Ambassador Joseph Hodges Choate and a sprinkling of high-ranking military officers represented the United States. Kilted highlanders mingled with turbaned officers from the British colonial forces. Flowered bonnets and parasols of titled ladies and the flags of the various nations lent color to the overall scene. The Palma Trophy Match at Bisley, full of the ceremonial pomp of Edwardian England, was probably one of the most elegant rifle matches ever held.

There were some disappointments in the entries. The Swiss, master riflemen of the Continent, whose expected presence had been looked forward to with great interest, had withdrawn almost at the last minute. The teams from Austria and Germany failed to appear. The Russians, an unknown quantity in the shooting world, were represented by a single forlorn Muscovite with a scant knowledge of English. The rest of the Russian team, still en route to Bisley from Siberia, was under the impression that the match was to be held in the following week. The Norwegian team reached Aldershot on the eve of the match.

The morning of the match dawned hot and sultry with no more than a breath of a wind. The shooting began at 9:40 in the morning on the 800-yard Stickledown Range. It immediately became apparent that the match was going to be a two-way duel between the British and the Americans. The Australians and the men from Natal, who had been expected to give strong competition, made slow starts from which they never recovered. The Canadians failed to shoot up to standards they had set in the prematch practice. Little was expected of the Norwegians or the French, since both teams were shooting under serious handicaps. The late arrival of the Norwegians after a long sea voyage put them at an immediate disadvantage, and their 6.5 millimeter Krag-Jorgensen rifles lacked the refinements that American armorers had built into the .30 caliber Krag. The Lebel rifles of the French had sights that were almost primitive compared to those of their rivals, and not one man on the French team, before arriving in England, had ever fired at a target beyond 600 yards. The surprise of the match, in fact, was not that the Norwegians and French lost, but that they shot so well in losing. The performance of the Scandinavians so impressed one British sportsman that he offered, on the spot, to pay their full expenses for a return match in the following year!

Before the match, the shooting costumes of the French—flat straw sailor hats and white linen dusters, which made them look like a delegation of meat-cutters—caused open amusement. At the close, due to the determination with which the French riflemen went about their work, the same scoffers found some merit even in their costumes.

In the 800-yard stage, the Americans trailed the British by a scant three points. The other teams were already being counted out of the running. At 900 yards, the British dropped eighteen points in their first twenty shots and the American team began to forge ahead.

The match resumed after lunch. Both the crowd and the heat had increased greatly, mirage and wind adding to the

124

SERJEANT HAYHURST
OF THE CANADIAN
TEAM

MAJOR GIBBS WHO
COACHED THE GREAT BRITAIN
TEAM

J. H. STEWARD

MR CHOATE
AMONG THE
SPECTATORS

Sketches made for the July 13, 1903, issue of *The Daily Graphic* illustrate
some of the shooting positions and the varied dress of the shooters at Bisley.

problems of the marksmen. It was at this point that a new coaching system developed by the National Rifle Association really proved itself. Each of the other teams on the field was coached by a single expert seated behind the firing line. The Americans used two members of each squad on the line itself to coach the shooter. No man touched off a shot until he and his two coaches all agreed that conditions were exactly right.

The marksmanship of the leading teams throughout the match was nothing short of superb. The scores of the British and American shooters were all the more remarkable since not one of the sixteen men missed the target. The lowest individual score by an American shooter was 191; the highest was 206, shot by Keough, out of a possible 225.

At 1000 yards, the British lost further ground and the United States won by a score of 1570. The British scored 1555; Canada, 1518; and Australia, 1501.

Except for those on the range at Bisley, the American who followed the progress of this match with the greatest interest was Theodore Roosevelt, America's most famous practitioner of the rifle. As soon as word of the American victory reached the White House, the President wired NRA Secretary Albert S. Jones: "Accept my heartiest congratulations for the American victory." This was the first public expression of personal interest in the affairs of the NRA by the President, an interest that lasted until his death.

The British accepted their defeat at the hands of the Americans with good grace,

125

but behind the scenes a storm was brewing around the American rifles.

Since the aperture sight was recognized as standard equipment on the American service rifle, the British could find no fault in its use in the Palma Trophy Match. They did, however, bar its use in the open military matches of their regular meeting, which immediately followed.

More serious criticism of the American rifles centered around their special barrels. The terms of the match were explicit that any rifles used should be of a type officially approved by the governments of the respective nations competing. Although the eight-groove barrel had been used experimentally on some test rifles, it had not been officially approved for military use. Approval for the purposes of this match would have been only a formality, but, somewhere, someone had been negligent. Both the members of the team and the officers of the National Rifle Association were completely unaware that the team was shooting with equipment not formally authorized.

Unaware of the storm that was building up in its wake, the team sailed for home after a royal send-off by their British hosts. They received an even more enthusiastic welcome on their arrival in New York on August 1, when they were met by General Spencer, J. A. Haskell, the vice-president of the NRA, and a large delegation of public figures. Colonel Bruce carried with him documents bestowing honorary life membership in the National Rifle Association of Great Britain on himself and all of the officers of the NRA. He had obtained his personally from the Duke of Cambridge at a banquet given in his honor at the Trocadero in London on the evening after the match.

As early as July 19, 1903, the *Volunteer Service Gazette*, the British counterpart of the *Army and Navy Journal*, had voiced this criticism of the American equipment: "The Americans used a rifle which in action and general construction is of Government pattern, but in the really vital matter of the rifling is of entirely different construction. It is not the Krag-Jorgensen barrel, but a special Stevens-Pope barrel. . . . Probably this rifling will be adopted by the United States Government in a new rifle; but it is not yet adopted."

This theme was expanded by newspapers abroad and in the United States. On October 26, the secretary of the National Rifle Association of Great Britain wrote to Secretary Jones of the National Rifle Association of America, requesting definite assurance that the rifles used by the Americans were of an approved design.

At the time the officers of the National Rifle Association were still under the impression that the new Springfield rifle would be released with rifling like that in the Krag-Jorgensens used by the American team. Then the Ordnance Department of the United States Army, as a matter of courtesy, sent one of the first Model 1903 Springfields to the British War Office. On inspection, it proved to possess four grooves imparting a twist of one turn

Sgt. J. H. Keough of Massachusetts led the United States team to victory in making the top score for the Palma Trophy at Bisley in 1903.

in ten inches. With this evidence in hand, the National Rifle Association of Great Britain lodged a formal protest. They were supported by a letter from Col. Frank E. Phipps, commanding officer of the Ordnance Department of the United States Army, who, in answer to direct questions from the editors of *Forest and Stream,* confirmed that the eight-groove, eight-inch twist barrel had never been officially approved by the Government of the United States.

This controversy dragged out for more than a year. Fearing that further debate would jeopardize the international competition that had been revived so successfully at Sea Girt, Rockcliffe, and Bisley, the NRA returned the Palma Trophy to the British Association. In keeping with their tradition for sportsmanship, the British, on their part, disclaimed any intention of reversing the results of the match, although they accepted custodianship of the Palma Trophy until such time as a return match could be arranged. The end result was to put the status of the Palma in limbo. Several years passed before the fine old trophy was brought back into play.

Behind the scenes in America very direct and important action had resulted from our 1901 loss of the Palma Trophy to Canada. From this came the introduction in 1902 of a bill sponsored by Congressman Frank Mondell of Wyoming to create in the War Department a "National Board for the Promotion of Rifle Practice."

The Mondell Bill of May 8, 1902, failed to pass. It incorporated suggestions that had been made by Gen. Bird W. Spencer at the January, 1902 meeting of the Board of Directors of the NRA. These were that the federal government sell surplus government arms to the militia organizations of the various states, authorize annual appropriations for transporting qualified teams from the state and federal forces to an annual national rifle and pistol competition, and establish machinery under which such national matches might be held.

The bill had the active support of President Roosevelt and his Secretary of War, Elihu Root, but it died with the adjournment of Congress. Early in 1903, General Spencer went to Washington to visit his friend Senator Dryden of New Jersey and outlined the proposal. Dryden immediately enlisted the support of Senator Redfield Proctor of Ohio, who reintroduced most of the wording of the old Mondell Bill as an amendment to the War Department Appropriations Bill. It became law in February, 1903. It authorized the establishment of the National Board for the Promotion of Rifle Practice, the National Rifle and Pistol Matches, and appropriations to transport teams of marksmen to the Na-

tional Matches from the various branches of the Armed Services and the National Guard organizations of the states.

Secretary of War Elihu Root, who had been an ardent supporter of this legislation, appointed the first members of the newly-born National Board on March 31, 1903. At its first meeting on April 21, 1903, it recommended: "That every facility should be offered citizens outside of the Army, Navy, Marine Corps, and organized militia to become proficient in rifle shooting, and that this purpose can best be accomplished by means of rifle clubs. The board therefore respectfully recommends the encouragement by the War Department of the organization of rifle clubs composed of those who would be eligible for service in time of war, but without special obligation for war service on account of such membership, under such regulations as may be prescribed by the Secretary of War."

The immediate effect of this law was to approve and lend the support of the federal government to the principles and program of the National Rifle Association of America.

The first National Rifle Match authorized by act of Congress was held at Sea Girt on September 8 and 9, 1903. Fifteen teams, including those from the Navy, Marine Corps, Infantry, and Cavalry entered the event, which was won by the New York National Guard, with a score of 2988. New Jersey's twelve, captained by General Spencer, placed second, while Massachusetts was third. The Cavalry team, pitting carbines against the long rifles of their rivals, turned in a brilliant performance. Even without the handicap of one shot per man at each distance that the rules permitted, they outshot the riflemen from Michigan and Vermont, and, with the handicap, outshot the Navy team. The highest individual score by a member of the Cavalry team was 237 points, made by a young West Pointer from the Class of 1900, Lt. Morton C. Mumma. He was destined, at a later date, to exert a profound influence on the affairs of the National Rifle Association of America.

In order to retain its identity with the National Rifle Matches, which represented only an extension of its own program, the National Rifle Association offered two of its own most cherished trophies, the Soldier of Marathon and the Hilton Trophy, as first and second prizes in the national competition. It should perhaps be noted here that the National Matches are sponsored by the National Board for the Promotion of Rifle Practice, and the NRA National Matches are sponsored by the National Rifle Association. It is customary, however, that these matches are held jointly, a practice recognized by provisions of the National Defense Act.

The regular matches of the NRA, which immediately followed the National Matches, were the largest ever held to that time. The President's Match was won by Lt. K. K. V. Casey of New York, the Leech Cup by Cpl. C. B. Winder of Ohio, and the Wimbledon Cup by Capt. W. H. Richard.

The matches of 1903 saw the inauguration of the Dryden Match, sponsored by Senator John F. Dryden of New Jersey. This was a team match, ten shots for each man at 200, 500, and 1000 yards, with ten men on each team. It was won by an Infantry team, whose members included Lt. Townsend Whelen, another young man who was destined to take a place among the all-time greats of shooting sports.

In 1904 the National Match was shot at Fort Riley, Kansas on August 22-25. Its scope was considerably expanded over that of the year before. In addition to the slow-fire, rapid-fire events were held at 200 and 500 yards, and the match closed with two skirmishers' runs. The National Guardsmen of New York again carried away the first

Secretary of War Elihu Root, whose dedication to marksmanship training and strong support of the legislation which created the National Board for the Promotion of Rifle Practice have helped to earn him stature as a great statesman.

prize, but the regular services showed marked improvement over their 1903 performances. The Navy, Infantry, Cavalry, and Marine Corps finished in descending order ahead of all other National Guard teams entered.

Most of the eastern National Guard teams that competed in the National Match were present that year at Sea Girt for the annual matches of the National Rifle Association, which were on September 1 through 10. Of the regular services, only the Marine Corps put in an appearance.

The President's Match was won by Pvt. Howard Gensch of the First Regiment of Infantry of New Jersey's National Guard. New significance to the name of this match was provided by none other than President Theodore Roosevelt, who, at its conclusion, personally wrote this letter of congratulations to the winner under date of September 25, 1904: "I have just been informed that you have won the President's Match for the military championship of the United States of America. I wish to congratulate you in person, and through you not only the First Regiment of the Na-

tional Guard of New Jersey, but the entire National Guard of New Jersey. As a nation we must depend upon our volunteer soldiers in time of trial; and, therefore, the members of the National Guard fill a high function of usefulness. Of course, a soldier who cannot shoot is a soldier who counts for very little in battle, and all credit is due to those who keep up the standard of marksmanship. I congratulate you, both on your skill and upon your possession of the qualities of perserverance and determination in long practice by which alone this skill could have been brought to its high point of development."

This was the beginning of a tradition that made a letter from the President of the United States the first prize in the President's Match for the military rifle championship of the nation.

In 1905, the National Rifle Association of America received another boost to its program when Congress passed Public Law 149. It was signed into law by President Roosevelt on March 3, 1905. The new law greatly broadened the function of the NRA by authorizing the sale at cost of surplus military rifles, ammunition, and other military equipment to rifle clubs meeting specifications laid down by the National Board for the Promotion of Rifle Practice and approved by the Secretary of War. These specifications were spelled out to the National Rifle Association by Capt. Grote Hutcheson of the National

Board to General Spencer, as president of the NRA, in a letter dated April 6, 1905. His suggestions dealt primarily with minor changes in the wording of the bylaws of NRA-affiliated clubs to permit them to purchase government equipment. These were translated into the form of a circular, 500 copies of which were mailed by the NRA to the boards of officers of National Guard regiments across the United States.

Under a resolution adopted by the National Board for the Promotion of Rifle Practice and approved by the Secretary of War on March 23, 1904, the members of all NRA-affiliated clubs were entitled to compete for a National Marksmen's Reserve qualification. Those making a total of 50 points in five shots each at the 200-, 300-, and 500-yard ranges were awarded a lapel button from the National Rifle Association and were recorded by the War Department as members of the nation's "Second Line of Defense." In the event of a national emergency, members of the Marksmen's Reserve were promised "First Consideration" by the War Department after volunteering for active duty. The National Rifle Association of America also had begun to award annually an enameled bronze medal as first prize in a championship match among members of each affiliated club.

These acts permitted a great broadening in the services of the National Rifle Association of America. Since 1871, it had functioned primarily as a national organization to promote marksmanship training in the militia and reserves of the several states. Until given the support of federal recognition for its services and launched on an expanded, attractive program for all American shooters, it had operated under severe difficulties. Here, indeed, was an important milestone in the proud role the National Rifle Association of America was destined to play.

# NRA to Washington-
# Camp Perry Replaces
# Sea Girt

As the new century progressed into its first few years, the .22 caliber rimfire cartridge came into use as a training cartridge—usually in connection with a "subcaliber" device inserted in the chamber of the standard military arm barreled for .22 caliber.

The *schuetzenverein* continued to flourish, sticking mostly to its own style of shooting but here and there beginning to affiliate with the National Rifle Association.

Prodded by the will to win long-range events, shooters and ammunition makers alike experimented continually with various forms for the new metal-jacketed bullets, and with various grain sizes and mixtures for the new smokeless powder. Cupro-nickel fouling was a great problem. The unexplained rusting of barrels despite faithful cleanings caused much discussion and brought forth many "cleaning solutions."

Gradually the picture of an expanded national shooting program began to take form. Although there had been some previous efforts within the organization to broaden its program and field of interest, most of these efforts had produced only temporary results. Throughout its existence during the Nineteenth Century and the first few years of the Twentieth, the NRA had placed nearly all of its emphasis on the improvement of military marksmanship. Affiliation with a military organization of some kind was all but a prerequisite to membership in the NRA or participation in its matches. The match-rifle events, which had given the NRA its greatest impetus in the early days, were invariably shot by members of National Guard units functioning as civilians. These matches were easily justified on the grounds that they paved the way for more accurate infantry weapons. This, too, was one of the original objectives of the National Rifle Association.

But by 1906 most of the original NRA objectives had been achieved. Its methods, once scoffed at in Washington, had been endorsed and adopted by the federal government. It had even attained a semiofficial status through the Act of Congress of 1903 that established the National Board for the Promotion of Rifle Practice and its extension under the Act of March 3, 1905. By 1906 each member of the armed forces was required to know his personal weapon intimately and to shoot it on the range at least once a year. Skill with the rifle had become an important criterion in judging the qualifications of the infantryman or marine.

Nearly every military post and camp, by 1906, had some form of rifle range based on standards developed by the NRA. The Army, handicapped by a lack of appropriations, was struggling to complete a major range installation at Fort Riley, Kansas. The matches of 1904, which had been held at Fort Riley, had already demonstrated the inadequacy of existing facilities. The Navy at Guantanamo, Cuba, was putting the finishing touches on one of the largest and most modern rifle ranges in the world. When completed it had 170 targets on a single line and accommodated 2000 shooters in a day. All of this was in marked contrast to the situation in 1871.

Similar progress had been made in the development of military firearms, developments that had been speeded on the ranges at Creedmoor and Sea Girt. The NRA matches had spurred American inventors to produce weapons with greater accuracy, higher velocity, and flatter trajectory. By 1906, under the conditions of the times, the rifle officially adopted by the United States seemed to have attained the ultimate plateau in reliability and effectiveness as a battlefield weapon. The new Model 1906 cartridge with its spitzer-point service bullet, whose basic design had been tested by the Palma Team of 1903, made the Model 1903 Springfield rifle one of the most accurate military arms in the world.

Although it had no inclination to reduce its interest in military marksmanship or to relinquish sponsorship of its military matches, the National Rifle Association in 1906 had traveled about as far as it could along the military route. And with the ascendancy of the National Matches, there was danger that its position in this field might eventually be overshadowed by the overpowering influence of the federal government itself. If it were to retain its leadership, it had to press forward into new and unexplored fields.

One path that suggested itself was the development of a closer affinity with civilian marksmen. There were hundreds of thousands scattered in small organizations and as individuals across the United States.

One hint of things to come appeared in the annual matches of the NRA at Sea Girt in September, 1906. On September 5, to implement its National Marksmen's Reserve program, the NRA scheduled a qualification event as part of the annual matches that was open to all riflemen who wished to compete for the Marksman Medal. The event was a huge success. Aspirants queued up all day in the hot sun for their turn on the line. Each competitor was required to shoot the hard-kicking standard-issue Krag at 200, 300, and 500 yards, five shots at each distance, kneeling at the shorter range. A minimum of 50 points out of a possible 75 was required for qualification, and many of those who lined up so confidently failed to make the grade.

In one of the lines there appeared a figure that seemed out of place in the pre-eminently masculine atmosphere of Sea Girt. For one of the hopeful riflemen obviously was not a man! Eyebrows were arched, cigars were chewed, and officials drew together in heated consultation. But try as they might, they could find nothing in the rules barring female shooters. The first lady in history was about to compete in a match of the NRA.

Under the existing bylaws, it would have been as improbable for a woman to join the National Rifle Association as it would have been for her to become a bank president. But nothing in the rules barred them from entering any all-comers' match open to civilians. A scattering of ladies had been at all of the larger matches to watch their husbands and sweethearts shoot. Under the tutelage of male escorts a few of the more daring had even ventured a trial shot or two with revolvers and light rifles. But not one of them would have dreamed of competing shoulder-to-shoulder with masculine shooters on the firing line of a military rifle match.

Elizabeth Servaty Topperwein of San Antonio, Texas, had no such compunctions. Although she lacked the fame and elfin beauty of Little Annie Oakley, "Plinky" Topperwein was possibly the greatest all-around marksman of her sex who ever lived. She could handle rifle, shotgun, or pistol with equal authority. Two months before arriving at Sea Girt, she had broken 485 out of 500 clay pigeons, shooting in gusty wind, in a single day at the trap range of the Texas Gun Club in San Antonio. She had shattered nearly all the records made by Annie Oakley both with the shotgun and with the rifle at thrown

targets. She could clip tossed coins consistently with the pistol, using either hand. She and her husband Adolph, exhibition shooters of the Winchester Repeating Arms Company, formed the most spectacular husband-and-wife shooting team in history.

Shooting rapidly because of her training in exhibition work, Mrs. Topperwein ran up sixty-one points to receive her medal to the cheers of the admiring males.

On March 9, 1903, the Executive Committee had unanimously passed a resolution, "That the National Rifle Association of America, recognizing the importance of training the young men of the country in rifle shooting, adopt a code for a course of rifle instruction, which code shall be the same as that proposed for the War Department for the State Militia, and that official score sheets be supplied to all ranges and to rifle clubs throughout the United States for the purpose of enabling citizens not connected with any military establishment an opportunity to qualify and become enrolled in the National Marksmen's Reserve; that each person quali-

Mrs. Elizabeth (Plinky) Topperwein, one of the greatest shooters of her sex, was the first woman to enter shoulder-to-shoulder competition with men in a formal match.

fying be entitled to receive a suitable decoration, and that a classified report be made to the War Department each year of those who have qualified under the code."

It was under the terms of this resolution that Mrs. Topperwein had qualified as a member of the Marksmen's Reserve. A companion resolution adopted on the same day stated: "That the National Rifle Association of America deems it expedient to take immediate steps to secure the affiliation with it of colleges, universities and other educational institutions of the United States for the purpose of stimulating and encouraging rifle practice among the American youth."

To implement these resolutions, General Spencer had sent circulars to all affiliated state clubs asking them to open their ranges to civilian use whenever they were not being used by state military units. Most complied, but a few were reluctant to accommodate any but National Guardsmen on their ranges. Urged to do so by the NRA, all affiliated organizations finally complied.

The youth program, however, had easier sailing. In April, 1903, Lt. Albert S. Jones, as secretary, had sent letters to the presidents of all major colleges and universities and the superintendents of the United States Military and Naval Academies asking their cooperation. Oddly enough, at that time, little emphasis was placed on marksmanship at West Point. The situation was little better at Annapolis, although the midshipmen were receiving more training in musketry than the future generals at West Point. The letter from NRA did much to correct this situation. It also resulted in the establishment of rifle clubs at the more prominent American universities and their affiliation with the NRA.

The broadening of the NRA program into the field of youth training, however, extended beyond the colleges. Shortly after his withdrawal from the affairs of the National Rifle Association, Gen. George W. Wingate became military instructor in the public schools

of New York City. This program, sponsored by the Grand Army of the Republic, was a predecessor of the high school cadet training program of later years. In this capacity Wingate, with the same energy and imagination that he had applied in the earlier years of the NRA, founded and became first president of the Public School Athletic League. Its purpose was to stimulate interscholastic competition in sports. It was only natural for Wingate to turn his thoughts to competitive shooting. In 1905, he started a rifle shooting program in the public schools, and by early 1906 he had organized teams that were competing intramurally in ten of the city's high schools.

Most of the student training involved use of the subtarget rifle, or "dotter," rather than live ammunition. The dotter was a patented device using a rifle fitted with a spring-activated stylus that snapped from the bore to mark a target. Since it involved very close-range work, the muzzle and stylus point being only a couple of inches from the target, standard long-range targets were reduced to scale.

The *Brooklyn Daily Eagle,* which had always taken a close interest in the work of the NRA and in target shooting in general, followed Wingate's program with more than passing interest. As a result, at Wingate's suggestion, it agreed to sponsor an interscholastic marksmanship match open to pupils of the New York high schools. The event, using subtarget rifles, was held at the Seventy-first Regimental Armory on June 1 and 2, 1906. Each member of the winning team received a medal designed by Wingate and struck at the expense of the *Eagle.*

The *Eagle* Interscholastic Rifle Match was highly successful. President Theodore Roosevelt, as soon as he heard of it, dashed off a characteristically spontaneous letter of commendation to its author.

The *Eagle* Interscholastic Rifle Match and its resultant publicity opened hitherto un-

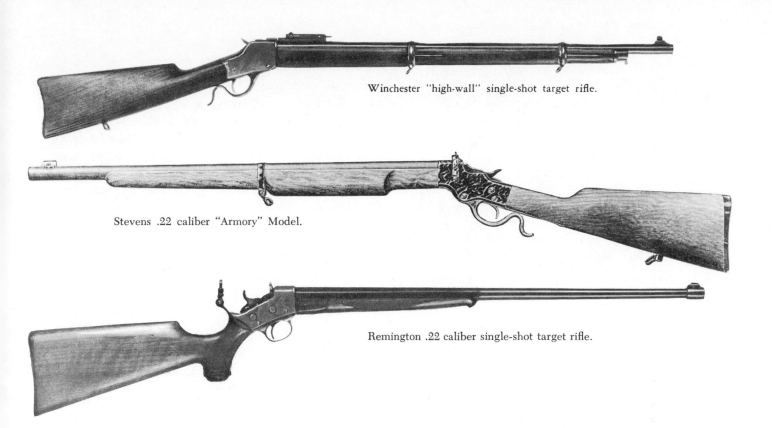

Winchester "high-wall" single-shot target rifle.

Stevens .22 caliber "Armory" Model.

Remington .22 caliber single-shot target rifle.

recognized vistas to existing shooting organizations. The New York State Rifle Association was first to recognize the possibilities and added an interscholastic rifle match to its summer program at Creedmoor. The event was applauded by *Shooting and Fishing* for offering the youngsters a chance to shoot with real rifles. Sponsored by the Lafflin and Rand Powder Company, which offered $200 toward the purchase of a suitable trophy, the match was open to teams from any college, high school, or elementary school in the United States and Canada.

This was not a hit-or-miss teen-age match, but a serious event conducted under the rules and standards imposed on the adult marksmen at Creedmoor. The youngsters even shot regular military service rifles, and the only concession to their junior ages was the use of reduced powder charges. Each was required to shoot five shots standing at 100 yards and five shots prone at 300. Ten teams competed in the event on July 26.

The success of the New York venture inspired the National Rifle Association to add a comparable event to its annual shooting program, which opened at Sea Girt on August 27, 1906. To accommodate the juvenile shooters it set aside a section of the camping area near the range specifically for their use under adult supervision. The opening match found more than 200 teen-age boys encamped at Sea Girt all anxiously waiting their turn on the firing line. The NRA youth program had started off in high gear!

The first youth's event sponsored by the National Rifle Association was an individual match open to any boy under eighteen years of age. Each was required to shoot fifteen shots with any rifle in any position at 200 yards. The Union Metallic Cartridge Company offered $200 in cash to be divided into sixteen prizes for the winners. Many of the youngsters shot with standard-issue Krags with reduced charges, but most used their own favorite .22s. The arms manufacturers were already turning out some excellent models for use specifically by boys. Remington had its rolling block, and comparable weapons were being produced by Stevens,

Gen. James A. Drain, NRA president (1907-1910).

Marlin, and other manufacturers. The Winchester single-shot musket, however, with weight, balance, and sighting equipment matching those of the Krag, was the favorite. Capt. Charles B. Winder, for whom the rifle was promptly nicknamed, had proved its capabilities by scoring a then unheard of 48 out of 50 points at 200 yards offhand with one of these rifles.

The matches of 1906 also saw the first handgun event directly sponsored by the National Rifle Association. It was partially influenced by emphasis on the pistol by the Armed Services in the National Matches, which preceded those of the NRA, and in part to an overlapping interest in both handguns and rifles by some of the newer members and directors. The United States Revolver Association held its own matches between August 26 and September 2, 1906, but this was a telegraphic event for the championship of the United States and only part of the match was shot at Sea Girt. The other contestants shot simultaneously at Chicago, St. Louis, Des Moines, and San Francisco, the results being exchanged by

James A. Drain purchased the magazine *Shooting and Fishing* after the death of Arthur Corbin Gould and changed the name to *Arms and the Man*, which was later turned over to the National Rifle Association and became *The American Rifleman*.

wire. The New York shooters at Sea Girt, led by John A. Dietz, Jr., made practically a clean sweep of these matches.

The telegraphic match, although economical to the participants, lacked the life and interest of shoulder-to-shoulder competition. The first major pistol match sponsored by the National Rifle Association was a lively affair with nine events providing variety and action. In addition to slow-fire at stationary targets there were rapid-fire matches, a bobber match, and a disappearing-man match. As expected, the experts of the United States Revolver Association took most of the first-place honors. Dietz alone won four of the eight matches and was one of three making perfect scores in a fifth. On the field that year were some of the great handgun experts of the times, LeBoutillier, Nathan Spering, Dr. R. H. Sayre, and A. L. Himmelwright. Adolph Topperwein competed in one match.

But men whose achievements with the rifle are remembered better than their skill with

pistols also placed high in these events. Sgt. Clarence E. Orr, winner of the President's Match of 1905, placed fourth in the Novice Military Revolver Match and eighth in the Any Revolver Match. He was one of those who tied for first place in the All-Comers Rapid-Fire Military Match. Capt. A. J. Macnab and Lt. Morton C. Mumma were among the other tying winners. Mumma also placed third in the Disappearing-Target Match.

The matches of 1906 did much to set the future course of the National Rifle Association of America, a course that would lead it into broader channels and greatly widened fields of service.

Two men must be credited with dedicated and very able guidance for the National Rifle Association of America in this period of its affairs. They were James A. Drain and Ammon B. Critchfield. Although in personality and in appearance each was the near opposite of the other they shared boundless energy, a love of shooting, and a capacity for hard work. Each also had a wealth of political, social, and business experience and a host of powerful friends. Each became active in the affairs of the NRA at about the same time.

Gen. Bird W. Spencer had helped to keep the National Rifle Association alive during its lean years, and under his guidance it had experienced healthy growth. In 1900 it was almost exclusively an organization of easterners. In 1906 it was drawing support from every state. In 1900 it had only 43 affiliated clubs. There were 108 in 1906. But Spencer was of a conservative cut who accepted change grudgingly. His first loyalty, too, had always been with the New Jersey State Rifle Association. Leadership of the national group had practically been thrust upon him rather than sought by him. Although the NRA made great progress under his administration, it had operated far below its potential.

The time was ripe for a fresh outlook. Conditions in America were changing. Com-

Ammon B. Critchfield, Adjutant General of Ohio, is generally considered "the father of Camp Perry." President NRA (1936-1937).

munications and transportation were improving daily, overcoming handicaps under which the organization had labored in the past. National interest in shooting was greater than ever before and it was flourishing in the political climate of the Roosevelt administration. Yet, the National Rifle Association under Spencer carried on much as before. It was at this point that James A. Drain and Ammon B. Critchfield arrived on the scene.

Brigadier General James A. Drain was a youthful, bustling, handsome figure of a man who, at the age of thirty-four had been appointed Adjutant General of the State of Washington, the youngest man in history to attain that post. Drain had been largely responsible for the legislation that gave the National Rifle Association its official recognition as spokesman for America's marksmen. In 1903, when this crucial legislation was pending in Congress, Drain contacted at his own expense most of the adjutants general of the other states, asking their support. He went to Washington to speak on behalf of the bill with congressmen, senators, and military leaders. He obtained enthusiastic support of the bill from Elihu Root, William

Howard Taft, and others prominent in public life.

Drain moved east in 1904. Since the death of Arthur Corbin Gould, *Shooting and Fishing*, with offices in New York City, had been languishing. Under Gould, although the magazine had no direct connection with the NRA, *Shooting and Fishing* had been an unofficial organ of the National Rifle Association, reporting all of its matches and meetings in detail. Drain purchased the periodical outright in 1906, renamed it *Arms and the Man*, and became editor and publisher. He continued the policy of its founder. He was elected a vice-president of the National Rifle Association in the same year.

The second dynamic personality now to become closely associated with the direction of the National Rifle Association was Adjutant General Ammon B. Critchfield of Ohio. In contrast to Drain, Critchfield was a heavy-set man whose fleshy appearance belied his

General Critchfield envisaged the flat fields bordering Lake Erie dotted with the tents of shooters and divided by excellent ranges for all distances in national marksmanship competition.

skill with the rifle both at stationary targets and in the more active Running Deer events. He became a vice-president of the NRA at the same time as Drain. Like Drain he was one of the youngest state adjutants general in history.

As Adjutant General of the Buckeye State beginning in 1903, General Critchfield had built an outstanding shooting program in the Ohio National Guard. The quality of Ohio's marksmen and the rate of improvement that they demonstrated in three years of national and international competition was amazing. Ohio was considered one of the "poorer" states; its shooters lacked the luxuriant range facilities available to those from the wealthy states of New York, Massachusetts, and New Jersey. But under Critchfield's encourage-

Camp Perry of the 1960s has developed into an efficient facility that has exceeded General Critchfield's fondest hopes.

ment, they more than made up in enthusiasm what they lacked in equipment.

Back in 1900, when the National Rifle Association was reactivated, Ohio was represented at Sea Girt only by Cpl. Charles B. Winder. The state rifle association had been unable to raise enough money to send a team. In 1901, a team of Buckeye shooters reached New Jersey but it placed last in a field of eleven in the Hilton Trophy Match and last in the Interstate Military Match. In the first National Rifle Match of 1903, the year Critchfield became Adjutant General, its shooters placed fifth of fifteen teams in the Hilton, seventh in the Dryden Match, and sixth in the Interstate. Winder had won a place on the Palma team by winning the Leech Cup, while Capt. William H. Richard had won the Wimbledon Cup.

In 1904, under Critchfield's tutelage, Ohio broke into the open. A five-man team of the Ohio State Rifle Association, which included both Winder and Richard, won the Interclub Match for the championship of the United States and another Ohio team placed a close second to New Jersey in the Dryden. In 1905, Sgt. Clarence E. Orr of Newark, Ohio, won the President's Match and Richard won the Leech Cup. In 1905, Ohio's shooters also won the Dryden Match.

Largely through General Critchfield's effort, the Ohio State Legislature in 1905 appropriated $25,000 toward the purchase and development of a state National Guard rifle range and camp. General Critchfield already had an area in mind. By personally searching the entire lake shore, he had found a level plain a mile long and a half mile deep along the southwestern shore of Lake Erie. It had ready access from rail lines; it was less than forty-five miles east of Toledo and just south of Put-in-Bay, the site of Commodore Perry's great triumph over the British in the War of 1812. As level as a table top, the land was only lightly wooded; it would require almost no clearing and a minimum of grading. Critchfield later wrote that "it seemed to just naturally be right at the right place."

At Sea Girt shooting was often interrupted by the tedious passage of a coasting freighter just behind the targets. Sand bars and a reef extending far out into Lake Erie would keep stray shipping at least seven miles offshore. At Sea Girt coastal fogs were a constant problem. The Ohio site was relatively fogfree. The Governor of Ohio had scarcely signed the appropriation bill before the Ohio State Rifle Association and the Ohio National Guard Association agreed to join in purchasing thirty additional acres as the site of a clubhouse.

Sea Girt in 1905 had become almost overwhelmed by the expanding shooting program, and its almost insular character made further expansion of its facilities impossible. The 1906 program at Sea Girt was a great success in terms of interest, but the facilities were swamped. With an unprecedented number of teams on the field for the National Matches, the matches of the NRA and the New Jersey State Rifle Association had to be delayed and were partly disrupted. The camping facilities, once the most modern of any military installation in the United States, had become outmoded and dangerously crowded.

Dissatisfaction with Sea Girt was growing both within the NRA and within the War Department. Either a new site had to be found for future matches, or the National Matches had to be divorced from those of the NRA. The latter course, which was narrowly averted, carried tragic implications for the future of both matches at that time.

Two alternatives to separating the matches presented themselves. One was to transfer the matches to the new range that was being built at Fort Riley, Kansas, by the Army. The War Department, including a strong element in the National Board for the Promotion of Rifle Practice, favored transfer to Kansas on the grounds that the location, near the geographic center of the nation, would be most accessible from all points in the country. But to the still eastern-oriented NRA, this suggestion was not acceptable. The range experts within the National Rifle Association examined the plans for the range and branded them a monstrosity, poorly planned and badly executed. They had also had a taste of the heat of the treeless plains at Fort Riley during the National Matches of 1904 and few looked forward to a return. If Fort Riley had been selected as the permanent site of the National Matches at that time the National Rifle Association quite probably would have divorced itself from the national program. Fortunately, because of the snail's pace at which development at Fort Riley proceeded it soon became obvious that the range would not be available in 1907 anyway.

The second alternative was to transfer both matches to the new installation that General Critchfield was building on the shores of Lake Erie. It promised everything that Fort Riley lacked. Critchfield's plan called for the most modern facilities in running water, sewerage, and electric lights. Its spacious campgrounds, easy access from all eastern and midwestern cities, and the quality of the planning of the range itself were major points in its favor. Critchfield promised to have 150 targets for known-distance shooting at 200, 600, and 800 yards, 4 revolver ranges, and 50 skirmish targets installed by the summer of 1907. Moreover, the Ohio range was becoming reality at a speed that made the federal project seem at a standstill. With this in mind, the Ohio State Rifle Association in January, 1907, through General Critchfield, made its bid for the transfer of the matches of the National Rifle Association to its new range.

General Spencer objected strenuously and understandably in view of his intimate association with Sea Girt. A majority of the Executive Committee, however, led by Critchfield and Drain, voted to transfer. Spencer resigned subsequently as president of the National Rifle Association and Drain was elected to succeed him. Drain and Critchfield immediately asked the War Department to transfer the National Matches to Ohio. With the installation at Fort Riley still languishing, the National Board for the Promotion of Rifle Practice had little choice. The National Matches of 1907 were scheduled to be held at the Ohio State Rifle Range in August. The new installation was dedicated as Camp Perry, in honor of the hero of Lake Erie, just before the matches opened.

James A. Drain and A. B. Critchfield brought to the National Rifle Association the youthful imagination, vision, and leadership it needed to function as a truly national body. Under the administration of General Spencer, the NRA had only one employee, Albert S. Jones, who as secretary received a salary of $1800 a year. His one-room office, cramped and crowded with supplies, in the People's Bank Building of Passaic, New Jersey, was furnished by General Spencer, as president of the bank.

As soon as he became president of the National Rifle Association, General Drain moved the headquarters of the Association back to New York City, leasing a suite of offices for one year at 299 Broadway near Duane Street, in what was then known as "Sporting Goods Row."

Although this arrangement was far better than the facilities at Passaic, Drain still felt out of touch with national affairs even in New York City. Both as president of the NRA and as editor of *Arms and the Man* he felt a need for establishing closer ties with the War Department and the affairs of the Board for the Promotion of Rifle Practice of which he was a member. Early in 1908, the National Rifle Association moved to Washington, D. C. Its offices were in the Woodward Building on Fifteenth Street, Northwest, two blocks

Under the administration of General Spencer, the NRA offices were in the People's Bank Building at Passaic, N. J. Shown here is an advertisement of that period.

from the White House, in the heart of the financial district. General Drain established offices for *Arms and the Man* almost next door in the Hibbs Building at Fifteenth and H Streets.

In moving to Washington, Drain offered his employees moving expenses, but only Albert S. Jones and Frank J. Kahrs, Drain's personal assistant and treasurer of *Arms and the Man* Publishing Company, accepted. Although there was still no direct official tie between the magazine and the National Rifle Association, the relationship between the two had become very close.

Affairs of the National Rifle Association had now moved along to a solid state of permanency—in location, in national affairs, and in objective services. And it would not be many years before the NRA would have its own magazine.

# 13

# International Shooting

# Junior Shooting

When Brig. Gen. James A. Drain became president of the National Rifle Association of America on January 9, 1907, he declared in his inaugural speech to the Board of Directors: "It is desired to accomplish everything possible toward making the Association one of genuinely national scope and to increase its usefulness to the country as an agency for the promotion of rifle practice."

Drain was a man whose aims were high. One of his first acts was to start a campaign to sign as many prominent citizens as possible as life members. And he began at the top with President Theodore Roosevelt himself. Early in February, 1907, he visited the White House to tell the President the importance of the National Rifle Association program in national defense. In a letter dated February 16, 1907, he invited the Chief Executive to lend his personal support by becoming a life member. Two days later he received President Roosevelt's reply: "I am so heartily interested in the success of the National Rifle Association of America and its work done in cooperation with the National Board for the Promotion of Rifle Practice that I take pleasure in sending you herewith my check for $25 for life membership therein."

Simultaneously, Drain approached most of the members of the President's Cabinet, both in personal visits and by mail. Secretary of War William Howard Taft became a life member on February 23, and two days later, Secretary of State Elihu Root sent his check, writing to Drain: "That the young men of America shall know how to shoot straight is one of the fundamental requirements of our scheme of national defense."

Within the next few weeks Drain signed as life members the Postmaster General, George von L. Meyer; Assistant Secretary of the Navy, Truman H. Newberry; Chief of Ordnance, Brig. Gen. William Crozier, USA; Army

142

President Theodore Roosevelt, American patriot, ardent rifleman, Life Member of the NRA.

# Successes—

# Program Moves Forward

Chief of Staff, Maj. Gen. J. Franklin Bell; and Senator George P. Wetmore of Rhode Island.

In campaigns of this kind, Drain operated at a distinct advantage over earlier officers of the organization. He was president of the National Rifle Association; he was chairman of the Executive Committee of the National Guard Association; and finally he was a prominent journalist and editor of one of the leading magazines dealing with military affairs. His weekly column, "National Guard Notes," in the pages of the *Arms and the Man* was "must" reading for officers of the organized militia. In one capacity or another, he had a ready entrée with any official concerned with military affairs.

In the autumn of 1907, Drain toured all of the states of the West and Southwest, where the National Rifle Association, to that time, had been weakest in representation. In each state he visited the adjutant general and, where possible, its governor as well. He urged states that were already participating in the NRA program to increase their activities in the national program. He encouraged those that had no state rifle association affiliated with the NRA to create them.

The results of this personal approach were highly successful. Many of the governors or adjutants general called special meetings of the high-ranking officers of their state militia to listen to Drain. Many signed life membership applications. Two states, South Dakota and Utah, asked Drain to stay long enough to perfect rifle associations in their National Guards. By the end of his tour, Drain had received additional affiliations from state rifle clubs in California, Kansas, Minnesota, Missouri, Oregon, Texas, and Washington.

To round out this campaign, Drain asked Secretary Albert S. Jones to

143

write to the adjutants general of all other states with unaffiliated rifle associations in an effort to bring them under the wing of NRA.

Drain's impact on the National Rifle Association was reflected in his report to the Board of Directors on January 8, 1908, one year after he took office. Between 1900 and January, 1907, the NRA had received only 72 new life memberships. In 1907 alone he added 87 new life memberships. In January, 1907, the organization had 20 affiliated state organizations; one year later the total stood at 29. The number of affiliated regimental clubs increased from 57 to 79, affiliated civilian rifle clubs from 63 to 72, college rifle clubs from 5 to 15, and school clubs from 11 to 29.

The liaison between the National Rifle Association and the National Guard organizations became much closer during Drain's administration than it had ever been before. In his report on his first year as president, he stated that it had been his policy to refer to the adjutants general for approval all applications of state clubs for affiliation with the NRA.

In the NRA major shooting program, as late as January, 1907, there was lingering doubt that General Critchfield and his associates in Ohio would have the range at Camp Perry completed in time for the matches of the approaching summer. Drain visited Ohio in February and found a miracle of achievement. The clubhouse was all framed, the range graded and the butts ready for the installation of targets. Gen. John C. Speaks, Critchfield's successor as president of the Ohio State Rifle Association, had appointed a liaison committee with the National Rifle Association under the chairmanship of Critchfield.

The result was that at 9:10 in the morning of August 19, 1907, when a shot from the Krag rifle of Cpl. L. B. Jarrett, Ohio National Guard, opened the first NRA competition at Camp Perry, the range was not only ready

but facilities had been expanded beyond the original plans. The area behind the firing line was a sea of canvas. Except for the officials and visiting dignitaries, who were quartered in the clubhouse, most of the teams camped in pyramidal tents furnished by the Ohio National Guard. There were mess tents, hospital tents, and tents for representatives of the sporting goods manufacturers. Tents housed the latrines and showers, luxuries compared to the facilities at Sea Girt, even if the water did run cold!

In its first year, Camp Perry had a raw unfinished appearance. Streets were rutted with the wheels of heavy construction equipment, and the freshly planted trees were spindly saplings leaning for support against the props to which they were tethered. The firing lines were pitted with holes where stumps had been dynamited from the sandy loam, and the newly seeded grass had made scant progress against the summer heat. General Critchfield and his associates had laid planks along the roadsides and paths, a precaution that was appreciated when a rain squall whirled in from Lake Erie on the second day, turning the camp into a quagmire.

Forty-eight teams, including those from the Infantry and Cavalry, the Navy and the United States Naval Academy, were on the field at the opening. Some National Guard teams from the wealthier states, the envy of less fortunate rivals, bunked in chartered Pullman cars, which lined the spur track out of Lacarne, within walking distance of the range. The others detrained at Port Clinton and bounced in over rutted roads in wagons and carriages rented from the local livery stable.

There had been commercial exhibitors at Sea Girt and Creedmoor, but the sporting goods manufacturers turned out in force at Camp Perry. The year 1907 saw the first "Commercial Row," a familiar feature of all NRA matches since that time. The hit of the commercial show that year was Tom Keller of the Peters Cartridge Company, who toured the establishment in a rented buckboard behind an ancient white nag named Alice. With his battered buckboard emblazoned with the Peters banner, Keller and Alice were everywhere, providing transportation for everyone from General Drain and Lt. Col. Robert K. Evans, the executive officer of the National Matches, down to individual team members hitchhiking from one point to another over the muddy range!

The suspense over the outcome of the individual matches of 1907 was higher than usual that year. Their results were to decide at least nine of the members of the team that would shoot against the Canadians, Australians, and British in September for the Palma Trophy.

Nearly four years had passed since the Palma Trophy had been in competition, and the dispute over the American rifles used in the match of 1903 still left its custodianship under a cloud of controversy. In December, 1905, General Spencer had started a three-way correspondence with Col. John Tilton, chairman of the executive committee of the Dominion of Canada Rifle Association and Maj. Gen. Lord Cheylesmore, chairman of the council of the National Rifle Association of Great Britain, in an effort to arrange a match in Canada in 1906. The British, however, were unable to finance the sending of a team across the Atlantic.

By 1907, however, the British organization was in an improved financial condition and it accepted an invitation from Australia to send a team to Sydney. En route, the British planned to stop at Ottawa for a friendly match with the Canadians. General Drain immediately pounced on this opportunity, renewing the NRA's challenge to the Canadians and British and extending it to the Australians. All three promptly accepted. The Palma Trophy would be shot for on the Rockcliffe Range near Ottawa on September 6, 1907, almost immediately after the close of the matches at Camp Perry.

Nine members of the American team were to be selected on the basis of their aggregate scores in a preliminary contest at Camp Perry on August 16 and 17, in the Wimbledon and Leech Cup Matches, and in the 800- and 900-yard stages of the President's Match. Three additional members were to be selected by the Executive Committee of the NRA. The eight members who would actually shoot were to be selected in Canada at Rockcliffe by the team captain on the basis of performance in prematch practice.

The Company Team Match opened the first NRA shooting season at Camp Perry on August 19, 1907. The Leech Cup Match was

Rain sometimes swept in from Lake Erie to create scenes like this at Camp Perry.

shot the second day. It was won by Capt. J. C. Semon of Ohio, who crowded out Dr. W. G. Hudson of New York, in spite of nine consecutive bullseyes scored by the shooting physician at 800 yards.

The President's Match was shot on the third day. On the previous day Maj. C. B. Winder, whose ancestral farm had become part of Camp Perry, was home in bed with a recurrence of malaria. In spite of his illness, the popular champion of Ohio shot well enough to place second to the winner, Sgt. W. A. Berg of the state of Washington. Under earlier rules, Berg would have been declared military champion of the United States. Under the new rules, however, the championship was decided on the basis of the aggregate score in the President's Match of the NRA and the Individual Rifle Match of the National Matches. In spite of this change, President Roosevelt sent a letter to Berg as well as to the new champion.

Dr. Hudson assured himself a place on the Palma Trophy Team of 1907 by placing second in the Wimbledon Cup Match to Capt. K. K. V. Casey of Delaware, one of the most popular marksmen in America, whose place on the team was a foregone conclusion.

The matches of 1907 saw the inauguration of the Herrick Trophy, a massive silver cup presented to the Ohio State Rifle Association by former Governor Myron T. Herrick. It was shot for in State Association Matches in a 1000-yard team match immediately after the matches of the National Rifle Association.

The big surprise of the matches of 1907 was the performance of the midshipmen of the United States Naval Academy, coached and captained by Lt. A. P. Fairfield. In the National Matches, this team placed fourth among forty-eight entered. Midshipman Willis A. Lee, shooting against 638 individual marksmen, many of whom had been competing for years, was first in both the Individual Rifle and Individual Pistol Matches. This was the first and only time both matches

were won by the same man, and Lee won them both on the same day. His teammate, Midshipman Harold Travis Smith, won the Military Championship of the United States with the highest aggregate score in the Individual Rifle and President's Match. It was an amazing sweep for a group of youngsters who had been shooting little more than a year.

The first annual meeting of the National Rifle Association of America that was not held on the east coast convened in the newly completed clubhouse at Camp Perry on August 22, 1907. Most of the business dealt with the approaching Palma Trophy Match. At this meeting Capt. N. B. Thurston was elected team captain; Capt. Frank E. Evans, USMC, team adjutant; and Lt. Morton C. Mumma of the Second U. S. Cavalry, team quartermaster. In the Camp Perry team events, Mumma had run up a personal score of 307, the second highest individual score of the match, although his team had placed third.

Thus organized, the American Palma Team set out for Canada in early September of 1907. They reached Ottawa in ragged physical condition after an almost sleepless thirty-hour rail journey. They had planned to make the trip in two easy jogs. But when they reached Montreal they found every hotel room filled with delegates to a convention. When they reached Ottawa more than half of the team was laid low by heavy colds. The British, Canadians, and Australians were already familiarizing themselves with the Rockcliffe range and had been able to practice several days before the travel-weary Americans arrived. Two days passed before the full American team could start serious practice.

Rockcliffe, when they finally were able to inspect the range, reminded Captain Thurston of Creedmoor. It was of comparable size, with fifty targets on a line, and with shooting toward the northeast.

The members of the first-string team, selected by Captain Thurston on the basis of their performance in practice were: Sgt. George E. Bryant, Capt. K. K. V. Casey, Dr. W. G. Hudson, Capt. William A. Tewes, Maj. C. B. Winder, Capt. C. S. Benedict, Capt. J. C. Semon, and Sgt. C. E. Orr. The team was armed with Krag-Jorgensen rifles using a relatively light load of powder behind a 203.5-grain pointed bullet. All individual matches at Camp Perry in 1907, by regulation, were shot with Krags, owing to the difficulty that many states had in obtaining the new Model 1903 Springfield.

The shooting began under fair skies on the morning of September 6. It was apparent from the start that the Americans were out to remove all doubt that they had won the previous Palma Match by anything but superior marksmanship. During the 800-yard stage, the Americans plopped bullet after bullet into the black with only an occasional flier ranging into the four ring. Out of a possible 120 bullseyes, the Americans scored 112 to end the stage with a whopping score of 590. From that point on it was not a question of who would win, but of how great the margin of victory would be. Just before the 900-yard stage a member of the Australian team called the pits. As he hung up the telephone he was heard to say: "The marker asked me if he could put his bet on the Australians and I told the beggar to put his coin on the U.S.A."

During the 900-yard stage the Americans doubled their lead over the second-place Australians. Great Britain had already been counted out of the running, although the British score exceeded the winning score in the last Elcho Shield Match. In an effort to match the accuracy of the flat-shooting Krags, the British were using heavy charges of cordite behind 225-grain bullets. By doing so, they achieved a high velocity, but the shooters suffered heavily from the recoil.

No one had ever seen shooting like that

The Governor Herrick Trophy went into competition in 1907.

of the Americans in 1907. At the close of the match, the average score per man was 214, one point higher than the existing world record which had been made with a match rifle! Seven of the eight shooters broke Keough's top score of 206 in the Palma Match of 1903. The final scores were: United States, 1712; Canada, 1671; Australia, 1653; and Great Britain, 1580. That year there was no quibbling over who had won the venerable Palma Trophy! Both President Roosevelt and King Edward VII of Great Britain wired congratulations to the winning team, and there was no perceptible difference in the warmth of either message.

Although there was some rationalization in the British and Canadian press, the members of the losing teams had only the highest praise for the conduct and ability of the American team. No one took the defeat more gracefully than the British National Rifle Association. Its team captain, Maj. P. W. Richardson stated: "We were beaten by better rifles in the hands of better marksmen, and we should let the matter rest on that until we meet the Americans again."

International matches were not the only endeavors to which General Drain's able talents were directed. The youth program in which the NRA had engaged especially appealed to his imagination. One of his first steps as president had been to appoint a committee of two, Gens. George W. Wingate and Ammon B. Critchfield, to study ways to expand the school shooting program. Their report, submitted to the Executive Committee on February 23, 1907, was detailed and comprehensive. The Executive Committee voted unanimously to continue its sponsorship of the school program, stating, "Boys and young men taught to shoot the rifle as a means of making them fit to serve their country in time of need are not on that account more inclined to warlike strife. . . . The National Rifle Association of America will at once put into operation those plans (drawn up by Wingate and Critchfield) under which an opportunity will be given to organize rifle clubs in all institutions of learning throughout the country."

To implement this resolution General Drain appointed a committee to draw up qualifications for both indoor and outdoor rifle matches. The NRA appropriated funds for suitable badges for youngsters who qualified. Because of the varying conditions in different communities and a general lack of rifle ranges in most urban areas, the committee struggled long and hard to devise a qualification course. It finally decided that, for indoor ranges using .22 rimfire cartridges, the distance would be fifty feet, with five shots standing and five shots prone at a target with a one-inch bullseye, worth 10 points. A minimum score of 40 standing and 42 prone position was required for qualification. Outdoors the distance was 200 yards with Krag rifles

under comparable rules of scoring, ten shots standing and ten prone on the NRA "B" target.

The first NRA schoolboy matches were shot at Creedmoor on July 21 and 22, 1907, and later matches were held in the same year at Wakefield, Massachusetts, and Washington, D. C.

This program, thanks to a built-in base of 6000 schoolboy marksmen trained under General Wingate's Public School Athletic League in New York City, was an immediate success. The Athletic League itself affiliated with the NRA in May, 1907, placing its already active program under the direction of the national organization. By June, New York City, Brooklyn, Rochester, Albany, Washington, D. C., Baltimore, Philadelphia, and Boston had active NRA high school rifle clubs. At the college level, St. John's College and the College of the City of New York joined in 1907.

Meanwhile, the National Rifle Association had been trying with little success to increase the emphasis on individual marksmanship at the United States Military Academy. Through *Arms and the Man*, General Drain circulated a report of the subcommittee on rifle practice of the Board of Visitors to the Military Academy that was headed by Gen. Bird W. Spencer. Spencer and his associates, in a detailed summary of conditions at West Point, decried the lack of shooting facilities and the shortsightedness of the faculty in failing to train future Army officers in a basic military skill. They recommended that if suitable range facilities could not be developed the government invest in the subtarget rifle machines that Wingate had used in his school program. A number of Wingate's trainees had qualified as expert marksmen the first time they used rifles with live ammunition!

The blistering report of Spencer's subcommittee brought a prompt but not too encouraging response from the Commandant of

148

Shooting on the Rockcliffe Range in Canada, marksmen of the United States brought the Palma Trophy home in 1907. Their score of 1712 topped Canada's 1671, Australia's 1653, and Great Britain's 1580

Cadets, Lt. Col. Robert L. Howze. The Commandant still stood firmly on his decision that the cadets could not spare time from formal studies to engage in anything but rudimentary rifle practice and no time at all for interscholastic competition. "Expert shooting," Colonel Howze protested, "is postgraduate work."

Meanwhile, as the future generals of West Point pored over their books and diverted themselves at football and baseball, the future admirals at Annapolis were shooting regularly on a first-class range, competing with teams from Maryland, the District of Columbia National Guard, and building one of the strongest rifle teams in the Armed Services of the United States.

The opening of a massive sportsmen's show in Grand Central Palace of New York City on December 23, 1907, offered an opportunity for the NRA to dramatize its program before the American public. The show was a major social event attended by thousands of national and international sportsmen. In addition to exhibitions of outdoor skills—wood-chopping, fly-casting and trick shooting—the vast hall sparkled with hundreds of commercial exhibits of the arms and sporting goods manufacturers.

The NRA leased the entire south end of the second floor, which it devoted to a public exhibit of the history of firearms. In addition to the antique and historical arms owned by its members, it displayed a collection of weapons, from matchlocks to the latest Springfield, that it borrowed from the Army.

The National Rifle Association also staged schoolboy and collegiate rifle matches in connection with this show on a fifty-foot tunnel range with six shooting ports. At three positions, special ramps permitted prone shooting. The rifles were Model 1903 Springfields fitted with adaptors to convert them to .22 caliber. General Drain and NRA Secretary Jones opened the range on December 23, 1907, in a personal ten-shot match.

This ceremonial match opened the Junior Marksmanship Competition in which any youngster of high school age or below could qualify for an NRA Junior Marksman's Badge. The entrance fee, including cost of cartridges, was thirty-five cents. A steady stream of boys passed through the course in the next few days.

An intercollegiate team match was held on the same range on Christmas afternoon. Yale, Harvard, Cornell, Columbia, and George Washington University participated. The match was won by Columbia. The NRA program closed on December 27 with a high school team match using the subtarget rifle machine in the main hall of the Palace.

By formulating its youth program the National Rifle Association opened new horizons beyond which lay a broad vista of untilled ground. At the time, however, it still seemed reluctant to explore further afield into the ranks of the more mature civilian shooters. International competition continued to get the top billing, and a chance for another meeting with the British, Canadians, and teams from other nations came earlier than expected.

Shooting had become a part of the program of the Olympic Games in Athens in May, 1906, but neither Great Britain nor the United States had sent teams. Only two years later, in 1908, the next Olympic Games were held in London and the British Olympic Association invited the United States to compete in a series of international rifle and pistol matches. General Drain on behalf of the National Rifle Association of America at first declined, stating that there was little probability that the NRA, on such short notice, could raise the funds needed to send the team.

On April 15, 1908, just after Drain's refusal had been publicized, the president of the NRA received a letter from C. W. Dimick, president of the United States Cartridge Company of Lowell, Massachusetts. The

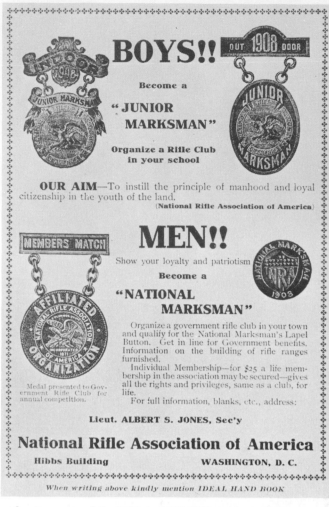

Advertisements of the NRA in 1907-1908 emphasized the youth program, but men's programs were not neglected.

ammunition manufacturer offered, "under proper conditions," to pay from his own pocket the expenses of any team selected by the NRA. Drain immediately asked Dimick to clarify his conditions and called a meeting of the Executive Committee to consider the offer.

With assurances from Dimick that he was interested only in seeing an American rifle team in the Olympic Games, the Executive Committee accepted the offer, and General Drain appointed a committee consisting of Brig. Gen. W. P. Hall, USA, and Brig. Gen. Lawrason Riggs, NRA vice-president and Commander of the Maryland National Guard, to select a team. General Drain him-

150

View of the rifle ra
at Bisley, Engl

self was elected captain of the team before the meeting adjourned.

This somewhat hasty action caused an immediate reaction among the other prominent ammunition manufacturers who suspected Dimick of ulterior motives. As soon as these protests were forwarded to him, Dimick protested that he had made the offer purely for patriotic reasons and that he would welcome the participation of any other company in financing the expenses of an American team. The response of the three other leading ammunition manufacturers was immediate. H. J. Leonard, assistant treasurer for the Winchester Repeating Arms Company, agreed to share in the responsibility but suggested that, to avoid the implication that the team was industry-sponsored, the NRA try to raise funds by public subscription. On May 12, 1908, William J. Bruff, president of the Union Metallic Cartridge Company, agreed to pay any share of the expenses that the NRA deemed necessary. Two days later J. G. Ewing accepted for the Peters Cartridge Company.

Although the eagerness of the ammunition manufacturers to participate had removed the NRA from the horns of one dilemma, it soon found itself on another. Now it was in the unenviable position of having to decide between the ammunition of one of four rival manufacturers for use in the forthcoming match. To resolve this problem, it scheduled a series of machine-rest tests at the Congress Heights Range of the District of Columbia National Guard with representatives of each company as witnesses. The winning cartridge was one made by the United States Cartridge Company, a load using a 180-grain bullet. While these tests were under way, Capt. K. K. V. Casey was at Springfield selecting by test the most accurate of a group of star-gauged Model 1903 rifles to be used by the American team.

Trials for the team were held at Camp Perry on June 10 through 12, 1908, and the first-string team selected on the basis of these matches consisted of Sgt. William F. Leushner, Maj. W. B. Martin, Capt. K. K. V. Casey, Maj. C. B. Winder, Capt. C. S. Benedict, and Cpl. I. L. Eastman. The rifle team, with General Drain as captain and Capt. Frank E. Evans as adjutant, sailed on the S.S. "St. Louis" on June 20, 1908.

In the meantime, the United States Revolver Association, on its own initiative, had raised funds to send to London a pistol team captained by Dr. Reginald H. Sayre, president of the USRA and a former treasurer of the NRA.

To the surprise of no one who had followed the Palma Trophy Match in Ottawa, the Americans, at every distance except 600 yards, outshot rival teams from the United Kingdom, Canada, France, Sweden, Norway, Greece, and Denmark. At 600 yards they trailed the British by only a single point. Shooting on their home range, the British provided much stouter competition than they had offered in the recent Palma Match. The consistently higher individual scores of the American shooters, however, gave them a lead which widened slowly throughout the match. At the end the Americans won their first gold medal in an Olympic shooting match, with a final score of 2531 to 2497 for the second-place British. Canada won the bronze medal.

The 1000-yard Individual Match Rifle event was won handily for the United King-

THE PALMA TROPHY

Emblematic of the Team Rifle Shooting Championship of the World, with the army rifle, at long ranges.

dom by Col. J. K. Millner, the grizzled veteran of the first Palma Match. Using his favorite Mannlicher, now fitted with a telescopic sight, the champion of the British Isles shot from his obsolescent back position, dropping shot after shot into the black for a near-perfect score of 98 out of a possible 100. No one on the American team begrudged him his gold medal. But the surprise of the match was the performance of K. K. V. Casey who won a silver medal with a score of 93 while pitting his iron-sighted Springfield against the scope-sighted and long-barreled match rifles of the best marksmen in the world.

The individual Running Deer competition was a British and Continental specialty. Only a few Americans entered the match and they fared badly against the Swedes and British. The Double-shot Running Deer Competition, however, was won by Walter Winans, an American resident of England, who competed as a representative of the United States.

Meanwhile, in the Olympic pistol matches, the Americans made a sweep, winning the fifty-meter team match by 50 points over the Belgians. In the individual pistol match the bronze medal was won by J. E. Gorman of San Francisco.

A gay welcoming party organized by the National Rifle Association greeted the team on its return to New York. The revenue cutter "Mohawk," placed at the disposal of the

NRA by Assistant Secretary of the Treasury Beekman Winthrop and crowded with dignitaries, fired a thirty-four-gun salute to the team as it sailed into the harbor—one shot for each point that it had exceeded the British score in winning the International Team Match.

Although somewhat overshadowed by the spectacular Olympic matches which shortly preceded them, the National Rifle Association and National Matches of 1908 were again held jointly at Camp Perry. During the year much of the raw sogginess had been removed by an extension of the drainage system and the landscaping had become well enough established to give the range an aspect of permanence. The 1000-yard range had been improved and the big concrete mess hall was nearly finished, its massive walls dominating the scene like an island in a sea of canvas.

There were fifty-one teams on the field that year and, because of the large number of entries, the National Rifle Association elected to combine the Wimbledon and Leech Cup Matches. After shooting seven shots each at 800 and 900 yards, the contestant then fired twenty shots at 1000 yards, the first seven of which concluded the Leech Cup round, the full twenty being used to determine the score in the Wimbledon.

General Drain hailed K. K. V. Casey's performance in this combined match as "the most wonderful shooting ever seen in America." Casey broke the record for both matches, scoring 97 out of a possible 100 in the Wimbledon and a near perfect 104 out of 105 in the Leech. The President's Match was won by Sgt. Arthur Brest of the Fifteenth U. S. Infantry, but Lt. S. A. Harris of the Fourteenth Infantry became Military Champion of the United States on the basis of his aggregate score in the President's and National Individual Rifle Match. Except for the victory of the Sixth Regiment of Massachusetts' Volunteer Militia in the Regimental Team Match, the National Matches of 1908 were won almost entirely by teams from the Regular Services.

During the Camp Perry Matches of 1908, a special dinner at the clubhouse honored the veterans of the various international matches in which the United States had participated since 1872. During the dinner, at the suggestion of Lt. Morton C. Mumma, USA, and Capt. Thomas Holcomb who had just returned from active duty in the Philippines to become a member of the first Marine rifle team, the guests were organized into the Association of American International Riflemen. General Bird W. Spencer was elected president of the honorary society whose membership was confined to the members and officers of teams that had shot in Palma and Olympic competitions.

The years 1907 and 1908 marked the development of the National Rifle Association of America into a truly national organization; it enjoyed broader public recognition and endorsement of its principles. In 1908, at its annual meeting, the National Guard Association of the United States unanimously en-dorsed the program of the National Rifle Association. In his address to Congress in January, 1908, President Theodore Roosevelt advocated the establishment at public expense of rifle ranges in all large public and military schools.

The most important immediate development, however, was the fruition of a suggestion made in 1907 by Lt. Gen. Arthur MacArthur that a special school to train instructors in small-arms firing for the Regular Army be established. This led to the creation in 1908 of the School of Musketry at the Presidio of Monterey, California, which provided extensive courses in combat and static marksmanship with all small arms used by the United States Army. A few years later the Army created a similar installation at Fort Sill, Oklahoma. With each year, the objectives of the National Rifle Association were finding more solid support.

The American champions after their 1908 Olympic triumphs at Bisley, England.

# 14

# The Years 1908-12

One of the greatest contributions that Brig. Gen. James A. Drain made to the National Rifle Association was in giving it a year-round program. A major weakness of the organization until that time was that, except for an occasional fling in the international arena, it lacked continuous activity to fill the gaps between its annual matches.

The first real break in this pattern came with sponsorship of the school matches. These, being based largely on indoor ranges, could be shot at any season and were most popular in winter when outdoor shooting was least attractive. To broaden the public interest sparked by this new activity, the Board of Directors in January, 1908, amended the Bylaws to create two new classes of membership—one for affiliated college rifle clubs and one for school clubs below the collegiate level.

Until this point the National Rifle Association, as an organization, had shown little interest in any weapons except the long-range match rifle and the military rifle and pistol. This is not to say that the officers, directors, and many members were not interested in other types of shooting. Drain, himself, was an avid big-game hunter. Many of the officers and directors were devotees of the *schuetzen* and gallery matches.

Gallery shooting at that time was the most popular form of organized shooting in America. The National Schuetzen Bund boasted 130,000 members in 160 clubs located in all parts of America. In May, 1907, its convention in Charleston, South Carolina, attracted nearly 6000 delegates. The more important matches of the National Schuetzen Bund were outdoor events, but it also devoted much of its energies to promoting indoor gallery shooting. Although the early masters of the *schuetzen* preferred rifles of .32 or .38 caliber for indoor as well as outdoor work, many, by the turn of the century, had adopted rifles chambered for the .22 rimfire cartridge.

This remarkable little cartridge gave its user several advantages over the large-bore, especially in terms of practice. Used within limitations of its range in a first-class barrel, it was supremely accurate. It cost little to shoot. It could be used satisfactorily at any distance between 25 feet and 100 yards. Its report was negligible, which made it ideal for use in confined quarters.

The active interest of the NRA in "miniature rifles" developed only a short time before the venerable National Schuetzen Bund passed from the scene.

Except for the schoolboy competitions, which had started two years earlier, the first major activity of the NRA involving .22 rifles came when the Association in January, 1909, accepted a challenge from the Miniature Rifle Association of Great Britain

# Period of Great Progress

to engage in a championship indoor rifle match. Each team was to compete on a range selected by its respective association and the results of each round of the match were to be exchanged by cablegram and mail. Australia's National Rifle Association accepted the same challenge to make the event a three-way match.

Under the terms, each team would consist of fifty men shooting rifles of not more than .230 caliber, thirty shots to a man. Any sights without glass, mounted ahead of the hammer, could be used. The seventy-five-foot target had a half-inch bullseye with quarter-inch concentric rings scoring from 1 to 9 points.

The first International Smallbore Match was shot by the American team at Zettler's Rifle Club, 159 West Twenty-third Street, New York City, on March 15 through 27, 1909. Many of the fifty shooters had played prominent parts in long-range matches at Camp Perry. Dr. W. G. Hudson made the highest individual score and William A. Tewes of New Jersey placed second, nosing out Harry M. Pope, the famous barrelmaker and one of the best gallery shots in America. The first match was won by Great Britain with a score of 14,585. The United States scored 14,179 to place second.

A telegraphic match, also won by Great Britain, was shot between April 10 and April 23, 1909. The rules were similar except that,

as a concession to the Americans, many of whom had been using scope-mounted rifles, telescopic sights were permitted. During the course of this second match Sir Thomas Dewar, the late Sheriff of London, announced that he was presenting a valuable silver cup as a trophy to be shot for annually in an international smallbore championship match.

The American team won the Dewar Trophy in 1910 by a margin of 100 points. In that match the number of shots per man was raised to fifty and telescopic sights were again banned. The shooting took place be-

The Dewar Cup, presented in 1909 by Sir Thomas Dewar for International Team Postal Competition.

tween June 6 and 11, and in making their total score of 24,539 points, the American marksmen demonstrated a remarkable improvement over their performance of the year before. Sgt. James H. Keough of the Massachusetts National Guard and W. C. Andrews of Cleveland's Cuyahoga Rifle Club each made 499 points out of a possible 500. The third-place Australians trailed the Americans by 646 points.

Turning to another field, and beginning in 1909, the National Rifle Association greatly expanded its school program. The impetus for this expansion was a highly successful interscholastic match in Washington, D.C. In 1909 there were rifle clubs affiliated with the NRA at six public schools in the nation's capital. Early in October of that year, General Drain, through an editorial in *Arms and the Man*, suggested that a match among teams representing these schools would be an inspiration and an example to the faculties of schools in other parts of the country. President Taft, vacationing in Gregory, Texas, immediately wired his encouragement. "I approve," the Chief Executive said, "the teaching under proper regulations of rifle shooting to our boys in the advanced grades." This official word of encouragement was all that was needed to set in motion the wheels of the Washington School Rifle Tournament.

Secretary of War Dickinson, who was a vice-president of the NRA, authorized the Association to procure an appropriate prize to be offered in his name to the winning team. Assistant Secretary of War Robert Shaw Oliver; Gen. William Crozier, Army Chief of Ordnance; the Du Pont Powder Company; two local newspapers, and the Washington Chamber of Commerce immediately pledged additional prizes.

The Marine Corps detailed officers to serve as range officials and enlisted men to serve as scorers and markers. The Army placed at the disposal of the youngsters 300 Model 1898 Government rifles and an adequate supply of ammunition. The District of Columbia National Guard offered the use of its Congress Heights Range.

The events, in addition to the NRA Junior Marksman's Qualification Match, included an interclub team match, an interschool team match, and an individual competition. Three hundred boys participated in this match on October 28, 1909.

The success of these activities caused the National Rifle Association to explore other avenues of action. One of the obstacles that confronted the NRA whenever it scheduled a match for civilian shooters was that of distance. The transportation of teams representing state or federal military units usually was paid for from state or federal funds. Civilian marksmen, however, had to pay their own way or to draw upon limited funds in club treasuries. As a result civilian representation at most matches was largely local.

In September, 1909, *Arms and the Man* ran an editorial, based on a suggestion by Frank J. Kahrs and Albert S. Jones, calling for the establishment of a National Smallbore Rifle League. The idea was based on the International Smallbore Match in which the competing teams shot on home ranges and exchanged the results by cable. Why not apply the same procedure to a national competition? By limiting it to indoor shooting the variables of wind, weather, and lighting would not influence the comparative scores.

The National Rifle Association accepted the suggestion and drew up regulations for the events. The competing teams shot on

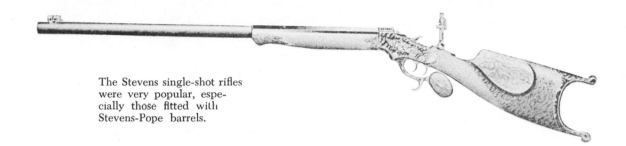

The Stevens single-shot rifles were very popular, especially those fitted with Stevens-Pope barrels.

their home ranges each Friday beginning on the first Friday of April, 1910, and continued on a round-robin basis until each team had competed directly with every other team. Marked targets were supplied and scored by the NRA. The shooting of each team was supervised by a local member of the National Rifle Association. Shooters were permitted to use any .22 rifle with iron sights, the rear sight mounted forward of the hammer, and shooting was at seventy-five feet on the standard gallery target. Each member of each five-man team fired twenty shots each week.

The first Interclub Smallbore Rifle League Match was won by a team representing the Rocky Mountain Rifle Club of Butte, Montana. The westerners scored 985 out of a possible 1000 in a shoot-off against the Winchester Rod and Gun Club of New Haven, Connecticut. Under previous conditions, it would have been almost impossible to have arranged a match between these two clubs.

The response of affiliated clubs to this program almost overwhelmed the tiny office staff of the National Rifle Association. Dozens of targets had to be marked and mailed to the competing teams and each mail during the tournament brought sacks of completed targets for marking and scoring. The brunt of this work fell on Albert S. Jones, the NRA secretary, and Frank J. Kahrs, who was delegated as a

staff writer of *Arms and the Man*. When the work load became too heavy, they often called upon Sgt. Ollie M. Schriver, a stocky young Marine, who was one of the best shots in the Corps.

The success of this match was so great that it soon became apparent that some division of the program would have to be made to handle the details efficiently. As a result, the original NRA Interclub League was split geographically through the Great Plains. The western division was supervised by the Pacific Coast Rifle and Pistol League, organized in May, 1910, under the presidency of Capt. E. C. Crossman. The Eastern Smallbore League remained under the direct supervision of the NRA. The winning team in each of these divisions shot against the winning team in the other division for the national championship. In the second tournament, which ran from December 24, 1910 to March 11, 1911, twenty-six teams competed. The rules at that time were changed to permit up to ten men in each club to shoot, but only the five best targets counted as the team score. Most of the shooters used Krag rifles converted to .22 caliber or Springfield rifles chambered for the .22 rimfire. In winning the national championship for the second consecutive year, however, the Rocky Mountain Rifle Club used Stevens' Ideal Model single-shot rifles fitted with sights designed by a local gunsmith.

Almost simultaneously with the origin of the Interclub League, the National Rifle Association initiated a League of College Rifle Clubs organized along similar lines. Twenty-one teams, of which twenty finished, entered the first Intercollegiate Smallbore Tournament, which opened on January 13, 1910 and closed on the following tenth of March. It was won by Washington State University. In the following year the championship went to the team from Massachusetts Agricultural College, whose shooters held it for three successive years. This tournament was separate from and complementary to the annual Intercollegiate Outdoor Rifle Match.

The regular Intercollegiate Match of 1910 was held on June 18 at the Congress Heights Range of the District of Columbia National Guard. This, too, was won by Massachusetts Agricultural College. Only four other teams entered and because of the poor representation the NRA decided to permit the teams in future years to shoot on their home ranges, exchanging results by telegraph or mail.

The National Rifle Association, at the same time, greatly expanded its public schools program. Forty-two schoolboy teams shot in the Interscholastic Rifle Matches of 1910. They were won by the DeWitt Clinton High School of New York City. The members of this junior team piled up scores high enough to match the best that had been made in the Intercollegiate Match. Their average score per boy was 182.1 out of a possible 200. As an incentive to participation in this annual match Col. John Jacob Astor in 1909 had presented a magnificent silver cup as a trophy to be held by the winning team. General Wingate presided over the ceremony in which the Astor Cup was first presented to a winning schoolboy team.

The success of the schoolboy program in the East and of the league tournament approach in general led Capt. Edward C. Crossman to suggest, in an article published in *Arms and the Man* on February 2, 1910, the establishment of a schoolboy rifle league. The first tournament of the Interscholastic Smallbore Rifle League was shot in the following winter, and the Astor Cup became the trophy for this match. A team representing Iowa City High School, Iowa, won. As a result of this activity alone, the NRA succeeded in affiliating seventy-three new school rifle clubs in 1910, most of which would have been unable to compete in NRA matches through any other medium than the postal tournament. Throughout 1910 the NRA concentrated on organizing schoolboy clubs throughout the United States. It mailed circulars to the principals and superintendents of high schools in every state and frequently followed them with personal visits. The NRA secretary, while attending the annual meeting of the National Guard Association in St. Louis in October, 1910, took time off from the meeting to organize

The Astor Cup, presented in 1909 by Col. John Jacob Astor for award in the interscholastic rifle championship match. It was won seven times by the fine Iowa City High School teams.

clubs in the public schools of that city. On his return trip to Washington he stopped off at Cincinnati long enough to organize school rifle clubs there.

Gen. James A. Drain stepped down as president of the National Rifle Association on January 12, 1910. Certainly, no earlier president had worked harder at his job with the exception of General Wingate, or had left a more enduring mark on the NRA. In his report to the Board of Directors in 1909, he was able to advise that eighty-eight new organizations had affiliated with the Association during the previous year; only one had dropped from the roster.

One of the objectives that Drain had worked for since he became president was to change the Bylaws to enlarge the representation in the Board of Directors. This was done in 1909. Under the amendment suggested by Drain, thirty-six members of the Board were to be elected from the Life Members, members of any affiliated organization, and such Honorary Directors "as have been or may hereafter be elected." Three directors were to be appointed annually by the Secretary of War, one of whom was to be a member of the General Staff, one representing the Infantry and one the Cavalry. Two more were to be appointed by the Secretary of the Navy—one from the Navy and one from the Marine Corps. The adjutants general of all states, with or without affiliated state organizations, were added to the Board of Directors. All members of the Board were to be elected and certified by the secretary before January 1 each year.

At this historic meeting, the Board authorized an annual membership class, open to any citizen of the United States on payment of dues of $2. The NRA had experimented briefly with annual member-

Gen. John C. Bates, NRA president (1910-1913).

ships ten years earlier but had dropped the class because of lack of public interest. Annual membership entitled the member to all reports, publications, and privileges except a vote in the elections of the organization.

General Drain remained active in the affairs of the NRA as a member of the Executive Committee after his retirement as president in 1910. He was succeeded to the presidency by Lt. Gen. John Coalter Bates of St. Louis, Missouri.

Bates was a sixty-eight-year-old professional soldier who had begun a long and distinguished military career as a first lieutenant in the Eleventh Infantry of the United States Army on May 14, 1861 and ended it, at his own request, on April 14, 1906, as Army Chief of Staff. His Civil War record was distinguished. He served the last two years as aide-de-camp to the Commanding General of the Army of the

Potomac. He commanded Bates's Independent Brigade at the opening of the Spanish-American War and at its end commanded the Third Division of the Fifth Army Corps in the Philippines. He was the first Regular Army officer since Sheridan to serve as president of the National Rifle Association. Few men better knew the value of well-aimed rifle fire in battle.

At this meeting Secretary of War Jacob McGavock Dickinson was elected second vice-president to replace Ammon B. Critchfield, and Brig. Gen. Carl A. Wagner replaced Ernest L. Isbell as treasurer. Among the eighteen new members of the Board of Directors were Secretary of the Navy George von Lengerke Meyer, the former Postmaster General; Brig. Gen. Robert K. Evans, who had served for three years as the executive officer of the National Matches; and Lt. Morton C. Mumma of the Second U. S. Cavalry, who had just been assigned as an instructor of military science at the University of Iowa.

Both Drain and Bates used their influence in stepping up the tempo of international competition. Back in October of 1908, Drain, on behalf of the NRA, had sent invitations to the rifle associations of nineteen nations asking them to send teams to compete in an international rifle and revolver tournament at Camp Perry in September, 1909. The tentative program listed a Palma Trophy Match, comprehensive team matches based on Olympic rules, and, for the benefit of the Continentals, 300-meter team and individual rifle events. Although many nations expressed interest, nothing came of this effort.

In 1909, however, the Republic of Argentina announced an elaborate Pan-American Exposition in connection with its centennial, which it was to celebrate in 1912. As its contribution to the national program the National Rifle Association of Argentina planned an inter-American shooting tournament in Buenos Aires. The Board of Directors of the National Rifle Association of America, at its meeting in January, 1910, accepted an invitation to send a team of riflemen to represent the United States. It was the first opportunity American marksmen had had to pit their skill against that of riflemen south of the border.

In the midst of all this planning and activity the NRA was continuing its regular program at Camp Perry each year. By 1911, the Association had fourteen major trophies in competition, several of which had been received in recent years. In May, 1909, the Winchester Repeating Arms Company commissioned Frederic Remington, the noted western artist, to execute an original bronze of a cowboy on a bucking horse. The Winchester Bronco Buster Trophy was offered as first prize in a regular NRA match in which the shooter tried to score as many hits as possible in one minute on a disappearing target at 200 yards.

In August, 1909, Maj. Gen. George F.

The Marine Corps Cup Trophy was donated to the NRA in 1909 by officers of the U. S. Marine Corps.

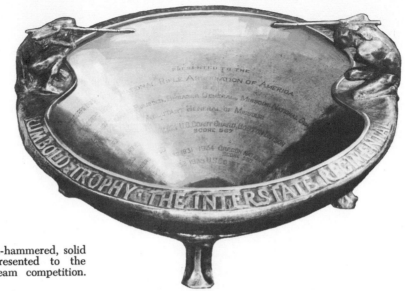

The Rumbold Trophy, a hand-hammered, solid silver punch bowl, was presented to the NRA in 1910 for annual team competition.

Elliott, Commandant of the Marine Corps, presented to the NRA a magnificent silver cup valued at $1500, which had been raised by donations from officers of the Corps. The Marines specified that it be shot for annually in the regular NRA matches in an event to be known as the Marine Corps Match. This was a squadded individual event with military rifles, 20 shots at 600 yards and 20 shots at 1000 yards.

Brig. Gen. Frank M. Rumbold of Missouri presented a huge hand-hammered silver punch bowl as a trophy for the winner of the Championship Regimental Team Match, which had been established at Sea Girt in 1906. Since then the winner had received a cash prize but no trophy.

Not to be outdone by their officers, the enlisted men of the Marine Corps in 1910 presented the National Rifle Association with a statue of a Marine rifleman financed by donations from men in the ranks. Known as the Enlisted Men's Trophy, it was to be awarded to the winners of a match for enlisted men from the Regular Services or National Guard.

A third trophy donated by Marines orig-

inated under unusual circumstances. In the National Rifle Matches of 1910 the Marine team made a score high enough to place it second and in line for a cash prize of $350. By actual score, the United States Cavalry team trailed in third position. During the course of the skirmish phase, however, one of the Marine coaches, carried away by the excitement and, in violation of the rules, blurted out a few words of encouragement to his team. Because of this infraction, the executive officer ordered the Marines' score in the skirmish phase to be thrown out, dropping the team to forty-second place.

The Marines took this ruling gracefully, but the cavalrymen did not. They protested the ruling so vigorously to the National Board for the Promotion of Rifle Practice that the Marine team was reinstated to second place, a gesture that cost the Cavalry team $150 in prize money. In appreciation for this sacrifice, Capt. William C. Harllee, the captain of the Leatherneck team, announced on October 8, 1910, that the team had voted unanimously to apply the full amount of its prize money toward the purchase of a cup to be awarded annually to the cavalryman making the highest score in the President's Match of the NRA. Few brighter examples of sportsmanship could be found in the annals of any sport!

One innovation that appeared in the NRA Matches of 1910 was a police revolver match. Police competition as an annual activity did not begin until the 1920s, but the 1910 match, small as it was in terms of entries, was an important step forward. Like marksmanship in the Army before 1870, the ability of all policemen to shoot was taken for granted. Some city police officers at that time were picked for their jobs because they had a reputation as marksmen, but the majority were selected because they were big enough to command respect or because they stood well with local political bosses. Few had any training and, in the majority of cases, a policeman never fired a shot until he was called upon to use his revolver in line of duty. The results were often disastrous.

Brig. Gen. James A. Drain suggested that the National Rifle Association schedule a police revolver match as part of its Camp Perry program. "These men ought, every one of them," Drain concluded, "to be expert shots with the revolver." The Match in August, 1910, which was won by the Chicago Police Department, was the fruit of this effort. Two years later, on May 30, 1912, *Arms and the Man* published a comprehensive course of rifle and revolver practice for police, which was drawn up by K. K. V. Casey.

Early in 1910, Congressman John Albert Tiffin Hull of Iowa, the chairman of the Committee on Military Affairs, introduced in the Sixty-first Congress a bill authorizing the War Department to issue free rifles and ammunition to organized rifle clubs "under such regulations as the Secretary of War may prescribe." When this bill later became law, the National Board for the Promotion of Rifle Practice became the agency for the distribution of the free materiel. Affiliation with the National Rifle Association became a prerequisite for qualification.

In the meantime the War Department, with the adoption of the Model 1903 Springfield as the official infantry arm, found itself with a surplus of Model 1898 Krags on its hands. On November 3, 1910, Secretary of War Dickinson authorized the Chief of Ordnance to set aside a supply of Krag rifles for sale to members of the National Rifle Association at $10 each and costs. All orders for these rifles were placed through the adjutant general of the state of residence of the applicant.

These two actions greatly advanced the program of the NRA. It was the first time that individual members at large of the NRA were given access to government equipment; earlier distribution had been only to affiliated military clubs, and ownership of the

The Cavalryman Cup was donated in 1911 by the 1910 U. S. Marine Corps Rifle Team to be awarded to the high-scoring cavalryman in the President's Match.

weapons was retained by the War Department. These rifles, however, were sold outright to individual members who could "sporterize" them for hunting, "accurize" them for target work, or scrub off the cosmoline and use them as they were. The only restriction was that they not be acquired for the purpose of resale.

While individual NRA members were receiving this welcome dividend, however, the Association itself, in addition to the Pan-American Match in Argentina, was faced with the problem of raising funds to finance the transportation and expenses of two more international teams in 1912. The Olympic Games were to be held in Stockholm, Sweden, in the summer of that year, and the NRA had already firmed up a Palma Match with the Canadians to be held in the autumn. With the International Smallbore Match, Interclub, Intercollegiate, and Interscholastic Tournaments now operating as annual affairs, 1912 was the most active in the history of the Association to that time.

The Enlisted Men's Trophy was presented to the NRA in 1910, and placed in team competition.

The Board of Directors on January 10, 1912, reelected General Bates as president and Lieutenant Jones as secretary. Col. H. G. Catrow became treasurer. There were changes in the three-man slate of vice-presidents. Col. Charles D. Gaither of Maryland became second vice-president and Brig. Gen. Elliott C. Dill, the Adjutant General of Maine, became third. The first vice-president, Brig. Gen. Charles C. Boardman, was retained in office.

The problem of raising $15,000 to send three international teams out of the country in one year weighed heavily on the deliberations of the Board that year. In 1911, the Association had started a drive to raise the required funds by private contributions, but almost on the eve of the Pan-American Games the effort was far short of its goal. Since the Board was committed to sending a team to Buenos Aires in April, 1912, it decided to apply all available funds to the expenses of that team and to redouble its efforts to raise the other funds needed. As its own contribution, it applied all life membership dues received between then and the opening of the Olympic Games to the Olympic Rifle Team expense fund.

Tryouts for the Pan-American Team were held on April 10 and 11; those for the Olympic Team were shot between April 29 and May 15, 1912. Both preliminary matches were held at the Marine Corps Range in Winthrop, Maryland. General Drain and Col. J. G. Ewing were named delegates to represent the National Rifle Association of America at the Pan-American Congress of Sharpshooters, which would meet in Buenos Aires during the Argentine matches.

Arthur P. Lane, one of the great pistol shots of all time, won three gold medals at the 1912 Olympics.

When the Executive Committee met on April 6, 1912, enough money had been raised to finance the Pan-American team expenses, but the Olympic fund was still too low to assure that the United States would be represented at Stockholm by a rifle team.

The Pan-American International Rifle Match, which was held on April 20, 1912, involved unfamiliar rules for the Americans. The shooting was at 300 meters at a bulls-eye 23 inches in diameter with concentric rings which were scored 9, 8, and 7 points, the overall target being one meter square. All teams were required to shoot with unaltered military rifles of their respective services. Each member of each five-man team was required to fire a total of 120 shots, 40 each in standing, kneeling, and prone positions. Col. Charles D. Gaither, the team captain, picked Stuart W. Wise, John W. Hession, O. N. Schriver, J. H. Kneubel, and W. H. Hyde to shoot for the United States. It was apparent, in the course of this practice, that Argentina would be the team to beat. Not only were

they on their home range, but they had consistently outpointed the Brazilians, Chileans, Peruvians, and Uruguayans throughout the practice session.

In spite of their handicaps, the American shooters outmatched the South American marksmen in every phase. The final scores were: United States, 4722; Argentina, 4597; Chile, 4122; Peru, 3912; Brazil, 3876; and Uruguay, 3460.

In the meantime, sufficient funds had been raised for the trip to Stockholm and the Olympic Team had been selected at an elimination match on the Marine Corps Range in Winthrop, Maryland, between May 16 and May 20.

In the London Olympic Games of 1908, the United States had entered only about half of the shooting events. The 1912 team determined to enter every event at Stockholm, regardless of American familiarity with the type of shooting involved. As soon as it was selected it encamped on the Naval Academy Range at Annapolis to begin intensive training. The men rigged their own Running Deer range to practice this sport at which the Scandinavians were known to excel. In the military rifle practice they shot only at 200, 300, 400, 500, and 600 meters on European targets to familiarize themselves with conditions they would face overseas. Scoring, also, was done by European standards with the center of the bullet hole determining its relative score. They used prone position exclusively, since the rules permitted any position. The rifle team was joined in practice by the pistol team which had been selected by the United States Revolver Association.

The rifle team sailed on June 14, accompanied by NRA Secretary Albert S. Jones, and reached Stockholm on June 29. In the prematch practice, team captain Harris Laning selected C. L. Burdette, A. L. Briggs, H. L. Adams, J. E. Jackson, C. T. Osburn, and

W. A. Sprout to represent the United States in the important Military Team Match.

Ten national rifle teams were on the field at Stockholm—the United States, Great Britain, Sweden, South Africa, France, Norway, Greece, Denmark, Russia, and Hungary. Although the Americans had felt some dismay when the Olympic Committee announced that there would be no events involving ranges over 600 meters, where American marksmen were at their best, their intensive practice at Annapolis began to pay off almost from the first shot. At the end of the 200-meter stage the Americans had a substantial lead, which they increased at every other distance. Only Great Britain and Sweden provided any serious competition. This was the first international match in which American riflemen had been pitted against those of Russia, who were represented at Stockholm by a fierce-looking crew of shaven-headed Muscovites in baggy uniforms. The Russian shooting form caused raised eyebrows and some amusement; its team insisted on shooting with fixed bayonets! In spite of their warlike appearance, the Russians finished next to last, beating only the hopelessly outclassed Hungarians.

The second day of the Olympic shooting program at Stockholm was devoted to the shotgun. The American shotgun team, which had been organized by the American Trapshooting Association, picked up a second gold medal for the United States by winning the team event. J. R. Graham of the shotgun team won a third gold medal in the individual trapshooting match with a score of 96 out of 100.

In the Individual Military Rifle Match, Osburn and Jackson of the United States placed second and third behind P. A. Colas of France. The Running Deer rifle team captained by Walter Winans, who had won the individual double-shot Running Deer events

Col. Morton C. Mumma, one of the nation's best marksmen, outstanding leader in marksmanship training.

for America in 1908, placed second to Sweden.

But the most popular marksman in the American ranks that year was Arthur P. Lane of New York City, a dapper but modest youngster of twenty who had been shooting only two years. Shooting in starched collar and business suit, the "boy wonder of Manhattan" swept the revolver matches and led the American pistol team to an overwhelming victory. Lane himself won three gold medals —in the duel-shooting match at thirty meters, the fifty-meter championship match, and the medal for the highest individual score in the team match.

A final gold medal was won by Capt. Fred S. Hird of Iowa in the fifty-meter miniature rifle match. Except for Lane's superiority over the French in the duel match, Hird's victory over the British in this event was the major upset of the Olympic shooting competition. The five shooters ranking behind Hird were all members of the British miniature rifle team.

There was yet another international match scheduled in July, 1912. In 1908, the National Rifle Association of America had joined the International Union of Shooting Federations and Associations, with headquarters in Paris. The ISU invited the National Rifle Association to send a team to Bayonne-Biarritz, France, to compete in the annual matches of the ISU between July 19 and August 1, 1912. Because of its involvement in the Olympic, Pan-American, and Palma Matches in the same year, the NRA was unable to take on these additional responsibilities. The Ohio State Rifle Association, however, picked up the gauntlet for the United States and sent a strong team of Ohio marksmen, captained by Ammon B. Critchfield. When it arrived in France, some of the other nations represented there objected to the American peep sight and the use of the sling, which had become a standard accessory in all American matches. Because of this the American team withdrew. The disappointed Ohioans participated as a team in the ISU match only as spectators, although some competed successfully in individual events.

The final international match in 1912 was the Palma Trophy Match, which was held at Canada's Rockcliffe Range on September 14. Because the War Department had decided against holding the National Matches in 1912 and because of the absence of many of the best American marksmen overseas in the international matches, the NRA returned to Sea Girt to hold its matches in conjunction with those of the New Jersey State Rifle Association, on August 24 through September 7. Although attendance was lower, there was more individual competition.

The Palma Team was selected largely on the basis of individual performances in the NRA Matches of 1912. Col. Smith W. Brookhart, Chief Ordnance Officer and Inspector of Small Arms Rifle Practice for Iowa, served as captain, while now-Captain Morton C. Mumma, who was still on detached service from the Second Cavalry as instructor of military science at the University of Iowa, became team adjutant. Mumma had been a member of the United States Cavalry team in 1903, 1906, 1907, and 1908; of the National Revolver Team in 1909 and 1911; and was the winner of the Marine Corps' Cavalryman's Trophy as the highest-scoring cavalryman in the President's Match of 1912.

In the prematch practice, F. H. Kean, E. H. Eddy, K. K. V. Casey, W. B. Martin, George W. Chesley, W. A. Tewes, J. H. Keough, and J. W. Hession of the American team were selected to do the actual shooting. The Canadian team, shooting improved Enfield rifles, gave the Americans the heaviest competition they had had in years, but the final score was 1720 to 1712 in favor of the American team.

By 1912, the National Rifle Association of America had grown tremendously in stature. Its marksmen had competed against and beaten in direct competition the finest riflemen of five continents, in some cases on their home ranges and in their own specialties. In a relatively few years it had emerged from an Eastern-oriented organization that was national largely in name to a strong association with a year-round program that extended into nearly every state in the Union.

Rockcliffe Range, near Ottawa, Canada, was the scene where this group of United States riflemen won the Palma Trophy in 1912.

# 15

# Stepped-up

# Shooting Programs—

# Shadows of War

The Battle of Lake Erie was fought and won on September 10, 1813, within sight of the shoreline of what later had become Camp Perry. Nearly a century later, in 1911, the Ohio State Rifle Association decided to celebrate the centennial of the American victory with a major shooting match at the state camp which bore the name of the American hero who had commanded that vital naval engagement. The officers of the state organization advanced the idea to the National Rifle Association, asking that the Palma Trophy be placed in competition as part of the 1913 Camp Perry program.

The rapid growth of American interest in international shooting in 1912 gave the idea broader scope. When final plans took shape, they included not only the Palma Trophy but the International Shooting Union and Pan-American rifle and pistol competitions as well. Combined with the National Matches and the annual matches of the NRA and Ohio State Rifle Association they made Camp Perry, in the summer of 1913, the axis of the shooting world.

At the Executive Meeting on December 5, 1912, General Bates appointed a committee under Col. H. G. Catrow of Ohio to petition Congress for federal assistance. The scope of the planning had already outstripped the resources of the NRA. Catrow and his associates visited Senator Henry S. du Pont, chairman of the Senate Military Affairs Committee. In reply to their request the senator from Delaware drafted a rider to the Army Appropriations Bill earmarking $25,000 to help the National Rifle Association meet the cost of the proposed matches.

In addition to providing the needed funds, the du Pont rider authorized the War Department to cooperate with the NRA in managing the matches and requested the State Department to lend its offices in extending invitations to national shooting or-

ganizations throughout the world. France had already accepted an invitation extended by NRA Secretary Jones while he was en route home from Stockholm in 1912.

The National Board for the Promotion of Rifle Practice assigned Brig. Gen. Robert K. Evans as executive officer of the National Rifle and Pistol Matches. The NRA asked this newly appointed Commander of the Army's Department of the Gulf to serve in the same capacity in the combined matches. No one had more experience than Evans. He had been executive officer of the National Matches for all but the first years of their existence.

General Bates, who had asked that he not be nominated for re-election, was replaced as president of the NRA in 1913 by Brig. Gen. Charles D. Gaither, Commander of the Maryland National Guard. Brig. Gen. Elliott C. Dill, Adjutant General of Maine, was elected first vice-president; Col. S. W. Brookhart of Iowa, second; and Maj. Carl T. Hayden of Arizona, third.

Winchester "Schuetzen" or free-rifle models employed the excellent single-shot action designed by John M. Browning.

Hayden, who for several years had captained the Arizona Rifle Team, had become a member of the Board of Directors in 1911, the year he moved east as Congressman-at-large for the Territory of Arizona. Colonel Catrow, whose efforts had led to the du Pont rider, replaced Brig. Gen. Carl A. Wagner as treasurer.

Because the War Department had decreed that the National Rifle and Pistol Matches, after 1913, would be held only in alternate years, the Board voted to reinstate the Hilton Trophy Match in the Association's annual matches. Since 1903 the Hilton Shield had been awarded by the NRA as second prize in the National Rifle Team Match. The Board also decided to revert to its original concept of the President's Match and make the score in that event the sole determinant of the military rifle championship of the United States. Since the start of the National Matches, the aggregate score in the President's and National Individual Rifle Matches had determined the championship. At the same time the directors increased the number of shots at 1000 yards in the President's Match from ten to fifteen and decreased the bullseye of the mid-range target to sixteen inches. To encourage civilian rifle clubs, which were playing an increasing role in NRA affairs, the Board announced a new match—a 500-yard event, twenty shots per man for teams of four from affiliated civilian clubs.

By April, 1913, plans for the combined matches began to take form. Invitations had been sent by the NRA to national shooting organizations around the world. An encouraging number of acceptances were on file in the NRA offices. Colonel Evans asked the War Department to assign 1000 troops and 100 officers to duty at Camp Perry as markers, scorers, and range officers.

Brig. Gen. Charles D. Gaither, NRA president (1913-1915).

The rules of the ISU and Pan-American Matches made it necessary to rebuild many range facilities at Camp Perry. Metric distances had to be measured off and new and unfamiliar targets printed. A Running Deer range, based on international specifications, had to be installed and disappearing targets for the pistol events improvised. To house the pistol and smallbore rifle ranges, the Ohio State Rifle Association built a large concrete structure near the present site of the water tower. The shooting positions were sheltered from weather by sheet metal roofing. It could accommodate forty simultaneous competitors equally divided between the rifle and the pistol. The first men to use it stuffed their ears with cotton and named it the "Boiler House," a name that lasted as long as the building itself.

Although the "free-rifle" which now had come into prominence resembled the *schuetzen* rifle, popular in America for years, European free-rifle rules were new to most Yankee marksmen. Where the *schuetzen* rifle was used in America primarily in the offhand position, the free-rifle was shot in three positions at distances much longer than those in most *schuetzen* matches. Tryouts for the American free-rifle team, using a rifle designed and built by the Winchester Repeating Arms Company, were held at Camp Perry on August 14, 1913.

The great matches of 1913 exceeded in scope, size, and worldwide interest any that had been held in America. France, Switzerland, Sweden, Argentina, Peru, and Canada sent their best marksmen to pit their skill against the Yankees. Canada had teams from each province as well as a national team hand-picked by the Dominion of Canada Rifle Association to shoot the Palma Match. There were teams from every state except five, and Hawaii and the District of Columbia were on the field. With those from the regular services, the forty-nine American teams were more by six than the previous record for American shoulder-to-shoulder competition.

There were some disappointments in the international response. Although Germany, Cuba, and Mexico had accepted the invitation, they failed to appear. The Cubans were unable to raise the necessary funds and the German government, preoccupied with building its war machine, blocked travel plans of its national team. Mexico had been among the first to accept. A few weeks later, on February 23, 1913, assassins killed both President Reyes and his vice-president and plunged the nation into chaos. The Mexican problem was one of the dark clouds hanging over Camp Perry that year. For a while it appeared that the matches might have to be cancelled and that the careful planning of the National Rifle Association would come to nothing. Fortunately, conditions stabilized enough for the matches to proceed, but many soldiers who shot in them headed immediately afterward for the Mexican border.

The NRA's Wimbledon Cup Match opened the combined matches on August 14. The highlight of the National Rifle Association Matches that year, however, was the performance of a scrub team of prominent shooters who entered the Herrick Trophy Match under the name of the "Usterwases." Shooting against twenty-seven formally selected entries, and competing as a lark, the remarkable veterans topped Iowa's official winning score and exceeded by six points the world's record for service rifles set by the 1912 Palma Team.

The NRA Matches of 1913 saw the first Individual Palma Match, a man-to-man event that was otherwise shot under rules of the Palma Team Match. The trophy, a large sterling silver cup supported on a wooden base by miniature service rifles, was presented to the National Rifle Association by the National Guard Association. One hundred and fifty-nine marksmen shot for it in the first contest. The first three places were taken by Canadians led by Maj. C. Hart McHarg. Two years later, McHarg became one of the first Canadian officers to die in action in France.

A new and short-lived feature of the National Matches, which were held on August 25, was a "surprise fire" event, developed at Monterey, California, as a substitute for the skirmish run which had been eliminated from the National Matches. Surprise fire involved disappearing silhouette targets at various unannounced ranges. Each target was visible only six seconds, in which the shooter had to drop to the prone or kneeling position and score as many hits as possible. It was a bruising course. The War Department soon dropped it because of the number of injuries—twisted ankles, wrenched elbows, and bruised knees suffered by overzealous marksmen.

The combined ISU and Pan-American Matches opened on September 1. The Swiss, master riflemen of the Continent, to no one's surprise, dominated the free-rifle events. The three-position 300-meter match was a specialty of the Alpine republic where every citizen was a marksman. They scored nearly 200 points more than the second-place French. But the Americans did better than anyone expected. Fighting it out with the Swedes in a neck-and-neck finish, they made third by a single point.

The American pistol team dominated the International Revolver Matches. They won both the Pan-American and the ISU International. Under ISU rules, the individual pistol championship was determined by the high individual score in the team match. The contest became a battle between Sweden's Carlberg and young A. P. Lane of the United States. Each finished with identical scores but the Swede won under the rules of scoring.

The two real upsets came in the smallbore rifle and Running Deer events. John Schnerring of the Frankford Arsenal won the former over the favored Europeans in a hotly contested match in the "boiler house." The Running Deer match operated as a continuous event throughout the nine days of the combined matches. This match was originated by and was a favorite sport of the Scandinavians, and the Swedes were odds-on favorites to win by a large margin. But Lt. C. T. Osburn, USN, turned in a perfect score of 50 points, and two other Americans ran up 49s. On the last day, in spite of patches and repairs, the Running Deer was so riddled that it refused to run any more.

Midway through the ISU and Pan-American Matches, Colonel Thurston, captain-designate of the American Palma Team, was called back to New York by illness in his family. Responsibility for selecting and leading the team fell on Capt. Morton C. Mumma, USA, statistical officer of the combined matches and one of the most experienced officers available. Since Thurston had delayed making his selection until the close of the earlier matches, this responsibility fell on the cavalryman from Iowa. Mumma had played a prominent role in the annual matches since 1907. In that year he had come into prominence as the high individual marksman in the National Team Match.

The team, picked by Captain Mumma on recent performance and past experience, was a strong one. The lead-off man was Lt. Col. C. B. Winder, one of the most seasoned

The Individual Palma Trophy, presented by the National Guard Association in 1913 for annual competition.

171

For over fifty years the NRA has given assistance to rifle clubs in many colleges, service academies, and secondary schools.

American riflemen with a distinguished record predating the turn of the century. Capt. Guy H. Emerson, another Ohioan, made the top score in the ISU long-range team match, and led the "Usterwases" in their informal romp in the Herrick. Capt. K. K. V. Casey of New Jersey had won so many trophies so often that Mumma selected him on past performance alone. Maj. Paul A. Wolf, USA, 2d Lt. R. Sears, USA, and 1st Lt. Littleton W. T. Waller, USMC, were all newcomers to international shooting. But all had turned in brilliant performances in the recent National Matches. George W. Chesley of Connecti-

cut held the record for the Palma course with military rifles and had just won the Leech Cup. Capt. C. G. Duff, Texas National Guard, and alternate in the 1912 Palma Team, had scored high in all of the individual matches he had entered.

In practice it appeared that Canada had the team the Americans would have to beat. Armed with new .303 Mark II Ross rifles, they turned in excellent scores in the prematch warm-up. The South Americans, represented by Argentina and Peru, had done little shooting beyond 600 yards, although the Argentinians had made surprisingly high scores in the recent Herrick Match. They had arrived in the United States two weeks ahead of any other foreign team and, as guests of the New Jersey State Rifle Association, had learned in a week-long session of practice at Sea Girt to stretch the range of their 7.65 Mausers. The Swedes, the only other team to enter the Palma, shot .256 Mausers using bullets too light for 1000-yard work in any kind of a wind.

And high winds greeted the opening of the match. The 800-yard stage turned into a three-way battle that was the closest fought in the history of the Palma. At this range the Canadians and the Americans finished with identical scores. The Argentinians dogged the heels of the leaders by a single point.

The Canadians had the finest team ever to represent the Dominion in an international shooting match, but at 900 yards their scores fell off badly. Their long bullets, designed for the Palma Match, had excellent accuracy in fair weather but the designers had failed to test them in wind. Near-gale winds off Lake Erie played havoc with the Canadian scores. While the more stable Springfield and Mauser bullets rarely strayed from the black, those of the Canadian Ross straight-pull rifles wan-

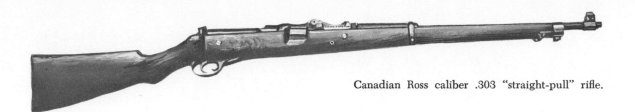

Canadian Ross caliber .303 "straight-pull" rifle.

dered all over the target. The match ended in a resounding victory for the United States. Argentina was second and Canada third. Sweden and Peru finished far behind.

Meanwhile, to round out a long string of international victories, the American Dewar Team, selected by the National Rifle Association to compete in the International Smallbore Match, defeated Great Britain. Two of the Americans made possible 500s.

A great deal more than the noise of riflefire and the smell of burned gunpowder was generated by American participation in international rifle and pistol competition in 1912 and 1913. Goodwill was one of the great dividends. The Association's all-out plunge into international shooting was so rewarding that continued participation was only natural. The Directors voted to send a Palma Team to Canada in 1914, to accept an invitation from the National Rifle Association of Peru to organize a team for the Pan-American Matches in Lima, and to enter the Sixth Olympiad in Berlin in 1916. The last acceptance was on the condition that the German Olympic Committee rescind its impossible insistence that all teams compete with German military Mausers. But all of these fine plans crashed to earth a few months later when the Kaiser's hordes swarmed into Belgium and lit the powder keg of World War I.

President Gaither's report to the Board of Directors in 1914 showed a substantial growth in civilian interest in the National Rifle Association. Gains in affiliated civilian clubs had more than offset losses in the number of affiliated National Guard regimental clubs, the mainstay of the early

NRA. Forty civilian clubs had applied for affiliation in the previous two months. The majority of the new affiliates represented school, college, and other youth groups. More than 15,000 schoolboy and college riflemen had been or were then enrolled in NRA tournament programs.

The school, college, and interclub winter tournaments were still growing in popularity and in public interest. Twenty-eight civilian rifle clubs were enrolled in the interclub tournament; thirty-four colleges and eighteen military schools were competing among themselves for NRA trophies. At the height of the season in 1914 targets poured into the NRA offices at the rate of 2200 each week. Each had to be marked, scored, and recorded, cramping limited office space and taxing the resources of the little office staff. In April, 1914, the National Rifle Association hired four more clerks and moved into more spacious quarters in the Woodward Building on Fifteenth Street, N.W., in Washington.

The NRA tournaments were developing some phenomenal marksmen. The top man in the 1914 interclub league was T. K. "Tackhole" Lee, of the Birmingham Alabama Athletic Club. Lee ran up an amazing record of 1999 out of a possible 2000. As a member of the Fifth International Smallbore Championship team on June 25, 1914, he shot a possible 500 against the British and then continued shooting for a score of 999 out of 1000. In 1915 he made it 2250 out of 2250!

In September, 1914, after considerable negotiation, the National Rifle Association overcame opposition to shooting by a dominant group in the National Council of the Boy Scouts of America. Merit badges in marksmanship were among the first offered by the Boy Scouts when the organization was established in the United States. But their issue had been suspended soon afterward. Concern for safety, and pacifistic influences, seem to have motivated the opposition, but a shortage of qualified instructors and merit badge counselors was also a major factor.

The Boy Scouts originated in Great Britain in 1908 with Maj. Gen. Sir Robert S. Smyth Baden-Powell and spread rapidly around the world. Baden-Powell, a leader of the British forces in the Boer War, had been impressed by the lack of basic woodcraft skill in the soldiers of his command. Tommy Atkins was as brave and staunch a soldier of the line as any in the world. But send him forward alone to scout the enemy and he might never return. City-bred and city-oriented, he knew nothing of reading compasses and maps or living off the land. It was, in part, to reinstill these skills in young Britishers that Baden-Powell formed the Boy Scouts. The familiar terms, "scout," "patrol," and "troop," reflect this early military consideration.

The Boy Scout movement reached the United States in several separate forms. One was the Boy Scouts of America, whose National Council was incorporated early in 1910. Another, with a rather close affinity to the National Rifle Association, was the Boy Scouts of the United States. It was organized by Col. Peter S. Bomus, the executive officer of the first National Rifle and Pistol Matches at Sea Girt. The Boy Scouts of America was an extension of the Sons of Daniel Boone, or Boy Pioneers, organized early in the century by naturalist-author Daniel Carter Beard.

Bomus founded his Boy Scouts of the United States without knowing that another organization was already on the scene, and his ideas differed considerably from those of Beard. In October, 1910, the Boy Scouts of the United States, Dan Beard's Boy Pioneers, and Ernest Thompson Seton's Woodcraft Indians formally merged under the National Council of the Boy Scouts of America. Early in 1911, the National Council held its first annual meeting at a banquet attended by President William Howard Taft. Seton became Chief Scout, while Beard, William Verbeck, and Colonel Bomus became national scout commissioners.

The first Boy Scout handbook, printed in 1910, contained specifications for a badge in marksmanship that, undoubtedly drawn by Bomus, closely followed the NRA Junior Marksmanship course. The second edition, released in 1911, brought the two programs into parallel by making qualification in the NRA Junior Marksmanship program prerequisite to obtaining a merit badge.

In 1911, however, America and the world had been at peace. Only a few, in or out of the Boy Scouts, could then see any value in teaching young boys to shoot. There were strong "peace" organizations active throughout the land who opposed anything smacking of militarism and who equated preparedness with a step toward war. Others feared that boys trained to shoot would menace songbirds by promiscuous hunting. Over Bomus' strenuous objections, the merit badge for marksmanship temporarily went into the discard.

By mid-1914, the dream of world peace had faded. Mexican unrest was threatening to spill over the Rio Grande; the Army was patrolling the southern border. The Atlantic Fleet had landed Marines at Vera Cruz and nineteen Americans had died in action. The European war was still far away but the guns that were battering Liége and Brussels boomed loud in the American conscience.

In the climate of 1914, marksmanship training took on a new aspect. As early as

November 24, 1913, the National Council of the Boy Scouts had agreed to cooperate with the NRA which, on its part, agreed to supervise Scout rifle practice and to furnish targets. On June 30, 1914, the National Council resumed issuing merit badges in marksmanship. The National Rifle Association, through its national offices and affiliated clubs, cooperated closely with the Boy Scouts in this training program, opening ranges to their use, coaching them in aiming and position, and supervising their efforts on the range. In October, 1915, the Executive Committee created a new class of NRA membership for affiliated Scout troops.

While a brighter climate prevailed in rifle training for the nation's youth, clouds gathered in another area. The National Rifle and Pistol Matches of 1914 were shot in divisions at four different ranges throughout the United States. The National Board for the Promotion of Rifle Practice had decided on this arrangement when the War Department elected to hold joint maneuvers in even-numbered years. Divisional matches were held in the autumn of 1914 at Sea Girt; at Florida's State Range near Jacksonville; at Fort Riley, Kansas; and at Portland, Oregon. The National Rifle Association, with no other alternative, followed the same pattern and split its own matches, under a reduced program, on a regional basis.

It was a noble experiment in economy but the results satisfied no one. The matches in Division E in Oregon were so poorly attended that no real competition developed. Attendance at Fort Riley resembled a local shooting match. Only the matches at Sea Girt and Jacksonville had any of the character and flavor of national events.

Storm clouds were fast gathering from many directions when, on January 13, 1915, the Board of Directors of the National Rifle Association elected a new slate

Col. William Libbey, NRA president (1915-1921).

of officers except for the secretary, Lt. Albert S. Jones, and one vice-president. Brig. Gen. Fred B. Wood, Adjutant General of Minnesota, advanced from second to first vice-president. Brig. Gen. Louis W. Stotesbury, Adjutant General of New York, and Brig. Gen. J. Van Holt Nash, Georgia National Guard, became the second and third vice-presidents. Col. Glendie B. Young of the District of Columbia National Guard became the new treasurer.

The new president was Lt. Col. William Libbey, a member of the Executive Committee since 1913. Dr. Libbey, sixty and white-bearded, was at once the most scholarly and most versatile of all the NRA presidents to that time. He held a Doctor of Science degree from Princeton where he was professor of physical sciences and Director of the Museum of Geology and Archaeology. He was a Fellow of the Royal Geographic Society and Royal Geological Society of Great Britain and of their national counterparts in France. He was an officer or member of a dozen American scientific organizations. He was an author of two books and a vice-president of two banks. He was also an expert rifleman and since 1908 had served as assistant inspector of rifle practice for New Jersey.

One of the problems that the new officers faced was an Executive Order, signed by President Woodrow Wilson in January, 1915, prohibiting the further sale of surplus government weapons to clubs affiliated with the NRA. He took the action to assure that as many serviceable rifles as possible would be retained in federal arsenals in the event of war. The sale of surplus Krag rifles had been a stimulant to the NRA program in recent years. The President's action, however, did not affect the issue of rifles and ammunition to the clubs, which began in 1914. The Executive Order was rescinded later in the year and the release of rifles was accelerated rather than checked when the government stepped up its preparedness program. The only hitch that developed was a temporary order by the Secretary of War in 1916, suspending distribution of rifles to clubs in Texas and New Mexico. He feared that American irregulars along the border would embarrass the United States by raiding into Mexico as a reply to the provocations of Pancho Villa.

The Board of Directors voted to stage the annual NRA matches in conjunction with the National Matches, which the War Department had elected to hold in October at the Florida State Range.

The NRA tournament program had been a major success and it was still growing. In 1915, the Board voted to expand it still further by creating two more leagues. The first was an Indoor Regimental Gallery League, open to teams of ten men from any affiliated regiment. It was to be shot with the U. S. Gallery-practice .22 Springfield on the fifty-foot indoor target, ten shots slow-fire prone, ten shots rapid-fire in the kneeling position with a time limit of ninety seconds.

The second new tournament involved an Interclub Outdoor Shooting League, open to all affiliated civilian rifle clubs. This was an extension of the Short-Range Rifle League that *Arms and the Man* had sponsored since 1913, under associate editor Frank J. Kahrs. As soon as the NRA announced that it was starting its tournament, General Drain turned the Short-Range League over to the national association. He would have had difficulty continuing it anyway, for Kahrs, effective May 1, 1915, had accepted a position with the advertising offices of Remington Arms Company in New York City. The Short-Range Rifle League, with rules almost identical to those of the NRA's announced Interclub League, provided a strong, pre-built foundation for the new venture.

The Interclub Outdoor Shooting League Tournament was designed as a miniature of the standard 300- and 600-yard course. All shooting was with .22 caliber rifles on targets reduced to scale. The 100-yard target had a six-inch sighting bullseye extending to the outer edge of the six-ring around a two-inch scoring bull. The 50-yard target was a small silhouette, four inches across the base, a reduced version of the NRA rapid-fire "D" target. Each entry was required to shoot ten slow-fire shots prone at 100 yards and ten shots rapid-fire at 50 yards in the kneeling position. The Interclub Outdoor Tournament was an immediate success; twenty-one teams enrolled before the full conditions of the matches were decided.

As a further extension of the tournament idea in 1915, the National Rifle Association established a Military Outdoor Rifle League open to teams from any affiliated National Guard unit. It was designed both to increase interest in NRA affiliation by National Guard organizations and to further rifle practice in the organized militia. On April 30, 1915, the Executive Committee voted to hold one simultaneous league match each year rather than extend it over a period of time, as most other tournaments were operated. It also voted to permit the use of telescopic sights by all contestants. The National Board for the Promotion of Rifle Practice immediately endorsed the new program and voted to donate trophies and medals to the winning teams.

Under usual circumstances it would have been a foregone conclusion that the first six winners each year would be from Iowa, Ohio, Maryland, New York, New Jersey, and Massachusetts with differences only in the order of finishing. Their marksmen had dominated the NRA matches for years. Teams from other states would have a tendency to avoid entering in the face of certain defeat. As an incentive to the weaker teams, the Executive Committee hit upon a novel method of classification that gave teams of neophytes chances for honors equal to those made up of experts. Classification based upon past experiences and performances had been used for years in the National Matches, but the teams were rated before shooting began. In the NRA Military Outdoor Tournament the teams were classified after the match on the basis of their scores. All teams started on even terms. The ten highest scores determined the relative standing of Class A teams. The eleventh place and twenty-first place scores determined the winners in Class B and Class C, who received trophies and medals as impressive as those of the Class A hot shots. Under this plan, known as the Lewis System, no one could predict whether his team would finish last in one class or first in another. A team that under usual scoring procedures would have finished far down among the also-rans could take pride if it ranked high in its own class or low in a higher class than it expected to attain. The only real losers were the trailers at the bottom of the lowest class. The forethought of the Executive Committee in devising this system did much to make the Military Outdoor Rifle League an immediate success at the 1915 matches coming up in Florida.

The new Florida State Rifle Range, on the banks of the St. Johns River, proved a colorful setting for the annual competition. The range was the pride of Brig. Gen. J. Clifford R. Foster, Adjutant General of Florida and a member of the NRA Executive Committee, who had been responsible for its construction. Dense stands of pine, rather than the usual water or sky, provided a backdrop for eighty targets that stood out sharply against the curtain of foliage. Magnolias and live oaks, bearded with Spanish moss, shaded the camp grounds. To New England and midwestern eyes, the entire scene had an exotic flavor.

The National Rifle Association Matches opened on October 7, 1915, with thirty-nine states and the regular services represented. Most of the NRA matches that year followed the usual pattern and were run with routine efficiency. The Leech Cup Match, however, because of the new rule permitting telescopic sights, produced unusually high scores. With military sights, a perfect score in any stage was an unusual performance. In 1915, nineteen men made possible 35s at 800 yards and four of these had perfect 70s after 900.

The National Rifle and Pistol Matches ran smoothly and without any major upset. The team match that year provided the greatest excitement as the Marine and Infantry, the leaders in a field of thirty-six, battled down to the last shots. The Infantry won by a four-point margin in the closest finish in the history of the National Matches.

For the next few years the programs of the National Rifle Association of America were dedicated to the urgency of war.

177

# 16

# NRA Gets a Magazine

# Small Arms Firing School

Between 1914 and 1917, the United States was drawn unavoidably toward involvement in the European war. In the first year it tried to remain neutral and aloof. But German excesses in Belgium strengthened American sympathies for the Allies. Then in 1915, Germany launched unrestricted submarine warfare against Great Britain, and American citizens died on the "Lusitania." From that point on, direct American involvement became only a matter of time.

The United States was ill prepared for conflict on the scale of that in Europe. In its 140 years of independence it had fought only one overseas war. And the Spanish-American War had been aimed at the tentacles rather than the body of an aging colonial octopus. The American military establishment was geared to defense rather than attack. In November, 1914, the Army numbered 97,760 and the Marines 10,000. The National Guard, scattered piecemeal throughout the various states and territories, contained 120,000 officers and men. With the Navy, the United States could put only 285,000 trained men in action.

As soon as it appeared that America could become involved in Europe, the federal government started to prepare for that eventuality. It initiated a recruiting campaign for the Armed Services and stepped up the production of weapons. In this climate the program of the National Rifle Association, which many had been inclined to regard as sport or play, took on grim reality and vital importance. It was the only non-military organization in the country designed to teach men to shoot. As such, it was creating a backlog of trained civilian riflemen who could carry their skill into the Services whenever the Army or Navy needed them. The value of its work had already been dramatized at Vera Cruz in April, 1914. When the Atlantic Fleet landed its Marines, Ensign W. A. Lee, who as a midshipman had starred in the matches of 1907, was in charge of one of the landing boats. When small-arms fire from the shore pinned down the men on his barge, he borrowed a rifle from a Marine and with deadly marksmanship picked off three of the enemy snipers.

There was a growing awareness in the Wilson Administration and in the nation

# Activated

at large that if America was forced into the war demands upon it for men and materiel would be sweeping. Lord Kitchener, the Commander of the British Armed Forces, had stated the basic need of the war as clearly as anyone in his general orders of September 2, 1914. Appealing for still more volunteers, Kitchener wrote: "Never mind whether they know anything about drill. It doesn't matter whether they know their right foot from their left. Teach them how to shoot and do it quickly."

As America gradually dropped its early attempts at neutrality and assumed a position of preparedness, the training program available through the National Rifle Association became attractive and useful to men who heretofore had been unaware of its existence.

In response to this new-found public interest and anxious to contribute to the national effort, the NRA immediately expanded its program and its field of activities. On July 29, 1915, it launched an intensive drive which in three months brought in 15,000 new annual members. Many prominent military and civilian

figures, among them Thomas Alva Edison, lent their support by becoming Life Members. The Association earmarked all Life Membership dues received during these years to a special trust fund for promoting rifle practice. It also started a drive to organize rifle clubs among the employees of industrial firms and the various government agencies. At the end of 1915, it had thriving civilian clubs in the various plants of General Electric, Goodyear Rubber, Willys-Overland, Jordan Marsh Company, Petroleum Iron Works, and Hydraulic Pressed Steel. It affiliated sixty clubs in the Order of Maccabees alone.

The War Department, through Assistant Secretary of War Henry Breckinridge, encouraged this effort. At the meeting of the Board of Directors of the NRA on July 29, 1915, Breckinridge announced that the Department was furnishing trophies and medals for teams from civilian rifle clubs in a national competition based on the rules of the National Team Match. Following the NRA's Lewis classification system, the participating teams were to be divided on the basis of performance into classes of ten with trophies for each winning club. Breckinridge's enthusiastic support of the NRA civilian program helped mold official attitudes which would have an important bearing on the future of the organization.

The role of the NRA in the war preparedness program was more clearly defined when it participated, in October, 1915, in the Conference of National Defense. This meeting was attended by the leaders of the more prominent veterans' organizations, the National Defense League, the Navy League, and the Army and Navy Union. By unanimous vote it endorsed a proposal advanced by NRA President William Libbey for a national shooting academy to train civilian rifle instructors in the event of war. This idea, too, had originated with Breckinridge, who suggested it in an address during the 1915 National Matches at Jacksonville. In this speech Breckinridge advocated the construction throughout the United States of a series of government rifle ranges that would be open to all civilian rifle clubs affiliated with the National Rifle Association. He also encouraged the National Rifle Association to expand as fully as possible its civilian training program as a contribution to the defense effort. Breckinridge's ideas, although they reached fruition after he left government service, formed the foundation of Section 113 of the National Defense Act of 1916.

At the meeting of the Board of Directors on January 12, 1916, President Libbey was re-elected to succeed himself for another year. In his report he was able to report a remarkable record of growth. Although the Board of Directors retained Colonel Libbey as president and Brig. Gen. Fred B. Wood of Minnesota as first vice-president, it voted replacements in all of the other elective offices. Brig. Gen. Charles F. Macklin, the new Adjutant General of Maryland, became second vice-president and Maj. William C. Harllee, USMC, third. Macklin's career was interesting in that, on his retirement as Adjutant General, he became Commander of the Maryland Naval Brigade with the naval rank of captain. Albert S. Jones, who had served as secretary of the National Rifle Association since its reactivation in 1901, was replaced by Brig. Gen. Fred H. Phillips, Jr., of Tennessee. Lt. Col. David M. Flynn became the treasurer.

It was at this point that the National Rifle Association acquired its first official periodi-

cal. Early in 1916, Gen. James A. Drain decided to retire from the publishing business to devote full time to his law practice. In discussing the idea with Frank J. Kahrs, who had recently resigned as treasurer of Arms and the Man Publishing Company to accept a position with the Remington Arms Company, Drain abruptly offered to sell the magazine to Kahrs for one dollar. *Arms and the Man* had proved no gold mine although it had become the leading magazine of its kind in America.

Kahrs, in view of the unsettled international situation, declined the offer but countered with a suggestion that Drain offer the publication to the National Rifle Association. *Arms and the Man,* under General Drain, had been the unofficial organ of the NRA for years. Kahrs himself had covered nearly all of its matches and activities under the pen name "Al Blanco."

General Drain offered *Arms and the Man* to the NRA, his offer was accepted, and on July 1, 1916, for the price of one dollar the Association had an official magazine. Seven years later, with the issue of June, 1923, the magazine's name *Arms and the Man* was changed to *The American Rifleman*, and it has been published continuously by that name since that time.

The change of ownership and editors was effected smoothly and without suspension of publication. General Drain's association with the NRA had been so close that the content of the old and the new magazine was almost identical. The masthead listed Fred H. Phillips, Jr., as editor and Kendrick Scofield as associate editor.

Important things were happening in that summer of 1916. The National Defense Act of June 3 was another milestone in the development of the National Rifle Association of America, and it incorporated into government policy many of the ideas that the NRA had

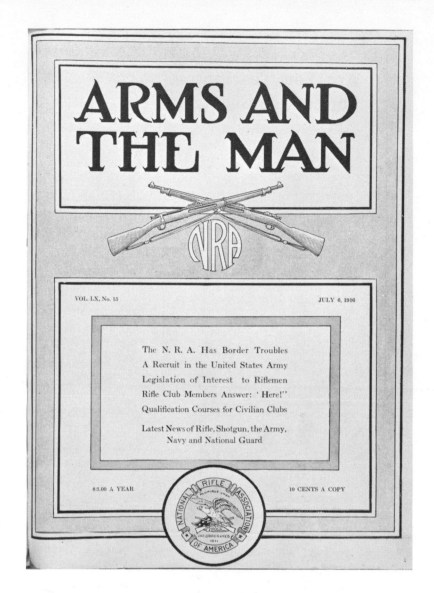

First issue of *Arms and the Man* after it had been acquired by the National Rifle Association, thus becoming the official NRA-owned magazine.

advocated for years. It earmarked $300,000 to promote civilian marksmanship training. It authorized the War Department to distribute appropriate arms and ammunition to organized civilian rifle clubs, under rules established by the National Board for the Promotion of Rifle Practice; it provided funds for the operation of government rifle ranges and the transportation of military instructors to assist civilian rifle clubs. It opened all military rifle ranges to civilian shooters. It provided $60,000 to transport civilian teams to the National Matches. Finally, it created the Office of the Director of Civilian Marksmanship under the National Board.

The 1916 annual matches of the National Rifle Association and the National Matches were again held jointly at the Florida State Camp. Col. Samuel W. Miller, USA, was executive officer, assisted by Maj. William C. Harllee of the Marine Corps and Col. John J. Dooley of the Maine National Guard. Harllee was vice-president and Dooley a member of the Executive Committee of the NRA.

Civilians did remarkably well in their first appearance in the National Matches. The Individual Rifle Match was won by W. K. Spencer of St. Louis, who by this achievement became the military rifle champion of the United States, although affiliated with no military organization. G. E. Cook of Washington, D. C., another civilian, won the National Individual Pistol Match.

Under the increasingly tense international situation, a close relationship sprang up between the military and the civilian rifle clubs. It had started under a program sponsored by the NRA in Washington at the Marine Corps range near Winthrop, Maryland. The Winthrop Range, built under the direction of Major Harllee in 1909, had been opened to local civilian teams and members of the NRA from Washington and Maryland under a policy initiated in 1913. The success of this activity was, in part, responsible for its extension as the preparedness program gathered steam.

Appointment to the position of Director of Civilian Marksmanship went to Col. Samuel W. Miller, the executive officer of the recent National Matches. Miller, a native of Pennsylvania, was a graduate of the Military Academy and Commandant from 1911 through 1914 of the School of Musketry at Monterey, California. He served only six months, however, before being called back to service with the Tenth Infantry when America entered the war. His replacement was Maj. Edwin V. Bookmiller, USA (Ret.), a veteran of the Spanish-American War, the Philippine Campaign, and the Peking Relief Column in the Boxer Rebellion. At the time of his appointment he was a military instructor at Georgetown University. At the request of the National Rifle Association, a retired Army officer was selected to prevent a rapid turnover in the position during the national emergency.

The War Department had expanded the National Board for the Promotion of Rifle Practice from nine to eleven members in 1916, the two additional members to be appointed from the Army. Although Colonel Libbey was the official representative of the National Rifle Association, the NRA was well represented by additional members on the board. Maj. William C. Harllee and Capt. Thomas Holcomb, Jr., the two Marine Corps representatives, were both officials of the Association, and Secretary Fred H. Phillips, Jr., appointed to represent the nation at large, became its recorder. Past President Charles D. Gaither was also a member.

At the first 1917 meeting of the National Rifle Association, the Board of Directors took important steps affecting the conduct of future matches. Its most sweeping innovation was to eliminate all cash prizes in events sponsored by the Association. Cash prizes had been traditional in practically all shooting matches since 1871. Some of the early shooters, like W. Milton Farrow, made a career of entering and winning matches in the United States and abroad. Professionalism had been a subject of debate in many meetings of the NRA since 1906. Part of this problem stemmed from its participation in the Olympic Games, which required that participants maintain an amateur standing. But since there were few experienced simon-pure amateurs among the leading marksmen of America or Europe, the definition had been stretched to embrace anyone whose main livelihood did not come from shooting.

But the year 1917 brought more important changes; on

As a wartime measure, approximately four million of these Model 1917 Enfield rifles in .30-06 caliber were produced in United States armsmaking plants.

April 6, 1917, the United States declared war on Germany. The best military minds of the time believed that no more than a million men would have to be drafted. No one dreamed that before the war was over additional increments would total three million Americans above that estimate!

At that time, the arsenals of America contained 800,000 Model 1903 Springfield rifles and production under an eight-hour day was 200,000 a year. At capacity, production could be increased to 500,000, still far short of the need. And the Springfield rifle did not lend itself to mass production at other plants without complete retooling. Fortunately, there were three private plants in the United States that had been tooled up to produce Enfield rifles under contract from Great Britain—Winchester, Eddystone, and Remington. On May 11, 1917, the Ordnance Department decided to accept the Enfield, modified to chamber the M1906 cartridge, as the standard infantry weapon. Government production of the M1903, at the same time, was stepped up to full throttle. Before the war was over nearly four million of the Model 1917 Enfield rifles were produced in American plants.

The Model 1917 was a sound and reliable weapon; but the adoption of a "foreign rifle" caused grumblings, and the grumblings grew into ugly rumors. Word soon had it that the Enfield was totally inaccurate and unsafe to shoot. One major contribution that the NRA made to the national war effort was in dispelling these rumors. Gen. George W. Wingate, the "father of American rifle practice," was assigned to test the Enfield. In a series of articles published in *Arms and the Man* he supplied a reassuring report. Wingate's verdict was that the Enfield in many respects was as good as the Model 1903 and totally reliable under battle conditions. By burying the rumors quickly and decisively the NRA did much to improve the morale of many Americans who found themselves carrying Enfield rifles into action in France.

The impact of the war on the National Rifle Association was immediate and heavy. Many of its more prominent members were National Guardsmen who were ordered immediately to the colors. Many of its affiliated clubs showed up en masse at recruiting stations to volunteer for active service. On May 9, 1917, an order signed by Adjutant General W. T. Johnson suspended the free issue and purchase of all rifles and ammunition to civilian clubs for the duration of the war. Some draftees already were drilling with broomsticks. Colonel Miller, the first Director of Civilian Marksmanship, had been recalled to active duty and reassigned as Commander of the Reserve Officers Training Corps Camp at Fort Niagara, New York.

One of the National Rifle Association's successful efforts at this time was in influencing members of affiliated clubs to volunteer for the Home Guard. The Home Club Target Association from the Department of the Interior was one of the first to respond to the call. Its members walked sentry duty before public buildings in Washington armed with antiquated .45-70 Springfields. The NRA editorially reassured them that the .45-70 was a proven manstopper quite adequate for sentry work. Later it succeeded in having the Home Guard armed with shotguns, which were more practical for street warfare.

In June, 1917, the Association launched a more important phase of its war program. Discovering that the Reserve Officers Training School at Fort Myer, Virginia, had no rifle range, it opened all of its local ranges to the trainees and succeeded in putting 2500 through a 40-shot qualification course.

By July 7, 1917, with .30 caliber ammunition almost impossible to obtain, the NRA launched a smallbore qualification course, which like its Outdoor Smallbore League

Tournament, was based on a reduced version of the military course. It devised scale-model targets that were shot at respectively with .22 caliber rifles at 50, 75, 125, and 150 yards. They were equivalent to the standard A, B, and C targets at 200, 300, 500, and 600 yards. The "D-4" target for rapid fire was a miniature of the standard D silhouette target reduced to 4¾ inches high and 6½ inches wide. Similar ranges were built up by affiliated rifle clubs throughout the United States. Thousands of prospective soldiers had an opportunity to familiarize themselves with conditions comparable to those on military rifle ranges. As the war effort intensified, some soldiers went into battle with little more training in musketry than they had received on NRA ranges before induction.

One of the most important training installations in the East at the beginning of the war in Europe was the Marine Corps' Winthrop Rifle Range near Indian Head, Maryland. It had been the first federal rifle range thrown open to civilian use. With the outbreak of World War I, it became the site of the Navy School for Small Arms Coaches, under the direction of Capt. G. K. Shuler, USMC. Shuler, who maintained a close association with the NRA during his duty in Washington, continued Harllee's policy of permitting civilian rifle clubs affiliated with the NRA to use the range. Moreover, he permitted them to qualify side by side with the Marines and blue-jackets and to learn the niceties of rifle practice under qualified instructors. By the beginning of 1917, Winthrop had graduated 800 Navy and Marine rifle instructors. But 6000 civilians, including 60 schoolboys from Washington, had qualified on its range. The range was absorbed in October, 1917, by the expansion of the Navy Proving Ground at Indian Head, and Shuler became one of the first members of the American Expeditionary Force to go into action in France. But by then Winthrop had served an important purpose, and its success

had planted the seeds of an idea in the minds of the leaders of the National Rifle Association.

In September, 1917, the War Department announced that it was bringing to America some British and French instructors to teach American recruits the art of war. The new program included a series of schools in musketry that would be directed by foreign officers. The National Rifle Association protested this decision. While its own members were being drafted and assigned to duty without reference to their special skills or were walking sentry duty as members of the Home Guard, the traditional capability of the American with the rifle was being overlooked by the War Department. Many of the Allied officers who were assigned to training duty in the United States had already expressed prejudices against the rifle. Although the British considered skill in marksmanship a useful quality in a soldier, some also believed that training accomplished marksmen was too time-consuming to be practical in time of war. The French view of the rifle was even dimmer. Several high-ranking French officers had publicly stated that a rifle was merely a useful handle for a bayonet. Soldiers, they claimed, could never be trained to shoot straight in the heat of battle. The *poilu* was taught to follow a screen of fire laid down by his deadly "seventy-fives" and to close with the enemy with grenade and bayonet.

The National Rifle Association differed sharply with the announced plans of the War Department. Within a few days their position received indirect but powerful endorsement. In France, Gen. John J. Pershing had become exasperated by the poor marksmanship among the recruits that were swelling his command. Some had never fired their rifles and many had never had a rifle in their hands before entering military service. Valuable time and energy had to be spent in retraining them overseas. And wartime France had few places where adequate rifle ranges could

184

be established without endangering civilians or the millions of Allied soldiers who crowded the territory behind the lines. The demands of war often made it necessary for Pershing to assign green troops to front-line duty before they had learned more than the rudiments of shooting.

Pershing's views of the rifle were quite different from those of the French and British and he stated them unequivocally in a communiqué to Secretary of War Newton D. Baker, which was made public on October 6, 1917: "You must not forget that the rifle is distinctively an American weapon. I want to see it employed. . . . Long experience with conditions in France confirms my opinion that it is highly important that infantry soldiers should be excellent shots. . . . I, therefore, strongly renew my previous recommendations that all troops be given a complete course in rifle practice prescribed in our firing manual before leaving the United States."

Two weeks later, on October 20, the NRA through *Arms and the Man* renewed its earlier pleas for action, stating: "It would be wise for the War Department to immediately establish a thoroughly up-to-the-moment school of musketry at State Camp, Florida, where shooting would be held throughout the winter, and there train a corps of competent coaches in some simple effective course. No time should be wasted. . . . The fact now stands out clear and plain *that our men must be taught to shoot.*"

The National Board for the Promotion of Rifle Practice met in Washington on January 8, 1918. It recommended unanimously that a "central school of musketry for the Army, Navy and Marine Corps" be established at the earliest possible date. In its recommendations it cited in full Section 113 of the National Defense Act of June 3, 1916: "The Secretary of War shall annually submit to Congress recommendations of an estimate for the establishment and maintenance of in-

Gen. John J. Pershing was one of the strongest advocates of marksmanship training. He gave staunch support to NRA programs.

door and outdoor rifle ranges under such a comprehensive plan as will ultimately result in providing adequate facilities for rifle practice in all sections of the country. And that all ranges so established and all ranges which may have already been constructed, in whole or in part, with funds provided by Congress shall be open to use by those in any branch of the military or naval services of the United States, and by all able-bodied males capable of bearing arms, under reasonable regulations to be prescribed by the Secretary of War. That the President may detail capable officers and non-commissioned officers of the Regular Army and National Guard to duty at such ranges as instructors for the purpose of training the citizens in the use of the military arm. When rifle ranges shall have been established and instructors assigned to duty thereat, the Secretary of War shall be authorized to provide for the issue of a reasonable number of standard military rifles and such quantities of ammunition as may be available for use in conducting such rifle practice."

Col. Morton C. Mumma was given the responsibility of organizing the very important new Small Arms Firing School in 1918.

The National Defense Act of 1916 was one of the most sweeping military laws ever enacted by Congress. It paved the way for the conscription of any able-bodied male citizen between eighteen and forty-five, increased the size of the Regular Army, provided for a College Reserve Officers Training Corps and a Federal Officers Reserve Corps. It was a long and complex Act, and until that time Section 113 had been all but overlooked. But read in the light of General Pershing's urgent appeals for trained manpower, it was a tacit endorsement of the program that the National Rifle Association had been advocating since the start of the war. Clear legal authority for the establishment of a small arms firing school obviously existed. All that was required was for the War Department to implement it.

The Secretary of War, Newton D. Baker, spurred by Pershing's appeals, endorsed the recommendations of the National Board almost as soon as he received them. On April 15, 1918, the Chief of Staff of the U. S. Army, Gen. Peyton C. March, signed orders authorizing establishment of "The Small Arms Firing School for the Instruction of Officers and Enlisted Men in Rifle and Pistol Shooting" at Camp Perry, Ohio. A companion order assigned Lt. Col. Morton C. Mumma, USA, as Commandant and charged him with establishment of the new school; Maj. Smith Brookhart of Iowa was chosen Chief Instructor.

This selection put the right men in the right jobs. Mumma was probably the most experienced rifleman in the Regular Army with a career that had started with a borrowed rifle when he was nine years old. He had won distinguished marksmanship rank with rifle and pistol and was a top man with a shotgun; he had been a high-scoring member of the Cavalry Rifle and Army Pistol teams and had won many individual honors both in the National and NRA Matches. He won the Marine Corps Cup twice and placed second in the President's Match once. He had been Adjutant of the Palma Team of 1912 and captain of the Team of 1913. While on assignment with the State University of Iowa as an instructor of military science, he had consistently turned out championship rifle teams in the NRA intercollegiate matches.

Senator Smith Brookhart of Iowa, while commissioned a major, was chief instructor at the Small Arms Firing School in 1918.

Brookhart, like Mumma a member of the Executive Committee of the National Rifle Association and of the National Board for the Promotion of Rifle Practice, was not himself an outstanding marksman. But he was a builder of marksmen. He had captained the high-scoring Iowa team in nine National Matches and the 1912 Palma Team. At the time of his appointment he was a captain in the Army Ordnance Department.

The Small Arms Firing School came into being on May 15, 1918. Addressing the first class of officers and enlisted men eleven days later, the Commandant, Colonel Mumma, assured his audience that hereafter the American soldier would be taught to place his shots. The American soldier was to be shown how he might become an accomplished "bullet placer"—and at the same time be best prepared to protect his own life. This was a bright milestone in the history of the United States Army, for straight shooting was indeed a principal business of its soldiers. The Commandant's words were received by the assembled officers and enlisted men with an enthusiasm which indicated the old shooting spirit of the armies of Washington and Jackson was still alive.

The primary objective, under a plan devised by Mumma, was to train instructors rather than expert riflemen. Each student, without regard for rank, was selected on the basis of his ability to teach. On returning to his regiment he was qualified to pass his new knowledge on down to the men in the ranks. Each trainee at Camp Perry underwent approximately a month of intensive training and shooting under the guidance of the best riflemen in the world.

Colonel Mumma's assistant commandant was Maj. Frank Lee Graham, a member of the Palma Team of 1912. The staff, personally selected by Mumma and Brookhart from the best contemporary marksmen, were men who were well known in national and international competition. Among them were veterans of the Palma teams—Chesley, Leushner, Preussner, and Keough; included were T. K. Lee, one of the greatest smallbore riflemen in the world, and President William Libbey of the National Rifle Association. Some had been called to active duty or reassigned from desk jobs at the request of Colonel Mumma.

On June 24, 1918, the National Board for the Promotion of Rifle Practice met at the clubhouse at Camp Perry. One of its principal recommendations was that the National Matches be resumed in the following autumn. The War Department had suspended the National Matches indefinitely because it felt that the necessary manpower and materiel could not be spared from the war effort. Canada, in 1914, for the same reason, had also suspended the annual meeting of the Dominion of Canada Rifle Association, which compared to the National Matches of the

United States. The Dominion was first to recognize the shortsightedness of this policy and in the winter of 1917-18 had announced that its national matches would be resumed as a device for training men to shoot. The United States profited by Canada's longer experience as a combatant. The War Department accepted the recommendations of the National Board.

It was evident that Board members were convinced that the National Matches could be staged without conflicting with the greater national interest, and would indeed further that interest, when they issued this statement: "It is believed that during the existing emergency that the holding of the National Match is deemed important and should be held, not only as an incentive to those already in the service, but as a medium for the development of competent coaches among units of the National Guard and civilians, whether they be members of the home guard, rifle clubs, colleges or schools. The necessity for teaching the citizenry of the United States to fire small arms accurately has never been more apparent than at the present time and the participation of a team from each State in the National Match in the opinion of this Board will do more to stimulate interest in and insure the promotion of rifle practice than any other action that could be taken by the Board."

The question of civilian participation in the forthcoming National Matches arose at the meeting of the National Board. Under regulations adopted just before America entered the war, each state was entitled to send one civilian team to the matches, but conditions had changed since 1916. Two able spokesmen on the Board strongly endorsed opening the matches to civilians. One was Colonel Mumma, whose views became the basis for the present association of the Small Arms Firing School with the National Rifle and Pistol Matches. "It appears to me," Mumma stated, "that great good could be accomplished if a plan were perfected whereby members of civilian rifle clubs could receive training at the Camp Perry school in connection with the National Matches. . . . There are plenty of men who will gladly take advantage of such an opportunity."

The National Board referred the matter to a committee, which endorsed it and forwarded it to the War Department, where it was approved. Under the Defense Act of 1916, most civilian male citizens were subject to possible military service, and it was logical that their usefulness would be enhanced by prior training with the standard infantry weapon. Since all Model 1917 rifles then being produced went directly to military units, few civilians were familiar with their construction or qualities.

The result of this discussion was an announcement by the War Department forming a marksmen school for civilian rifle teams to precede the National Matches of 1918. The official decision went beyond the recommendations of the National Board. Although only one civilian team from each state could travel to the National Matches at federal expense, the War Department opened the National Matches and the Small Arms Firing School to all civilian or school teams that traveled to Camp Perry at their own expense.

A second spokesman for civilian participation in the National Matches was Major Harllee, who announced that the Navy was opening all of its ranges except two to the public. Official orders confirmed this on August 19, 1918, and they included a full course of training for all civilians who wished to learn to shoot under Marine or Navy instructors. Ten days later on August 29, the Navy opened its rifle range near Caldwell, New Jersey. The purchase of its 5000 acres had been negotiated by Harllee. Three miles long and a mile deep, it was then the largest rifle range in the world.

The National Matches of September, 1918

From a modest beginning in 1918 the Small Arms Firing School at National Matches now attracts thousands of participants in rifle, pistol, and junior sections.

at Camp Perry, combined with those of the National Rifle Association and the Small Arms Firing School, were among the largest ever held to that time. There were fifty teams and 6000 individual marksmen in attendance. The NRA Matches were shot under an abbreviated program with only six events scheduled. These were the Wimbledon, Leech, Marine Corps, President's, Members', and Individual Pistol Matches. All events were shot with the Model 1917 Rifle and the Colt Model 1911 Pistol. Marine Corps shooters dominated most of the events.

The success of the Small Arms Firing School in producing outstanding military marksmen was overlooked by neither the War Department nor by Congress. Early in October, 1918, Congress appropriated $10,-000,000 for a greatly expanded version of the Camp Perry model on the banks of the Chattahoochie River near Columbus, Georgia. Its 120,000 acres would accommodate 12,000 student officers in a single class,

or 144,000 in one year. This was the Infantry School of Arms, later named Fort Benning. Its original composition combined the old school of Musketry from Fort Sill, the Small Arms Firing School from Camp Perry, an experimental section, a trench warfare section under foreign officers, and an automatic weapons section.

The Infantry School of Arms was the development of an idea the National Rifle Association had been advocating since the beginning of the war. It came into being too late to play a significant role in the war effort; Colonel Mumma and his staff arrived there in early October, 1918, only a few weeks before the Armistice was signed. But it developed into the most important Army training complex in America, next to the Military Academy, and its establishment was an important tribute to the programs so diligently pursued by the NRA. Truly the tree planted at Creedmoor was spreading its roots and its branches in an ever widening circle.

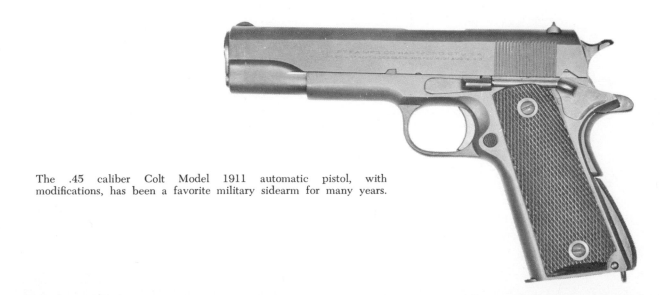

The .45 caliber Colt Model 1911 automatic pistol, with modifications, has been a favorite military sidearm for many years.

# Postwar Program – National

# Caldwell, N. J. – The Smallbore

Franklin Delano Roosevelt, then Assistant Secretary of the Navy, knew how to handle a Springfield rifle and had an active role in the National Board for the Promotion of Rifle Practice.

On November 11, 1918, the world was at peace for the first time in four years. In the National Rifle Association there was speculation what this abrupt change might mean to its future. Since 1915, its program had been geared to the war effort, and under the stimulus of preparedness its membership had increased rapidly. But many of its newer annual members had joined primarily to prepare themselves for military service. Would they continue their interest in shooting now that the national emergency had passed? Millions of men had learned to handle a rifle in the Armed Services. How many would continue to shoot for sport in time of peace? No one in late 1918 knew the answers. And on them depended the future programs of the NRA.

Demobilization, when it started, came rapidly. Construction of the new Infantry School of Arms in Georgia ground into low gear just as it was starting to gain momentum. Its select personnel was discharged or reassigned. On February 1, 1919, Col. Morton C. Mumma was reassigned from his duties as Executive Officer of the Small Arms Firing School to Commandant and Director of

# Matches at

# Comes of Age

Military Instruction of the ROTC at the State University of Iowa.

Although demobilization progressed rapidly, the War Department continued its interest in marksmanship training. The lessons of the war were still fresh, and the NRA program neatly fitted the needs of peacetime preparedness. On November 16, 1918, Capt. Richard D. LaGarde, USA, became Director of Civilian Marksmanship, and the National Board for the Promotion of Rifle Practice was reorganized to be made up of twelve members "thoroughly informed of marksmanship." Its chairman was Assistant Secretary of the Navy, Franklin Delano Roosevelt. Colonel Mumma, Lt. Col. William C. Harllee, USMC, William Libbey, Smith W. Brookhart, and Brig. Gen. Fred H. Phillips were retained from the earlier board, and the new members included Lt. Col. Townsend Whelen.

The newly constituted Board went to work early in 1919, voting unanimously to recommend the continuation of the National Matches, with a period of instruction for civilians preceding the 1919 national competition. It also urged that purchase privileges

be restored to civilian rifle clubs "under a system of reasonable prices." It adopted tentative changes in regulations governing the free issue of arms and ammunition, making it possible for NRA-affiliated rifle clubs to draw modern military weapons and increased allowances of ball cartridges.

The Board of Directors of the National Rifle Association met close to the same dates as the National Board. Colonel Libbey again succeeded himself as president. Lt. Col. David M. Flynn was retained as treasurer, and Brig. Gen. Fred H. Phillips, Jr., as secretary. Lt. Col. William C. Harllee, Lt. Col. Smith W. Brookhart, and C. C. Crossman were the first, second, and third vice-presidents.

In view of the changed conditions brought by the end of the war the NRA Board voted to take all steps possible to rehabilitate old and to organize new state organizations. It also voted to consider the feasibility of giving pistol shooting greater prominence in the NRA program. For several years the United States Revolver Association had been having organizational problems. Like the NRA it had lost many of its annual members during the

Savage Model 1919 clip-fed repeating .22 caliber match rifle.

The Winchester Model 52 soon became one of the most popular of the smallbore target rifles.

A prototype of the Springfield .22 caliber rifle, which became known as the Model 1922, was first shown by Julian Hatcher, then a lieutenant colonel at Springfield Armory.

war, but unlike the NRA it had been unable to recruit new ones. It lacked a national headquarters and its officers were scattered throughout the nation. It had no house organ. In an effort to assist its sister organization, the National Rifle Association between 1917 and 1918 had given the USRA space in *Arms and the Man* for a page of news items written by C. C. Crossman, who was at the time a vice-president of the NRA and president of the USRA. This had been instrumental in holding the revolver association together after the war. Most of the USRA matches were conducted by mail or telegraph, in contrast to the shoulder-to-shoulder events of the NRA. There was still room for expansion in the NRA handgun field without conflicting with the program of the USRA.

Both the National Board for the Promotion of Rifle Practice and the Board of Directors of the NRA in 1919 gave careful study to the continuation and expansion of work with the .22 caliber rifle. Because of a shortage of .30

caliber ammunition during the war, many affiliated clubs of the NRA had practiced with the .22. Many had grown to like it. In the meeting of the National Board it was suggested that the authorities add a smallbore event to the National Match program.

One of the drawbacks to this suggestion was that there was no magazine-equipped bolt-action .22 rifle in production at the time. Springfield and Krag rifles had been adapted to .22 caliber by plugging the magazine and inserting auxiliary barrels. These, however, were makeshifts with poor accuracy beyond seventy-five feet, and they had to be loaded singly. In response to the NRA smallbore qualification program, the United States Cartridge Company had developed a new NRA cartridge which, in the hands of C. S. Landis, who tested it for the Association, grouped forty-nine out of fifty shots in a two-inch circle at fifty yards.

The Savage Arms Company then produced its .22 NRA bolt-action rifle in June, 1919. Winchester followed six weeks later with its "experimental target rifle," the forerunner of its famous Model 52. Both rifles were well-stocked, loaded from detachable magazines, and had pinpoint accuracy. Two years later the federal government unveiled the first model of the Springfield rifle specifically designed for .22 caliber shooting. The prototype was exhibited to the National Board at its annual meeting by Lt. Col. Julian Hatcher of the Springfield Armory.

The .22 rifles being very popular with young shooters, the question arose at the 1919 meeting of the National Board whether or not the National Defense Act of 1916 imposed an age limit on civilians eligible to shoot at government rifle ranges. Many base and post commanders had barred shooters below the age of eighteen and above forty-five on the grounds that they were not eligible for military service. The Army Appropriations Bill for the fiscal year ending June 30, 1920, clarified this in accordance with the views of the NRA and the National Board for the Promotion of Rifle Practice. It authorized the expenditure of $10,000 in these terms: "to establish and maintain indoor and outdoor rifle ranges for the use of *all* able-bodied males capable of bearing arms under reasonable regulations prescribed by the National Board for the Promotion of Rifle Practice and approved by the Secretary of War" (italics added by editor).

Further, the Board appropriated $300,000 for the promotion of small-arms target practice on military ranges and authorized "such ranges and galleries to be open as far as practicable to the National Guard and organized rifle clubs under regulations prescribed by the Secretary of War."

Finally, the National Board decided that the National Matches of 1919 should be held at the new, sprawling Navy Rifle Range near Caldwell, New Jersey. Lt. Col. William C. Harllee, who had helped plan and build it, was named Executive Officer. Among the eight assistant executive officers were Lieutenant Colonels William Libbey, Smith W. Brookhart, and Townsend Whelen; Maj. Richard D. LaGarde, the current Director of Civilian Marksmanship; and Capt. G. L. Wotkyns. The Adjutant for the matches was G. K. Shuler, the former Executive Officer of the Navy Rifle Coaches School at Winthrop, Maryland. Lt. Col. Julian S. Hatcher was Ordnance Officer and Thomas G. Samworth of Delaware was Statistical Officer. Capt. Edward C. Crossman (not to be confused with C. C. Crossman), one of the most enthusiastic smallbore shooters in the country, was placed in charge of the miniature rifle range.

The Advisory Board for the National Matches of 1919 included three of the surviving past-presidents of the NRA—Generals George W. Wingate, Bird W. Spencer, and James A. Drain. The other members were Brig. Gen. Robert K. Evans, USA; Rear Adm. Charles P. Plunkett, USN; Maj. Gen. George F. Elliott, USMC; Brigadier Generals Clifford R. Foster, Ammon B. Critchfield, and Fred Phillips, Jr., and the former Assistant Secretary of War, Henry C. Breckinridge.

The Board decreed that the National Matches of 1919 were to be shot exclusively with the Model 1903 caliber .30 Springfield rifle and the Model 1911 caliber .45 Colt pistol. It again changed the course of fire to require several positions at 500 yards. Among them was the squatting position, which had been developed and taught at the Navy School of Rifle Coaches by Shuler. The position was a controversial one. The Navy swore by it as a highly practical combat position. The Army shunned it as undignified and awkward. But the Army was overruled, and the squatting position remained.

In January of 1919 the selection of Caldwell as the site of the matches seemed pure inspiration. It was the newest and largest range in America, and it was only an hour's run from New York City. Its "Century Butt" held 100 targets and there was ample room for 150 more.

Colonel Harllee and his staff were all enthusiastic and practical riflemen. Capt. Edward C. Crossman, a man of boundless energy and limitless imagination, threw himself into the task of devising a unique smallbore program. "There ought," he wrote on April 5, 1919, "to be nothing under 50 yards and there ought to be events out to 200 yards." Such distances with .22 caliber rimfire rifles had been considered impractical. But Crossman had tested the new rifles and cartridges and had found them to be adequate for such distances. The .22 was new in the regular National Rifle Association Matches and Crossman, its most ardent advocate, was determined to make it an outstanding success.

Crossman's program, like the NRA smallbore qualification course, was based on scaled-down targets. Most of the twenty-five

miniature rifle events were patterned after standard NRA and National Match events. There was a Smallbore Wimbledon—20 shots per man at 200 yards; a Smallbore Marine Match; a Smallbore National Individual Match and National Team Match; and others based on reduced versions of the largebore models. There was also a Ladies' Sweepstakes. To add still more flavor, the Dewar International Miniature Rifle Match was to be shot at Caldwell against the British, for the first time since the beginning of the war. A whole new range, with butts constructed of timber, was built to accommodate the new system.

Colonel Harllee, in preparation for the matches, installed 100 new midrange targets for the regular events. A detail of sailors and Marines under his command cleared brush at one end of the huge range to accommodate fifty new short-range targets. They erected tents and installed boardwalks. Then, just as the first teams arrived on the scene, disaster struck!

Heavy rains battered New Jersey for nearly a week in mid-July. On July 23, as the Passaic River turned into a torrent, a dam on one of its tributaries near Morristown let go. A sheet of water rolled out over the Caldwell Range, turning it into a shambles. Tents were flooded; the boardwalks floated through the camp like battering rams; and Crossman's wooden smallbore butts piled into the Century Butt nearly a quarter of a mile away. The sailors and Marines, working around the clock, towed floating material back into position behind boats.

It was a credit to the Navy and the Marine Corps that any matches were held that year. Harllee, however, was a stubborn Marine with a reputation as a drop-of-the-hat fighter. On August 4, 1919, when the Small Arms Firing School opened, on schedule, everything was back in place. Little sign of

The Crescent Cup, offered to commemorate building of the Navy Rifle Range at Caldwell, N. J.

Even the boardwalks floated away when flood waters swept over the Caldwell, N. J., range. The tent city on the left was "Commercial Row," where guns and accessories of the various manufacturers and dealers were displayed.

the disaster was apparent except for puddles and pools of water that dotted the landscape.

But the standing water provided ideal breeding places for the notorious Jersey mosquito, and when the shooters began to arrive, newly hatched and hungry mosquitoes by the millions were already there. The wind squalls of the previous week were replaced by hot, humid, and lifeless air which created heavy haze and morning fogs. Targets disappeared when viewed through rifle sights.

The Leech Cup Match opened the NRA Matches. Surprisingly, it was won by W. H. Richard with the first perfect score on record, in spite of the fog and mosquitoes. The Wimbledon Match was won by John W. Hession of the New York Athletic Club and a man destined to make quite a name for himself as a marksman.

The Class A National Matches of 1919 were swept by Marine Corps shooters. A feature attraction of the National Matches was the presence in the competition of three of the nation's most decorated Marine heroes. Lt. Col. Thomas Holcomb had commanded the Second Battalion of the Sixth Regiment at Soissons, St. Mihiel, Belleau Wood, and Meuse-Argonne, while Maj. Littleton W. T. Waller, Jr., had distinguished himself as commanding officer of the Sixth

Marine Machine Gun Battalion in the same actions. Maj. Ralph S. Keyser had commanded a battalion of the Fifth Marines at Belleau Wood and Soissons.

In keeping with the plans of the Board of Directors, greater emphasis that year was placed on the pistol than in the past. A. P. Lane added the first prize medal of the NRA Individual Pistol Match to his many national and international honors. There were other new features; one was a trapshooting match, and the other a Police Revolver Team Match. The latter was a major disappointment; only the Philadelphia Police Department was represented. The NRA matches, that year, however, were the largest held to that time. There were seventy-two separate teams on the field, with hundreds of entries in the individual events.

The smallbore matches were popular with everyone. Nearly all of the .30 caliber shooters tried their hands with the .22s. On August 25, 1919, the newly reinstated Dewar International Smallbore Match was shot against the British in the customary cable match. The American team turned in a record performance, scoring 7617 out of a possible 8000 points against 7523 for the British, who shot on their home range across the Atlantic. One member of the winning team was Mrs. E. C. Crossman, the first woman to compete in an international rifle event.

The success of the .22 caliber matches at Caldwell led the NRA to standardize smallbore rifle shooting throughout the nation, and it established a committee under the chairmanship of Lt. Col. Townsend Whelen for that purpose.

For a postwar year, 1919 went into the record books as an active and progressive one. Starting the new year 1920, the National Board for the Promotion of Rifle Practice and the Board of Directors of the National Rifle Association met on January 14 and 15. The slate of officers of the NRA remained the same as for 1919 except for the three vice-presidents. Lt. Col. William C. Harllee, USMC, became first; Lt. Col. Smith W. Brookhart, second; and Col. George W. Burleigh, NYNG, third vice-president. The Board of Directors voted a new class of membership to accommodate veterans' organizations and such organizations as the American Trapshooting Association and the United States Revolver Association. It also endorsed American participation in the shooting phases of the Seventh Olympic Games, which were to be held in Antwerp in the upcoming summer. The Olympic Committee appointed by the National Board included President Libbey and Secretary Phillips of the NRA; Lt. Col. George C. Shaw, USA, and Lt. Col. Townsend Whelen, USA; Comdr. C. T. Osburn, USN, and Maj. Littleton W. T. Waller, USMC.

With international competition now restored to the American marksmanship program, tryouts for the Olympic Rifle Team were held on May 24-29 at the Marine Corps Rifle Range, Quantico, Virginia. One hundred of the best rifle shots in the United States competed for places. The selected members included ten marksmen of the Army, four from the Marines, two from the Navy and two civilians.

Our Olympic Rifle Team, under the captaincy of Lt. Col. George C. Shaw, USA, with Capt. Paul W. Mapes, USA, as adjutant and Colonel Libbey as liaison officer, sailed for Antwerp on June 21, 1920. The Army provided transportation. This was the first time the government had helped in financing the travel of an Olympic shooting team.

Tryouts for the Revolver and Pistol Team, also held at Quantico, were shot under match conditions on June 21-23, with Reginald H. Sayre, president of the United States Revolver Association, as team captain. Sayre, however, was prevented by an emergency from accompanying the team, and responsibility for leadership fell on Lt. Col. O. F. Snyder. The pistol team included some of the long-famous names in handgun shooting—A. P. Lane, Dr. H. A. Bayles, and Dr. J. H. Snook. But its roster also contained a newcomer to international shooting, a tall, handsome New York attorney named Karl T. Frederick, who in the trial matches seesawed with Lane as the winner and second-place man in every event.

Upon arriving in Belgium the Americans found neither practice facilities nor ranges up to American standards. The pistol team had to practice on temporary targets in a vacant

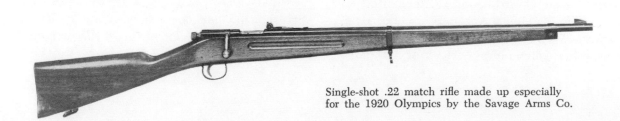

Single-shot .22 match rifle made up especially for the 1920 Olympics by the Savage Arms Co.

The year 1919 brought with it an end to shooting in anger, but Allied forces overseas engaged in closely contested marksmanship matches.

The Roumanian Trophy offered by Queen Marie for the Inter-Allied Competition at Le Mans, France.

The Gold Cup Trophy, presented by the Chinese Republic for first place in a pistol-shooting match among the Allies at Le Mans.

The General Pershing Trophy, presented for team competition at the Inter-Allied Games at Paris.

field several miles from its camp. The rifle team found it necessary to practice on the U. S. Army Rifle Range at Weissenthurm, Germany.

The Running Deer event was held near Antwerp in connection with the shotgun events. The American team placed third among four entries in the single-shot and fourth in the double-shot Running Deer contest. The remarkable expatriate, Walter Winans, who had upheld American honors in the nation's first participation in this Olympic event, was conspicuous by his absence. Weeks earlier, at the age of seventy-eight, he had run up a new double-shot world's record in the Running Deer event at Bisley, while trying out for the British Olympic team. A few days later, he died.

In the Military Rifle Matches held forty-five miles southeast of Antwerp at Beverloo Camp, the United States did better. It placed second to Denmark among a field of fifteen in the Team Match, 300 meters, standing; and in the individual match under the same rules, Comdr. Carl T. Osburn, USN, picked up the first gold medal for the United States.

Lawrence A. Nuesslein of Washington, D.C., took a bronze medal in a shoot-off with a Belgian.

From that point on, the Americans began to sweep the field. They took gold medals in the 300-meter and 600-meter prone team matches, the 300-meter free-rifle team event, the individual free-rifle match, and both team and individual matches in the miniature rifle events. In winning the free-rifle events, the Americans used "as-issued" Springfield rifles. Nearly all of the other teams shot special rifles equipped with set triggers and tailored stocks.

American dominance of the miniature rifle events, thanks to recent NRA emphasis on smallbore shooting, also came as a surprise. Just before it sailed, the American team had discovered that the rules in the smallbore matches would permit only the offhand standing position, forty shots per man. This, in essence, was the old *schuetzen* game, which had dropped from popularity in the United States at the beginning of the war. The team was not even equipped with a suitable rifle. When J. J. Dooley of the NRA Board of

197

Directors learned of this, he rushed to Massachusetts and contacted George Lewis of the Stevens branch of Savage Arms Company. Lewis and his top gunsmiths worked almost around the clock to build rifles especially designed for the Olympic match. Dooley had delivered them just as the team was sailing for Belgium.

The pistol team picked up three gold, one silver, and two bronze medals in its four matches. Frederick won the 50-meter individual and placed third in the 30-meter individual match, which was won by a Brazilian. In the 50-meter individual match DeCosta of Brazil broke his pistol, borrowed a .22 Colt from Captain Snyder of the American team and ammunition from Lane, and then proceeded to win second place.

American trapshooters also turned in outstanding performances, sweeping both the team and individual championships. Americans took the first five places in the individual match. The Olympic matches of 1920 placed the United States solidly on the top of the shooting world in every team event involving rifle, shotgun, and pistol, except the Running Deer match.

Their European marksmanship victories behind them, our teams returned home. They, and other American marksmen, began planning for the big National Matches to be held in August, not many weeks away. After an absence dictated by the recent war, the National Matches and the National Rifle Association Matches were returned to Camp Perry in 1920 with Col. Morton C. Mumma as executive officer. Most of the civilian marksmen that year were dressed in the new khaki NRA official uniform—riding breeches, wrap-around puttees, and pleated shooting jacket topped by a wide-brimmed Anzac-style hat.

By 1920 postwar doubts about shooter interest had been dispelled. The Association had 766 affiliated organizations distributed through every state and territory, and many of these had teams on the field at Perry. Camp Perry also had been refurbished and expanded. It now boasted fifty 200-yard targets and one hundred each for 600-yard and 1000-yard shooting. The course of fire in the National Match was restricted to 200, 600, and 1000 yards by a decision of the National Board.

The clubhouse at Camp Perry was operated as a hotel and restaurant by the state of Ohio that year for the first time. And for the first time the "Squaw Camp," for visiting ladies, married couples, and a scattering of lady shooters, was established.

Camp Perry's "Squaw Camp," where married couples, women shooters, and visiting ladies were housed.

Two important new trophies appeared in 1920. One was the now famous Nathan Hale Trophy, awarded to the individual making the highest score with rifle and pistol on a course the same as the first stages of the National Individual Pistol and Rifle Matches. It was presented to the NRA by the Camp Perry Instructors' Association, which had been organized by Colonel Mumma when the Small Arms Firing School moved from Perry to Fort Benning. The second, presented by Mrs. K. K. V. Casey, was for the winner of the NRA Grand Aggregate, the highest combined scores in the more important individual NRA matches.

Capt. Edward C. Crossman was again in charge of the small-bore range at Camp Perry and added a few new events to those he had devised at Caldwell. Several were for juvenile shooters. One thirteen-year-old girl, Marjorie Kinder, fired more than 500 shots every day in the Junior Reentry Match "C" to place among the winners. Marjorie had been at Caldwell the year before and had been an attentive student at the Small Arms Firing School, a lone girl among dozens of male shooters.

The National Rifle Matches, which were held on August 20 and 21, were won for the first time since 1915 by the Army, which managed to wrest supremacy from the Marines. Marine Corps shooters, however, dominated the pistol matches.

With the successful Olympic Matches and reactivation of the National Matches at Camp Perry, 1920 was a far better year than many had expected, and the NRA headed into a new year with high hopes for the future. Colonel Libbey, after ably guiding the affairs of the Association for five years, stepped down as president at the annual meeting on January 12, 1921. His successor was Lt. Col. Smith W. Brookhart. At its meeting, the NRA Board voted to continue the system of entrance fees and money prizes, which had been reinstated after a year's trial without cash incentives. It also voted to accelerate its activities in college shooting programs.

At a meeting of the National Board on January 13, 1921, Col. C. E. Stodter of the United States Cavalry was appointed Director of Civilian Marksmanship. Major LaGarde, the former DCM, on the same day became a member of the NRA Executive Committee, as did Lt. Col. A. B. Critchfield of Ohio and Lt. Col. D. C. McDougal, USMC. The National Board again selected Camp Perry as the site of the National Matches, which were scheduled to be held with the Small Arms Firing School and the

The Nathan Hale Trophy, first offered in 1920. The figure was produced by sculptor F. MacMonnie in 1890.

NRA Matches between July 26 and August 26, 1921. Later, the program had to be postponed until August 27 to September 22. The Board also named Lt. Col. Mumma as Executive Officer of the National Matches of 1921.

The increasing activities of the NRA kept its staff busy, and the months passed quickly until another big Camp Perry gathering of the nation's top shooters was close at hand. Shortly before the annual rifle and pistol matches were scheduled to open, the National Rifle Association was invited to send a team to represent the United States in the 1921 International Shooting Union Matches at Lyons, France, to be held August 5-15. The invitation was accepted promptly. Notice was short and provided no time for tryouts; the ten-man American team consisted almost entirely of Olympic shooters who had represented the United States in Belgium the year before. Lt. Col. O. F. Snyder, who had led the Olympic pistol team, was team captain. The Navy came to the assistance of the NRA by transporting the team on the battleship "Utah." The Americans this time had specially stocked and specially fitted Springfield rifles to use in the free-rifle events. Each was offered a choice of four stock styles ranging from the straight issue stock to an intricate *schuetzen* style with a deep-crescent buttplate. Although they had almost no time to practice, the Americans turned in remarkable performances, with a record score in the team match. They beat the second-place Swiss by 82 and France, Italy, and Holland by from 400 to nearly 1000 points. Walter R. Stokes of Washington, D. C., won the individual championship, taking first place in each of the standing, kneeling, and prone events.

So sweeping was the American victory that the Swiss protested the use of "special equipment" by the United States team. The protest was especially interesting since the Swiss not only used, but had originated most of the same special equipment that the Yankee marksmen employed against them! The protest was disallowed.

Back in the United States, less than two weeks later, the combined NRA National Matches of 1921 got underway and were the largest and most successful held to that time. Colonel Mumma, as Executive Officer, selected assistant executive officers that included all of the surviving presidents of the NRA—Wingate, Spencer, Drain, Gaither, Libbey, and Brookhart. Mumma himself served as commandant of the Small Arms Firing School, with his old assistant, Smith W. Brookhart, serving as Director of Instruction. In 1921 the school graduated 500 qualified rifle instructors.

The matches were remarkable for the scores made by individual competitors. Record after record went by the board. The excellent 1921 match ammunition and the general use of telescopic sights permitted some of the most remarkable shooting ever seen. In the Winchester Match, Marine Gunner C. A. Lloyd made 101 consecutive bullseyes at 600 yards. Then Sgt. T. B. Crawley, USMC, ran up a string of 176 at 800 yards. Another Marine, W. D. Adkins, shot 91 straight bulls at 1000 yards! Adkins also won the Wimbledon Match with the first perfect score on record.

The expanded NRA pistol program, in general, was enthusiastically received, and there were many participants in all events. It also attracted to Camp Perry shooters like A. P. Lane

Remington-made Russian Model 1891 rifle, manufactured during World War I period in caliber 7.62 mm.

and Karl Frederick, who later played an important role in the NRA program.

The 1921 Matches also saw a marked expansion of public interest in the smallbore matches. Nearly all of the prominent firearms and ammunition manufacturers that year offered trophies or prizes for matches featuring the .22. There were so many first-class smallbore shooters at Perry that year that no effort was made to hold tryouts for the Dewar International Championship Match. The officials of the NRA merely selected the most likely prospects from among those competing in the NRA events. On September 18, 1921, this American pickup team soundly beat the best marksmen in Great Britain by more than 100 points and the Canadians by more than 400.

A short time after the Camp Perry matches, on October 15, the NRA announced the most elaborate gallery program to date. It included twenty-eight separate rifle competitions to run continuously between December 3 of 1921 and May 15, 1922. Then on November 1, 1921, the Board of Directors announced a new home-range gallery series for handgun shooters. The program included four individual and team tournaments, with all matches shot at twenty yards. The committee also voted to organize a team for international competition in 1922. In preparation, it retained the mandatory standing position in its gallery matches in an effort to develop free-rifle experts for international competition.

By early 1922, the National Rifle Association was finding many new and hitherto unexplored avenues in shooting sports of interest to its expanding membership. Thomas G. Samworth joined the staff of *Arms and the Man* as its second associate editor in January, 1922. Its pages now included articles on hunting, shotgunning, handguns, ballistics, and new shooting products. Many articles dealt with the conversion of American and foreign military rifles to sporters. Regular notices of action by

Lt. Col. Smith W. Brookhart of Iowa, best known as Senator Brookhart, NRA president (1921-1925).

the DCM made their appearance for the first time. On October 15, 1921, Col. C. E. Stodter, Director of Civilian Marksmanship, had announced the availability of new Russian 7.62 caliber rifles at $10 each with ammunition at $8 a thousand. These had been manufactured in the United States by Remington and the Westinghouse Company and were undelivered at the close of the war. Prewar Springfield rifles had been available through the NRA and the DCM since March, 1919, at $23.40 each.

The Astor Cup in 1922 was won by a rifle team composed entirely of girls from the Central High School of Washington, D. C. Moreover, they won with a perfect score. Shooting horizons were beginning to widen!

The National Rifle Association had made the transition from war to peace and had gained in the process. It had an active and varied program of interest to anyone concerned with shooting in any of its many phases. As a result it had grown greatly in prestige and membership. But darker days loomed on the horizon ahead.

# More International Victories - Greater Police Participation - Administrative Structure Strengthened

18

At the suggestion of the National Board for the Promotion of Rifle Practice, the National Matches of 1922 were scheduled to be shot at Camp Perry on September 2 through 28. Following custom, the NRA Board of Directors voted to hold its own matches in conjunction with the National event. The two matches had become very closely associated.

Dark clouds, however, had built up again on the horizon. Congress, during the later years of the war and its aftermath, with the lessons of the Argonne, Saint Mihiel and Belleau Wood still fresh and with the commanding voice of Gen. John J. Pershing ringing in its ears, had been generous with the marksmanship training program. But by 1922 the lessons and the voice had begun to fade. Congress was looking for ways to cut the budget and, with the "war to end wars" already fought, where better to cut expenses than in the military? The great war machine which General Pershing had led to the rescue of the Allies had been trimmed to bare bone; now the Administration and Congress were working over the skeleton with scraping knives. In this spirit of economy they eliminated the appropriation providing federal assistance to the states for sending National Guard teams to the National Matches. And no civilians were to travel at government expense. There had been 150 such civilians at the 1921 matches.

The slash created a major upset in the shooting program and led to speculation that there would be no National Matches in 1922 except among teams representing the Regular Services. The Dewar Match, which was scheduled to be held on September 24, seemed doomed to cancellation.

As it turned out, these predictions proved overly pessimistic. The National Rifle Association immediately canvassed the adjutants general of the various states, urging them to send representative teams. The result was an almost spectacular response. Thirty states sent National Guard teams at their own expense and the Militia Bureau managed to dredge up enough

"Kernel Mumma's Amatures" proved their professional talent by making a world record. From left: Capt. G. Wotkyns, G. H. Emerson, F. J. Kahrs, Midshipman M. C. Mumma, Jr., Col. M. C. Mumma, Maj. Don Preussner, Capt. W. H. Richard, Capt. C. J. Van Amburgh.

funds to finance the travel of one civilian team from each of the nine Army Corps areas.

The uncertainty that prevailed almost up to the time of the matches cut attendance and caused some losses of affiliated clubs who felt that the economy drive had doomed the Association. What it actually did was to prove that the NRA program had matured enough to stand on its own legs. Most of the clubs that strayed away soon drifted back to the fold.

The combined 1922 NRA and National Matches opened on schedule at Camp Perry with Lt. Col. Morton C. Mumma as executive officer and Maj. Frank Maloney, first vice-president of the NRA, in charge of the Small Arms Firing School, which opened the program on the first week of September. Those who attended Camp Perry that year found many improvements. A new paved road to the range from Port Clinton replaced the former dirt road, and buses ran regularly to Lacarne.

There were also major changes in scoring procedure. So many bullseyes had been made in the previous year that ties were commonplace. To separate the near-perfect shooters from run-of-the-mill experts, the National Board, at its meeting in January, 1922, adopted the "nickel" target featuring a 12-inch inner V-ring in the bullseye of the B target and a 20-inch V in the C target. From that point, the overall score and the number of shots in the inner rings determined the winner.

In the NRA's Herrick Trophy Match, justification for the new system was proved by several unofficial teams equipped with special rifles and sights. The Herrick Match was the highlight of the 1922 Matches, owing to the unusual number of unofficial teams entered in addition to those officially representing the Infantry, Cavalry, Coast Artillery, Navy, Marine Corps, National Guard, and state civilian clubs.

Under the rules, only one team from each of the Regular Services and one National Guard and a civilian team from each state could shoot for record. The twenty-nine official teams were required to use the service weapon with issue sights. Spectator interest centered on the performance of the six unofficial teams, which shot the course although their scores were not to be recorded. The unofficial teams were allowed to use any special equipment they wished. The conditions under which they shot, however, were comparable to the Palma Match, where the use of special sights and match rifles was allowed.

Five of these teams were second teams of the Regular Services or National Guard, but one, known as "KMA" team, for "Kernel Mumma's Amatures," was a pickup group organized by the Executive Officer of the Matches. Its members were Capt. W. H. Richard, Guy H. Emerson, Frank J. Kahrs, Don Preussner, Capt. Grosvenor L. Wotkyns, Capt. C. J. Van Amburgh, Lt. Col. Mumma, and his son Midshipman Morton C. Mumma, Jr. With the exception of young Mumma, the team consisted of some of the most prominent shooters in America. Nearly all were veterans of one or more international matches and all had competed regularly in national events.

Midshipman Mumma had not won a place in this elite company purely through parental indulgence. Although he was an unknown to most of the spectators, he had fired on the Iowa Civilian Team in 1919-1920 and had won the

Harry Pope, expert rifle shot and famous barrel maker, wishes "bon voyage and good luck" to the United States team as it embarks for Europe.

NRA High School Championship in 1921. In the opening phase at 800 yards, the KMA team, shooting scope-sighted experimental models of the Model 54 Winchester, dropped only four points, a new world's record for the distance. Midshipman Mumma was one of five finishing with a perfect score. The record stood only five minutes. The official Massachusetts National Guard team, using issue sights on regulation rifles, broke it by a single point. Then this record, too, toppled as the unofficial Infantry team turned in a clean score for the distance. Of the 150 shots fired by the KMA and unofficial Infantry teams, 146 were in the bullseye and 112 of these were in the V ring! To cap this remarkable shooting performance, the official Marine Corps team, placing second to Massachusetts, equalled the previous world's record. Young Mumma continued his perfect performance at 900 yards, and then at 1000, to finish the course with the first perfect score on record. In the official scoring, the Massachusetts National Guard took the Herrick Trophy from the Marines for the first time in nearly ten years.

Another surprise of the matches of 1922 came

when Loren M. Felt, a civilian from Illinois, won the Leech Cup Match. Felt had come to Perry at his own expense to compete in the smallbore matches. He had done little .30 caliber shooting before attending the Small Arms Firing School at Camp Perry that year. His performance was demonstrable justification of the NRA's smallbore program as a training ground for military marksmen.

The Dewar International Championship Smallbore Match was shot against Great Britain by an American team captained by Col. C. E. Stodter, the Director of Civilian Marksmanship, with Frank J. Kahrs serving as team coach. The smallbore experts ran up a score of 7685, and when the cablegram arrived from London it revealed the Americans had won the Dewar Trophy by a solid 45-point margin.

While these matches were being shot, a team of American riflemen captained by Maj. Littleton W. T. Waller, USMC, was in Milan, Italy, competing in the ISU matches. With Lt. Comdr. E. E. Wilson as Adjutant and Lt. Comdr. C. T. Osburn, USN, as coach, the team consisted of Lawrence Nuesslein, W. R. Stokes, Maj. J. K. Boles, USA; Sgt. Morris Fisher, USMC, Capt. Joseph Jackson, USMC, and Lt. Comdr. A. D. Denny, USN. It was equipped with specially built free-rifles worked up for it at the Marine Corps Depot of Supplies in Philadelphia and employing barrels made by Harry Pope. The team arrived in Milan on September 20, 1922, after an almost incredible battle with European customs officials. At Cherbourg, French customs officials refused to let the members of the team carry either rifles or ammunition as part of their personal baggage. At Paris, the baggage car in which the equipment was carried was shunted to Koblenz, and Major Waller was forced to leave the team and chase the errant car. It finally arrived in Milan one day before the match.

Although these difficulties made prematch practice impossible, the Americans turned in an outstanding performance. Walter R. Stokes, a relative newcomer to international shooting, outshot Lynhard of Switzerland by two points to become the Individual World's Free-rifle Champion. In the team match they won over favored Switzerland by twelve points and decisively defeated Denmark, Sweden, and Holland.

The year 1922 did not turn out so badly after all, and there was optimism for the future when the Board of Directors met on February 14, 1923 at the Willard Hotel in Washington. At the meeting Smith W. Brookhart, who had just been elected to the United States Senate from Iowa, was continued as president and Ammon B. Critchfield of Ohio became third vice-president, replacing Brig. Gen. W. W. Moore. The secretary's report showed a gain of 5000 individual members over the 13,000 in 1922 and an aggregate membership of 150,000 in affiliated clubs. At this meeting, Brig. Gen. Harry B. Smith of Indiana, Maj. Littleton W. T. Waller, USMC, and Lt. Col. R. D. LaGarde of the District of Columbia were elected members of the Executive Committee. Lt. Col. Morton C. Mumma, USA, was the representative of the Assistant Secretary of War and Maj. W. W. Buckley, USMC, that of the Assistant Secretary of the Navy.

Many of the historical trophies of the NRA here gained official approval and date from this meeting in 1923. They included the "Remington Trophy," the Western Cartridge Company "Marksman Trophy," the "Hercules Trophy" of the Hercules Powder Company, the "Peters Trophy," the Winchester "Plainsman Trophy," and the United States Cartridge Company "Scout Trophy." All of these awards were for smallbore shooting, but in the same year the Navy Cup was presented for use in a new high-power rifle event. In the following year the Coast Artillery trophies were presented to be awarded to the Marine ranking highest in the National Individual Match and to the Coast Artilleryman ranking highest in the President's Match.

Smallbore shooting was now standing solidly on its own feet. It was enormously popular even with men who had made their mark with military rifles. Frequently, at Camp Perry, the captains of Service and National Guard teams had to go to the smallbore range to round up their shooters for the next match. And if there were doubts as to recognition of the military value of the program as a training ground, they were effectively dispelled by a general order issued on February 12, 1923, by the Chief of Staff, Gen.

1922 International Rifle Team at tryouts. (l. to r., front) Maj. J. K. Boles, USA; Maj. L. W. T. Waller, Jr., USMC; Lt. Comdr. C. T. Osburn, USN. (Standing) Capt. Joseph Jackson, USMC; Lt. Comdr. A. D. Denny, USN; Lawrence Nuesslein; Sgt. Morris Fisher, USMC.

John J. Pershing. In this order, the outspoken and high-ranking advocate of military marksmanship directed: "The expenditure of 500 rounds of ammunition, caliber .22, is authorized for each officer and enlisted man of the Regular Army participating in the National Rifle Association Matches. . . . Pending the issue of suitable arms and ammunition, the expenditure of company funds is authorized for the purchase of suitable arms and ammunition to enable organizations to participate in matches with .22 caliber rifles conducted by the National Rifle Association to which members of the military services are eligible."

In 1923 the NRA greatly expanded its smallbore program. An Outdoor Smallbore Program for beginners was initiated with two classes, one for those shooting target rifles and a second for those forced by circumstances to employ light sporting rifles. Expert riflemen's decorations were awarded to those qualifying in either class. As a further stimulus to free-rifle shooting in the United States, the NRA also developed a free-rifle match for .22 caliber rifles, under rules identical to those applying in international competition except for the distance and size of targets.

In June, the name of the Association's magazine *Arms and the Man* was changed to *The American Rifleman*, and following the change in name its coverage and size increased appreciably. In the next few months, four men, whose names were to become bywords

206

The Du Pont "Bowman" Trophy

Hercules Powder Co. Trophy

The Winchester "Plainsman" Trophy

U. S. Cartridge Co. Trophy

Peters Cartridge Co. Trophy

Western Cartridge Co. Trophy

Many of the arms manufacturers and powder and ammunition companies offered trophies in 1923.

President's Match, Coast
Artillery Corps Trophy

Coast Artillery Corps Trophy
for Marines

The Navy Cup

The Navy Cup and two Coast Artillery trophies were among the many fine awards in 1923 competition.

with shooters everywhere, began their long careers with the NRA. One was Maj. Julian S. Hatcher, who had served on the staff at the Springfield Armory and was already a leading authority in America on small arms and ballistics. His column, "The Dope Bag," was carried as a regular feature dealing in the technical aspects of firearms and shooting.

A column covering "Shotgun and Field Shooting" was written for each issue by Capt. Charles Askins, Sr., the leading authority in his field. "Rifles and Big Game Hunting" was the assignment of Maj. Townsend Whelen, one of the leading target shots in the United States who had spent years in exploring and hunting in the wilder portions of the world.

The fourth man was C. B. Lister, who had worked for the Du Pont Company. His first assignment with the staff of the National Rifle Association was to prepare a column called "NRA Notes," covering the programs and activities of affiliated clubs and headquarters affairs.

Another addition was a column of "DCM News" written by Colonel Stodter, the Director of Civilian Marksmanship. With its new status the official organ of the NRA also acquired its first art editor, Charles Dunn. For the collectors, there was a column called "Firearms of Yesterday."

There was a substantial growth and expansion of the overall program of the National Rifle Association of America in 1923 in spite of recurring governmental economies and cutbacks that often made it touch and go whether the National Matches would be held. At its annual meeting the NRA Board of Directors had decided to hold the International Shooting Union Matches in conjunction with the National and NRA Matches. These were scheduled to be held during most of the month of September, 1923, with Colonel Mumma again serving as Executive Officer. It also voted to hold another Palma Match and sent invitations to national shooting associations throughout the world. Because many national shooting groups felt that the proven superiority of the Springfield rifle over any other service weapon gave the Americans an advantage, the Board changed the rules to permit foreign teams to use the service weapon of any nation or privately built rifles under eleven pounds.

Col. C. E. Stodter, the Director of Civilian Marksmanship, again captained the International Smallbore Team that

The Appreciation Cup, donated in 1922 by the Cavalry to be awarded the high-scoring Marine in the President's Match.

The Infantry Trophy, designed by E. M. Viquesney, was first competed for in 1922.

The Farr Trophy was placed in competition in 1922 to commemorate the great score made by seventy-one-year-old Geo. R. Farr.

Behind the origin of many trophies and the matches in which they appear are to be found outstanding examples of good sportsmanship.

would defend the Dewar Trophy, while Maj. Littleton W. T. Waller was elected again to lead the Free-rifle Team in the International Matches.

Tryouts for the International Free-rifle Team were held on August 13-15, 1923, at Army posts throughout the United States. This was the first time that a thorough national effort had been made to obtain the best American free-riflemen.

Retrenchments in federal spending were more stringent in 1923 than in previous years, and no civilian teams traveled to Camp Perry at government expense. The National Rifle Association, however, was able to prevail upon the major railroads to offer half-fare rates to civilian shooters traveling to the range at personal expense.

The National Matches of 1923 had both bright spots and disappointments. In spite of the federal austerity program, more than a hundred civilian shooters attended, and the state and federal services turned out more than a thousand marksmen. The attendance of police at Camp Perry, after several years of lukewarm interest was gratifying. The police departments of Toledo, Buffalo, Portland, Oregon, and New Orleans, and the Delaware and Hudson Railroad Police all sent teams.

After a major outbreak of mail train robberies, Colonel Mumma, of his own initiative, had developed a course in shooting for railroad mail clerks. Practically all of the country's 10,000 mail clerks were armed but few had any training in the use of their weapons. The NRA police training program, as part of the Small Arms Firing School, was largely an extension of activity in this general field.

The 1923 National Matches were again dominated by Marine shooters. After a heavy downpour they were shot in a sea of mud. The Palma and International Rifle Matches both had to be shot as walkovers; no foreign competition appeared in either match. The Palma Match, shot by a pick-up team which included Guy H. Emerson of Ohio, turned in a surprising performance, since it shot without the stimulus of true competition. Lt. G. W. Trichel, USA, turned in the first perfect score ever recorded in the Palma Match, and the team score was 52 points higher than the record made by the Palma Team of 1912. This team was captained and selected by Maj. K. K. V. Casey.

The International Free-rifle Team shot on September 18, 1923, under the direction of Maj. Littleton W. T. Waller as

*In June, 1923, the name of the NRA magazine Arms and the Man was changed to The American Rifleman.*

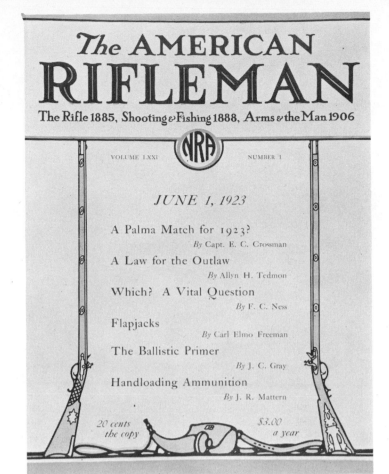

captain. It, too, broke the world's record for the team event.

A novelty of the matches of 1923 was the appearance of an informal muzzle-loading rifle match, which came about largely by accident. It may have been one of the first such matches held in America since the 1800s. Capt. John G. Dillin of Pennsylvania brought to the matches a historical rifle that reportedly had killed Indians in the early days of Pennsylvania. Someone suggested that it be used in a match. Veteran riflemaker Harry Pope fired the first shot at the old traditional X-target. Since there were no other muzzle-loaders on the range, all competitors shot the same rifle.

The Dewar Match held particular international interest in 1923. The British score, which had already been made and leaked by a British newspaper, showed that the American shooters had heavy competition. The British had tallied a score only a few points below the winning score of the United States in 1922. The Canadians had also entered the field. However, Colonel Stodter's smallbore marksmen turned in a magnificent performance, winning with an average score three points per man higher than those of the year before.

After the 1923 matches the police marksmanship program of the National Rifle Association gained real momentum. On November 17 of that year the Denver Police Department staged a turkey shoot as a feature of a police benefit program. The Director of Public Safety for the city was appalled by the poor quality of the marksmanship displayed by his officers and immediately ordered that all patrolmen and detectives on the force undergo a thorough course in marksmanship training. The course was based largely on that developed by the NRA.

A year earlier the entire New Jersey State Police force had affiliated with the NRA, and several years later Chief of Police R. Lee Heath of the Los Angeles Police Department decided

to do something about the shooting inadequacies of his force. Capt. Edward C. Crossman, long a director and prominent member of the NRA, was asked to develop the course. A modern pistol range designed by Crossman was built by the city. Before the end of the year, twenty city police teams were competing regularly on the range. The Los Angeles police nearly all became members of the NRA.

As the year 1924 rolled around, it was destined to see four important international matches. One was the Dewar International Smallbore Match, in conjunction with the National and NRA Matches at Camp Perry. The ISU Matches were held at Rheims, France, on June 7-12 and 17-22 and the Olympic Matches at Chalons, France, on June 24-29, 1924. Pan-American Matches were held in Lima, Peru, November 11-29.

The Olympic Rifle Team organized by the

Looking very pleased at winning the Argentine Trophy in the 1923 International Free-rifle Match, from left: Sgt. Morris Fisher, Maj J. K. Boles, Sgt. Dennis Fenton, E. N. Moore, Maj. L. W. T. Waller, Comdr. C. T. Osburn, Lawrence Nuesslein, and Walter Stokes.

National Rifle Association was selected in preliminary tryouts in each Army Corps area and a final tryout at the Marine Corps Range at Quantico, Virginia, where thirty-one finalists were whittled down to twelve. The team was captained by Maj. Littleton W. T. Waller, and its expenses were financed entirely by public subscription through the National Rifle Association.

Since both the ISU and Olympic Matches were held in France, it was necessary to send only one team, but a larger one than would have been needed to compete in the Olympic Matches alone. Its members included Marcus Dinwiddie, only seventeen years old, then the youngest shooter ever to compete in an international match. In the Olympic Smallbore Match young Dinwiddie turned in a brilliant performance, breaking the world's record, only to have his own record broken by a French shooter before the match was over.

For the major events the American team was equipped with Army Springfield rifles with set triggers, heavy barrels, and other features to adapt them for match shooting. Sgt. Morris Fisher, USMC, and Comdr. C. T. Osburn, USN, ran up scores of 95 to place first and second in the Olympic Individual Match, and Walter Stokes placed fourth in the same match. The American Rifle Team easily won the Olympic Team Match by 30 points. But the surprise of the day was the performance of a team from Haiti, which, although it placed third, made a

score identical to that of the second-place French. Equipped and trained on American lines, the team had been organized by Col. D. C. McDougal and Maj. H. L. Smith of the United States Marine Corps.

The United States picked up a bronze medal in the Running Deer Single-shot Team Match, and Maj. J. K. Boles, USA, won the Single-shot Individual Running Deer Match for another gold medal.

Meanwhile, the pistol team, managed by Dr. Reginald H. Sayre, had finished fourth in a field of thirteen in the ISU team match at Rheims. In this match they shot under an extreme handicap since all of the other teams were equipped with long-barreled free-pistols with set triggers and custom stocks. As a result, the National Rifle Association started a campaign to develop an American free-pistol that would permit American shooters to compete on even terms with the Europeans.

To cap an outstanding performance by American shooters in 1924, the trapshooting team won its team match against a field of twelve opposing teams.

When the American teams returned to the United States Colonel Stodter learned that he had been replaced as Director of Civilian Marksmanship under a regulation that prohibited Army officers from serving more than four years in the nation's capital. He was transferred to the Second Division Cavalry in Texas. Colonel Stodter had given an entirely new dimension to the office of DCM. He had conducted a regular column of DCM notes in *The American Rifleman*, captained or coached several international smallbore teams, and had been active in developing the improved M1922 Springfield rifle. He remained an ardent shooter until his death in 1965, a refined gentleman respected by all who knew him.

Colonel Stodter was replaced as Director of Civilian Marksmanship in 1924 by Lt. Col. George C. Shaw, USA, another distinguished soldier and rifleman. Colonel Shaw's military career began in 1898 as a member of the District of Columbia National Guard. He had been awarded the Congressional Medal of Honor in World War I. A member of the Infantry rifle teams of every year between 1904 and 1908, he had captained the team in 1909, 1910, and 1911. He was a member of the U. S. Palma Team of 1901 and he had captained the Olympic Rifle Team of 1920.

The National Matches of 1924 at Camp Perry got off to a good start and the NRA Matches were the largest held to that time. Maj. Gen. George C. Rickards, USA, Chief of the Militia Bureau, had been instrumental in reinstating the policy of sending civilian teams to Camp Perry at government expense, through an order of the Secretary of War. Lt. Col. Morton C. Mumma again served as Executive Officer. In the 200-yard Rapid-fire Match, which opened the NRA program on September 15, there were 1031 entries, and 1142 shooters participated in the Marine Corps Match. The Police Matches continued to gain in popularity. There were ten entries in 1924 with teams from Detroit, Chicago, Toledo, New York City, the Pennsylvania State Police, and the Delaware and Hudson Railroad Police. The Chicago team, with a longer record of participation in NRA matches than any other, won the event.

The Dewar Match, with the American team captained by Lt. G. L. Wotkyns, was shot under rather difficult conditions. Unusually cold weather had swept down from Canada on twenty-five-mile-an-hour winds, and the weather turned damp and cold with the threat of snow. Few of the shooters were dressed for such inclement weather, and for a while it appeared that the American team might have to forfeit the Dewar Trophy by default. Wotkyns, however, decided to make a try in spite of the weather. His shooters not only won the Dewar Trophy for the sixth consecutive American victory, but broke the world's record in doing so. Sgt. Ollie N. Schriver, USMC, shot a phenomenal 397 out of a possible 400 and led the Americans to a 7779 to 7753 victory over the British. Schriver already had won the National Trophy Match with another world's record score.

The annual meeting of the National Rifle Association was held at Camp Perry on September 22, 1924, and was exceptional for the number of state adjutants general who attended. It was addressed by Maj. Gen. George C. Rickards, who had pessimistic news for his audience.

"You all know," General Rickards stated, "that at the present time retrenchment is the order of the day, the cry is economy. . . . If the budget goes through as it is now made up, there will be no participation of National Guard teams in the National Matches next year."

At the conclusion of General Rickards' address, Brig. Gen. Fred H. Phillips, Jr., reported

Major Townsend Whelen joined the NRA writing staff in 1923, specializing in big game hunting and rifles.

that he had found considerable sentiment "that the National Matches not be held in 1925" and that the budget contained no item from which the expenses of the National Matches might be paid.

At Camp Perry, the Directors of the National Rifle Association agreed to join with the National Board for the Promotion of Rifle Practice in organizing, equipping, and financing a team to compete in the Pan-American Matches in Lima, Peru. Members selected for the American team were all veterans of international competition. Sgt. Morris Fisher held the championship of the world for free-rifle shooting, and about half of the other members had shot in the recent Olympic and ISU Matches. The team was captained by Capt. John H. Kneubel, Jr., and coached by Capt. Joe Jackson, USMC, and Capt. E. C. Crossman of Los Angeles.

The American team swept the rifle matches, smashing all records by a hundred or more points, and winning the Argentine Cup in a sweeping victory over Cuba, Argentina, and Peru. Fisher won the Visitors Cup and Lt. Sidney Hinds won the individual championship. The Americans also won the Peruvian Trophy Match.

The United States finished 1924 as champions of the world in nearly every form of shooting used in international competition, including several specialties that until then had been considered peculiarly European.

Meanwhile, the growth and development of the National Rifle Association appeared to be continuing smoothly and with considerable speed.

Advertising had become an important source of revenue, ranging from full-page advertisements by the major arms and ammunition manufacturers down to individual trades or personal sales advertised in "The Arms Chest," a new section of classified ads in the back of the magazine. Early in 1925 the NRA acquired an advertising manager, J. R. Mattern; and C. B. Lister moved up to the position of associate editor with T. G. Samworth, who had brought him to the NRA.

The first 1925 meeting of the Board of Directors was held in Washington on February 11. Senator Francis W. Warren of Wyoming was elected NRA president. The business of the meeting centered principally on plans for sending an American team to St. Gall, Switzerland, to shoot in the ISU Matches in the coming summer. There was no inkling of the internal problems that lay ahead.

The first indication that anything was amiss came in March, 1925, when the National Board for the Promotion of Rifle Practice moved its offices from the Woodward Building and relieved Brig. Gen. Fred H. Phillips, Jr., of his duties as executive officer and recorder of the Board. His replacement was Lt. Col. George C. Shaw, the Director of Civilian Marksmanship. Ever since its inception, the National Board and the NRA had shared offices, and the secretary of the NRA had traditionally served as the recorder of the National Board. The move by the War Department was not alarming, but the manner in which it was done caused some apprehension among members of the Executive Committee and the Board of Directors. The NRA, therefore, launched an investigation.

The investigation by the NRA subcommittee appointed for this purpose focused sharply on the affairs of Secretary Fred H. Phillips, Jr. Phillips was a handsome and engaging man and, during his term of office, the NRA had enjoyed good growth. Ever since he had come into the organization, however, the importance, responsibility, and power of the secretary had grown and expanded. Instead of serving as custodian of a few trophies and accounts ranging into a few hundred dollars, as in the days of Albert S. Jones, the secretary in 1925 dealt with accounts ranging into hundreds of thousands of dollars, and supervised a salaried staff of nearly twenty people. He also had one-man control over a national magazine.

The subcommittee presented its findings at special meetings on May 11 and 12, 1925. It recommended, because of a list of unfavorable findings, that Phillips be replaced. At a subsequent meeting of the Board of Directors in June, after extensive study and debate, amended recommendations of the subcommittee were approved and Phillips' connection with the NRA was terminated.

C. B. Lister was appointed by the Board to fill out the unexpired term of the secretary as acting-secretary, and Thomas G. Samworth was named editor of *The American Rifleman*, to replace Phillips in that capacity. The Board before adjournment voted to continue the subcommittee to study the Association's legal framework.

These decisive steps taken by the Board provided a very favorable turn in the affairs of the Association, leading within the next year to great organizational improvement. Competent counsel was employed to review the Bylaws, and an auditing committee was appointed, consisting of Col. A. J. Macnab and R. B. Reynolds.

On September 10, 1925, a general meeting of the NRA was held at Camp Perry. Apprised of a need to revise the Bylaws, members present immediately voted to change them to make the Board of Directors a body of sixty Life Members divided into three classes of twenty each, with the classes to serve staggered terms of three years.

The affairs of the Association then drifted along on a reasonably smooth course into the first months of 1926. A crucial meeting of the Board of Directors, presided over by General Ainsworth, the first vice-president, was held on February 10 at the LaFayette Hotel in Washington, D.C. Senator Warren was retained as president, and the administrative affairs of the Association were allocated to a secretary responsible directly to the Executive Committee.

Brig. Gen. Milton A. Reckord of Bel Air, Maryland, was elected to this post. General Reckord had a distinguished career as a soldier and as a businessman. Born in Bel Air in 1879, he had risen through the ranks of the Maryland Guard after enlisting as a private.

Senator Francis W. Warren of Wyoming, NRA president (1925-1927).

The Mexican Border Campaign found him a major in the First Maryland Infantry. In World War I he led the 115th Infantry as a colonel, winning in action in the Battle of Meuse-Argonne, both the Distinguished Service Medal and the Croix de Guerre with Palm. At the time of his election as secretary of the NRA, he was Adjutant General of Maryland and a former president of the National Guard Association.

The close studies of its affairs had disclosed some hidden weaknesses in the Association's structure which those in charge of its destiny promptly cured. As a result, the Association gained rapidly in stature and membership, and was able to state without fear of rebuttal: "In the final analysis, the National Rifle Association of America is the average rifleman—no more, no less. The Association is not a mystical organization of a few individuals and a few officers in Washington. . . . It is rather an organization of everyday citizens who believe in the rifle as a means of recreation and national defense, banded together for the purpose of advancing the sport, and, in a sense, pooling their resources in order to accomplish a most worthy end."

# 19

# Youth and Police NRA Given Support and Other Nationa

General Reckord brought to the National Rifle Association a zeal for work, a great personal prestige, and an impeccable reputation. He was known and widely respected by the leaders of the veterans' organizations and the military and political leaders of the state and federal governments, and he had a wide acquaintance among business and financial leaders of the nation. He had the ability to lead and to build. General Reckord gave the NRA precisely the quality of leadership it needed to overcome any problems it faced and to emerge stronger than ever.

The police program was expanded as soon as General Reckord became the executive officer of the National Rifle Association. He announced an entirely new incentive to police officers to gain familiarity with their personal weapons. He initiated two pistol tournaments, open only to members of law enforcement agencies. These tournaments operated under a postal system that permitted the officers to shoot on their home ranges, outdoors or indoors. In addition to medals and qualification decorations the NRA offered cash prizes to the winning teams and leading individuals in the two tournaments. Los Angeles, which had been among the first cities to develop a police marksmanship training program, adopted the NRA-based program immediately. The Los Angeles program developed by Capt. Edward C. Crossman, was already well-established. The city was the first to offer increased pay to policemen who qualified as experts with the pistol.

Brig. Gen. Charles D. Gaither, the former president of the NRA, on his appointment as Commissioner of Police, had started a similar program in Baltimore, Maryland. On his first inspection tour, General Gaither was horrified at the quality of the pistols carried by his men. They were required to purchase their own handguns, but there were no standards. Many had purchased second-hand pistols of ancient vintage, inadequate power, and poor accuracy. Some guns were almost inoperative. Others would have been a greater hazard to the user than they would to a criminal at whom they might be aimed.

# Programs Move Ahead by American Legion Organizations

Maj. Gen. Milton A. Reckord, whose long tenure as executive officer of the NRA was a vital factor in building the Association to its present high stature.

General Gaither, himself a crack shot, quickly changed all this. He required every man on the force to buy a new pistol of standardized caliber and to learn to use it. He set up a target range on city land and ordered every man on the force to spend several hours each week in practice. Among officers on the Baltimore Police Force there was one young recruit who had been regarded with amusement by his fellow officers because he insisted on perfecting his skill with his handgun. General Gaither promptly promoted him to sergeant and placed him in full charge of the training program. The instructor became a captain, while some of his earlier detractors, less enthusiastic about the General's reforms, were still pounding beats as patrolmen. By 1926, Baltimore had one of the best-trained police departments in the United States.

That good progress was being made was apparent in General Reckord's first report to the Executive Committee on January 15, 1926. He was able to report that there had been a sharp upswing in membership during the previous year. Annual membership had risen from 15,173 to 22,054, and Life Members had increased from 245 to more than 1500.

Another field of expansion into which the NRA moved immediately was youth training. A short time before General Reckord entered on his managerial duties the Executive Committee had unanimously voted to accept responsibility for managing the Winchester Junior Rifle Corps. This organization of school-age shooters had been created in 1917 by the Winchester Repeating Arms Company primarily as a promotional program. From the beginning it overlapped to a degree the NRA youth program, after which it was loosely patterned, but it possessed a few features that were peculiarly its own and which gave it much of its appeal to youngsters. The NRA Junior Marksmanship Program required the participants to shoot on a formal range. Members of the Winchester Rifle Corps could qualify anywhere, provided the shooter could obtain adult witnesses to authenticate his targets. The principal feature, however, was a graduated series of qualification courses through which each participant moved

215

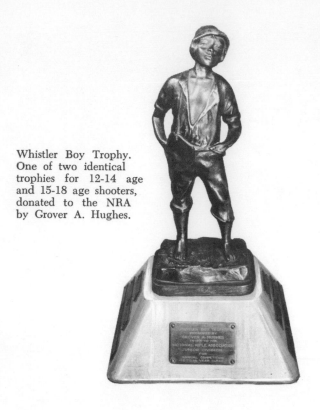

Whistler Boy Trophy. One of two identical trophies for 12-14 age and 15-18 age shooters, donated to the NRA by Grover A. Hughes.

by stages as his skill increased. Medals and other prizes recognized each stage of proficiency as the shooter moved up the ladder to expert status.

The Winchester Junior Rifle Corps was a huge success. By the time the NRA assumed its direction, it had qualified 135,000 boys and girls who had been organized in 3000 active clubs and supervised by more than 500 volunteer instructors.

Since its inception, the directors of the Winchester Junior Rifle Corps program had cooperated closely with the NRA. The Winchester Company in 1922 financed the transportation and billeting of nearly a hundred Corps members at Camp Perry, where a special camp was set up for their use. But excellent as it was, the WJRC suffered from the stigma of commercial sponsorship, even though the requirement that all contestants use Winchester products was implied rather than stated. It had also grown so rapidly and so large that it had become a financial liability rather than an asset to the sponsoring company. By turning the direction of

the WJRC over to the National Rifle Association, the Winchester Company hit upon a solution that was satisfactory to all. It permitted the program to continue without the handicap of product selection and removed the burden of management from its own staff to that of the NRA, which was happy to receive it.

Although there were differences between the WJRC and the Junior Marksmanship Program of the NRA, there were also close similarities; both were organized on a postal basis, with targets shot by the youngsters scored at a central office. The NRA combined the two programs into one that included the best features of each.

The youth program was but another of the many activities to which the attention and boundless energy of the new secretary were directed. One of General Reckord's first moves after he assumed operational leadership of the National Rifle Association was to consolidate the offices of the organization on one floor of the Woodward Building. Until then, the offices had been scattered inefficiently over three floors.

Now well-composed and efficiently housed, the NRA staff was prepared for the National Matches of 1926. That year, however, the Matches were operated on a greatly reduced scale with little more than token support from the federal government, an economy-minded War Department having eliminated funds for the National Matches from the budget. Brig. Gen. Bird W. Spencer, the former president of the National Rifle Association, stepped into the breach to offer the use of Sea Girt, on behalf of the New Jersey National Guard, as the site of the Matches. Then Maj. L. W. T. Waller, Jr., and Col. A. J. Macnab, who had been executive officer of the Matches of 1925 and had been General Pershing's instructor of rifle practice overseas, prevailed upon the Commandant of the Marine Corps to assign Marines as support personnel. General Spencer served as

216

commandant of the Matches, while Col. D. C. McDougal, USMC, was executive officer.

This was the last of many major contributions of General Spencer to the program of the NRA. A few years later, on July 28, 1930, he died in the clubhouse of the rifle range to which he had devoted so much of his life.

Because of almost a total lack of support from the War Department, the 1926 NRA and National Matches were conducted on a divisional basis, with simultaneous matches shot between September 4 and 14 at Wakefield, Massachusetts; Fort Screven, Georgia; Harrisburg, Ohio; Fort Lawton, Washington; and at Sea Girt. All of the NRA Matches, except the Leech Cup Match, which was conducted at Fort Lawton, were shot at Sea Girt.

At Sea Girt, on September 11, 1926, the Directors voted to elevate General Reckord from secretary to executive vice-president and promoted C. B. Lister to secretary. The meeting also confirmed the promotion to president of Lt. Col. F. M. Waterbury, who had been the first vice-president. Colonel Waterbury, who had been Ordnance Officer of the New York National Guard, had served in an acting capacity since July, 1926, when Senator Francis W. Warren, the president, resigned because of the press of his official duties. The Directors also further enlarged C. B. Lister's duties by electing him to the dual office of secretary-treasurer.

Under the new Bylaws an orderly method of succession to the presidency was established for the first time. The president was selected from the slate of vice-presidents but could serve only two one-year terms. Usually this honor

Lt. Col. F. M. Waterbury, NRA president (1927-1928).

went to the first vice-president, while the two remaining vice-presidents moved up in rank and a new third vice-president was elected. Continuity of administration was provided through the offices of executive vice-president and secretary-treasurer.

In his report to the Board, General Reckord announced an expanded program of activity. *The American Rifleman*, now published monthly instead of semimonthly, had been refurbished and expanded in size and coverage. Thomas G. Samworth, its former editor, had resigned to devote full time to his book publishing business.

General Reckord also reported that funds for the National Matches upcoming in 1927 seemed to be assured, although a strong faction in the

Scene at the Sea Girt Range.

This man with a gun will always remain the symbol of freedom and patriotism.

War Department was still pressing for their abolishment. At its annual convention in Philadelphia in October, 1926, the American Legion resolved: "That we heartily endorse the work of the National Rifle Association of America in its efforts to spread the doctrine of rifle marksmanship in high schools and colleges throughout the nation and urge that our individual members and posts cooperate in every way in the furtherance of this work, and we favor the holding of the National Matches annually and the participation of the United States in International competition."

This resolution was inspired by an address to the Legionnaires by General Reckord. It was implemented immediately by many Legion posts throughout America. Rifle clubs were established or sponsored by many local posts. One individual Legionnaire, Walter C. Mayer, a former Marine captain, in the following year alone organized forty-two Legion rifle clubs in Nassau County, New York.

In the previous September, 1926, the Reserve Officers Association at its national convention in Norfolk, Virginia, resolved: "That we favor all of the aims and purposes of the National Rifle Association of America." In its meeting on November 17, 1926, the National Guard Association commented in a similar resolution on "a splendid and patriotic work by the National Rifle Association." General Reckord spoke at both of these meetings.

As a result of widespread support such as this for NRA objectives, the National Budget again provided funds for the National Matches and free ammunition to clubs affiliated with the NRA.

Under a new policy, beginning January 1, 1927, the National Rifle Association sent its magazine to all annual members; before that time it had been mailed without charge only to Life Members and to the secretaries of affiliated clubs. This new policy automatically increased circulation, broadened the magazine's appeal to advertisers and, for the first time, provided a direct liaison between the offices of the Association and all the members. L. J. Hathaway became editor the following June. *The American Rifleman* began to sparkle with a more interesting content for its expanded reader audience.

At a meeting early in 1927, a decision was made to participate again in the International Shooting Union Matches, which were to be held in Rome, Italy, in the following summer. President Waterbury was authorized to travel to Europe in April, 1927, to attend a meeting of the International Olympic Committee in Monaco with a view toward restoring shooting events to the program of the 1928 Olympic Games.

The NRA also gave special attention to the conduct of the Dewar International Smallbore Match. In 1926, for the first time since the

218

The Minuteman Trophy, a bronze statuette of the "Minute-man of Concord" was approved for purchase by the Acting Secretary of War, Dwight F. Davis, in 1925. The sculptor of this famous figure was Daniel Chester French.

Match originated in 1912, the British had won the Dewar Cup and in doing so had set a new Match record. The Americans, shooting at Sea Girt, had been handicapped by a limited field and a strong wind. But this did not detract from the marked improvement in British small-bore shooting nor obscure the probability that the next American Dewar team would have to set a new record if it hoped to bring the Cup back to America.

The Dewar team in the past had been selected from shooters on the field at Camp Perry. In 1927, it was decided to expand the field of selection to a truly national level by picking future teams from participants in the national postal matches, many of whom were unable to travel to Camp Perry.

The 1927 ISU Matches rapidly approached, and at Rome on May 22 the United States free-rifle team suffered its worst defeat since entering the International Shooting Union competition. Free-rifle shooting had never been very popular in the United States, although American shooters had done reasonably well against the Europeans. Free-rifle shooting had been de-

veloped by and was practically the national game of the Swiss. Since the end of World War I, Swiss shooters had dominated the Matches. In 1927 Switzerland again proved unbeatable, breaking the existing world's record by ten points. Its team defeated second-place Sweden by nearly 90 points and the United States by 123.

The American team shot under a handicap when Maj. Harry L. Smith, the team captain, was taken ill soon after he arrived in Rome. Capt. Joseph Jackson, who had been the team coach, filled in for him. But there were no alibis or excuses. The Americans had been outshot in a specialized sport by superior teams with superior equipment. The defeat was softened only by Lawrence Nuesslein's victory in the International Individual Smallbore Rifle Match. In the NRA, however, the results caused second thoughts about future participation in international free-rifle competition.

While interest in free-rifle shooting was declining in America the interest in smallbore shooting was growing. The 1927 Dewar International Smallbore Team, which shot against the British in the traditional telegraphic match at Camp Perry in August, beat the former record by 14 points and brought the Dewar Cup back to the United States. The wisdom of the Board of Directors in expanding the American field of entries was proven when the British had surpassed their own 1926 record by a solid 10 points but still lost the match by 4 points.

At the Camp Perry Matches of 1927 E. M. Farris of the Ohio Railroad Company organized the Railroad Man's International Smallbore Match. The teams were made up of British and American railroad workers. It was shot, under the same terms and rules applying in the Dewar

Match, for a prize presented by the Pennsylvania Railroad Company. In the inaugural match, the American railroad men romped away with the prize, defeating the British by 12 points per man.

The most significant development at the Camp Perry NRA-National Matches in 1927 was the increased interest in the NRA Police School. This was a part of the Small Arms Firing School. Sixteen teams had shot at Camp Perry in 1925. The members of these teams, however, were the best police marksmen in the United States, and they needed little additional training. Earlier, however, in 1920, the NRA polled the police departments of all cities of 25,000 population or more to find the status of police marksmanship training. Only three had definite programs. By 1925 the NRA had established its police marksmanship qualification course, and in 1927 more than 2000 policemen all over the United States qualified in the course. Many departments sent officers to Camp Perry in 1927 to train as instructors. From that time on, police marksmen were always among the leading contenders in the annual NRA pistol matches. Before 1925, policemen were conspicuous by their absence in national competition.

Publicity by the NRA on the success of these programs and its active sponsorship of a police training program were directly responsible for elevating the standards of the American police forces. In 1927, the NRA established a Police Division. Eugene F. Mitchell, who came to the staff from Colt's Patent Firearms Manufacturing Company, directed the program, supervised the tournaments, and traveled extensively to attend police conventions and civic groups. Mitchell edited the police tournament news and wrote a regular police column in *The American Rifleman*.

The expanding program soon made it necessary to seek more space. In November, 1927, the NRA moved to the Barr Building on K Street,

N.W., off Farragut Square. This was then one of the newest office buildings in Washington. The NRA suite of fifteen offices occupied 4650 square feet of the eighth floor, while additional space in the basement housed the NRA Service Company.

The NRA Service Company was created in 1927 to supply targets, target rifles, shooting accessories, and match ammunition to the members at moderate prices. Equipment of this kind was not then readily available through retail outlets in small cities and towns. Only a few manufacturers produced quality material suitable for target shooting. During the first few years it was a relatively simple operation handled by C. B. Lister in his capacity as secretary-treasurer. As more and more manufacturers entered the market with products designed for the target shooter, the operation became more complex. By 1928 General Reckord found it necessary to employ O. N. Raynor as a full-time director of the retail outlet. In that year alone, the Service Company sold more than 3,000,000 targets.

At the height of the operation, in early 1929, the NRA Service Company offered all forms

"Ride 'em Cowboy" Trophy, sculptured by Joy Clinton Shepherd, was donated in 1925 by Col. Frank A. Scott.

of target shooting equipment—quality rifles and ammunition, special sights, slings, and shooting jackets. After five years of operation, however, the NRA Service Company was drastically curtailed for several reasons, and especially because other sources of supply had become readily available to shooters.

Another annual meeting rolled around, and on January 27, 1928, Lt. Col. Lewis M. Rumsey, Jr., became president of the National Rifle Association of America. At the meeting of the National Board for the Promotion of Rifle Practice, Brig. Gen. Frank D. Henderson, USA, was named executive officer of the next National Matches, although at the time it was still uncertain whether or not any matches would be held. The War Department again had knocked funds for them out of the appropriation bill.

Faced with this on-again off-again official attitude, General Reckord determined to do something about it. He had the support of the leading veterans' organizations, the National Guard Association, and the Reserve Officers Association as well as that of the NRA. At his request, Congressman Speaks of Ohio introduced an amendment to Section 113 of the National De-

fense Act making it mandatory that an annual appropriation for the National Matches be included in the budget of the War Department. This first attempt failed, but Congressman Speaks then introduced an amendment to the Army Appropriations Bill which provided an item of $500,000 for the conduct of the Matches of 1928 and to finance the expense of the military members of the American International Free-rifle Team. This bill passed on March 20, 1928.

Through the intercession of Senator Smith W. Brookhart, Senator James of Michigan joined Congressman Speaks in reintroducing Speaks's earlier amendment to the National Defense Act. This effort was successful and President Calvin Coolidge signed it into law on May 28, 1928. It provided:

> Section 1. That there shall be held an annual competition known as the National Matches, for the purpose of competing for a national trophy, medals and other prizes to be provided, together with a small-arms firing school, which competition and school shall be held annually under such regulations as may be prescribed by the Secretary of War.
>
> Section 2. The National Matches Competition in this act shall consist of rifle and pistol matches for the national trophy, medals and other prizes mentioned in Section 1 above, to be open to Army, Navy, Marine Corps, National Guard or Organized Militia of the several states, territories and the District of Columbia and civilian military training camps, rifle clubs and civilians, together with a Small Arms Firing School to be connected therewith and competitions for which trophies and medals are provided by the National Rifle Association of America; and for the cost and expenditures required for and incident to the conduct of the same, including the personal expenses of the National Board for the Promotion of Rifle Practice, the sum necessary for the above named purposes is hereby authorized to be appropriated annually as part of the total sum appropriated for national defense.

"The Last Drop" Trophy, by Charles Schreyvogel, was donated to the NRA in 1925 by the Hon. Benedict Crowell, former Asst. Secretary of War.

Lt. Col. Lewis M. Rumsey, Jr., NRA president (1928-1930).

At Camp Perry in 1928 the rivalry in all the matches was very keen. This was especially noticeable between the teams of the Navy, the Marines, and the Coast Guard. This latter team entered the National Matches for the first time. The Marine team, captained by Maj. Julian C. Smith, showed surprising strength.

Major Smith, schooled under Col. William C. Harllee, knew the fundamentals of both rifle and pistol shooting very well. He had graduated that year from the Army's Command and Staff College at Fort Leavenworth, and fifteen years later was destined to be the general in command of the Marine division which stormed ashore and took Tarawa in the Pacific.

One of the problems facing Major Smith's Marines and other shooters in 1928 was the unreliability of the 1928 ammunition, but he solved this problem and, although forced to make a hurried selection, chose his Marine shooters well. Chief Marine Gunner Otho Wiggs won the 1000-yard Wimbledon; Sgt. Bernard G. Betke won the Marine Corps

Cup, the first shooter to register a "possible." Gny. Sgt. Morris Fisher won individual honors in the Navy Match. Sgt. Harvey R. King won the President's Match. Then the Marines proceeded to win the National Board individual and team pistol matches, led by Sgt. Melvin T. Huff. Sgt. Carl J. Cagle won the National Trophy Individual Rifle Match, and in the final National Trophy Match, in which ninety-five teams were entered, the Marines scored 2733, topping the score of their nearest rival, the Navy team, by 29 points. Marines also won the Herrick and Rumbold trophies. It was indeed a good year for the Marine team captained by Maj. Julian C. Smith.

After the Olympic Games back in 1924, a dominant group within the International Olympic Committee had succeeded in eliminating all sports not of major spectator interest and those that it called "mass athletics." Among those events dropped under this arbitrary ruling was shooting. The National Rifle Association and the International Shooting Union bitterly protested this decision and conducted a running fight to have rifle and pistol shooting reinstated. Their efforts remained unsuccessful until the 1930s.

The staunchest support in these efforts came from William Randolph Hearst and his powerful chain of newspapers. Hearst himself had started and sponsored a school rifle-shooting competition based on the NRA program. In 1928, he underwrote the travel expenses of the civilian members of the International Free-rifle Team to Amsterdam, Holland, after the NRA was unable to raise the necessary amount by public subscription. His personal donation exceeded $8000. In 1929 the Hearst newspapers were the largest single contributor to a comparable fund to send the Free-rifle Team to the ISU Matches in Stockholm, Sweden.

During these years under General Reckord's guidance the National Rifle Association developed into the leading authority on shooting in the United States. Gifford Pinchot, the "father of American forestry," and an enthusiastic hunter, often visited the offices of the NRA to discuss shooting with General Reckord and his staff. The expert staff of the "Dope Bag" —Charles Askins, Maj. Julian S. Hatcher and Lt. Col. Townsend Whelen—became the last word on technical shooting questions. In 1928 alone the "Dope Bag" staff processed more than 5000 letters on hunting equipment, ballistics, reloading, and the selection of arms and equipment for special tasks. By this time *The American Rifleman* had become self-supporting for the first time. It boasted a circulation of 30,000 and a substantial list of paying advertisers.

In an effort to reach a wider audience than the members and newsstand purchasers of *The American Rifleman*, the NRA on January 26, 1929, launched its Publicity Bureau under the direction of C. B. Baker. The Publicity Bureau, through a newsletter to newspapers and magazines, gave national publicity to recreational shooting for the first time. Many of its news items featured the Junior Marksmanship Program, which had a broad appeal to newspaper editors. The Junior Rifle Club Program then had more than 3000 individual members in 540 separate clubs scattered all over America.

When the time came again for our best shooters to head for Ohio, it developed that, in attendance, the 1929 Camp Perry Matches were the most successful held to that date. There were 17,521 individual entries that year compared to 13,619 in 1928. The presence of a uniformed detachment from the Royal Canadian Mounted Police lent international flavor and a dash of color. The Mounties had come down from Canada to shoot in the police matches against American law officers. The police turned out in force in 1929; eighteen teams shot in the shoulder-to-shoulder competition. Police officers also won most of the pistol events, a far cry from the situation that had prevailed only five years earlier.

U. S. Coast Guard "Alexander Hamilton" Trophy.

Col. G. H. Clarke "Duelist" Trophy.

The "Daniel Boone" Trophy.

Gen. George A. Custer Trophy.

The Capt. E. H. Clarke Memorial Trophy.

The Lee O. Wright Memorial Trophy.

The latter years of the 1920s, as in the earlier years of that decade, brought many trophies into competition.

Capt. John G. W. Dillin again brought his Kentucky rifle to Camp Perry to use in the "Davey Crockett Match." Dillin was the author of *The Kentucky Rifle*, which was published by the NRA under a cooperative arrangement with the author. It did much to stimulate gun collecting in America and to revive interest in muzzle-loading weapons of the past.

The American Dewar International Smallbore Team led by Col. William A. Tewes shot at Camp Perry on September 6, 1929. Favored by excellent weather, the American team topped the British by 106 points. In winning, they shattered both the record set by their own shooters in 1928 and that of the British in 1927.

A high point of the Dewar Matches of 1929 was the performance of little Mary Ward, a nineteen-year-old schoolgirl from Chicago, who became the second woman in history to qualify as a member of an international rifle team. But this was the least of her attainments. She was the only member of either team to make a possible score of 200 at 50 yards, and she dropped only 5 points in the 100-yard stage to produce one of the best scores in the match against the leading smallbore shooters in the world.

On October 30, 1929, America awoke after its free-spending postwar spree with an ice bag on its head. The Great Depression had begun.

The National Rifle Association, because most of its assets were fluid, did not immediately feel the effects of the economic collapse. There was little sign of despair or concern when the Board of Directors met on January 30, 1930. At this meeting the Hon. Benedict Crowell became president of the NRA. The Directors voted to issue charters without charge to all clubs made up of 100 per cent NRA individual members and to waive annual dues for such affiliated clubs. One year later there were thirty-one "100 per cent clubs" on the rolls of the Association.

The NRA also decided to raise funds to help defray the expenses of sending another International Free-rifle Team to compete in the ISU Matches in Antwerp, Belgium, on August 9, 1930. Final tryouts were shot on June 2, 1930. The team was led by Maj. J. K. Boles as captain, with Maj. Julian S. Hatcher as adjutant and Lt. Sidney R. Hinds, serving as team coach.

The cry was "Beat the Swiss," although Finland, Italy, Denmark, France, Holland, and Belgium were also in the matches. It had been the Swiss marksmen, piling record on record every year, who had handed the United States its most humiliating defeats.

The 1930 International Free-rifle Team that disembarked in Belgium was the strongest that the United States had ever sent overseas. They were superbly trained and superbly armed. A majority of the members used rifles based on the Springfield action, but nearly half were armed with customized Martini rifles, each fitted precisely to the physical requirements of its user. Their ammunition was a special low-velocity load that had provided almost pinpoint accuracy in machine-rest tests.

The Match was shot on August 7-9, 1930, and the American shooters proved that they were

There were matches for the old muzzle-loading long-rifles at Camp Perry as well as matches for the most sophisticated shooting equipment.

The Hon. Benedict Crowell, NRA president (1930-1932).

up to the standards of their equipment. They came within one point of beating the existing Swiss record of 5442, set a new record for the prone position, and beat the Swiss shooters by 34 points. They brought the famed Argentine Cup back from Switzerland where it seemed to have found a permanent home.

With an American victory under its belt, the National Rifle Association was able to suggest, with honor, that the United States withdraw from the International Free-rifle competition in favor of an annual shoulder-to-shoulder small-bore match with the British at Bisley, England. The first such match was held in 1931. Gen. John J. Pershing, famed commander of the American Expeditionary Force of World War I, presented a handsome trophy for this competition.

Turning from the international scene to one closer home, the Camp Perry Matches of 1930 were a major success in spite of the depression, and they were marked by a growing emphasis on smallbore shooting. More than 1600 individuals participated in the Small Arms Firing School, and the number of law enforcement officers in the Police School increased 250 per cent over the attendance in 1929. In an international match against a team from the Royal Canadian Mounted Police, a team of American police officers won by a margin of 176 points. The American International Smallbore Team, captained by Dr. Emmet O. Swanson of Minneapolis, a veteran of the victorious free-rifle team and just back from the Antwerp Matches, beat the British by 10 points. The star performer was Frank T. Parsons, Jr., another veteran of the free-rifle team, a former national .30 caliber intercollegiate rifle champion and then coach of the George Washington University Rifle Team.

The year 1931 ended on a healthy note inso-

far as the marksmanship program was concerned, even though the national economy was staggering, and news that the International Olympic Committee had reinstated shooting in the program of the Olympic Games of 1932 brightened the annual NRA meeting on January 30, 1931. On the strength of this the Directors appointed an Olympic Rifle Committee, under the chairmanship of Maj. Gen. Milton A. Reckord and an Olympic Pistol Committee headed by Karl T. Frederick.

As soon as these committees started their deliberations they found themselves working under an almost insurmountable handicap. The International Olympic Committee, in an effort to eliminate any hint of professionalism from the games, ruled that it would bar from competition anyone who had accepted a cash prize or who had competed in a contest in which a cash prize had been offered. Since the beginning of competitive rifle shooting, cash prizes had been customary in America, even in some junior events. In the early 1920s there had been a short-lived effort to eliminate them from the NRA matches, but this quickly had been voted down. Although by the 1930s the cash prizes even for major matches were small, they were still cash prizes. There was scarcely a single experienced target shooter in America or in the world who could meet those standards set by the Olympic Committee in 1931.

Although the task was all but impossible, the two Olympic Committees set out to build teams meeting the standards of amateurism laid down by the governing body of the Olympic Games. Both were forced to draw upon unknown shooters of little competitive experience. Final tryouts for both teams were shot in late May and early June at clubs affiliated with the NRA and the USRA. Col. William A. Tewes was captain of the rifle team. Col. Roy D. Jones of Springfield, Massachusetts, captained and managed the pistol team.

Selecting the team members was practically all of the responsibility that the Olympic Games Committee permitted these two shooting committees to exert. Neither was consulted on the arrangements of the match or on the construction of the shooting facilities. This slight was further complicated when the Olympic Games Committee announced that Sgt. John H. March of the Los Angeles Police Department would be "in charge of shooting" at the Olympic Games in Los Angeles. This came in spite of the fact that the same committee had invited the National Rifle Association and the United States Revolver Association to assume charge of the shooting facilities.

The result was a fiasco. The Olympic Games Committee selected the Los Angeles Police Range as the site of the shooting matches. Although good enough for police practice it was neither designed nor built for formal competitive shooting, especially that contemplated for the Olympic Games. The Olympic Games Committee had laid out several thousand dollars in redesigning the police range and in extending the fifty-yard concrete-lined pits the full width of the range. Above the permanent concrete structure at the firing line it erected a second

About to embark for the 1931 International Smallbore Match at Bisley, England, are the two youngest members of the U. S. Team, Gale Evans and L. A. Wilkens (right). Both shot Model 52 Winchester rifles.

story of timber with an overhang of six feet at the rear in an effort to stretch the normal fifty-yard distance to fifty meters. Above all was a ten-foot-wide porch roof shading the elevated firing points.

The spectators occupied the concrete lower platform while the shooters were expected to perform in the elevated structure, which shook and vibrated whenever one of them changed position. When the Olympic Rifle Committee reached Los Angeles, they found that, with this glorious structure complete, the shooting house was several yards too near the fifty-meter targets and out of parallel with the line of targets. To attain fifty meters the shooters had to press back against the rear wall, so that men moving from one point to another interfered with those who were shooting. When the foreign teams arrived, most of them flatly refused to shoot until the range was almost completely rebuilt.

Although the American Olympic Rifle and Pistol Committees had leaned over backward in abiding by the rules of amateurism laid down by the Olympic Games Committee, they soon found that their competitors had taken the rules more lightly. General Reckord, Karl Frederick and Colonel Tewes had been associated with international shooting long enough to rec-

Some shooters preferred the single-sh match rifles like the Ballard shown he which were often fitted with special barr made by such highly regarded craftsm as Axel Peterson and Harry Pope.

ognize men who had been shooting in international circles for years. Frederick and Tewes had competed personally, for cash prizes, against a number of them. If they had protested, however, the entire shooting program would have been eliminated, and rather than precipitate this they decided to make the most of a bad situation.

The terms of the pistol match were entirely unsatisfactory to the Americans, although the range deficiencies were less serious than those affecting the rifle competition. Precision was subordinated to speed. Although billed as a "revolver match," no one used anything but autoloading pistols. Renxo Morigo of Italy won the match with a remarkable score of six hits in two seconds.

The rifle team fared almost as badly against the Europeans as the pistol team. The terms of the match favored the Europeans since it was essentially a smallbore free-rifle match in the prone position. Each shooter fired two stages of thirty shots each at fifty meters. William G. Harding shot well, although he had far less experience than his rivals, finishing only 2 points behind the winning score. But Bertil Ronmark of Sweden won the match in a shoot-off against Gustavo Huet of Mexico.

Both General Reckord and Karl Frederick protested the planning and programming of the shooting events in their report to the Olympic Games Committee The shooting events were a major disappointment to those involved, especially since the Games themselves had been characterized by detailed preparation and careful planning. But at least to the shooting world they were better than no participation at all, and they provided a basis on which future competition could be built.

A far better situation existed at the first International Smallbore Match, which replaced the traditional International Free-rifle Match and was shot at Bisley, England, in July, 1931 by a team selected by a committee under the chairmanship of General Reckord. The ten-man team was captained by Maj. Julian S. Hatcher whose rank through these pages rose to Major General; Charles H. Johnson, who traveled to England at his own expense, served as team coach. A majority of the team members were equipped with heavy-barreled Winchester Model 52s, but there was a scattering of other rifles such as the Peterson-Ballard, BSA, and Hubalek-Ballard. The team was selected in a nationwide competition in which 2000 individuals participated.

The match was shot on the Running Deer Range at Bisley, which the British had converted temporarily into a smallbore range. The Americans were intrigued by the unorthodox shooting style of the British. In contrast to the sprawling prone position common in America, most of the Englishmen shot with legs together and bodies in line with the target. W. Wildgoose, the high-scoring English shooter compounded this lack of orthodoxy by wearing a bowler hat while shooting with crossed feet. But in spite of this, the British finished with a 2-point lead. Major Hatcher returned home with some notes designed to bring American sighting equipment up to the quality of the superb sights on the British Vickers rifles.

The Pershing Trophy, symbol of victory in the first International Smallbore Match at Bisley, was not to be placed in competition again for several years because of economic problems and other factors unfavorable to shoulder-to-shoulder international competition. But a hot contest was assured when competition for this handsome trophy was resumed.

20

# The Depression —

# to the Brink of

The full impact of the Great Depression hit the National Rifle Association of America in the early 1930s. There was little room in the federal budget for more than the barest essentials, and the appropriations for the National Matches were an early casualty. Revival of the Bisley International Smallbore Match also went by the board, and the National Rifle Association, which had been collecting contributions to help send a team of riflemen to England in an effort to retrieve the Pershing Trophy, deposited $1500 in an earmarked savings account to use for this purpose in better times. Then the International Shooting Union cancelled its scheduled matches. The only major international shoulder-to-shoulder rifle competition in 1932 was the limited program staged in the Los Angeles Olympic Games.

From 1932 through 1934 the NRA held its annual matches on a regional basis. In 1932 they were shot at eight "little Camp Perrys," located on military ranges in eight of the nine Army Corps areas—at Wakefield, Massachusetts; Quantico, Virginia; Camp McClellan, Alabama; Camp Perry, Ohio; Fort Sheridan, Illinois; Fort Des Moines, Iowa; Fort Bliss, Texas; and Fort Lewis, Washington. The matches at Fort Des Moines were supervised by Col. C. E. Stodter, USA, the former Director of Civilian Marksmanship, who after a series of assignments elsewhere, had become Commanding Officer of that post.

The 1932 matches set the pattern for this period of economic depression, although in 1934 the regional matches were held at sixteen separate locations. There was a marked decline in .30 caliber shooting during these three years, largely because of the expense of ammunition and the cost of suitable shooting facilities. The War Department found itself unable to support the full-scale civilian marksmanship program.

After limping along for two years under these discouraging circumstances, the .30 caliber program received another stunning blow in 1934. Under President Franklin D. Roosevelt's drastic reorganization of the Executive Branch, the Director of the Budget was authorized to veto the spending of any funds authorized by Congress. In that year the War Department appropriations contained an item of $75,000 for use by the National Board for the Promotion of Rifle Practice. Budget Director Douglas promptly vetoed it and eliminated for another year any assistance to the 1600 clubs affiliated with the NRA. The action was taken over the protest of Secretary of War George H. Dern.

Loss of the War Department appropriations was only one hardship imposed by the federal government on the National Rifle Association; for a while after June 13, 1933,

228

# Shooting Activities

# World War II

the NRA was forced into a struggle to maintain its identity. Through coincidence, the federal government leased office space for its National Industrial Recovery Administration in the Barr Building, which already housed the offices of the National Rifle Association. Then it abbreviated its name to the National Recovery Administration and emblazoned its blue eagle and the initials "NRA" on placards, posters, and stationery that were known to every American. The officers of the National Rifle Association, which for more than half a century had been *the* NRA, strongly protested the infringement of their trademark. More seriously, the identity of initials and addresses often caused delays in the delivery of mail. Sacks of targets, used in NRA tournaments, were delivered to puzzled clerks in the offices of the National Recovery Administration, while the National Rifle Association staff sorted through pleas for financial aid to locate its own correspondence. The problem was not fully solved until May 12, 1935, when the Supreme Court voided the National Industrial Recovery Act.

While the .30 caliber program bucked the strong currents of economic depression, the smallbore program floated along with the tide. Riflemen who could not afford the ten-cents-a-shot luxury of .30 caliber shooting could still scrape up a penny a shot for the .22. Clubs that found the construction of a .30 caliber range beyond their means could still improvise a 50- or 100-yard smallbore range. With new recruits flowing into the smallbore field from schools and boys' clubs and with veteran bigbore shooters turning to the .22, the smallbore program experienced a surprising growth. Between 1932 and 1935 it was the main support of the NRA program.

In 1932, largely through interest in .22 caliber shooting, there were 361 clubs newly affiliated with the NRA. In the same year the National Rifle Association signed 2807 new Life Members, many of whom entered under a two-dollars-a-month installment plan conceived by C. B. Lister. In the same year the home office issued 40,909 Junior Qualification Awards; as of February 1, 1934, the number increased to more than 42,000, the largest number in the history of the organization to that time. Many of these clubs were in public schools, but a

This emblem of the National Recovery Administration, which was housed in the same building as the National Rifle Association and used the same NRA initials, caused great confusion in mail and otherwise.

NRA MEMBER

U.S.

WE DO OUR PART

substantial number were in Boy Scout troops, boys' clubs, and local YMCA organizations. The American Legion was extremely active in promoting the organization of school clubs.

The success of the smallbore program permitted an expansion into other fields. In May, 1933, the NRA initiated a new outdoor pistol league, and in 1934 it issued the first of its 16 mm. films designed to promote shooting safety. On April 10, 1935, it initiated an all-risk insurance policy program for members in cooperation with the Fireman's Fund Insurance Company of Chicago.

One casualty of this period, however, was the NRA Service Company, which, with changing conditions, had become a liability rather than an asset to the Association. In 1932, the NRA operated at a deficit for the first time since its early years, although it had just about broken even in 1931. Part of the drain was traceable to the Service Company, and the Board of Directors voted to eliminate the sale of firearms and accessories and to confine its operation to the sale of official targets. Three years later the NRA Service Company was eliminated entirely and the target business transferred under a franchise to the National Target Supply Company.

Because of the increased interest in smallbore shooting, there was no curtailment of the international telegraphic smallbore program. The Dewar Match was shot at Camp Perry on September 6, 1932, by a team led by Capt. E. M. Farris, USN, which defeated the British shooters 7872 to 7838. In the International Railroad Match, however, the British scored their first victory. A third international telegraphic match shot that year was the Fidac Inter-Allied Smallbore Competition, the American phase of which was also conducted at Camp Perry, on September 4, by a team of the American Legion. Easily outpointing their British, Yugoslavian, and Belgian counterparts, the American veterans picked up their fourth straight victory since the inception of the match in 1929. In 1933 they made it five in a row.

Although there were no federal appropria-

Bausch and Lomb's "Bronco Buster" Trophy was presented in 1933 and is a specimen of Frederic Remington's brilliant work.

tions for the conduct of the National Matches in 1933, some federal assistance was provided for the National Smallbore Matches held at Camp Perry on August 28 through September 4. Most of it stemmed from the personal interest of Chief of Staff General Douglas MacArthur, through whose intercession Col. C. E. Stodter was assigned as executive officer. The Matches were on a scale much reduced below the normal Camp Perry program, but the National Smallbore Tournament was a major success. It produced some of the most spectacular light rifle work seen to this date. Thurman Randle made perfect scores of 400 in the Dewar Course three consecutive times. The American Railroad Team, shooting against the British, set a new record that was higher than the score made by the British Dewar Team and the American Dewar Team, and exceeded 7900 points for the first time in history.

The 1933 National Smallbore Tournament saw the introduction of a new international competition among teams representing the United States, Great Britain, and Germany. Operated like the Dewar Match, on a telegraphic basis, it was initiated in a spirit of international goodwill by the Rhenish-Westphalian Explosives Company of Nuremburg, Germany. Fifteen years earlier some of the

The Rattlesnake Trophy, placed in competition in 1938, was also the work of the great artist Frederic Remington.

first participants could have traded shots under less amicable circumstances. American shooters took the first match for a clean sweep of the international smallbore field in 1933.

The success of the National Smallbore Tournament in 1933 inspired Frank J. Kahrs of Remington Arms Company and Henry Marsh of the Hercules Powder Company to suggest an expansion of the Eastern Smallbore Tournament and its transfer to Camp Ritchie, Maryland. Until that time the finals of the Eastern Smallbore Tournament had been shot traditionally on July 4 each year at Sea Girt. Located in Maryland's Catoctin Mountains, a few miles south of the Gettysburg Battlefield, Camp Ritchie had been planned and built by Gen. Milton A. Reckord in his capacity as Adjutant General of Maryland as a training ground for the National Guard.

With its picturesque mountain setting, clear air, stone buildings, and the most modern smallbore rifle range in America, Camp Ritchie was superior in many ways to Sea Girt. Most important, summer fogs often rolled in off the Atlantic at the height of the shooting season at Sea Girt and forced delays in the shooting program. At Camp Ritchie the bullseyes stood out crisp and clear. It was here that the Eastern Smallbore Tournament opened on June 30

and closed on July 4, 1934, supervised by a committee headed by Frank J. Kahrs. With General Reckord in overall command, Maj. Harry L. Smith, USMC, served as executive officer. The first Eastern Smallbore Tournament at Camp Ritchie was an outstanding success. One hundred and eighty smallbore riflemen competed at 50, 100, 150, 175, and 200 yards, and ninety pistol shooters at 15, 25, and 50 yards. Thurman Randle was the star of the rifle tournament, setting a new record of 196 bullseyes at Ritchie in the Swiss Match, a popular suspense-filled "miss and out" event.

Major Smith also served as the executive officer of the Sixteenth National Smallbore Rifle Championship Tournament which followed at Camp Perry on August 19, 1934. His chief range officer was a young Marine captain, Merritt A. Edson, who at this point began a long and important association with the NRA.

If the marksmanship demonstrated in 1933 at Camp Perry had been outstanding, that in 1934 was superlative. Great Britain, Canada, Australia, and South Africa had all entered the Dewar Match against the United States; and the British shooters, led by E. G. B. Reynolds, who punched out a perfect score, had set a new world's record by a margin of a dozen points. With this incentive before them, the American shooters proceeded to beat the British by 32 points for a new Dewar record of 7940. Sam Bond and W. B. Woodring each matched Reynolds' perfect score. Bond then shot in the Rhenish-Westphalian Match (which came to be abbreviated as the RWS Match) and turned in another perfect performance to lead the Americans to a 60-point victory over Great Britain while defeating the Germans by nearly 100 points. The American Legion team then set a third world's record in the Fidac (Federation Inter-allies des Anciens Combattants) Match to defeat the teams of Great Britain and Belgium, and the American Railroad Team completed another sweep for the United States by defeating teams of Great Britain and Canada.

While smallbore shooting had held the center

Brig. Gen. G. A. Fraser, NRA president (1932-1934).

of the stage during the preceding years, .30 caliber shooting came back into its own in 1935. The War Department Appropriations Bill for that year provided $350,000 for the conduct of the National Matches and for the use of the National Board for the Promotion of Rifle Practice. America was climbing out of the abyss of the Depression but toward the precipice of World War II. The recent Japanese invasion of Manchuria, civil war in Spain, and the saber-rattling of Mussolini and Hitler were gradually forcing a more critical analysis of America's military preparedness. President Franklin D. Roosevelt signed the bill authorizing the National Matches of 1935 on April 9 and designated Camp Perry as their site.

The first full-scale program since 1931 opened at Camp Perry on September 1, 1935, with the Small Arms Firing School and closed on September 10 with the completion of the National Rifle and Pistol Matches. There was a sharp step-up in participation by civilian shooters.

There were changes and innovations at the 1935 Matches. In 1934 the National Rifle Association had relaxed the rules for its state matches by permitting the use of "any .30-06 rifle weighing less than nine pounds and equipped with metallic sights." On July 5, 1935, at Camp Ritchie, the NRA Executive Committee had voted to open a number of the military rifle matches to shooters of "any rifle." Using a .300 Holland and Holland rifle, Ben Comfort broke the long-standing monopoly of the .30-06 in NRA matches by winning the Wimbledon Cup at Camp Perry.

The Executive Committee had also announced a new system of cash prizes for the 1935 annual matches. Under it all cash prizes were for a guaranteed amount and each medal winner received a definite prize. One hundred dollars went to each winner of the Wimbledon and President's Match; winners of the Leech, Navy, Marine Corps, and Coast Guard Matches each received $60, and $50 was provided for the winner of each single-stage match. Under the new prize rules, those who did not wish to jeopardize their amateur standing by accepting cash prizes were permitted to refuse the cash and accept a certificate as a declaration of their amateur status.

Although overshadowed again by the reinstated .30 caliber devotees, the smallbore shooters turned out in 1935 at Camp Perry in larger numbers than ever before. They also again clinched the domination of the United States in the international smallbore field. A team captained by Homer Jacobs defeated Great Britain in the Dewar Match by 18 points and easily outshot the teams representing Australia, Canada, South Africa, and India, which finished in that order. In the RWS Match a team captained by Dr. Emmet O. Swanson soundly trounced the Germans and retained for the United States the handsome RWS Challenge Cup.

By this time most of the leading marksmen were looking forward to the Olympic Games of 1936. The National Rifle Association again accepted an invitation to organize a team of American riflemen to participate in Berlin and appointed General Reckord chairman and C. B.

Lister secretary of the American Rifle Shooting Committee. Karl T. Frederick, then president of the NRA; Maj. Julian S. Hatcher, USA; Gustavus D. Pope, the NRA vice-president; Maj. L. W. T. Waller, Jr., and Russell Wiles served as members. Karl T. Frederick doubled as a member of the Olympic Pistol Shooting Committee, organized by the United States Revolver Association under the chairmanship of Dr. I. R. Caulkins.

American shooters had been chafing at the bit ever since the disappointing Olympic fiasco in Los Angeles in 1932. The National Rifle Association of America, its counterparts in other countries, and the International Shooting Union had prevailed upon the International Olympic Committee to relax its rigid rules of amateurism. Under the new rules, anyone was eligible to compete if he had not accepted a money prize between August 1, 1934 and the opening of the Olympic Games. Since nearly all shooters aspiring to enter the Eleventh Olympiad had abstained from collecting prize money, the change seemed to assure that the United States would be represented in Berlin by its best riflemen.

Then the International Olympic Committee announced the rifle shooting program—a single event with miniature rifles, identical to that held in Los Angeles in 1932, instead of the hoped-for military-rifle matches. The American Olympic Rifle Shooting Committee protested in vain, and then rejected the crumbs held out to the shooting world. The Committee voted not to participate in the rifle event. In his report, General Reckord called the program "totally inadequate and in no sense designed to meet the requirements of amateur rifle competition."

The Board of Directors of the NRA backed this decision with a resolution stating, "Solely because of the inadequate rifle shooting program for such Olympic competition, the Association does not approve the sending of a rifle team to such Olympic Games."

By 1936, the National Matches and high-power rifle shooting in general had been re-

Mr. Karl T. Frederick, NRA president (1934-1936).

stored to a normal schedule. The annual appropriation for the National Board for the Promotion of Rifle Practice had been restored to $500,000. The 1936 Camp Perry Matches, which were held August 24 through September 12, were reminiscent of those of the 1920s in attendance and in scope of program. There was a substantial increase in the number of pistol events.

A feature of the 1936 Matches was the dedication on September 1, 1936, of the bronze plaque to Brig. Gen. Ammon B. Critchfield on the mall in front of the headquarters building at Camp Perry. Critchfield himself was present to receive this recognition in a touching ceremony in which shooters from all over America, the Ohio National Guard, and officials of the NRA joined in their tribute to him.

Under the revised Bylaws, the administration of the National Rifle Association had followed a generally predictable and stable pattern. The active program was carried on by the executive vice-president with the assistance of the secretary, whose offices were in the national headquarters. The president customarily served for two one-year terms, and the first vice-president

Mr. Gustavus D. Pope, NRA president (1937-1939).

then moved into the leading office. In January 1933, the slate of officers included Brig. Gen. G. A. Fraser, Adjutant General of North Dakota, as president; Karl T. Frederick, first vice-president; Gustavus D. Pope, second vice-president; and Maj. L. W. T. Waller, Jr., USMC, as third vice-president.

In 1934 Karl T. Frederick had succeeded General Fraser, and Pope and Waller graduated to first and second vice-presidents respectively, while Lt. Col. Nathaniel C. Nash, Jr., of Boston was elected third vice-president. At the close of Karl T. Frederick's term of office as president, the NRA deviated from this set pattern for one year by making General Critchfield its leading officer in recognition of his long services to the organization. Gustavus D. Pope did not become president until February 5, 1937.

The meeting of the Board of Directors of February 5, 1937, at which Gustavus D. Pope became president, was an important milestone in the development of the National Rifle Association. It was at this meeting that the Board created the Executive Council by amendment of the Bylaws. The first members of the Executive Council elected at that time, were the four

immediate past-presidents: Brig. Gen. Fred M. Waterbury, Lt. Col. L. M. Rumsey, Karl T. Frederick, and Brig. Gen. Ammon B. Critchfield.

There was ample evidence at this meeting that the Association had weathered the worst of the Depression. The Board unanimously approved the sending of a team to Bisley, England, to compete for the Pershing Cup in a match scheduled for July 5 through 10 in the following summer. It adopted a resolution calling for the introduction of rifle practice in the programs of the Civilian Conservation Corps and voted to contact the head of the Works Progress Administration to urge plans for constructing rifle and pistol ranges.

The report of the secretary showed that the circulation of *The American Rifleman* was climbing to 56,000, that the magazine had increased in size and coverage, and that it had a healthy list of paying advertisers. In February, 1937, it had carried its first full-color advertisement—a four-page spread purchased by the Packard Motor Car Company.

With the recovery of the American economy, the shooting program had returned to its pre-depression level. The shooting programs of 1937 and 1938, with increased support from the Administration and Congress, were the most comprehensive held since the 1920s. Where there were only thirty-six registered tournaments in 1936, there were nearly a hundred in 1938. The NRA also named the first All-American rifle and pistol teams, patterned after those of foot-

The Critchfield Trophy, presented in 1934 by the Riflemen of Ohio, commemorates the work of Brig. Gen. A. B. Critchfield, "the father of Camp Perry."

ball and baseball. In the collegiate rifle tournaments, the ten top-ranking scorers were designated "Golden Bullets." The leading college marksman of that year, and captain-designate of the first All-American team, was Midshipman W. L. Kitch of the United States Naval Academy.

The return Bisley Smallbore Match, annually planned and annually cancelled for six years, finally came about in 1937. The team that shot against the British on July 9, 1937, was selected entirely on the basis of individual performance in the registered smallbore tournaments. It was captained by Ned Moor, Jr., with Thurman Randle serving both as team coach and a shooting member. The other members were Dr. Russell Gardner, E. A. Craven, William P. Schweitzer, W. J. Summerall, L. A. Pope, William B. Woodring, D. Carlson, and Merle Israelson. General Reckord accompanied the team to Bisley as the official representative of the NRA. Frank J. Kahrs, of the Remington Arms Company, also traveled with the team to film a motion picture of the event.

The Match was a cliff-hanger with the outcome in doubt almost to the final shot. Dr. Gardner and Merle Israelson each dropped only 1 point, while only one member of the British ten matched their individual scores. When the final shot was fired, however, the British won, for the second time by a margin of 2 points.

Although disappointed, the Americans took their defeat in good grace. But while they were in Europe, the team decided that American shooters should again try their hand in the International World Championship Matches of the ISU, which were scheduled to be held in Helsinki, Finland, in July, 1937. With this in mind, General Reckord selected for the American ISU Team Schweitzer, Woodring, Mrs. Kay Woodring, and John B. Adams, all of whom volunteered to pay their own expenses. Mrs. Woodring was not selected only because she was the wife of the team captain. In her own right, she was one of the leading marksmen in the world, having finished near the top in the annual tournament. Shooting against the teams of twelve other nations, this team brought back to the United States the fifty-meter prone championship of the world, salve for the disappointment over the outcome of the Bisley Match.

The loss of the Pershing Trophy for another year was softened still further by the victory of the American handgun shooters in the first International Pistol Team Match, later called the Mayleigh Match; this was patterned after the Dewar Match and operated on a telegraphic basis. The British shot their phase of the Match on July 9, 1937, the same day the Pershing Team was competing shoulder-to-shoulder at Bisley. An American pistol team, shooting at Camp Perry, defeated the British by 148 points. The British riflemen, however, won the Dewar Cup by beating the United States, Canada, New Zealand, and South Africa. The American phases of these telegraphic events were shot as part of the National Matches at Camp Perry.

The 1937 Eastern Smallbore Tournament again was held at Camp Ritchie, Maryland, on a range greatly improved and expanded by WPA labor in the previous spring. These matches were the first interstate shooting events ever covered by radio, although earlier in the year the state matches in South Carolina had been carried by a local broadcasting company. Bob Longstreet, sports announcer for station

The Critchfield-Herrick Trophy, presented in 1938, is a silver and bronze plaque.

Shooting shed at the Petersham range
during the Bisley matches of 1937.

WFMD of Frederick, Maryland, assisted by William F. Shadel, public relations director of the NRA, conducted a half-hour running commentary on the shooting through a hookup between his station and WBAL in Baltimore.

The success of this venture led Shadel to seek a comparable coverage of the National Matches at Camp Perry. Although he was unsuccessful that year, the Mutual Broadcasting System, through station WLW of Cincinnati, covered the Herrick Trophy Match at Camp Perry on September 3, 1938, on a nationwide hookup.

As the international situation worsened, support for and interest in the National Matches increased. In 1938, the Budget Bureau again reduced the funds for the conduct of the National Matches by $153,000, but the sum was restored by the House of Representatives. The last peacetime matches before the outbreak of World War II were hailed as "the best ever held." Certainly, they produced some of the most spectacular shooting that ever had been seen. The Dewar Match was highlighted by four perfect individual scores by American shooters, who defeated the British with a near-record score and brought the historic cup back to the United States. Americans swept the smallbore field in the international events, winning the RWS, Railwaymen's and Fidac Matches by some of the highest scores ever recorded. In the individual events, Bill Woodring became the first man in history to win the national smallbore championship in three consecutive years.

Sparked by such all-time great marksmen as Harry Reeves and Alfred Hemming, the Detroit

Police Team set three world's records and ran up a total of eleven victories; Reeves and Hemming broke the two-man team record three times in 1938, raising the top score by 35 points. In the National Match, the Detroit Police were beaten only by the United States Infantry. Police teams from all over the nation attended the matches in that year and were strong contenders or winners in all events open to them. This was a far cry from the situation in the early 1920s when the policeman who could hit a man-sized target at fifty feet was the exception rather than the rule. Much of this improvement was attributable to the NRA Police Marksmanship Program and Police Revolver Tournaments.

In the pre-Perry Matches at Detroit, Reeves had shot a 200 "possible" and then shot an additional string of ten 10s for a perfect score of 300. At Camp Perry he walked away with the NRA .22 Pistol Championship, placed first in the .45 Timed-fire Match, and set a new record for the .45 Slow-fire. Charles Askins, Jr., of the United States Border Patrol, broke the Center-fire Slow-fire Pistol record by 3 points, tied the world's record for .22 caliber Slow-fire and equaled the record in the .45 Medalist Match. With such talent on the field, the American International Pistol Team had little difficulty in running up a higher score than the teams of Canada and Great Britain.

Exceptional shooting performances were not confined to the handgunners and smallbore fanciers. The Marine Corps Rifle Team, armed with .300 H & H Magnums, ran up a new record in the 1000-yard Herrick Trophy Match with a score of 797-122 Vs.

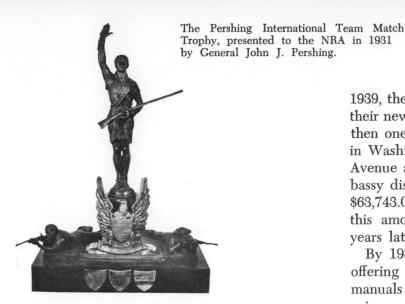

The Pershing International Team Match Trophy, presented to the NRA in 1931 by General John J. Pershing.

The years leading up to World War II saw continued organizational growth and expansion of programs within the NRA. As early as 1937, the organization had developed to the point where increased staff specialization became necessary. By 1939, there were five separate divisions, each headed by a staff member responsible to General Reckord and C. B. Lister. In January 1939, these included: Frank L. Wyman, in charge of competitions; F. M. Hakenjos, extension; L. Q. Bradley, membership; William F. Shadel, public relations; and Herbert Goebel, club service and junior rifle program. Each of these members also served in editorial capacities on the staff of *The American Rifleman;* Shadel was associate editor under Editor L. J. Hathaway.

Because of this growth, office space available in the Barr Building, which a scant ten years before had seemed commodious, now became cramped and crowded. In 1938, the Executive Committee had authorized the management to purchase a building of its own. In January,

1939, the National Rifle Association moved into their new quarters, an old mansion in what was then one of the most exclusive neighborhoods in Washington. Located at 1600 Rhode Island Avenue at Scott Circle on the edge of the embassy district, the building and land then cost $63,743.05. The Association borrowed most of this amount, but paid off the mortgage two years later.

By 1939, the National Rifle Association was offering its members a full line of books and manuals on shooting and firearms at bargain prices. Among them was *The Handloader's Manual* by Maj. Earl Naramore, one of the first publications on this subject available in the United States. With the slackening of the Depression, the size of the official magazine was expanded from thirty-eight to seventy-two pages and appeared on higher-quality paper.

A firearms safety program began to take shape at the NRA annual meetings in February of 1938. A feature of those meetings was a Round Table Conference on Safety under the chairmanship of Edwin Pugsley, chairman of the Safety Committee of the Sporting Arms and Ammunition Manufacturers' Institute. On the panel with Mr. Pugsley were Fred C. Mills, National Safety Director of the Boy Scouts of America, and Seth Gordon, chairman of the Board of Game Commissioners of Pennsylvania and former secretary of the American Game Association. By 1939 the program suggested by the group was gaining momentum but its full development had to be postponed until after the war. Although the NRA for years had promoted the cause of firearms safety through news items and publicity releases, it did not, at

Shooters from the United States who traveled to Bisley in 1937 were: *Seated, from left:* Pope, Hamer, Carlson, Swanson, McGarrity, Lambert, Israelson. *Standing:* Gardner, Craven, Randle, Moor, Woodring, Summerall, Canfield.

that time, have a centralized program built around this activity.

The 1939 meeting of the Board of Directors convened in the new national headquarters on February 3 and 4; it was the largest meeting of its kind held to that time. The directors elected Col. L. W. T. Waller, USMC, of Meadowbrook, Pennsylvania, to succeed retiring President Gustavus D. Pope, who became a member of the Executive Council. Under changes in the Bylaws adopted four years earlier, the offices of second and third vice-presidents had been phased out. Col. Nathaniel C. Nash, Jr., of Boston, was elected to fill the single vice-presidency. All other officers retained their positions.

Colonel Waller had been active in the affairs of the National Rifle Association since long before World War I. He had started his competitive shooting career in 1906 at the Marine Corps Barracks in Norfolk, Virginia, where his father at that time was a Colonel in Command. In 1908, teamed with then-Captain Thomas Holcomb, he helped win the two-man team match in Peking, China. In 1913, he and Thomas Holcomb had shot together as members of the Marine Corps Team in the National Matches, and Waller finished second in the National Individual Rifle Match. In the same year, he was a member of the Palma Team. He organized and captained the American Free-rifle Team that defeated the Swiss at Milan in 1922, and in 1925 he was captain of the International and Olympic Rifle Teams in France.

Target shooting was only one of Colonel Waller's many interests. He was an all-around hunter—big game, waterfowl, upland birds—and a skeet and trap shot of national prominence. He was also a past treasurer of the American Game Association.

In addition to these varied interests, Colonel Waller brought to the presidency of the NRA a broad personal knowledge of the practical value of marksmanship. After his service in China, he had seen action at Vera Cruz in 1914 and had distinguished himself as a battalion commander with the Second Marine Division in France. His decorations included the Navy Cross, Purple Heart, French Legion of Honor, and Croix de Guerre with three palms.

The two guest speakers at the members' banquet in 1939 were Brig. Gen. H. A. Pickert, Commissioner of Police of Detroit, Michigan, who urged the training of citizens in small arms marksmanship as an aid in law enforcement; and Brig. Gen. George C. Marshall, Deputy Chief of Staff of the Army, whose themes were the importance of the foot soldier to national defense and the value of the NRA program in developing trained riflemen capable of springing to the defense of America.

Approaching war clouds cast their shadow over the shooting program of 1939 as the shelter of isolationism behind which America had sought refuge showed glaring holes. France and Great Britain were beginning to stiffen their backbones against Nazi aggressions, and the United States was moving slowly into a posture of defense. A Pershing Trophy Match against the British, planned early in 1939, was nearly cancelled. Bisley in the summer of 1939 was being used to train British troops. The Miniature Rifle Association of Great Britain, however, was able to obtain use of the Ham and Petersham Range on the outskirts of London, and scheduled the Third International Smallbore Match for July 9, one week earlier than originally planned.

The American team that year was one of the strongest smallbore teams ever sent abroad. Its members were selected from the eighty high-

This residence at 1600 Rhode Island Avenue, Washington, became the headquarters of the NRA in January, 1939.

ranking shooters in the NRA tournaments in a final competition that involved shooting the Dewar Course twice in succession. Captained by Dr. Russell Gardner, with Ralph McGarity as Team Adjutant, and J. C. Lippencott, Jr., as Team Coach, it consisted of William Schweitzer, Jr., R. C. Pope, J. O. Miller, Merle Israelson, Carl Jackson, Charles Hamby, Carl Frank, Harold Allyn, John Wark, and R. D. Triggs, with Willis Kenyon and R. C. Berkheister as alternates. Gardner, Schweitzer, and Israelson were veterans of the 1937 team. Bill Woodring, who had won the National championship three years in a row, qualified but was unable to leave the United States because of business commitments. The Americans, after twice losing the earlier matches by a margin of 2 points, won the match by 3950 to 3831.

Part of this success was attributable to British sportsmanship. In the earlier matches, they had selected their shooters just before the competition, throwing against the Americans men who were at the peak of their form. Someone in the British Association suggested that this gave them an unfair advantage over the Americans, who had to be selected weeks before the event. So, in 1939, the Pershing Team for Great Britain was selected at the same time as the American, eliminating whatever advantage this time factor may have given.

But Colonel Waller had other ideas of the reason for the American victory. At the traditional farewell ceremony in honor of the team before its embarkation for England, Colonel Waller presented Dr. Gardner with a small pocket knife. While captain of the American International Rifle Teams in Italy, France, and Switzerland, he had carried the same knife. While his team was shooting, he had relieved the tension by whittling on a bit of wood. When he whittled, the team seemed to shoot at its best; when he stopped, their shots wandered out of the black. When he forgot to carry the knife, his team lost. But when he carried it, his shooters invariably won, even when pitted against the superlative free-riflemen of Switzerland.

Col. L. W. T. Waller, NRA president (1939-1941).

On the Ham and Petersham Range, Doctor Gardner tried Colonel Waller's magic whittling knife on a "lucky" tent peg donated by Asst. DCM Maj. G. G. Parks, USA. As the shavings curled from the steel, the American team, bucking cloudy, blustery weather, shot as no comparable team had ever shot before, winning by 19 points. Schweitzer rolled up a high score of 398, and the average for the ten shooters was 395 per man for a total only 50 points short of a perfect 4000. More important factors of course contributed to the American victory, and if there may be some sort of moral to the knife story, it might be that anything which reduces tension and inspires confidence is useful in competitive shooting.

Whatever his sentiments about the effectiveness of his "whittling stick," Colonel Waller publicly acknowledged the sportsmanship of the British in permitting the two teams to shoot on an equal basis. In this spirit of good feeling, he, on behalf of the NRA, invited the British to come to Camp Perry in the following year to try to regain the Pershing Trophy. This return match failed to materialize. By August, 1940, Great Britain was shooting for her life.

# American Gunowners Help

# NRA Contributions to the

Between 1934 and September, 1939, the world, like an old lady crossing a river on ice cakes, had jumped awkwardly from crisis to crisis. During these years, Hitler, in defiance and contempt of the former Allies, rearmed Germany, reoccupied the Rhineland, occupied the Sudetenland and carved up Austria and Czechoslovakia. Mussolini sent bombers and machine guns against the spears of Haile Selassie's warriors of Ethiopia. The war lords of Japan launched their armies against China and bombed and sank the U. S. gunboat "Panay." The rest of the world cringed before these bullies and debated what, if anything, to do about them.

No one who attended the National Matches of 1939 would ever forget them. Halfway through the program, on September 1, word arrived that Hitler had invaded Poland, and World War II was on. Eight days later, President Roosevelt signed an order declaring a limited national emergency; from that point on the course of life of every American was changed. Many of the National Guardsmen and reservists among 4000 spectators on the field at Camp Perry left soon afterward for active duty. The matches themselves suddenly took on an added urgency. Feelings of concern for the international situation were tempered by confidence as the eight-man rifle team of the U. S. Marine Corps ran up a perfect score in the Herrick Match and the Infantry won the National Team Championship. The Marines, in making their record-shattering score of 800 at 1000 yards, placed 160 shots in the five ring and 123 of these in the V!

There was also unexpected and subdued drama in the Rhenish-Westphalian Smallbore Team Match, which was shot on September 3, 1939. This match had been introduced after World War I as a goodwill gesture by former enemies of the United States. The posted scores read: "United States, 3971; Great Britain, 3921; Germany, not reporting." On September 2, the American Dewar Team defeated the British. These were the last major

# to Rearm Britain

# War Effort

**21**

international rifle competitions until the close of the war.

Col. Oliver S. Wood served as executive officer of the National Matches that year, assisted by Maj. Francis W. Parker, Jr., in charge of the smallbore program and Maj. Merritt Edson, USMC, as assistant range director. Col. Francis C. Endicott, USA, who had served for several years as executive officer of the National Matches, had been appointed Director of Civilian Marksmanship and executive officer of the National Board for the Promotion of Rifle Practice.

The Matches of 1939 were marked by a continued acceleration of the handgun program. The NRA Grand Aggregate Pistol Match, similar in principle to the Critchfield (.22 caliber) and Wright Memorial (.30 caliber) Aggregate Matches, was first shot in that year. The winner was determined by his aggregate score in eight matches.

Another innovation in 1939 was the advent of the M1 (Garand) Rifle on the range at Camp Perry, although none was used in active competition. As America debated its future role in the rapidly developing hostilities abroad, only 200 of these rifles were available for "instruction only" at Camp Perry on the eve of World War II.

At its meeting in 1939, the Executive Committee voted to open a new series of international pistol matches as a feature of the Pan-American Exposition. The team, selected on the basis of performance in the NRA Registered Pistol Tournaments, consisted of Alfred Hemming, Emmet Jones, Harry Reeves, Corp. G. Huddleston, USA, Walter Walsh of the Federal Bureau of Investigation, Harold Cline, and Norman Adair, with

The M1 (Garand) rifle made its appearance at Camp Perry for the first time in 1939.

past NRA president Karl T. Frederick as Team Captain. American participation was largely in response to the interest shown by Mexico in sending to Camp Perry a team representing the Mexico City Police.

The Matches were shot in Mexico City on February 17-19, 1940. They were won by Mexico which handed the United States its first major loss in the Pan-American pistol competition. Cuba and Canada, the other two entries, placed third and fourth.

It took two years and Pearl Harbor to bring America into direct involvement in World War II. But the presence of the war brought many changes in the program and personnel of the National Rifle Association, as it did in all American organizations and institutions. "Preparedness" and "defense," rather than neutrality and non-involvement, became the watchwords of America. When the NRA met in Washington on February 2, 1940, the Board of Directors and 225 members heard Assistant Secretary of War Louis Johnson and Chief of Staff General George C. Marshall endorse the program of the National Rifle Association as a major factor in preparing the United States to meet threatened dangers. This was the second banquet of the NRA addressed by General Marshall in two years.

Secretary of War Johnson awarded Number 1 ranking insignia to Alfred Hemming and to William B. Woodring in recognition of their respective championships in the pistol and small-bore rifle tournaments. Hemming, in 101 times over the National Pistol Course, had an average of 95.63; Woodring in shooting the Dewar Course 42 times, averaged 99.65. Those attending the meeting that year were given a conducted tour of the newly opened museum in the new NRA Headquarters. At that time it contained 250 items representing the development of firearms and a number of valuable weapons of historic interest.

The first of many important changes in personnel in the NRA staff occurred with the death on April 15, 1940, of Herbert Goebel, who had joined in 1926 when the organization assumed operation of the Winchester Junior Rifle Corps Program. In addition to the youth program, Goebel at the time of his death was in charge of Club Services. Responsibility for the youth program fell on Goebel's assistant, C. Richard Rogers, who had become a member of the staff in 1937; Evan Lloyd, the office manager, assumed temporary charge of the Senior Club Division. Three months later, on July 1, 1940, J. Russell Lent was engaged as the new director of the Senior Club Division.

J. Russell Lent, at the time of his appoint-

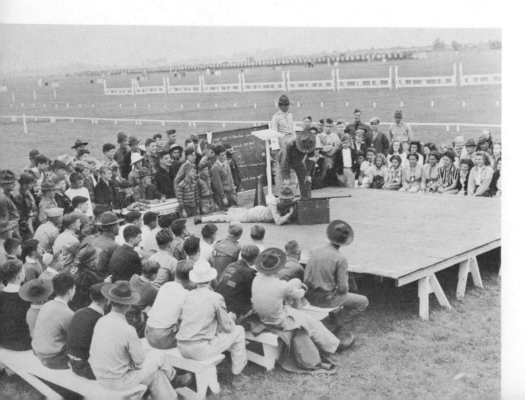

As shadows of war deepened, young men and women gave serious attention to instruction in handling firearms.

ment, was president of the Connecticut State Rifle and Pistol Association and a director of the NRA. In February, 1940, he had been elected to the Executive Committee but resigned this post when he became a member of the office staff. The vacancy in the Executive Committee was filled on July 6, 1940, by the election to the Committee of Fred C. Mills, National Safety Director of the Boy Scouts of America.

The last full-schedule National Matches before America entered World War II were held in 1940 largely because of the personal interest of Gen. George C. Marshall, a man who was not swayed by arguments that the role of the rifleman had been totally eclipsed by the long-range bomber and the armored tank. Except for his intercession, the National Matches might well have been cancelled. Many of the National Guard units were on active duty, and extensive joint maneuvers were to be held in Louisiana during the summer, overlapping the scheduled dates of the National Matches, August 18 through September 7. No federal troops would be available for range duty during this period. If the matches were postponed, school, collegiate, and ROTC teams could not attend.

General Marshall personally requested the advice of General Reckord in resolving this dilemma. Rather than accept outright cancellation, General Reckord, supported by Col. F. C. Endicott, executive officer of the National Board, and Col. Oliver S. Wood, executive officer-designate of the National Matches, agreed to a postponement to September 1 through 21. This eliminated all schools and eighteen ROTC units that had planned to send teams to Camp Perry, but most of the National Guard and federal military organizations participated. The program had already been curtailed by the cancellation of the RWS and Fidac Matches, and the conduct of the Dewar and International Pistol Matches remained in doubt.

Although attendance was smaller than usual, the participants of the National Matches made

C. Richard Rogers, administrative assistant, a member of the NRA staff since 1937, contributed greatly to the research and compilation of this book as secretary to the NRA History Committee.

up in serious dedication what they lacked in numbers The United States Infantry won the National Team Match with the highest score made in fifteen years; the superb handgunners of the Detroit Police again ran away with most of the pistol trophies, breaking the standing police team record by 35 points. Harry Reeves clinched his firm grip on the NRA all-around pistol championship and set a new Camp Perry record for .45 caliber timed-fire.

The only international event in the Camp Perry program of 1940 was a two-way competition with the Canadians in the Dewar Cup Match. The reason for the lack of participation by the British was obvious; England was reeling under the German *blitzkrieg* and facing triumphant German armies across the narrow moat of the English Channel.

After Dunkirk, only the British Navy, a pitifully outnumbered RAF, and twenty miles of water separated Great Britain from defeat. Practically all of the arms and equipment of the British Expeditionary Force had been destroyed

Lt. Col. N. C. Nash, Jr., NRA president (1941-1942).

New York City, established the American Committee for the Defense of British Homes. The most conspicuous advertisement in the November, 1940, issue of *The American Rifleman* was a full-page notice requesting all members of the National Rifle Association to send pistols, rifles, shotguns, and binoculars to the embattled British. "Send a gun to defend a British home," the notice urged in bold type. "British civilians, faced with the threat of invasion, desperately need arms for the defense of their homes." The grim plight of the British was emphasized by a direct appeal to NRA members by a British military spokesman: "Send us anything that shoots," he pleaded.

The American Committee for the Defense of British Homes collected more than 1500 rifles and pistols and 100,000 rounds of ammunition, mostly from members of the NRA, by the end of the following December. Before the emergency passed, the National Rifle Association alone collected more than 7000 small arms for shipment to England to rearm the police and Home Guard units of the embattled kingdom. All of this equipment was given to Britain without compensation.

The urgency and value of the small arms shipments to beleaguered Britain can best be judged from these words of Winston Churchill: "When the ships from America approached our shores with their priceless arms, special trains were waiting in all the ports to receive their cargoes. The Home Guard in every county, in every town, in every village, sat up all through

or abandoned at Dunkirk. Although the "Miracle of Dunkirk" had snatched 338,226 troops from the jaws of Hitler's panzers, most of the survivors disembarked without even their rifles.

Every usable weapon, regardless of its age or condition, had been collected for use in the defense of British soil. Shotguns, sporting rifles, and pocket pistols were the standard armament of many Home Guard units assigned to front-line duty along the English Channel. There were few of even these arms; anti-firearms regulations adopted before World War I had all but disarmed the British civilian.

At the height of this threat a group of American citizens, headed by C. Suydam Cutting of

The William Randolph Hearst Rifle Trophy is a Seventeenth-Century flintlock inlaid with ivory and pearl and is awarded to the ROTC or service academy competitor making the highest score in the National Trophy Individual Rifle Match.

the nights to receive them. Men and women worked day and night making them fit for use. By the end of July we were an armed nation, so far as parachute or airborne landings were concerned. We had become a 'hornet's nest.' Anyhow, if we had to go down fighting (which I did not anticipate), a lot of our men and some women had weapons in their hands . . ."

The war hung heavily over the deliberations of the Board of Directors of the NRA at its meeting on February 7, 1941, in the Mayflower Hotel in Washington. Colonel Waller was absent on foreign duty with the Marine Corps, and General Reckord had asked that he be relieved of his duties as executive vice-president, since he had been ordered to active duty as commanding general of the Twenty-ninth Division at Fort George G. Meade, Maryland. At this meeting Col. Nathaniel C. Nash, Jr., succeeded Colonel Waller as president, and Judge Hilliard Comstock was elected vice-president. Colonel Nash, an old-time rifleman and for many years a leader of the very active Massachusetts State Rifle Association, was an officer of the Massachusetts National Guard. Judge Comstock, of the Superior Court of California, became the first officer of the National Rifle Association from the west coast. As the retiring president, Colonel Waller was elected to the Executive Council.

At the request of General Reckord, the Board of Directors conferred on C. B. Lister the necessary executive powers to carry on in the absence of the executive vice-president. The Executive Committee also confirmed the elevation of L. Q. Bradley from the post of director of membership to assistant secretary and the appointment in 1940 of Frank C. Daniel as office manager. Before adjourning, the Board of Directors voted to offer to the government of the United States free and unrestricted use of 3500 rifle and pistol ranges owned or controlled by its affiliated clubs. The national emergency had already curtailed much of the NRA shoot-

ing program. Sale of surplus military weapons had been suspended and the issue of ammunition by the DCM cut off.

During 1941, changes in personnel in the headquarters staff came rapidly. Fred Hakenjos, executive assistant, who had joined the staff in 1934, resigned to accept a position with the Hercules Powder Company under Col. Henry N. Marsh. By the end of 1941, nearly half of the members of the staff, including Office Manager Frank C. Daniel, were on leave of absence or preparing to leave for duty with the Armed Services. On April 1, 1941, L. J. Hathaway, who had served as editor of *The American Rifleman* for fourteen years, resigned for reasons of health, and William F. Shadel, head of the Publicity Bureau, became the new editor.

As America drifted closer to war, the National Rifle Association searched for its most appropriate role in the national emergency. It began by

Judge Hilliard Comstock, NRA president (1942-1944).

developing a series of 16 mm. films on small-arms marksmanship. Master prints of these films were later made available to the Army Service Forces, Army Air Force, and Navy and Coast Guard, from which hundreds of prints were made for distribution to training centers. Its film on pistol marksmanship was the only one of its kind available during World War II.

In anticipation of the national need for trained riflemen, the NRA developed a preinduction Smallbore Service Course based on the .22 caliber rifle. The targets followed the standard military qualification course with the 200-yard .30 caliber targets reduced to a 50-foot scale. The course included ten shots standing, ten shots kneeling or sitting, ten shots prone in slow fire, and two five-shot strings of rapid fire, each with a forty-second time limit. By the end of the war the NRA had conducted 2862 preinduction training classes in 1278 communities, providing training for 158,956 men.

In spite of the rising international crisis, the National Matches were scheduled to be held on August 31 through September 7, 1941.

Through the interest of Col. F. C. Endicott, the federal government helped defray the expenses of two high-scoring members from each of the state organizations affiliated with the NRA. With troops in training and the use of military ammunition curtailed, the .30 caliber championship was cancelled. Under the circumstances the NRA made tentative plans for the annual smallbore matches to be shot at the L. A. Young range at Detroit and the pistol matches on the Ohio State Rifle Association's range at Mount Giliad. However, efforts to get the use of Camp Perry for the matches finally succeeded, and 481 pistol shooters and 700 smallbore marksmen competed on this familiar acreage. The Detroit Police again carried away most of the honors in the handgun competition; Harry Reeves again won the all-around pistol championship, and Alfred Hemming, his teammate, the .22 caliber championship.

On September 6, 1941, at its annual members' meeting, the National Rifle Association publicly offered its services to the nation through Fiorello H. LaGuardia, Director of Civilian Defense. In reply to its resolution offering its cooperation, LaGuardia replied: "I believe the members of your Association can contribute substantially by enrolling and participating in the auxiliary police and other civilian defense forces now being established by the local and state governments."

In response to this suggestion, the NRA immediately launched a training program for members of the Home Guards which the states were organizing to replace National Guard units ordered into federal service.

Direct American intervention in World War II, with the bombing of Pearl Harbor on December 7, 1941, found the National Rifle Association already geared to the national emergency. It voted to curtail for the duration all competitive shooting, including the scheduled Pan-American Games, and recommended that all arms and ammunition available be used for training civilian defense organizations and members of the Armed Services. It sent a letter to the chairman of each state civilian defense agency offering the services and facilities of its state affiliates. It also launched a training program geared to teach marksmanship to a million men.

In February, 1942, Colonel Nash submitted his resignation as president for reasons of health and was elected to the Executive Council. Judge Hilliard Comstock then took the reins of the presidency. Thurman Randle, one of America's highest-ranking smallbore shooters, was elected vice-president. Randle, when not engaged in shooting, was a leading sporting goods dealer in Dallas, Texas.

Under C. B. Lister, the staff of the NRA, riddled with calls to service, worked unceasingly to carry out its important program. One of its first steps was to develop a pistol training manual for use by plant guards and auxiliary policemen. This was followed by publications on plant protection and the use of shotguns for guard duty. Two thousand each of these manuals were printed and distributed through Civilian Defense offices during the war. In conjunction with its preinduction training program, it printed and donated 20,000 manuals on instruction in small arms marksmanship. In May, 1942, it launched a campaign to collect serviceable M1917 and M1903 rifles from its members and other citizens for donation or resale at cost to the Army; through its affiliated clubs it established 200 offices where arms offered under this program could be inspected. Most of the weapons collected were used by the War Department for arming internal security units. Late in 1942, it offered the services of its members and affiliated clubs in handloading ammunition for use by plant guards. On November 23, 1942, the Provost Marshal General issued to managers of war plants a special circular, Paragraph 3d of which stated: "It may be possible for plants to make arrangements for reloading by members of the National Rifle Association. Inquiries on available facilities should be directed to the National Rifle Association, 1600 Rhode Island Avenue, Washington, D. C., with full details on the types of ammunition to be reloaded."

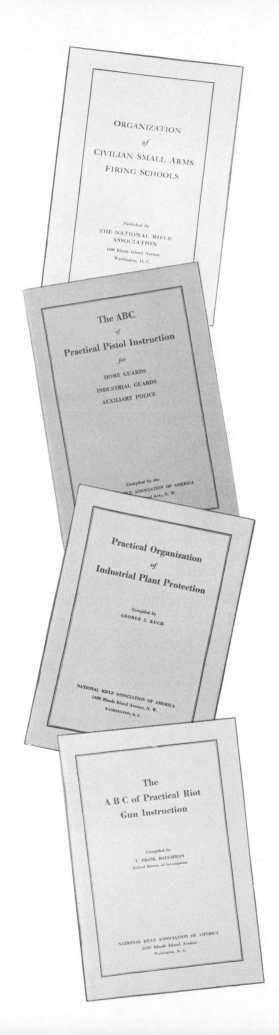

247

Gen. Thomas Holcomb, USMC, an expert marksman who for many years was connected with NRA activities.

Thurman Randle, vice-president of the NRA, entered the Navy with the rank of lieutenant commander in 1942 and was assigned to duty at the Sachuest Range of the Newport Naval Training Station with a staff of junior officers under his command. All were members of the NRA. They were among 300 key small-arms instructors selected by and recruited from the NRA during the war by the Army Service Forces, Navy, and the Army Air Force. Both Randle and Col. Francis W. Parker, Jr., who became National Rifle Association president and vice-president, respectively, for 1944 and 1945, served out their terms on active service.

The program of the National Rifle Association in these years was devoted almost entirely to the war effort. C. B. Lister, in charge of the office activities in the absence of General Reckord, carried on under increasing difficulties. Eleven of the officers and staff members had entered the Armed Services by the spring of 1944, when the Allies stood poised for their leap across the English Channel. Then William F.

Shadel, the editor of *The American Rifleman*, received his credentials as a war correspondent for the Columbia Broadcasting System and shipped to England to cover the invasion. His duties as editor were assumed by Associate Editors C. M. Palmer, Jr., and E. B. Mann. *The American Rifleman* featured articles by Shadel, based on personal experiences and interviews, up until the end of the war. Other worries faced Lister by this time. There was a serious paper shortage and quality paper, severely rationed in 1943, became almost impossible to obtain in 1944. The size of *The American Rifleman* had to be cut almost in half, and mail deliveries were delayed as the tempo of the war increased.

In spite of these difficulties, the remaining staff carried on an active program, furnishing range construction plans to contractors for the Armed Forces and to camp and station commanders. The staff and affiliated clubs in the Washington area conducted special small-arms instruction classes for more than 700 Army and Navy reserve officers and served as technical advisors to the War Production Board in situations having to do with small arms and ammunition.

Yet, faced with these additional duties and mounting problems, the staff managed to mail *The American Rifleman* on schedule every month. During this period, in part because the poor paper available reproduced photographs poorly and partly because of a shortage of photographic supplies, it made wider use of art work. Pulitzer prize-winner, James T. Berryman, joined the staff as art director in January, 1943, and the pages of *The American Rifleman* sparkled with his animated drawings for many years. The articles reflected the nature of the times. Most of the type in each issue was devoted to discussions of American and foreign ordnance, narratives of the front-line fighting in Europe by Bill Shadel, letters from servicemen and interviews with or articles by prominent soldiers, marine or naval heroes. In an exclusive interview published in January, 1944, in *The American Rifleman,* Gen. Alexander A. Vandergrift, successor to General Holcomb as Commandant of the United States Marine Corps, stated: "The rifle is the basic weapon of the Marine Corps."

General Holcomb, who had been actively associated with the National Rifle Association since the turn of the century, had been appointed by President Roosevelt to be U. S. Minister to the Union of South Africa. Upon his retirement as Commandant of the Marine Corps, he had become the first Marine to wear the four stars of a general.

The conduct of the annual meeting of the Board of Directors in the headquarters building in Washington on February 2 and 3, 1945, reflected the intensity of the national war effort. Only twenty-one members of the Board attended, and the meeting was brief. The Board did little more than go through the formality of re-electing the incumbent slate of officers and pass a resolution endorsing the enactment of the Universal Military Service Bill, then being debated by Congress.

The most important actions of direct concern to the organization were the establishment of a postwar contingency fund and authorization of the establishment of branch offices in various sections of the country. The first of these opened one month later in Elkhart, Indiana, under the direction of W. Dow Smith.

This was one of the few meetings that General Reckord had missed since his election to the office of executive vice-president. After relinquishing command of the Twenty-ninth Division, he had become the first National Guard officer to be appointed a commander of an

Lt. Comdr. Thurman Randle, NRA president (1944-1946).

Army Corps Area. He served as Commanding General of the Third Corps Area for two years and then was ordered to Great Britain and assigned to the staff of the Supreme Headquarters of the Army Expeditionary Force. During the war he won his second and third Distinguished Service Medals; his second Croix de Guerre with Palm; a Bronze Star; the British decoration, Knight Commander of the Order of the Bath; and the French Legion of Honor.

By the summer of 1945, with Germany beaten, the outcome of the war was no longer in doubt. The questions were, how long would it take and what would it cost to bring the remaining members of the Axis to their knees. Then in the mornings of August 6 and 9, 1945, Hiroshima and Nagasaki dissolved under mushroom-shaped clouds. Less than a week later, on August 14, Japan sued for surrender.

In the National Rifle Association, as in every other segment of American life, it was a time to remember well the lessons of the past and to plan wisely for the future.

# 22

# Rapidly Expanding Membership—
# Administration,    Procedures,

With the end of the war and the beginning of demobilization, the staff members, officers, and directors of the National Rifle Association who had seen active military service began to filter back. Many had attained high ranks and had won distinguished honors. At least three prominent members—Brig. Gen. Merritt A. Edson and Col. D. M. Shoup of the United States Marine Corps and Comdr. John D. Bulkeley of the Navy—wore the star-studded, pale-blue ribbon of the Congressional Medal of Honor.

Organizations do not receive medals, but the work of the NRA during the recent war did not go without official notice. On November 14, 1945, President Harry S. Truman sent this letter to the National Rifle Association:

> The tradition of the citizen soldiery is firmly, and properly, imbedded in our national ideals. Initiative, discipline, and skill in the use of small arms are essentials for the development of the finished citizen soldier.
>
> The National Rifle Association, in the periods between our last four wars, has done much to encourage the improvement of small arms and of small arms marksmanship in the regular services, as well as in the National Guard, reserve units, and the civilian population.
>
> During the war just ended, the contributions of the Association in the matter of small-

arms training aids, the nation-wide preinduction training program, the recruiting of experienced small-arms instructors for all branches of the armed services, and technical advice and assistance to Government civilian agencies aiding in the prosecution of the war—all contributed freely and without expense to the Government—have materially aided our war effort.

> I hope that the splendid program which the National Rifle Association has followed during the past three-quarters of a century will be continued. It is a program that is good for a free America.

Similar letters of commendation were received from General George C. Marshall, Chief of Staff, and from Fleet Admiral Ernest J. King, Chief of Naval Operations. General Marshall wrote in part on October 30, 1945:

> The record of the National Rifle Association during the war has been one in which its members should take great pride. The nation is fortunate in having such an organization upon which it can rely for the continued development of proficiency in the use of small arms by the citizens of this country.

Admiral King, on November 1, 1945, wrote:

> The Navy places strong emphasis upon the importance of proper instruction in the use of small arms as a fundamental in training for

# Changes in and Bylaws

President Harry S. Truman, recognizing the important role played by the NRA in the war effort, thoughtfully sent a letter voicing the nation's appreciation.

naval gunnery. When we were compelled to enter the war in 1941, the need for greatly increased training facilities and well trained officers and men in the use of small arms became more and more urgent.

The problems we faced in connection with meeting this need were many. The National Rifle Association of America came to our assistance with facilities and expert instruction, which proved invaluable to our small-arms program. Such assistance, rendered willingly and unstintingly in the interests of our country, is deserving of the highest praise and is sincerely appreciated by the Navy.

By the early months of 1946, nearly all of the staff members on active service during the war had reported back for duty. Maj. Gen. Milton A. Reckord had reassumed his duties as executive vice-president in December, 1945, and immediately reorganized the staff and program for an expected period of postwar growth. Secretary-Treasurer C. B. Lister relinquished the emergency executive power that he had been granted for the duration of the war but retained editorship of *The American Rifleman.*

The Seventy-fifth Annual Meeting of the National Rifle Association, held at the Statler Hotel in Washington, D. C., in February, 1946, was the first peacetime meeting in four years. The "Diamond Jubilee" banquet was attended by

no fewer than thirty-four general officers of the Army and Marine Corps, by many admirals and a large representation from both houses of Congress. The principal speaker was General of the Army Dwight D. Eisenhower, who stated: "An organization such as the National Rifle Association of America, utterly selfless in its aims, can do more than any other single group in achieving the cooperation we need [to maintain world peace]."

In its business session the Board of Directors elected Col. Francis W. Parker, Jr., as president. Colonel Parker, with Comdr. Thurman Randle, his predecessor as president, had served out all but a few months of his two-year term as vice-president on active wartime duty with the Armed Forces. Colonel Parker, a patent lawyer in Chicago, has been continually active in the councils of the NRA since 1922, serving on the Board of Directors, the Executive Committee, and the Executive Council.

Maj. Gen. Julian S. Hatcher, USA, resigned from the Board of Directors to accept

251

Col. Francis W. Parker, Jr., NRA president (1946-1948).

appointment as head of an enlarged Technical Division in NRA headquarters. General Hatcher, who had retired as Chief of Field Service of the Army Ordnance Department and who had served as coeditor of the "Dope Bag" in *The American Rifleman* from 1922 to 1931, was a leading authority on small arms in the United States. In appointing General Hatcher to head the Technical Division, the Board accepted the resignation of Fred C. Ness, who had been a member of the "Dope Bag" staff for eighteen years. It also established a field office at Tulsa, Oklahoma, under the direction of Ray B. Whitaker, an outstanding tournament shooter and an active participant in the programs of the American Legion and the Veterans of Foreign Wars.

With authority from the Board, General Hatcher built an outstanding technical staff, retaining A. H. (Al) Barr, and transferring J. L. Murphy from his post in the Club Activities program. Murphy had joined the NRA staff in October, 1944. He was a trained architect and a specialist in the construction of rifle and pistol

ranges and clubhouses. General Hatcher also employed John S. Rose, who held a degree in wildlife management from Ohio State University and was in his own right an outstanding marksman, having won the National CMTC-ROTC rifle championship in 1939 (Citizens Military Training Corps-Reserve Officers Training Corps).

Rounding out General Hatcher's technical staff was Edwards "Pete" Brown, Jr., recently released from his duties as a lieutenant commander with the Navy Bureau of Ordnance. Before the war he had been a member of the technical staff of the Western Cartridge Company, specializing in ballistics. He had won major events in three National Matches, had served as a member of the RWS Team of 1937 and as coach of the 1938 U. S. Dewar Team.

The immediate postwar growth of the National Rifle Association under the leadership of General Reckord, C. B. Lister, and their staff was almost phenomenal. In August, 1945, the NRA had 86,000 members; one year later the membership totaled 155,000; by the time another year rolled around membership passed the quarter-million mark, and affiliated clubs totaled 4800.

In spite of this growth, recreational shooting consisted primarily of anticipation of the future. All of America's arms and ammunition plants had converted to the production of military materiel; and retooling was a long and slow process. Stocks of sporting ammunition of all kinds were at all-time lows, and no military ammunition had been authorized for release through the DCM. In December, 1945, Col. Emerald F. (Tod) Sloan, Director of Civilian Marksmanship, and a member of the Executive Committee of the NRA, announced that wartime restrictions on the activity of his office had been lifted. He released several thousand surplus Model 1903 and M1917 rifles, but the flood of applications forced him to suspend sales a few weeks later.

For a while it appeared that there would be no National Matches at all in 1946. Camp Perry, during the war, had been federalized and converted to a prisoner-of-war camp. In the spring of 1946 it was still on a caretaker status pending a decision on its disposal by the War Department. Most of its once-fine ranges were dotted with the barracks and houses of its former involuntary tenants. Largely through the intercession of Brig. Gen. Sidney Hinds and Colonel Sloan, executive officer of the National Board, the smallbore and pistol phases of the National Matches were shot between August 31 and September 8, 1946. The National Rifle Association paid the travel expenses of eighty shooters, five from each regional tournament.

Facilities at Perry that year were at a subsistence level. The clubhouse was closed; there was no junior camp because of the late dates during which Camp Perry was available; and there were no facilities at the camp for family housing. In spite of these handicaps, there was a great enthusiasm among those who attended and great hope for the future. Even with a restricted program and limited facilities, the fact that Camp Perry was back in operation with the first peacetime rifle matches in years was enough to kindle a great feeling of satisfaction.

Harry Reeves, freshly back from duty in China with the Marines, demonstrated his amazing skill by winning the national pistol championship for the third consecutive time;

As a military commander and as President, Dwight D. Eisenhower has always shown an approving interest in the services of the National Rifle Association.

but much of the drama came in the smallbore rifle events.

Garrett Wayne Moore of Washington, Pennsylvania, handicapped by an artificial leg and a borrowed rifle, walked away with the National Smallbore Championship. But the hit of the rifle events was Arthur E. Cook of Washington, D. C., whose small stature and round boyish face belied his eighteen years. Shooting with a case of hay fever so serious that he was half-blinded, he placed tenth in a field that included such great marksmen as Moore, Carlson, Schweitzer, and Triggs in the National Smallbore Championship. In winning the Junior Championship he became a member of the coveted "400 Club." Then in the International Dewar Match, he helped the United States run up a score of 7949 with a personal score of 399 in defeating Great Britain and Canada in the first major international rifle match since 1941.

At the annual meetings held in Washington in February, 1947, General Reckord was formally elected vice-president and treasurer. In

253

Maj. Gen. Julian S. Hatcher, one of the leading authorities of America in weaponry, was long an influential and highly respected member of the NRA staff.

C. B. Lister, a man who handled many jobs in the administrative work of the NRA and helped to keep it moving forward in difficult times.

assuming these responsibilities, he relinquished some of his administrative duties to C. B. Lister, who, while retaining his post as secretary, became the first officially designated executive director of the Association.

The mushroom-like growth of the NRA after the war forced a further expansion and reorganization of the managerial staff. By 1947 there were three assistant secretaries—each specializing in a particular field—L. Q. Bradley, membership; Frank L. Wyman, club activities; and Maj. Gen. Julian S. Hatcher, technical. John Scofield, whose father had been an associate editor of *The American Rifleman* in its early days, succeeded to the post of managing editor in May, 1947, and John A. Harper replaced him as associate editor.

The NRA voted to assist the National Skeet Shooting Association in 1947. The skeet organization was reorganized and incorporated in June of 1947 under the laws of the state of Delaware as a nonprofit organization. Its officers were John A. LaFore, Jr., president; Alex H. Kerr, vice-president; C. B. Lister, secretary-treasurer; and Col. E. F. Sloan, manager. Its

254

operating offices were next to the headquarters building of the NRA in space which NRA owned.

Intercollegiate shooting competition was resumed for the first time since 1940 in a match conducted in twelve locations across the country on March 29, 1947. University of Maryland shooters, led by Arthur E. Cook, broke the previous record established in 1940 by the University of Iowa. Cook was Number One on the All-American First Team in 1947 with the highest rating ever achieved by a collegiate rifleman.

By 1947, with the restoration of production of sporting arms and ammunition, the shooting program picked up momentum. But there were still no .30 caliber events in the National Matches held at Camp Perry in August of 1947. As in 1946, only the smallbore rifle and pistol events were shot.

Although the housing conditions were improved they were still below standards. But more than 700 competitors from every state were on the field. Through the interest of Gen. A. A. Vandergrift, Marines served as support personnel of the National Matches.

Young Arthur E. Cook was again the sensation of the smallbore events, cracking the old Camp Perry record over the 50-yard Iron Sight Course with a 400-36X, six Xs better than the old mark. Jack Lacey of New Haven, Connecticut, equalled Cook's score but was outranked for first place. Defending champion G. Wayne Moore and Charles C. Whipple each had perfect 400s with 35 Xs and 33 Xs respectively at this distance—all better than the

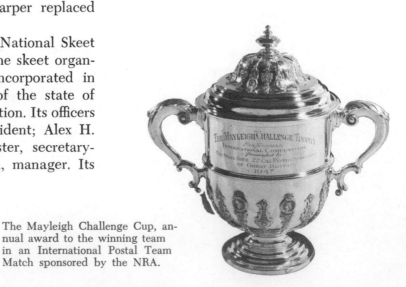

The Mayleigh Challenge Cup, annual award to the winning team in an International Postal Team Match sponsored by the NRA.

earlier record. On the second day, Moore dropped to third place. Then in one of the most dramatic finishes in a Camp Perry Match, Moore pulled up from behind on August 7 to retain his National Smallbore Championship with the highest aggregate score ever recorded at Camp Perry—3194 out of a possible 3200.

The big surprise in the pistol matches was the unseating of Harry Reeves as National Pistol Champion by S/Sgt. Huelet L. (Joe) Benner, USA, of Fort Knox, Kentucky.

Lady shooters placed high in both the smallbore and the pistol events. Mrs. Adelaide McCord won the women's title for the fourth consecutive year, but she received heavy competition from Elinor Bell of Los Angeles, a newcomer at Camp Perry, and from little sixteen-year-old Audrey Bockman, the new Junior Smallbore Champion, who finished only 3 points below the champion in the final tally.

Punching holes in targets was not the only activity to receive major NRA attention, and in 1946 and 1947 the NRA began to place more emphasis on developing programs for the hunters, many of whom had little interest in target shooting. Early in 1947 the Technical Division began collecting information from hunters to determine the most efficient deer rifle and load, and the most effective placement of the shot. More than 4500 deer hunters

Dr. Emmet O. Swanson, NRA president (1948-1949).

returned reports that included anatomical diagrams of deer. An analysis of the material by John S. Rose showed that at that time, the .30-06 with 180-grain loads was being used by more deer hunters than all other cartridges combined.

In addition to this survey the expanded interest of the National Rifle Association in the hunting sportsman was evident in an increased number of articles on deer and other big-game loads, conversions of military weapons to hunting use, shotguns, sportsmanship, and gun safety in the field. Some of the most experienced hunters in North America were regular contributors to *The American Rifleman*.

In early 1948 General Reckord elected to retain his dual offices of executive vice-president and treasurer. Dr. Emmet O. Swanson of Minneapolis, at forty-two, then became the youngest president in the history of the NRA. Dr. Swanson, a dentist by profession, had been a member of two international rifle teams and was one of the ranking smallbore marksmen in the world. The new vice-president was Maj. Gen. Merritt A. Edson, USMC, who, as the leader of Edson's Raiders that spearheaded the attack at Guadal-

255

Frank L. Wyman, whose special talents for organization and field operations have earned for him a high place in the NRA hall of fame.

Huelet L. (Joe) Benner, a great pistol champion who with Harry Reeves could always be counted on to be a top contender in any handgun match.

canal, had been awarded the Congressional Medal of Honor.

As a result of panel discussion in the 1948 general members' meeting, several changes were voted in the rules of competition. Among these were the return to four shooting classifications—Master, Expert, Sharpshooter, and Marksman. Before the war there had been subdivisions in the Marksman category—Marksman First Class and Marksman. Definite geographic boundaries in the regional tournaments were eliminated, permitting members to attend the regional of their choice. Approved in principle was the idea of an official twenty-five-foot gallery target for junior instruction and qualifications with $CO_2$ rifles. The fifty-meter experimental target, which had been adopted tentatively two years before, was made official.

One of the most important decisions made in February, 1948, was to revise the procedure for future meetings. Until that time, the annual meeting of the Board of Directors had been held, according to the Bylaws, in February, in Washington, D. C.; the members meeting had been held at Camp Perry in conjunction with the National Matches. Many members, particularly the growing number in the western

and southern states, found it difficult or impossible to attend. From this point on, the business meetings were to be held in conjunction with an Annual Convention, meeting at various locations throughout the country as determined by the Board of Directors.

The National Matches were not held at Camp Perry in 1948 because of lack of appropriations, but American participation in international competition resumed in that year. Looking forward to the first Olympics since the beginning of World War II, committees had been appointed as early as 1946 with Karl T. Frederick chairman of the Olympic Pistol Committee and General Reckord as chairman of the Rifle Committee.

The Olympic pistol and rifle matches were scheduled to be shot at the famous Bisley Range outside London on August 2 through August 6. The nature of the events and the custom-made weapons of their competitors placed the Americans again at a disadvantage and they fared poorly. As an indication of the accuracy of the specially designed European automatic pistols, when Huelet Benner shot a higher score in the main pistol event than ever recorded by an American he placed only fourth. Bob Chow of San Francisco led the American rapid-fire shooters with an expert performance, getting in all sixty hits for a score of 553 of a possible 600, but placed thirteenth! The only gold medal was brought back to America by Arthur Cook, whose smallbore score 599 of 600 with 43 Xs nosed out the second-place shooter by one X.

The Seventy-seventh Annual Meetings, which became in effect the first annual convention of the National Rifle Association, were held in the Shoreham Hotel in Washington, D. C., on October 25-28, 1948, with Frank C. Daniel serving as convention secretary. It set the pattern for the modern meetings which members and friends of the NRA know today—complete with commercial exhibits, field trips, and a welter of committee and executive business activity.

The address of welcome to more than 700 delegates was given by Gen. Jacob L. Devers, Chief of Field Forces of the United States

Army. General Devers was an active proponent of individual marksmanship and had required all Army recruits to undergo seventy-two hours of basic training with the rifle.

In lieu of the Camp Perry Matches, the 1948 National Smallbore Rifle and Pistol Matches were shot at Quantico, Virginia, on October 25-27, as part of the NRA convention. Public interest in the outcome of both the pistol and rifle events ran high and centered on the leading contenders. Both events had taken on the aspect of two-man contests.

In the smallbore match Olympic Champion Arthur Cook, still looking like a high school freshman, was gunning for the national title of G. Wayne Moore, who until then had held off all comers. In the pistol matches, big, rock-steady Harry Reeves was determined to regain his national title from Sgt. Huelet "Joe" Benner, whose shooting arm was equally firm.

The smallbore matches opened under cloudy skies with blustery winds that gusted to thirty miles an hour. Otherwise there may have been revisions in the record books. Cook, showing more skill in doping the wind, pulled into the lead in the opening event with 393 to 388, a lead that Moore was only beginning to overcome by the end of the matches. Over the eight-match course, Cook won four, split two, and dropped two to win the title of National Smallbore Champion of the United States.

The suspense in the pistol matches was almost as high, but Reeves, determined to regain his championship, outpointed Benner in seven of the twelve stages and lost only two. In winning, Reeves set a new record for the longest tenure as champion in the history of pistol competition.

At the 1948 business meeting, there were significant changes in the staff organization of the

Harry Reeves, perennial pistol champion, one of the all-time greats in handgun marksmanship.

National Rifle Association. Since his return from the war, General Reckord had held the dual offices of executive vice-president and treasurer. With the great expansion of the program of the NRA, fiscal matters became increasingly complex. General Reckord after his federal service in the war also had returned to duty as Adjutant General of Maryland in 1945, and his additional official responsibilities made it increasingly difficult for him to devote the required time to the mounting financial affairs of the NRA. In the annual meeting, Louis F. Lucas, a member of the firm that had conducted the annual audit of the National Rifle Association's books, was elected treasurer and appointed business manager. F. L. Wyman became secretary.

The year 1948 was one of unprecedented growth in terms of club activities. At the end of the year there were more than 6500 affiliated clubs, including 2800 junior groups, 700 of which were in secondary schools; 1400 new clubs were organized between January and December, 1948. The 1948 registered tournament program also set new records, with 495 separate tournaments, an increase of 127 over the previous year.

YOUR NRA

FORMATION FOR MEMBERS OF THE
NATIONAL RIFLE ASSOCIATION
OF AMERICA

257

Despite all this postwar enthusiasm for the shooting sports, the .30 caliber shooting program was slow in recovering from its disruption by the war. Between 1945 and 1950, the spotlight was on the smallbore and pistol shooters. Camp Perry was still unavailable for full-scale matches as late as 1949, and the pistol and smallbore events were held in that year at separate locations—smallbore at Camp Dodge, Iowa, and pistol at Fort Sheridan, Illinois. Col. Francis W. Parker, Jr., past NRA president, served as executive officer of the National Pistol Championship Matches. The bigbore shooters suffered a further disappointment when lack of facilities forced the cancellation of the proposed .30 caliber events at Camp Dodge.

Both the smallbore and pistol events were shot on September 1-6, 1949. The smallbore matches at Camp Dodge brought a major upset when Robert Eric McMains, a newcomer to national shooting, walked away from all other contenders to become the new National Smallbore Champion. Arthur Cook, the odds-on favorite to retain his title, finished far down in twenty-ninth place.

Meanwhile, in the handgun competition at Fort Sheridan, it looked like practically no contest. Harry Reeves, the only man considered capable of topping Joe Benner, was suffering from a ruptured back muscle. In spite of his

difficulty, Reeves made a real fight for his title. In the aggregate, however, Benner rolled up a score of 2592 while Reeves trailed in second place with 2579.

Bringing a climax to the widespread NRA activities for 1949, the Seventy-eighth Annual Meetings (and second convention) were held in Denver, Colorado, on October 17-21, in accordance with the procedures adopted in 1948. At this time, General Edson,who had become the Director of Public Safety of Vermont on his retirement from the Marine Corps, succeeded to the presidency of the NRA, and Harry Linn became vice-president. Among the twenty members of the Board of Directors elected to three-year terms at this time was Mrs. Alice Bull of Seattle, Washington, the first woman ever elected to the Board.

With this meeting in Denver's Shirley-Savoy Hotel on October 19, 1949, an era in the administrative history of the National Rifle Association closed with the voluntary retirement of Maj. Gen. Milton A. Reckord as executive vice-president. Except for his absence during the war, General Reckord had guided the affairs of the Association continually since 1926. By his energy, courage, and executive ability, he had been a dominant force in building the NRA into a dynamic and influential organization representing all aspects of American shooting activity.

The post vacated by General Reckord was filled by C. B. Lister, who had assumed executive leadership of the NRA during General Reckord's absence during World War II. Lister also retained his previous title of executive director and editor of *The American Rifleman*. Louis Lucas was re-elected as treasurer and Frank Wyman as secretary. Under the Bylaws General Reckord relinquished his position on the Executive Committee but immediately became a member of the Executive Council.

More than 1000 delegates and guests, the largest number ever recorded at an NRA social function, heard Lt. Gen. Robert L. Eichelberger, USA, who had commanded the Eighth Army in the Pacific, address the annual banquet in

Mrs. Alice Bull of Seattle, first woman to be elected to the NRA Board of Directors.

prophetic terms; he stated, on the eve of the Korean War:

> Some well-meaning people have urged the general registration with the police of all privately owned firearms as a means of curbing crime and fifth column activities. These people are poor students of history. . . . In spite of strict government control of the manufacture, distribution and possession of firearms, the fifth column groups made sure they were powerfully, although illegally armed. It is my hope that this will never happen here. . . . If war starts today, we are going to have a lot of boys lying in the mud with rifles.

To round out the shooting events for 1949 the International Shooting Union Championships were shot in Buenos Aires, Argentina, during November 4-13. They were the first ISU Matches in nineteen years in which the United States was represented by a complete team.

The Americans faced extremely stiff competition in these matches, the rifle team placing fifth in a field of seven in both the smallbore and the important Argentina Cup Free-rifle Matches. Art Jackson won a gold medal for the United States in the 50-100-meter prone match, and the American center-fire pistol team won with a one-point margin over the Swiss. Harry Reeves missed out on a gold medal by firing on the wrong target.

Not only war clouds and shooting matches occupied the minds of those entrusted with the direction of the National Rifle Association. The original Bylaws of the Association were written in 1871 and were last overhauled fully in 1926 when the organization had a relatively simple program, a small staff, and comparatively uncomplicated administrative problems. They had been drafted, in short, for an organization quite different from that which now existed. As early as 1948, need for major revisions became apparent. The former Competitions Committee, which originally had functioned as a subdivision of the Executive Committee, had been re-established as three standing committees, which included active shooters who were not always members of the Board of Directors. A Challenge

Maj. Gen. Merritt A. Edson, NRA president (1949-1951).

and Protest Committee, whose members were not necessarily members of the Executive Committee, was acting on challenges, protests, and reclassifications, which had formerly been decided by the Executive Committee or by the headquarters staff. A Finance Committee, which had formerly merely supervised investments, had assumed broadened budgetary powers. These assignments had been made administratively by the Executive Committee to meet changing conditions.

The need for a full revision of the Bylaws became obvious, and the Executive Committee appointed a Bylaws Revision Committee under the chairmanship of Col. Francis W. Parker, Jr. Serving with Colonel Parker in the revision of the Bylaws were Harry D. Linn, J. Alvin Badeaux, Marvin Driver, Karl T. Frederick, John Schooley, Dr. Emmet O. Swanson, George Whittington, Carl Kastner, W. Owen Keller, and Rear Admiral Morton C. Mumma, Jr.

The annual meetings and convention of the National Rifle Association for 1950 were scheduled to be held on October 2 through October 6 in San Francisco. However, postponement for one year was forced by the deteriorating situation in Korea. The scheduled National rifle and pistol matches also went by the board in 1950. They had been scheduled as a feature

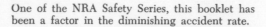
One of the NRA Safety Series, this booklet has been a factor in the diminishing accident rate.

of the NRA meetings, like those held previously.

A meeting of the Board of Directors was held in San Francisco, however, on October 6, 1950, and it is one of the landmarks in the development of the National Rifle Association as we know it today. Here was adopted the final draft of the the vitally important revised Bylaws.

The modernized Bylaws defined more clearly the obligations and privileges of individual members and affiliated organizations and provided for the calling of special meetings upon request of 5 per cent of the Life and Endowment Members as well as upon request of the president, the Board of Directors, or the Executive Committee. They also required the publication in *The American Rifleman*, at least thirty days before the annual meeting, of all names of nominees to the Board of Directors selected by the Nominating Committee; provided for the additional nomination of candidates by any five members entitled to vote, and specified election by secret ballot, by members attending the annual meeting. Two years later, another revision established the mail ballot.

One important provision changed the procedure for electing members of the Board of Directors. Under the old rules, only Life or Endowment Members could make prenominations of candidates; the new Bylaws permitted any individual or affiliated organization to make prenomination recommendations to the nominating committee.

Under the new Bylaws, also, the president was required to appoint annually four standing committees to provide rules and program recommendations on high-power rifle, smallbore rifle, pistol, and junior activities, each in its respective field. Any recommendations made by

the committees became effective unless acted upon to the contrary by the Executive Committee.

The Bylaws also established Junior Patrols, affiliated groups of from three to nine youngsters under the supervision of an adult instructor. This permitted supervised shooting programs in rural communities where there was an insufficient number of boys or girls to form full-fledged junior clubs.

The year 1951 saw many changes in the programs and staff of the NRA; some the result of growth, others due to unexpected circumstances. Five members of the staff, including John Scofield, managing editor of *The American Rifleman*, were called to active service with the outbreak of the Korean War.

Sweeping changes in the staff organization came with the death of C. B. Lister on May 14, 1951, a tragic loss to the National Rifle Association. Lister, still an active man of fifty-two, had started his career with the organization as advertising and promotion manager in 1921 when the NRA had about 3500 individual members and 450 affiliated clubs. During the long tenure of office of Maj. Gen. Milton A. Reckord from 1926 to 1949, Lister had been General Reckord's "right-hand man." Even before 1926, he had played a vital role in tripling the membership of the organization by broadening its appeal to civilian shooters. He was a leader in the fight to preserve the rights of Americans to keep and bear arms. He was also largely responsible for the development of the youth program through a genuine interest in youngsters. He was a member of the National Council of the Boy Scouts of America, a director of the Boys Club of Washington, and had been active in many other civic organizations.

During General Reckord's absence on active military duty in World War II, the task of managing the affairs of the NRA in this difficult period fell upon C. B. Lister, and the important contribution of the NRA to the war effort had been accomplished under his guidance.

After Lister's death, the Executive Committee

met to select his successor. Effective June 15, 1951, Maj. Gen. Merritt A. Edson, USMC (Ret.), resigned his post as NRA president and Commissioner of Safety of his native state of Vermont to accept the position. General Edson had retired from the Marine Corps in 1947. In World War II he had seen forty-four months of continuous active service in the Pacific Theatre. He was an outstanding rifleman, having served as a firing member, coach, or captain of a dozen or more Marine Corps teams. As a leader and organizer of the First Marine Raider Battalion, and commanding officer of the Second Battalion, Fifth Marines, he had been one of the first in the American land forces to take the offensive against the Japanese. His personal gallantry in action had won him the highest military honors available to a member of the Armed Services.

Under the leadership of General Edson there were also major shifts in the program of the NRA. In the early 1950s there was major concern for the future of high-power competitive shooting. A survey of the members made in 1950 indicated that only one in ten was actively participating in .30 caliber shooting, while 75 out of each 100 were active in smallbore practice, and one in four was shooting pistols.

Bigbore shooting had never fully recovered from World War II, and the Korean conflict was another setback. Suitable ranges were scarce in a nation rapidly shifting to an urbanized society, and the expansion of suburbia was robbing many local clubs of their shooting facilities. The intermittent loss of Camp Perry had forced the NRA to farm out its matches to scattered military posts instead of holding them at a centralized location each year. The influence of the National Board for the Promotion of Rifle Practice had decreased for lack of appropriations. General Edson made the correction of these deficiencies a personal campaign, and he was successful in all of them.

A revealing aspect of a membership survey was that 44 per cent were big game hunters and 53 per cent were interested in varmint or predator shooting. Under the urging of General Edson, hunters received increasing attention. An outgrowth of the expanded emphasis on the hunting shooter was the NRA Uniform Hunter Casualty Report. With larger numbers of hunters in the field, hunter safety had become of major concern to the organization. During the 1940s New York, Michigan, Minnesota, and Pennsylvania had been conducting statewide surveys of hunting accidents, but there was no uniform system of gathering facts on a national scale. In most states, hunting accidents were considered entirely in the province of state or local police. Many newspaper reports included death from heart disease and en route traffic accidents as "hunting fatalities."

The idea of the Uniform Report had been conceived by C. B. Lister in 1945 and spelled out by him in an address before the Tenth North American Wildlife Conference. By 1946 the NRA had begun to gather facts with which to develop a uniform system of reporting. In 1950 the International Association of Game, Fish and Conservation Commissioners adopted the NRA standards and urged its members to cooperate with the NRA in gathering the necessary details. In the first year that this program was effective, thirty states and two Canadian provinces participated. In subsequent years most of the states and several Canadian provinces have contributed annual reports to the program.

At the 1949 ISU World Championships in Buenos Aires, Arthur C. Jackson won the gold medal for his best score in the Prone Championship Match.

# 23 Hunter Safety Program Acclaimed — The Korean PreinductionTraining Program

Further evidence of the NRA's expanding services came with introduction of its Hunter Safety Training Program. The idea of training youngsters for hunting had been proposed well before World War II by Seth Gordon, then secretary of the American Game Association, in a speech at the Annual Meeting of the NRA. His idea was adopted on a local scale by various clubs affiliated with the NRA. Then in July, 1949, in compliance with a newly enacted law, the New York State Conservation Department ruled that no hunter below the age of seventeen who had not held a license before could hunt until he had received instruction in safe gun-handling from a state game protector. This put an enormous workload on already overworked game protectors, and the Conservation Department asked members of the National Rifle Association to take over some of the responsibilities. On February 10, 1950, the New York State Legislature passed a bill authorizing qualified NRA members to serve as instructors in the Junior Hunter Training Program. The New York program was so successful in reducing hunting accidents that the NRA, in 1952, expanded it to a national program.

In 1951, the twenty-fifth anniversary of the NRA Junior Program, more than 200,000 boys and girls were participating in one or more of the NRA junior activities. There were more than 3000 junior clubs in local schools or at installations maintained by cooperating organizations. These included Future Farmers of America, 4-H Clubs, the Boy Scouts of America, Veterans of Foreign Wars, the American Legion, and high schools and colleges. In 1950 the NRA had initiated a fifteen-foot air gun program in which youngsters could qualify for medals with BB guns

# Nationally

# War — NRA

# Reactivated

under qualified supervision. A twenty-five-foot air gun course using pneumatic or $CO_2$ guns was already in force. These programs were designed to train boys and girls in the safe handling of arms where ranges for powder guns were not available.

In 1951 the NRA expanded its shooting program, although the future of competitive high-power shooting was now clouded by the Korean War. The 1951 National Matches were opened by the Executive Committee at its meeting of July 28, 1951, to any NRA member.

During World War II, the NRA Preinduction Training Program had graduated more than 1,750,000 trainees in basic military marksmanship. In 1950 as war clouds darkened in Asia, it reactivated this program, and by February, 1951, eighty-seven training schools were being conducted by NRA affiliated clubs for citizens subject to military service. In addition to preinduction trainees, the clubs were again schooling civil defense workers in basic pistol marks-

manship in cooperation with police departments, and auxiliary police, plant protection, and civil defense organizations. Many of the nation's best-known tournament shooters devoted much of their time to this work.

The program brought a warm endorsement from Gen. Lewis B. Hershey, Director of Selective Service, who, on March 9, 1951, wrote to General Edson: "I have a high appreciation of the value of marksmanship training. Its importance in the preparedness of individuals who may be called upon to defend our country cannot be overemphasized. It is reassuring to know that the patriotic efforts of your organization will again afford an opportunity for prospective servicemen to become better trained in the safe and efficient use of small arms."

This sentiment was echoed by General of the Army Omar N. Bradley, Chairman, Joint Chiefs of Staff, in an open letter to the members of the NRA, published in the May, 1951, issue of *The American Rifleman,* which read: "It is reassuring to know that the National Rifle Association is actively supporting our national preparedness by fostering the skill which helped make America free—rifle marksmanship. Your present program for preinduction training in small arms is an outstanding example of your many contributions to the essential partnership of civilian and military effort in national security. . . . It is my conviction that America's heart is strong, that America's soul is sound, and that America's spirit is equal to the challenge of this dangerous decade. The activities and the aims of your association, which contribute to the health, the citizenship and the preparedness of America, strengthen this conviction."

The Eightieth Annual Meetings (billed as "The Third Annual Convention") were held in San Francisco on October 8-12, 1951. Although designated as the "Second Convention," the meeting of 1950 had consisted of fundamental business sessions when the full-scale convention had to be cancelled as a result of the Korean

The National Pistol Championships of 1951 were fired at the Lake Merced Range of the San Francisco Police Department. Huelet Benner was the winner with a score of 2629 out of a possible 2700.

War. The 1951 convention, however, was complete with commercial exhibits, forums conducted by the various committees, and a welter of general and committee business.

National preparedness was foremost in the thoughts of the members with the sobering example of Korea fresh in mind. Rear Admiral Morton C. Mumma, Jr., explained the workings of the newly enacted Selective Service System and commented: "Since virtually all of our young men will have served or be serving in the next five years, it is not hard to see our responsibility . . . in helping prepare them for that service through training with small arms."

Brig. Gen. Merrill B. Twining, USMC, shared these views. "Korea taught that Americans cannot trade life for life with the Communist hordes," he stated. "What we must do is to shift the emphasis on the American fighting man from mass to quality."

Harry D. Linn, former Secretary of Agriculture of Iowa, and a past president of the Iowa State Rifle Association as well as former National Marksmanship Chairman of the American Legion, became the new president of the National Rifle Association to fill the vacancy left by the resignation of General Edson on his election as executive director. J. Alvin Badeaux of Thibodeaux, Louisiana, was elected vice-president.

As a feature of the Eightieth Annual Meetings (Third Convention) of the NRA, the National

Rifle and Pistol Matches of 1951 were shot in California from September 27 through October 6, under a divided program. The smallbore matches and the National Pistol and Revolver Matches were held at separate ranges in San Francisco, and the .30 caliber events at Camp Matthews with the cooperation of the Marine Corps. These were the first national high-power events since 1940.

The NRA Match Rifle Championship was won by Tom Barnes of Billings, Montana. The Service Rifle National Championship was taken by Lt. Remes Delahunt, USMC, with an M1 rifle, the first time the Garand rifle had been used in a National Match. Olympic Champion Arthur Cook, now a lieutenant in the Air Force, won the Navy Cup Match and then established

One of the various guides prepared by the National Rifle Association in the interest of firearms safety.

his versatility by setting a new record of 99-13V for the 200-yard offhand match with the largebore match rifle. Raymond W. Ickes, son of the former Secretary of the Interior, won the Marine Corps Match with a record 100-16V.

The historic 1000-yard Wimbledon Cup Match was won by Capt. Richard F. Hanson of Michigan with 100-17V, and the President's Match by Lt. Arthur Jackson, USAF, who, according to tradition, received a letter of congratulation from the President of the United States. The National Women's Championship was taken by Alice Bull of Seattle, Washington.

M/Sgt. Huelet (Joe) Benner, shooting shoulder-to-shoulder against his arch rival, Harry Reeves, won the National Pistol Championship.

Reeves, Benner, Cook, and Jackson were veterans of the 1951 ISU Matches, which had been shot at Buenos Aires, Argentina, in the previous February. Captained by Emmet O. Swanson and shooting against the best of eleven other countries, this squad won more individual places than any previous American team in international competition, although it was the smallest in the field.

As the Korean War sputtered into an uneasy truce with the removal of General Douglas MacArthur from command on April 11, 1951, the world entered a long phase of armed peace broken by sporadic flare-ups of actual combat. With the emphasis shifting to a national policy of containment of Communism, the National Rifle Association increasingly emphasized peacetime shooting. Reflecting its broadened program, it expanded its "Dope Bag" forum, under Gen. Julian S. Hatcher, to include L. R. Wallack and Frederick Rudolph Etchen, Jr. Bob Wallack was a gunsmith of Mayfield, New Jersey, a leading authority on bench-rest shooting and a specialist on gun barrels, who had designed a number of improved wildcat cartridges. Rudy Etchen, although only twenty-eight, had won more shotgun shooting titles

Mr. Harry D. Linn, NRA president (1951-1953).

than any other American and was captain of the All-American Professional Trapshooting Team of 1951. His home was in Sun Valley, Idaho. He became the first shotgun specialist on the "Dope Bag" staff since the retirement of Charles Askins, Sr., many years before.

A major change in advertising policy was announced in April, 1952, by General Edson. Under this policy *The American Rifleman* was to reject any advertisement of goods or services not connected with shooting and any goods or products of no practical value to shooters.

Under the newly adopted revised Bylaws, the standing committees, as direct representatives of the membership, assumed a much more prominent position in the affairs of the organization and now handled many details formerly assigned to the overworked Executive Committee.

In 1952, the standing committees included the Finance Committee, under the chairmanship of Adm. Morton C. Mumma, Jr.; a Development and Promotion Committee, under Karl T. Frederick; Protest, under the chairmanship of Frank T. Parsons, Jr.; Bylaws, under

1951 U. S. Pan-American Team, Buenos Aires, Argentina. (l. to r.) Arthur E. Cook, Arthur C. Jackson, Dr. Emmet O. Swanson, Harry Reeves, Huelet L. Benner.

Francis W. Parker, Jr.; Junior and College, James Affleck, chairman; and three Competitions Committees—Smallbore, C. M. Styer, chairman; High-power, Carl Kastner, chairman; Pistol, C. A. Brown, chairman.

One matter of major concern in 1952 was the decline since 1941 of the National Board for the Promotion of Rifle Practice. With the creation of the Department of Defense, the National Board had remained attached to the Department of the Army, and over the years it had declined gradually until it had become little more than the governing body of the National Matches. No funds for civilian marksmanship were provided in the Department of Defense Appropriations Bill of 1952. Since 1949, the Board had met only occasionally, and most of its meetings had accomplished little. In April, 1952, the NRA recommended that the National Board be elevated to the level of the Department of Defense as a training agency for all of the armed services.

As a result of this activity, Congress appropriated $100,000 for the National Board for the Promotion of Rifle Practice for 1953. After an initial request for $130,000 had been stricken from the Defense Appropriations Bill in the House, an amendment to restore that amount was submitted by Senator Henry Cabot Lodge of Massachusetts. In the Conference Committee, the sum of $100,000 was restored, and the bill was passed by Congress.

The year 1952 was an Olympic year and, for the first time in history, an American team had the task of competing in the ISU World's Championships and the Olympic Games in the same month. Frank Parsons served as captain of the 1952 International Team. He had been a firing member of every U. S. International Team from 1930 to 1949. The 1952 ISU Matches were shot in Oslo, Norway, between July 6 and 16 and the Olympic Matches in Helsinki, Finland, immediately after the ISU Matches. The team traveled to Europe with funds raised through public subscription by the NRA.

The first event to be fired was the ISU center-fire pistol match with factory model pistols—thirty shots slow fire and thirty intermittent rapid fire on the International Silhouette Target, visible for three seconds at seven-second intervals—an innovation in ISU Matches. The American team won this match and Harry Reeves, Lt. Col. Walter Walsh, and M/Sgt. Huelet (Joe) Benner finished first, second, and third in the individual scoring. Although the smallbore team placed third, Lt. Arthur Jackson won the individual prone championship with the only 400 "possible" shot in the matches, and Lt. Arthur Cook took third place. In the kneeling stage Dr. Emmet O. Swanson finished third with a 392 out of 400, only one point behind the Finnish winner. Out of eleven teams entered in the three-position match, the United States placed fifth. In the four-man team English Match—30 shots per man at 50 meters and 30 shots at 100 meters, prone—Jackson, Verle Wright, Cook, and Swanson won by 4 points over second-place Norway, and Jackson won another gold medal for his individual performance.

In the free-pistol event, American shooters placed fourth, although they came within one point of the existing world's record. The new record, set by Swedish shooters, was a fantastic 2718, which was 47 points above the earlier record. Benner placed third in the individual scoring.

In the free-rifle match, the Americans finished fifth, although they were shooting rifles not of true free-rifle design. To cap the American performance, Benner set a new individual record in the silhouette pistol match to lead the United States to a record-setting team victory.

After this excellent performance, the American Olympic contingent moved to Helsinki where the competition opened on July 21, 1952. The program consisted of three events—Free-pistol, 300-Meter Rifle, and Olympic Silhouette Pistol. Benner won the first event for the United States—the first time an American had won it since Karl T. Frederick's performance in 1920. This was the only medal won by the United States in the Fifteenth Olympiad shooting program.

The 300-Meter Rifle Match was won by A. Bogdanov of the USSR in the first appearance of Soviet shooters in Olympic competition.

Less than a month after the Olympic Matches the Eighty-first Annual Meetings of the National Rifle Association were held in Jacksonville, Florida, on August 15 through August 24, in combination with the National Smallbore and Pistol Matches. Every state in the Union, Hawaii, and Puerto Rico were represented in the registered attendance of 974; of these, 650 were active competitors in the matches. A new feature adopted at this 1952 meeting was the round-table discussions of various aspects of shooting sports.

In the pistol matches, which were shot at the Jacksonville Police Pistol and Rifle Club, William Toney, Jr., of the U. S. Border Patrol interrupted the long seesaw tenure of championship held jointly by Harry Reeves and Joe Benner for more than a decade. The NRA pistol team championships, however, were all won by the Army, and the national women's pistol championship was taken by Mrs. Maria Hulseman, a housewife from Towson, Maryland. Another newcomer, Robert Perkins of Fresno, California, became the new national smallbore champion.

The National High-power Rifle Matches were shot on the range at Fort Benning, Georgia, from August 27 through September 2. They were dominated by the Marines. The NRA Match Rifle Championship was won by Lt. Col. Walter Walsh, USMC, formerly with the FBI, and the Service Rifle Championship was won by another Marine, Maj. Robert A. Dawson of Barstow, California. The Army staged a comeback in the National Trophy Match to win the national team championship. Alice Bull of Seattle, a director of the NRA, was the ranking

The very successful 1952 American ISU shooters at Oslo, Norway. Standing (l. to r.): Walter Walsh, William Mc-Millan, Huelet Benner, Harry Reeves, Robert Sadager, Thomas Sharpe, Arthur Cook, August Westergaard, William Devine, William Hancock, Verle Wright, Arthur Jackson. Kneeling: Charles Rau, Frank Parsons, George Leppig.

woman shooter at Fort Benning, and the 1000-yard Wimbledon Cup event was won by a civilian, newspaperman Glenn Taylor of Phoenix, Arizona, with every shot in the bullseye and 16 Vs.

In 1952 England took the Dewar Cup back home in a six-way competition that included the United States, Great Britain, Canada, New Zealand, South Africa, and Ceylon. The American team, captained by George Whittington, shot at Jacksonville on August 24, under conditions of poor visibility and a gusty wind.

General Courtney Hodges, Commanding General of the Army Field Forces, was so delighted when Capt. Ben C. Curtis became the first Regular Army man to win the National Trophy Individual Pistol Match that he ordered the .45 pistol used by Curtis be engraved and presented to him.

As a result of the Annual Meetings of 1952 there were realignments of staff responsibility within the NRA beginning in 1953. Louis F. Lucas, NRA treasurer, became Deputy Executive Director; C. Richard Rogers was the new Director of Promotion and Public Relations; Secretary Frank L. Wyman, Director of Clubs and Competitions; and Assistant Secretary Frank C. Daniel, Director of Business Administration.

By 1953, there was only one field office of the NRA, although there was still need for representation on the west coast. Col. Emerald F. (Tod) Sloan, in September, 1952, resigned his position as Managing Director, Secretary, and Treasurer of the National Skeet Shooting Association to accept the post of Western Representative. From 1945 to 1947 he had served as executive officer of the National Board for the Promotion of Rifle Practice and Director of Civilian Marksmanship.

The dates of the Annual Members Meeting of 1953 were advanced to March 25-29 after a year of unprecedented growth, and held in Washington, D. C., for the first time since 1948. The number of members had increased by 16,000 in 1952, and Life Memberships were being processed at the rate of five per day. The organization was also functioning on a healthy financial basis; income during the year exceeded expenses by $41,000 as opposed to a loss of $16,000 in 1951.

At this meeting a Gun Collectors Committee, with Francis W. Parker, Jr., as chairman, was added to the list of Standing Committees. Congressman Cecil R. King of California was vice-chairman.

J. Alvin Badeaux of Louisiana replaced Harry D. Linn as president, and Rear Admiral Morton C. Mumma, Jr., whose father had been a guiding light in the affairs of the NRA during the early years of the century, became vice-president. J. Alvin Badeaux was a business executive of Thibodeaux, Louisiana, president of the Lafourche Sportsmen's League, and a past president of the Louisiana State Rifle Association. He was an active shooter, a sportsman and leader in state conservation affairs. He had become a member of the NRA Board of Directors in 1946.

The annual banquet was attended by many congressional and military leaders, and the major address was presented by Congressman Dewey Short of Missouri, chairman of the

Shooters on the firing line for the 1952 Olympic Matches at Helsinki, Finland.

268

House of Representatives Armed Services Committee. Pressing official duties prevented President Dwight D. Eisenhower from attending but, in declining he wrote, on February 4, 1953:

> I am very appreciative of your invitation to the eighty-second annual banquet of the National Rifle Association of America on March twenty-sixth.
>
> Having such pleasant memories of a similar occasion in 1946, I regret very much that the many problems facing me in these early weeks of my administration have compelled me to decline almost all functions of an unofficial nature. I'm sure you can understand the necessity for this decision.
>
> Because of my genuine interest in the purposes of your organization, I am especially sorry that I am unable to be with you. I hope that the splendid program which the National Rifle Association has followed for more than eighty years will be continued.

The spring and summer months passed quickly for the NRA officers and staff, absorbed in the demands of an expanding program. Soon it was time for the "big shoot." The National Rifle and Pistol Matches returned to Camp Perry in 1953 through the courtesy of the Ohio State National Guard. General Lemuel C. Shepherd, Jr., Commandant of the U. S. Marine Corps, was personally interested and a full

The range of the Jacksonville Police Pistol and Rifle Club was the site of the 1952 NRA National Smallbore and Pistol Matches.

battalion of Marines was assigned to operate the range. A complete program was scheduled for the first time since 1940, when the last high-power events had been shot on the Ohio range, and it included all of the customary side features—Small Arms Firing School and Commercial Row.

Owing to the expansion of the Erie Proving Ground at Camp Perry, adjustments in the schedule were necessary. In the old days it had been possible to schedule high-power, smallbore, and pistol matches on the same days. The Erie Proving Ground had absorbed the old Police School area, the former pistol and smallbore ranges, and thirty targets of the 1000-yard range. Because of this, it was necessary to shoot the various types of matches consecutively.

Although the range was reduced in size, it had been improved in housing facilities. Camp Perry at the height of the shooting season was no longer a tent city. During the war, much of its grounds had become studded with prisoner-of-war huts and officers' houses, and those that remained, with some refurbishing, provided more comfortable housing, especially in inclement weather.

The National Matches were shot on August 20 through September 7, 1953, opening with the Small Arms Firing School. An important feature of the matches was the reinstatement of the Pershing Trophy Match, with American smallbore shooters again competing shoulder-to-shoulder with British marksmen for the first time since 1939. A substantial sum was donated

Camp Perry's facilities improved as time went by, changing from a tent city to more substantial housing.

toward the British travel expenses by William Schweitzer, one of America's outstanding small-bore marksmen.

There were 2542 shooters registered at Camp Perry in 1953, representing forty-six states, Hawaii, and Alaska, Great Britain, Canada, Mexico, and Colombia. Instruction in the Small Arms Firing School centered on the M1 rifle, which was used in all military events.

The pistol matches were full of surprises, but Reeves and Benner were again dueling it out in their familiar domination of the National Pistol Matches; Harry Reeves chalked up his fifth national championship since 1940. Lucile Chambliss of Winter Haven, Florida, became the first woman to place in the Mayleigh Cup International Pistol Team and in doing so made the fourth-highest score in the American ten-man team. Kathleen Walsh, the fifteen-year-old daughter of Lt. Col. Walter Walsh, placed third among the women pistol shooters.

Individual scores in the smallbore events were so high that the higher ratings were determined entirely by the number of Xs. In the 50-yard any-sight match, the 243rd place also showed a score of 400 out of a possible 400! John Crowley of Connecticut became the new national smallbore champion in the most hotly contested national match on record. In the NRA Women's Championship, Mrs. Neva Seagly of Topeka, Indiana, and Mrs. Viola Pollum of Brookville, Pennsylvania, battled down to the final shots in the Grand Aggregate until Mrs.

Pollum was declared the winner by the margin of a few Xs.

The International Dewar Match was shot under perfect weather conditions on August 25 and the American team won with a new record of 7984, defeating a British team that had already set a new record of 7977 in their phase of the match in England. The Pershing Trophy Match, held on the same day with teams from Canada and Great Britain competing, was won by the United States with another record score of 3990, ten points ahead of the British and twenty-four more than the Canadians. All three teams on the field in 1953 broke the existing record. As in the Smallbore Matches, most of the high-power events were decided on the number of Vs rather than on numerical score. Nearly all of the leading shooters in all events placed all of their shots in the bullseye.

As a result of the activities of the new Gun Collectors Committee, shooters interested in firing old firearms received special consideration

270

The Hankins Memorial Trophy, donated to the NRA in 1953 for the high-scoring Reservist in the President's Match.

at the National Matches. The original Gun Collectors Committee had been expanded to include several new members prominent in this field. Muzzle-loading matches for both pistol and rifle were included in the program, and Commercial Row featured a number of exhibits of antique weapons.

Several new trophies made their first appearance at the National Matches in 1953. One was the Whittington Trophy, a handsome cup presented to the NRA by George R. Whittington as a prize to the annual Junior National Smallbore Champion. It was won for the first time by Charles Rogers of Arizona.

A significant staff change occurred with the employment of Walter J. Howe as editor of *The American Rifleman.* Howe brought to the magazine in 1954 a firm professional background in both journalism and firearms. A licensed gunsmith, he had served as Chief Armament Inspector at Fort Dix, New Jersey, during World War II, worked with Criminal Investigation Division agents on cases involving firearms, and was a student of ballistics. After the war he had served as gun editor of the *Sporting Goods Dealer,* as editorial director of *Hunting and Fishing,* and as assistant director of research and development for the Marlin Firearms Company. He was the author of *Professional Gunsmithing,* one of the authoritative books in its field.

The year 1954 was one of decision. Rising costs were beginning to catch up with the organization, and in 1953, for the second time in three years, the financial report had shown a deficit. Much of this was due to expenses in

Mr. J. Alvin Badeaux, NRA president (1953-1955).

connection with staging the Camp Perry Matches. Income had not gone up significantly since 1949, but it now cost nearly $97,000 more to publish and distribute *The American Rifleman.* There were three possible solutions—raise the dues, reduce the services to members, or increase membership. The Board of Directors in the Eighty-third Annual Meetings at the Shoreham Hotel in Washington, D. C., on March 27 to April 4, 1954, decided on the latter course.

This was the first time that members of the Board of Directors were elected by mail ballot. Under an amendment to the revised Bylaws adopted in 1953 any Life Member was entitled to vote by mail; previously he had to be present at the annual meeting to cast his ballot.

There was a great expansion of exhibits at the meeting of 1954. In addition to 2500 members and guests participating in the activities of the meeting in Washington, 2000 non-members paid admission to see the displays of shotguns, rifles, pistols, and shooting equipment. One entire section of the exhibit hall was devoted to antique arms. Among those who visited the displays was Vice-President Richard M. Nixon.

271

The Whittington Trophy, donated in 1952 for annual award to the National Junior Smallbore Rifle Prone Champion at the National Matches.

Walter J. Howe, director of the NRA Editorial Division (1954-1966), was responsible for great organizational efficiency in producing the Association's publications. His reports at the annual meetings were always informative and well documented.

In recognition of the outstanding support he had given the Association, particularly in connection with the National Matches, the Executive Committee elected General Lemuel C. Shepherd, Jr., Commandant of the Marine Corps, as the first Honorary Life Member.

Many NRA projects not directly involved with competitive marksmanship were making good progress. The Hunter Safety Training Program had received enthusiastic support in every part of America. New York, New Hampshire, Massachusetts, and California already recognized the NRA program by law.

Through the efforts of the Standing Committee on Gun Collecting, collectors received their first tangible benefits from affiliation with the NRA when a meeting was arranged between the collectors' representatives and the Alcohol and Tobacco Tax Division of the Internal Revenue Service in an attempt to have the National Firearms Act amended to exempt antique guns. Under the Act as it had passed, a firearm, other than one of .22 caliber, was defined as any rifle or shotgun with barrel less than eighteen inches long or pistols and revolvers equipped with attachable shoulder stocks. These provisions had been aimed clearly at sawed-off weapons and concealable foreign machine pistols favored by gangsters of the Prohibition Era. But the wording in the Act made

it include such choice collectors' items as the pre-Civil War Colt Dragoon caplock pistol with shoulder stock and a large number of short-barreled muzzle-loading weapons of no use to Twentieth-Century criminals.

Out of this meeting, less than nineteen months later, came an amendment signed into law by President Eisenhower on August 16, 1954, exempting from the provisions of the National Firearms Act all percussion and flintlock weapons.

In July, 1954, the Technical Staff was expanded by the addition of Col. E. M. Harrison, USA (Ret.), to assist General Hatcher. During his career in the Army, Colonel Harrison had served as Chief of the Small Arms Branch, Chief of the Small Arms Section of the Technical Staff in the office of the Chief of Ordnance, and Chief of the Arms and Ammunition Division at Aberdeen Proving Ground. He graduated in the Class of 1924 from the U. S. Military Academy and had done postgraduate work in ballistics at Massachusetts Institute of Technology.

At Camp Perry there were 2190 active competitors on the field for the National Matches of 1954, which opened on August 11 under the joint auspices of the National Rifle Association and the National Board for the Promotion of Rifle Practice. The range was again made available through the Adjutant General's Department of the Ohio National Guard; the Infantry Center at Fort Benning sent personnel to conduct two Small Arms Firing Schools; the Army's Chief of Ordnance provided weapons and ordnance specialists to issue and repair rifles and pistols; the Marine Corps provided personnel to operate and staff the range; and the Coast Guard supplied a patrol boat to keep small craft away from the firing zone on the lake behind the targets. Col. Noah J. Rodeheffer, USMC, served as executive officer. There was a full schedule of matches in the almost month-long program. This comprehensive program set

Gen. Lemuel C. Shepherd, Jr., Commandant of the U. S. Marine Corps, a firm advocate of rifle practice, provided manpower support and otherwise helped returning the National Matches to Camp Perry 1953 and subsequent years. He was an Honorary Life Member of the NRA.

Deputy Secretary of Defense Robert B. Anderson, who addressed the NRA annual banquet in 1955, is presented with a traditional long-rifle and powder horn by President J. Alvin Badeaux. Actor Fess Parker participated in the ceremony.

the pattern for National Matches since that time.

All was not concluded on a joyful note, however, for in the International Dewar Cup Match the American team took its worst beating in history. For the first time it finished third, being defeated both by Great Britain and by Canada.

A few months after the firing had ceased at Camp Perry, the International Shooting Union's 1954 World Championships were shot in Caracas, Venezuela, from November 15 to 27. The American rifle and pistol squad, with Frank T. Parsons as captain, Col. Charles G. Rau, USA, executive officer, and Maj. Harold J. Thomas, USMC, as adjutant, was again financed by private donations raised from its members by the NRA. The team consisted of ten riflemen and eleven handgunners. Eight skeet shooters competed through the courtesy of the National Skeet Shooting Association.

This was the largest shooting squad to represent the United States in years and one of the strongest in terms of performance in the elimination matches that selected its members. Twenty-eight of the fifty-five member nations in the ISU were represented—nineteen with complete teams, among them one from the Soviet Union, newcomers to international team shooting. Although the Americans finished somewhat higher in their relative positions than they had since their re-entry into the field of international shooting, the results of the

matches were something of a shock. When the smoke had cleared, the Russians had won nine team and eight individual championships, setting world records in all but three! They swept all rifle events except for one—the English Match, which was won by the United States team, with a Canadian picking up the individual championship. The Venezuelan Pistol Match was won by 2d Lt. W. W. McMillan, USMC. Huelet Benner won the fifty-meter free-pistol event for one of the two lone non-Russian triumphs in the pistol matches. But it was suddenly obvious that the USSR was far ahead of the United States and the rest of the world in their team organization and training methods.

These thoughts were in the minds of many when they attended the Eighty-fourth Annual Meetings of the National Rifle Association, held at the Willard Hotel in Washington on March 29 through April 3, 1955. The 1955 meetings reflected the growth of the NRA into an organization representative of all forms of shooting. More than 6000 members and non-members visited the dazzling displays of firearms and shooting equipment in the exhibit halls, and 3000 members attended one or more of the many business meetings and shooters' forums. Maj. Gen. Lewis B. Hershey, USA, Director of Selective Service, opened the meetings with an address on the role of firearms in American life.

273

Rear Admiral Morton C. Mumma, Jr., NRA president
(1955-1957).

The treasurer's report showed that the NRA was again operating in the black with a small surplus. The Executive Committee, in December, 1954, had voted to increase the annual dues to $5. Effective July 1, 1955, the stipulated contribution for Life Membership was increased from $75 to $100 and for Endowment Membership from $200 to $250. Only 1611 new members had joined in the twelve months of 1954, but 640 of these were Life Members.

Deputy Secretary of Defense Robert B. Anderson addressed the annual banquet and outlined the five-point National Reserve plan that President Eisenhower had presented to Congress in a special message of January 13, 1955. Secretary Anderson stated:

> In your 84 years you have contributed greatly to the safe and productive exercise of a basic right of American citizens—the right to keep and bear arms.
> Remember the importance of this. It is a right exclusive among free peoples. . . . here in America, we have the situation in which

your activity constitutes a positive force on the side of the government, for you are directly contributing to the development and spread of one of the most basic military skills necessary to its defense.

> Throughout our history, the trained rifleman has ever been a mainstay in our struggles for independence and security in a world which unfortunately has not found its way to any orderly existence.

Secretary Anderson was presented with a replica of an authentic flintlock rifle made by gunsmith Cecil Brooks of Lowell, Ohio, in a special ceremony that has since become a tradition at NRA banquets. Fess Parker, star of the television serial "Davey Crockett" carried the handsome rifle to the podium for presentation by retiring NRA President Badeaux.

The second Honorary Life Membership awarded by the National Rifle Association was given to Maj. Gen. Milton A. Reckord in recognition of "his outstanding service to the National Rifle Association of America on a national scale. . . ." The citation and certificate, presented at the annual banquet, were accompanied by a bronze medallion struck in the General's likeness. "The present stature of the National Rifle Association of America," President Badeaux stated, "is a direct result of the leadership and direction of General Reckord in the years in which he was connected with it."

At this banquet the United States Air Force presented to the National Rifle Association the Twining Cup, in honor of General Nathan Twining, to be awarded annually to the high Air Force man in the Pistol Championship Aggregate at the National Matches.

Rear Admiral Morton C. Mumma, Jr., USN (Ret.), became the new president of the National Rifle Association. A graduate of the Class of 1925 at the U. S. Naval Academy, he had a distinguished record both as a sailor and as a rifleman. He had commanded the Motor Torpedo Squadrons of the Seventh Fleet in World War II and distinguished himself in action

against the Japanese. As the son of the originator of the Small Arms Firing School, he had
received expert training in rifle and pistol shooting, firing high-power rifles at an age when
most youngsters were still using slingshots. He
graduated in the first Small Arms Firing School
in 1918, and became the first shooter to make
a perfect score over the Herrick Trophy Course
while still a midshipman at Annapolis. He was
a firing member of the Navy teams of 1925 and
1927, coach in 1927 and 1928, and he coached
the U. S. Naval Academy teams of 1932-1935
and 1938-1940. He had been elected to the
Board of Directors of the NRA in 1945.

The new vice-president was George R. Whittington, a lawyer and businessman of Amarillo,
Texas, and holder of state smallbore rifle championships in Texas, Oklahoma, Louisiana, and
New Mexico.

At this point in the National Rifle Association's history vital decisions bearing on its future
growth faced the Directors. Plans for a new
building were formalized at the business session. The NRA had outgrown the existing building that it owned at 1600 Rhode Island Avenue,
N.W., in Washington, and had been forced to
rent space on L Street to house its records and
supplies. In 1945 it had acquired ownership of
property at 1232 Sixteenth Street, N.W., adjacent to its headquarters. An application to

Col. Joel D. Griffing, chairman of the Building Committee
for the new headquarters building, worked tirelessly from
the time the plans were drawn until construction was completed. He was a member of the NRA Executive Council.

the Zoning Commission of the District of
Columbia for the construction of an office building, for permission to acquire the buildings at
1228 and 1226 Sixteenth Street, and to construct
an eight-story building fronting eighty feet of
Sixteenth Street had been approved in 1954.
These properties had been purchased. A resolution of the Board of Directors "To ratify, confirm, approve and adopt all acts of the Officers,
Directors and Committees," in respect to these
actions was approved on April 2, 1955.

A good share of the spectacular growth of the
NRA after World War II was attributable to the
leadership of Maj. Gen. Merritt A. Edson as
executive director. A man of vigor, imagination,
and foresight, his writings and speeches all
showed that he foresaw an even larger and
more dynamic National Rifle Association in the
future. Unfortunately, he failed to live to see
the full fruition of his planning. He died suddenly at his home in Washington on August 14,
1955, slightly more than five years after assuming the administrative leadership of the NRA.

275

The Twining Cup, in honor of Gen.
Nathan Twining, an annual award to the
high-scoring Air Force shooter in the
Pistol Championship Aggregate at the
National Matches.

# 24

## The President
## of the United States and
## Other High-ranking Officials
## Praise Services of the NRA

During the interim period between General Edson's death in August, 1955, and the next annual meeting in March, 1956, Louis F. Lucas, as deputy executive director, carried on the management of the program and the leadership of the staff of the NRA.

In March of 1956, Lt. Gen. Floyd A. Parks, USA (Ret.), was elected to succeed General Edson as executive director. The new executive director, then sixty years old, had a distinguished military record. In 1918 he had enlisted as a private and, after working his way up through the ranks, had retired only one month before his election to office in the NRA as Commanding General of the Second Army with the rank of lieutenant general. During World War II, he had served as Chief of Staff of the First Allied Airborne Army and had been among the first American soldiers to enter Berlin. He was a close personal friend of President Eisenhower.

The election of General Parks climaxed a long and intensive search for the best-qualified man by two special committees appointed by NRA President Mumma. When General Parks's name was offered in nomination, he was elected by unanimous assent.

The meetings of 1956, eighty-fifth in the Association's history, were held at the Sheraton-Park Hotel in Washington, D. C., and found the NRA in sound financial condition, although it had lost about 12,000 annual members as the result of the recent increase in dues from four dollars to five dollars. New Life and Endowment Memberships had more than made up for the difference. To stimulate the endowment membership, the Board of Directors took formal action so that Life Members could become Endowment Members on payment of $150.

Secretary of the Army Wilber M. Brucker, guest speaker at the annual banquet, stated, in part: "During the last 85 years, the National Rifle Association of America has been a potent influence in stimulating and perpetuating . . . interest in marksmanship which has paid off so handsomely in the test of war. It has performed a splendid service to America. . . ."

President Mumma read letters of greeting from many of the military and political leaders of the United States. Among them was this telegram from the President of the United States, Dwight D. Eisenhower: "Please extend my greetings to the members and guests of the National Rifle Association on the occasion of its eighty-fifth annual banquet. I applaud the Association's encouragement of marksmanship, of continuing importance to our national security, and I wish all of you a highly successful and enjoyable meeting."

Much of the interest of the visiting members was in the progress of the new headquarters building, which at that time was little more than a gaping excavation and a pile of blueprints in the office of John McShain, Incorporated. The McShain Company had constructed, among other buildings in Washington, the Pentagon and the Jefferson Memorial. Ground for the new building had been broken in a ceremony on December 11, 1955, when President Morton C. Mumma, Jr. lifted the first spadeful of earth.

The new building was very badly needed. The old mansion, which the NRA had occupied for sixteen years, had been designed as a residence rather than an office building, and its facilities had become cramped and crowded as membership rose from 50,000 to nearly 300,000 and employees from 47 to 140. In 1956, the NRA offices were scattered in four buildings over a twelve-block area in Northwest Washington, and the lack of unified facilities had become a major handicap to efficient operation.

Lt. Gen. Floyd A. Parks, NRA executive director (1956-1959).

The new eight-story building of reinforced concrete and steel with a front of blue-tinted glass between columns of white marble, was as modern as tomorrow. The plans provided for all of the many needs of the Association that its staff had found wanting in the old headquarters —modern testing equipment for the Technical Staff, up-to-date office equipment, centralized air conditioning, a museum, a library, and a twelve-point indoor rifle and pistol range.

The response of the members to the efforts of C. A. "Smitty" Brown and his Building Fund Committee was both generous and enthusiastic. By March 31, 1956, more than 10 per cent of the needed funds had been raised. By January 1, 1958, this amazing support by the membership had enabled the NRA to pay off the mortgage and the Association was beginning to replace the funds used from the NRA reserve.

During the construction period, until April, 1957, the NRA staff continued to occupy its scattered locations in Washington. The new facilities were behind rather than on the site of the old headquarters building, which remained in use for several more years. The rifle range, in the sub-basement, and the museum, then on the fourth floor of the new building, were not furnished until after the building was occupied. Both facilities were dedicated on December 5, 1958.

The range is operated by the NRA Program Division and is made available to clubs, leagues, tournaments, and individuals on a fee basis. It also provides facilities for courses of instruction. The museum houses an outstanding collection of historical firearms, which have been collected by the Association since 1926, also specimens of each arm as it has come in production by American and foreign arms manufacturers, and many trophies offered in various NRA rifle and pistol matches.

Turning from operational activities to action in the field, the National Matches of 1956, held between August 19 and September 8, again broke records of participation with 3165 registered shooters on the firing lines. Fifty per cent more people attended the Small Arms Firing School than had attended in 1955, a total of 2185.

Competition in all matches was exceptionally keen, and there was a sharp increase in the number of women shooters registered. In 1956, an all-women's team competed in the National high-power rifle matches for the first time in history and gave an excellent account of itself in a predominantly male sport. This team, composed of Mrs. Alice Bull, Mrs. Irene Paulson, Miss Marlene E. Bellinger, Mrs. Leona Acker-

land, Mrs. Laura Boyd, and Miss Pat McDowell, represented the Seattle Police Athletic Association. In the handgun matches, Mrs. Gertrude Backstrom, another Washington State shooter, won her second women's pistol championship in two years, and Mrs. Viola Pollum retained her women's smallbore crown.

In the smallbore matches, J. Kenneth Johnson of Washington, Pennsylvania, won the national championship on his second visit to Camp Perry, beating Oliver H. Lauderman, who, for the second consecutive year, lost by a margin of only a few Xs. Presley W. Kendall of Meyers, Kentucky, won the Junior National Smallbore Championship.

M/Sgt. Huelet (Joe) Benner, holder of the National pistol record, won his fifth national championship in 1956. The National High Power Open Rifle Championship was also won by a defending champion—SFC Loyd G. Crow, Jr., USA, while S/Sgt. James E. Hill, USMC, took the Service Rifle Championship. In the historic Wimbledon Cup Match M/Sgt. Francis E. Conway, who had won the cup in 1955, repeated his performance with an identical score in 1956. Marine Corps teams dominated both the National Pistol and National Rifle Trophy Matches. The Maryland National Guard team won the Hilton Trophy as the high-ranking National Guard team on the field.

Much of the interest of those at Camp Perry in 1956 centered on tryouts for the team that would represent the United States at the Olympic Games in Melbourne, Australia, in the following November and December. Eight members were selected in special elimination competitions. Dr. Emmet O. Swanson was named team captain and Lt. Col. Ellis Lea, USA, team coach.

The trip to Melbourne proved to be another disappointment; although the American team shot reasonably well, it was mauled badly by the Europeans. The Russians were particularly

The first unit of the new headquarters building was built immediately behind the old home which had served as the headquarters since 1939.

strong. Sparked by their ace riflemen, Anatol Bogdanov and Vassili Borisov, the Soviet team won three gold, four silver, and one bronze third-place medal in seven shooting events. In five of these matches European shooters took first, second, and third. By contrast American shooters took only a single medal, a third-place win by CWO Offut Pinion, USN, in the Free-pistol Match. Except for this one pale victory the highest-ranking American shooter in all events was Lt. James M. Smith, USA, who placed eighth in the 300-meter Free-rifle Match.

The American showing was especially bad in the smallbore prone events, which had been considered an American specialty for years. Canadian shooters took the gold and bronze medals in this match and a Russian took the silver.

The American team offered no alibis. Their equipment was good and the men had done their best. General Parks, who had accompanied the team to Melbourne, commented on the results and their reasons in a signed editorial in the February, 1957, issue of *The American Rifleman:* "The answer to me is plain. If we want to beat the European nations in international shooting events, then we must want to win as earnestly as they do, we must work as hard as they do and with the singleness of purpose which they, as nations, apply to their shooting. . . . The National Rifle Association must take the lead by developing and promoting more matches built around international courses of fire. . . . Initially the Armed Forces must actively support the effort because, as of now, they alone can provide the international-type ranges and the intensive training that the shooters must have in order to win today. . . . The Congress of the United States must support the effort by recognizing the vital function the National Board for the Promotion of Rifle Practice has to create the same sentiment for proficiency in marksmanship in this country that

Mr. George R. Whittington, NRA president (1957-1959).

exists in the other countries throughout the world."

The strengthening of American performances in international shooting was one of General Parks's major contributions during his brief tenure of office as executive director of the NRA. Much of his energy was devoted to implementing the program that he outlined in that editorial. American shooters, accustomed to the American course of fire, were out of their element when thrown suddenly into the international arena where the distances, targets, and rules were all unfamiliar. Before each Olympic or ISU Match, Americans had only a few days of practice under these conditions before being pitted against Europeans who had practiced most of their shooting lives under international rules. And America had nothing to match the intensive subsidized training program that the Soviet Union, with political motivation, was using to turn out finished shooters and athletes for international competition.

Going into 1957, the NRA faced new opportunities and new problems. At the annual

279

Qualified NRA instructors devote much time and energy, without compensation, for the benefit of Boy Scout and other youth training activities.

meeting of the NRA in Washington's Shoreham Hotel on March 23-28, the Board of Directors made important changes in the Bylaws to bring them into complete compliance with the Membership Corporation Laws of the State of New York. One change increased the size of the Board from sixty to seventy-five members. Another amendment provided that the Executive Council, the Executive Director, and Deputy Executive Director should sit with the Executive Committee with voice but without vote.

The Executive Committee approved two recommendations of the Hunting and Game Conservation Committee, which had been established in 1956. One was that the NRA establish a program to recognize proficiency in hunting by awarding a lapel button to any member killing a buck deer with antlers having at least four points on one side. The second provided for issuing a citation to any NRA member taking the outstanding deer trophy in the United States. Two years later this program was expanded to include antelope and other big-game animals.

This reflected a rapid expansion of the sphere of interest of the National Rifle Association into all aspects of the shooting sports, and these efforts had brought in 100,000 new members in 1956. The activities of the Gun Collectors Committee had resulted in a further expansion of

interest. Forty-two gun collectors associations and the North-South Skirmish Association had become affiliated with the NRA. Vice-President Richard Nixon, an interested visitor to the exhibits of historical weapons at the Annual Meetings, became a Life Member on July 29, 1957.

In 1957, all officers of the organization were continued for another one-year term with the exception of the president and vice-president, who under the Bylaws were limited to two terms. According to custom, Admiral Morton C. Mumma, Jr., as the retiring president, moved to the Executive Council, and Vice-President George R. Whittington became president. Irvine C. Porter of Birmingham, Alabama, was elected vice-president.

At the annual banquet, Senator Carl Hayden of Arizona who, in the early days of Camp Perry, had captained a team of riflemen from the National Guard of the Territory of Arizona, received the third Honorary Life Membership bestowed by the NRA. Senator Hayden had been a staunch supporter of the NRA programs throughout his long career in Congress, which had begun before Arizona became a state.

The guest speaker at the banquet was Lt. Gen. Lewis B. Hershey, USA, Director of the Selective Service System. He received the presentation flintlock rifle made by Cecil Brooks, in the traditional ceremony at the close of his address.

A high point of the Annual Meetings was the ceremony in which the new headquarters building was turned over to the National Rifle Association by the contractor as ready for occupancy.

These efficient new facilities at headquarters made possible increased services in the field. Youth work was an area which benefited. Cooperation between the Boy Scouts of America

280

and the National Rifle Association had been close ever since the early days of the Boy Scout movement in the United States. C. B. Lister, General Edson, and General Parks had all been active in Scout work, General Parks as a member of the National Council. These ties were strengthened in 1957, when, at the request of the Boy Scouts of America, the NRA again organized and supervised a shooting program at the Fourth Annual Boy Scout Jamboree in Valley Forge State Park, Pennsylvania, on July 12-18. It had successfully conducted such a program the previous year at the California Jamboree. Expanding it for 1957, the NRA planned the construction of a 100-point safety range built in four 25-point units for the Pennsylvania location. Volunteer members recruited by the National Rifle Association assisted in the program as instructors without compensation. In the course of the Jamboree they gave rifle instruction to 21,199 Scouts.

As a result of the success of this program, the Boy Scout Week National Safety Good Turn Program on February 7-13, 1957, featured rifle safety training on a national scale.

In the big league of shooting, the National Matches of 1957 were organized by the Second Army, which furnished personnel to condition the range at Camp Perry and to serve as markers and scorers. Army Chief of Staff Max-

Senator Carl Hayden of Arizona, who had supported NRA activities during his more than a half century in public office, received thunderous applause when he appeared at the 1957 banquet and was awarded Honorary Life Membership.

well D. Taylor was among those who watched the activities from August 9 through September 10.

A number of prominent trophies were donated to the National Board for the Promotion of Rifle Practice and went into competition that year for the first time. Among them were the Mellon Trophy, presented to the high-scoring National Guard team in the National Pistol Matches; the Leatherneck Trophy for the high civilian team in the Infantry Trophy Match; and the U. S. Coast Guard Memorial Trophy to the high-scoring Reserve Team in the National Trophy Pistol Match.

The President's Hundred and the President's Retreat were reinstated at the National Matches of 1957. The top-scoring 100 competitors in the President's Match were singled out for special recognition in a retreat ceremony in which they passed in review before the winner and former winners of this historic match. The high man in 1957 was Lt. Joe A. Deckert, USAR, who also distinguished himself by winning the Leech Cup Match. The International Aggregate was won by Col. Emmet O. Swanson, past president of the NRA, and the Wimbledon Cup Match by S/Sgt. Patrick O. Jones, USMC.

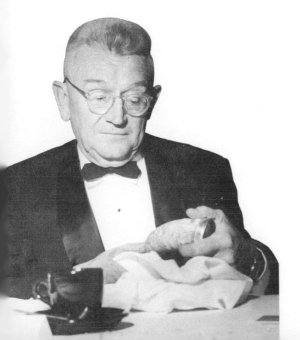

Lt. Gen. Lewis B. Hershey, a strong advocate of NRA marksmanship programs, was the banquet speaker in 1957.

In the President's Match the high-scoring Air Force man was Capt. Morton C. Mumma III, who won the Vandenberg Cup. Captain Mumma represented the third generation of champion rifle shooters of this family, each representing a different branch of the Armed Services, who had competed at Camp Perry in the past half-century.

In the handgun matches, Lt. W. W. McMillan, USMC, won the Regular Service Championship, and Mrs. Gertrude Backstrom not only won her third National Women's Championship but the Civilian Pistol Championship as well, the first woman in history to win this distinction.

The new champions in the Smallbore Matches were John Moschkau, winner of the Critchfield Trophy, Bertie Moore, National Women's Smallbore Champion, and Jimmie J. Williams, winner of the Whittington Trophy in the junior division.

In the National Trophy Matches, the Army showed great strength. At the suggestion of General Parks, the Army had developed a tournament system to select its eighty-five best shooters. These men had undergone intensive prematch training and practice at Fort Niagara in New York. Although a Marine, T/Sgt. Paul V. Bailey, won the National Trophy Individual Rifle Match, the Army for the first time in years won the National Team Match.

There were several novelty matches involving antique arms at Camp Perry in 1957. One was the North-South Skirmish, staged by the North-South Skirmish Association. The other was a crossbow match.

The Annual Meetings of the NRA, which had been held in Washington for several consecutive years, moved to Texas on April 12-17, 1958, and convened in the Adolphus Hotel in Dallas. More than 2000 members attended the meetings. It was at these meetings that the NRA Hunting Awards Program, which had been highly popular among deer hunters, was expanded to include trophy-size antelope. The Directors also agreed to use Boone and Crockett Club standards as the official criteria for judging trophies.

President Whittington, Vice-President Porter, Secretary Daniel, and Executive Director Parks were all continued in office for another year, according to custom. The Board of Directors, however, voted to recombine the offices of Treasurer and Deputy Executive Director and Louis F. Lucas was elected to fill this dual position.

J. H. Fauntleroy, the former treasurer, now headed the Membership Division, and C. Richard Rogers, former assistant secretary, was made director of a new Special Service Division. F. L. Wyman now directed the Program Division, William Binswanger, an ex-

The Leatherneck Trophy, replica of the famous "Iron Mike" statue.

The General Mellon Trophy, a miniature of a Kodiak bear.

The U. S. Marine and the Kodiak bear have something in common—they are rugged and fearless.

282

The Association of the United States Army Trophy.

The General Shepherd Trophy features Iwo Jima classic.

In the wake of wars, trophies honored the image of valiant men who had fought for our freedom.

panded Business Division, and Walter J. Howe, the Editorial Division.

Shifting the action from Texas to Ohio, the National Matches of 1958, held at Camp Perry on August 7 through September 6, were the longest ever held to that time. When they opened, however, most of the "big guns" of former years were in Wiesbaden, Germany, training for the thirty-seventh ISU World Championship Rifle and Pistol Matches, which were scheduled for Moscow on August 17-25. As a result, nearly all of the winners that year were newcomers to shooting fame. But there were exceptions. The most prominent was Gertrude Backstrom, unbeatable in the Women's Pistol Match for the fourth consecutive year. Mrs. Backstrom also outshot all the male competitors to win the Center-fire Rapid-fire Match.

Middleton W. Thompkins became the bolt rifle champion, while T/Sgt. V. D. Mitchell of the Marines won the National Service Rifle Championship. The prizes for his victory were the Du Pont Trophy and a selected M1 rifle.

Robert K. Moore, Janet S. Fridell, and William L. Madden won the National Smallbore Championships in the open, ladies', and junior divisions.

While the Camp Perry Matches were in progress, the largest team of shooters ever to represent the United States overseas in an international match were competing in the thirty-seventh World Championship, which was held on August 15-25, 1958. Moscow was host to the ISU Matches that year, and the Union of Soviet Socialist Republics went out of its way both to provide ideal facilities for the matches and to continue its winning streak in international shooting events. It succeeded on both counts.

The American shooting squad was captained by Col. Perry D. Swindler, USA (Ret.). Eighteen of the twenty-six members were Army men, four were Marines, three were civilians, and one, CWO Offut Pinion, the lone representative of the Navy.

The predominance of Army marksmen in this squad was a tribute to the effort that the Army had exerted in training men for international shooting in keeping with the advice of General Parks. This was the first ISU Match in many years in which an American team competed in the Running Deer event and they did surprisingly well, using the new M14 rifles in 7.62 mm. caliber. In the team match they placed second. Lt. Joe A. Deckert, USAR, gained

Mr. Irvine C. Porter, NRA president (1959-1961).

first place in the Individual Double Shot Match and James F. Davis of Falls Church, Virginia, second in the Single Shot event. Lt. Verle F. Wright took the individual championship in both the prone and kneeling position in the important 300-meter position match, and the American team placed fourth in the overall scoring. The United States also won the Clay Pigeon Match and placed fourth in Skeet.

In terms of victories, the American showing was little better than that at the Melbourne Olympics. Out of fourteen matches, the USSR won twelve team events and picked up eight individual championships. What these results failed to show, however, was the relative improvement, in all events, of the American shooters as a result of improved training methods. American marksmen in nearly every match crowded the Soviet shooters down to the final shots. The results were a source of encouragement to General Parks and others in the United States who had advocated the new training system. In future years it was to pay off in dominance by American shooters in the international shooting field.

Unfortunately, General Parks did not live to see this development. Only a few weeks after his return to the United States he was hospitalized at Walter Reed Army Hospital. He died on March 10, 1959, almost on the eve of the Annual Meetings, at the age of sixty-three.

General Parks's death cast a pall over the deliberations of the Board of Directors and Executive Council in their meetings in the Sheraton-Park Hotel in Washington on March 21-27. For the third time, Louis F. Lucas, Deputy Executive Director, became the ranking administrative officer of the NRA on the vacancy of the superior office. At the meeting in 1959 an amendment of the Bylaws changed the title of the executive director to executive vice-president, reverting to that held by General Reckord in his early days as administrative head of the NRA. Another change at the same time made Mr. Lucas' title that of executive director.

Vice-president Irvine C. Porter, a prominent attorney from Birmingham, Alabama, became the new president, and John M. Schooley of Denver, Colorado, the new vice-president. Mr. Porter had become a member of the Board of Directors in 1953, and was president of the Alabama State Rifle Association. An excellent marksman, he, like most members of the Board of Directors, was an active participant in shooting competition.

President Porter, in his acceptance address, pledged to work for the establishment of permanent range facilities throughout the United States, to attempt to consummate lease negotiations concerning Camp Perry, and to continue the work of General Parks in strengthening the National Board for the Promotion of Rifle Practice.

The M14 military rifle, caliber 7.62.

To find a successor to General Parks, the new president of the NRA, as his first order of business, appointed a select "Executive Vice-President Vacancy Committee" from the Board of Directors and Executive Committee. Its members were Maj. Gen. Milton A. Reckord, Col. Joel D. Griffing, AUS, Harlon B. Carter, Frederick M. Hakenjos, Leon C. Jackson, and Judge Bartlett Rummel, with George R. Whittington, the retiring president, as chairman.

The deliberations of the Committee to recommend a successor to General Parks were completed on October 31, 1959, when Deputy Assistant Secretary of the Army, Franklin Lewis Orth resigned from government service to accept the post of executive vice-president of the NRA.

Mr. Orth brought to the NRA a broad background of military, civic, and legal knowledge and personal experience in shooting. Born in Milwaukee, Wisconsin, in 1907, he had graduated from the School of Economics and the Law School of the University of Wisconsin and had practiced law in partnership with his father between 1931 and 1941. He entered World War II as a captain in the Infantry, and, as a member of Merrill's Marauders served on extra-hazardous duty in long-range penetrations behind the Japanese lines in Burma. As the commander of a regimental combat team, he led guerrilla-type operations against the enemy. He left the service with the rank of colonel.

One of the first steps taken by Franklin L. Orth as executive vice-president of the National

The Vandenberg Cup was won in 1957 by Capt. Morton C. Mumma III of the Air Force, third generation of high-scoring shooters bearing the same name.

Rifle Association was to help organize a long-range plan of far-reaching goals for the Association.

In the six years following and up to the preparation of this history of the Association, the activities of the NRA have reached such a broad scope that they can best be described here by summarization.

Supporting Franklin L. Orth as executive vice-president, the NRA has been led by a continuing group of dedicated officers and directors —prominent, highly respected and successful men in private life who serve without pay.

John M. Schooley succeeded Irvine C. Porter to the presidency at the meeting in 1961. At the time of his election he was Manager of Safety and Excise and an ex officio sheriff of Denver, Colorado. A former special investigator for the Alcohol and Tobacco Tax Divisions of the Internal Revenue Service, Mr. Schooley is one of America's leading pistol shots. He has been Western Regional Pistol Champion as well as State Pistol Champion of Colorado. He holds a Lifetime Master rating with the pistol.

Judge Bartlett Rummel of the Superior Court of Washington became president in 1963. He is the leading expert on firearms laws in North America. His column, "A Court Case of Consequence," and related articles have appeared in every issue of *The American Rifleman* since

Mrs. Gertrude E. Backstrom, a perennial women's champion, and first of her sex to win the Civilian Pistol Championship.

285

Franklin L. Orth, NRA executive vice-president.

Mr. John M. Schooley, NRA president (1961-1963).

1957. Judge Rummel is a big-game hunter and an outstanding marksman with both rifle and handgun. He holds a Lifetime Master rating with the high-power rifle and an Expert rating with smallbore rifle and pistol. He is a former member of the National Council of the Boy Scouts of America and has been active in Scout work for more than twenty-five years.

Harlon B. Carter, who succeeded Judge Rummel in 1965, is a resident of Garden Grove, California, and is Regional Commissioner for the Southwestern States of the U. S. Immigration and Naturalization Service. He directed the U. S. Border Patrol Academy from 1948 to 1950 and was largely responsible for the outstanding performance of the pistol teams from that institution. Mr. Carter captained the Border Patrol Pistol Teams at Camp Perry. He holds several state pistol and rifle championships and a Distinguished Marksman rating with both rifle and handgun.

The incumbent vice-president as of 1966 is Harold W. Glassen of Lansing, Michigan, an attorney and a member since 1947 of the Michigan Conservation Commission. He is a prominent member of the International Association of Game, Fish and Conservation Commissioners. Mr. Glassen is an outstanding wingshot and an avid upland game hunter and gun-dog breeder. He has served as chairman of the Hunting and Game Conservation Committee and the Finance Committee.

In the fields of national and international match shooting the past six years have produced a proud record. By 1959 the NRA had begun to institute international-type shooting events in its program. The results of this training became evident when on August 27 through September 7, 1959, the Pan-American Games Rifle and Pistol Matches were shot in the United States on the Municipal Rifle and Pistol Range of Waukegan, Illinois.

Because the matches were held at home, the United States was represented by one of the largest and strongest teams ever organized for an international event. The members were selected in nationwide tryouts, and those who qualified received further training and practice on the International Ranges at Fort Benning. Americans won sixteen of the individual and team events over a field of fifteen national shooting teams from the Western Hemisphere.

286

Judge Bartlett Rummel, NRA president (1963-1965).

Mr. Harlon B. Carter, NRA president (1965-1967).

They placed second only in the individual and team smallbore rifle prone matches.

With the exception of former Olympic Champion Arthur E. Cook, who won the Smallbore English Individual Match for the United States, and the veteran shooter Verle F. Wright, most of the Americans were newcomers to international shooting. One was a slender young divinity student from the University of Nebraska, Gary L. Anderson, whose performance was good but not spectacular.

In 1960, the United States was represented in the Olympic Games in Rome, Italy, by a strong team of rifle, pistol, and shotgun shooters. Capt. William W. McMillan, USMC, won the gold medal for first place in the 25-meter Silhouette Pistol Match after a dramatic shoot-off with a representative of the Soviet Union and one of Finland. Sgt. James E. Hill, USMC, won the silver medal for second place in the Smallbore Prone Match.

Further American improvement was evident on June 8-17, 1961, when the Norwegian Shooting Association staged the Moving Target World Shooting Championships, sanctioned by the ISU, in Oslo. The scheduled matches included Running Deer, Skeet, and Clay Pigeon. The United States sent a seventeen-man team to participate in all events.

The American team won the Clay Pigeon Match, and Francis Eisenlauer of California lost the individual championship in a shoot-off only after tying for first place. The performance of the American shotgunners in these events was particularly significant since at that time there was only one trap range in the United States suitable for international clay pigeon shooting. The rules of international trapshooting are quite different from those common in American matches. Fifteen traps located 16½ yards from the shooting stations throw targets at unpredictable heights and angles, and a second shot may be fired without penalty.

Loyd G. Crow and John R. Foster swept the Running Deer Matches for the USA, and Russian shooters trailed in second and third places in the individual scoring. Foster beat out L. Lustberg of the USSR in the Running Deer Aggregate by a single point.

The result of these matches gave encouragement to the NRA, which was already planning ahead to the thirty-eighth ISU World Cham-

287

pionships, which were scheduled to be held in Cairo, Egypt, on October 11-18, 1962.

The strongest international shooting squad since World War II represented the United States at Cairo. There were forty-one other national teams on the field, but the competition soon resolved into a two-way battle between the USSR and the United States. Of thirty-nine gold, silver, and bronze medals in the thirteen team events, Russian and American teams took eleven each. Of fifty-one individual medals, the USSR won seventeen and the USA gathered fifteen. If the Americans had not been plagued with sickness that robbed many of their key shooters of their full potential, there is every likelihood that they would have won more of the events.

The star of the thirty-eighth ISU Matches was Sgt. Gary L. Anderson, USA, who won both the Smallbore Rifle and 300-meter Free-Rifle Aggregate World Championships. He also won gold medals in both the Smallbore Rifle Standing Match and the 300-meter Free-Rifle Prone Match and set three new world records.

The American Skeet Team also set a new world's record. In all, the American shooting squad won five firsts, two seconds, and eight thirds in individual events and two firsts, eight seconds, and one third in team competitions. American women shooters, in their first attempt

Mr. Harold W. Glassen, NRA vice-president (1965-1967).

at international shooting, won three seconds and one third.

The Fourth Pan-American Games in São Paulo, Brazil, on April 20 to May 5, 1963, saw even more improvement in the American performance. There a twenty-four-man American shooting squad won all seven team events and all individual events except one. In so doing it established six new Pan-American shooting records and exceeded the world's record in two events. One of the world's records beaten was in the Free-Rifle Team Match.

To encourage this improvement still further, the National Rifle Association in June, 1964, announced a new competitive program for international skeet and a modified form of international clay pigeon shooting. NRA shotgun qualification ratings and awards over these international courses of fire were established and were later adopted also by the National Skeet Shooters Association. NRA also set up instruction programs, complete with manuals, film strips, the registration of training courses, and the certification of instructors. It established a proficiency classification system for shooters in both categories. In 1964 it was operating sanctioned

Lt. Gary L. Anderson, a consistent winner for the United States in international competition.

tournaments over international skeet and clay pigeon courses and an NRA Modified International Clay Pigeon Course.

The pay-off for all of this effort came in the Eighteenth Olympiad in Tokyo, Japan, on October 15-20, 1964. American riflemen dominated the three rifle events. Anderson won a gold medal and Martin L. Gunnarson a bronze in the 300-meter Free-Rifle Match; Lones W. Wigger, Jr., won a silver medal and Tommy G. Pool a bronze in the Smallbore Rifle Prone Match; and then Wigger picked up the second American gold medal in the three-position Smallbore Rifle Match. In the Clay Pigeon Match, William C. Morris III placed third and won the first Olympic medal taken by an American trap-shooter since 1920.

Seven of the eighteen shooting medals offered at Tokyo went to Americans, while the Russians won only two.

America was now back on top of the shooting world. On July 2-18, 1965, a U. S. Army rifle and pistol team from Fort Benning, whose members included Wigger, Anderson, Gunnarson, Pool, and Foster, shot in two invitational shoulder-to-shoulder International Matches at Emmen/Lucerne, Switzerland, and at Wiesbaden, Germany. These matches produced the most spectacular scores ever recorded. The best shooters from Switzerland, Austria, France, West Germany, Roumania, and the Soviet Union were on the field and competition was keen. World's records fell like duckpins. Eighteen of the winning team and individual scores tied or broke the world's records. Of these, thirteen were made by Americans.

No history of the National Rifle Association could be complete if it did not include a review of the problems its members have faced, and continue to face, through firearms legislation. Before summarizing the wide range of current NRA services and outlining the modern mission of the Association, an analysis of firearms legislation is now in order.

Shooters of the USA went often to the winner's steps following their victories at the Tokyo Olympics.

# 25

# Firearms Legislation

# A Review of Pertinent Facts

# NRA Policy

**A** better understanding of the entire subject of firearms legislation may be had if we review briefly steps already taken or contemplated in this field.

Until 1911 there were few other restrictions on the gunowner than a rather general prohibition against carrying concealed firearms. The right of the citizen to carry firearms openly or to keep them in his home or place of business without restriction was accepted almost universally by state law, and the federal government found no reason to enter the regulatory picture.

This traditional pattern changed on May 25, 1911, when Timothy D. Sullivan rammed through the New York State Legislature "An Act to Amend the Penal Laws in Relation to the Sale and Carrying of Dangerous Weapons." Introduced on January 5, 1911, the Sullivan Act had been passed and signed into law by the governor before those interested in keeping firearms could marshal opposition against it. The law was the parting gesture of a machine politician in the final plunge of his decline from power. Only months after he introduced the bill, and hounded by charges of corruption, Sullivan was committed to an institution for the insane. He was killed by a railroad train on September 1, 1913, after escaping from custody.

The radical feature of the Sullivan Act was its provision for a police or court-issued license to possess a firearm. Under the theory that the way to eliminate crime was to remove the instruments used by criminals, the police of New York City made it almost impossible for anyone to own or to purchase a handgun, regardless of his or her need. As the opponents of the law predicted, crime rates in New York continued to rise as rapidly as before and more rapidly than in many jurisdictions where no restrictions prevailed. The supporters of the Sullivan Act responded by tacking on new amendments, all designed to make the law even more restrictive than before. Those who wanted to acquire a pistol for illegal purposes, of course, paid no attention at all to the Sullivan law and purchased their weapons through "fences" or brought them in from outside. But those who wished to defend themselves against robbers, rapists, or prowlers were told that they should leave police matters to the police and were denied permits! Any law which, like the Sullivan Act, depends on the cooperation of the criminal has no chance of being effective.

The Sullivan Act led to dozens of injustices by overzealous police and prosecuting attorneys. In several instances men went to jail for holding robbers at bay with unregistered pistols while their would-be attackers were released under technicalities. In one classic case, a young woman who found a handgun on the seat of a street car and thought it her civic duty to carry it to the nearest police station, was promptly clapped into jail for carrying a concealed weapon! It was such injustices and efforts to extend the provisions of the Sullivan Act to other states that hardened opinion in the NRA against unwarranted and unjust firearms restrictions. These injustices continue in New York and the recent cases of two women who defended themselves from attackers with weapons—and were promptly arrested—led a western newspaper to publish a very critical editorial headed "When Self-Defense Is Made a Crime."

Under the conditions that prevailed in the 1920s and early 1930s, however, tighter regulation of the sale and use of firearms soon became inevitable. Before World War I, crime had been largely a state or local matter, except in cases of robberies of the mails or other felonies involving interference with interstate commerce. Prohibition had spawned an entirely new breed of criminal—highly mobile, backed by a staff of well-organized specialists. Such were the empires of Al Capone and "Dutch" Schultz. The automobile had bred another—the free-wheeling desperadoes like John Dillinger, the Barkers, and "Pretty Boy" Floyd—who specialized in hit-and-run bank holdups that were often accompanied by violence. The operations of these bandits were so flagrant that many states organized vigilante groups to help capture bank robbers. The Iowa Bankers Association and the Illinois Bankers Association both established vigilante groups of armed citizens in 1925. Los Angeles, in a similar effort, placed police-trained citizens under arms with special permits allowing them to carry concealed pistols. This approach, diametrically opposite to that taken in New York City, brought an immediate drop in the rate of violent crimes and robberies.

Although most of the pressure during the 1920s was for stricter control of firearms by the states, there was growing agitation for some form of federal regulation. This led in 1927 to the enactment of the federal law prohibiting the shipment of pistols through the mails except to officers of the law or to military personnel. President Calvin Coolidge actively discouraged the enactment of more rigid firearms restrictions on the grounds that he doubted their value in disarming the criminal.

After three years of study by an eminent committee, under which Karl T. Frederick served as a special consultant, the Commissioners on Uniform State Laws in 1926 adopted the Uniform Firearms Act. The Commissioner of Police of New York City, however, immediately wrote a strong letter of dissent to the Executive Committee of the Conference of Commissioners on Uniform Laws, charging that the proposed law would hamper law enforcement and open the doors to unrestricted traffic in firearms by criminals. The Commissioners sent the proposed law back to the subcommittee for further study. Both the subcommittee and the Commissioners as a body found the charges laid against the model law to be entirely false. In August, 1930, the Conference approved the model act for the second time.

The Uniform Firearms Act had a significant influence on the thinking of lawmakers wrestling with firearms legislation during the next decade. Before, the only model had been New

York's Sullivan Act; the Uniform Firearms Act, although some of its features were ill-conceived, provided an alternative. During the 1930s it was adopted in part or in full by some states, and it formed the basis of the law adopted by Congress for the District of Columbia.

In 1927, Karl T. Frederick was elected to the Board of Directors of the National Rifle Association; he became a member of the Executive Committee in 1928. He and Maj. Gen. Milton A. Reckord formed a formidable team in defense of the rights of the lawful gunowner from that time until Frederick's death on February 11, 1963.

A major assault on the rights of the law-abiding citizen to bear arms for the defense of his home and family began with the 1930s. Much of it stemmed from an organization calling itself the National Council for the Prevention of War. Although its goals were laudable, this organization labored under the delusion that war and the causes of war could be eliminated if weapons of warfare could be elimi-

nated. It had developed in 1922 out of the ashes of World War I and had emerged full-blown in the uneasy climate of the late 1920s. With a budget that in spite of the Depression increased from $150,000 in 1929 to $200,000 in 1930, it threw its full resources behind the anti-firearms fight. While most of the existing laws sought to restrict the use of firearms, the bills proposed by the National Council for the Prevention of War sought to abolish firearms along with all other instruments of war. Its monument, and that of counterpart pacifist groups in other countries, was the series of disarmament conferences of the 1920s and early 1930s which permitted the unchecked rise of Fascism, Nazism, and Japanese imperialism, and led directly to World War II. During this period the National Council picked up some important allies in state legislatures and in Congress, and much of the energies of the National Rifle Association were devoted to keeping track of new firearms bills and reporting them through *The American Rifleman* to its membership.

As the number of firearms proposals, good and bad, increased, usual channels of communication became too slow. Lags between the introduction of a bill and its publication in the NRA magazine often prevented the Association from alerting its members in time for them to take effective action. As a result, in 1934, the NRA launched its Legislative Division, under the direction of C. B. Lister. As soon as action was needed, the affected members were notified at once by mail and advised of the provisions of the proposed bills. The NRA did not then, nor has it since, employed anyone to lobby for or against legislation. It merely has provided the facts and an appraisal of the bill in question and left further action up to the discretion of individual members.

In the opening days of the Seventy-third Congress there were seven bills dealing with firearms in the House and five in the Senate.

ONE WAY TO WEAKEN AMERICA

Tom Ellinwood in the *Arizona Daily Star*.

Maj. Gen. Milton A. Reckord, left, winner of many decorations from his government for meritorious service, and eminent New York attorney Karl T. Frederick, former NRA president, discuss some of the reasons they have firmly opposed ill-conceived laws that would encroach on the constitutional right to possess arms for lawful purposes. Both men were elected Honorary Life Members of the NRA.

The House Ways and Means Committee devoted a full executive session to the discussion of firearms control. The result of these efforts was the enactment on June 26, 1934, of the National Firearms Act.

The original version of this act, favored by Attorney General Homer S. Cummings, imposed unduly severe conditions on all firearms, a move that was vigorously opposed by members of the National Rifle Association. General Reckord, Karl Frederick, and others of the NRA were engaged during this period in an almost endless round of hearings before various Congressional committees. They were supported by testimony from Charles V. Imlay of the Conference of Commissioners on Uniform State Laws; by Col. John Thomas Taylor, legislative representative of the American Legion; and by Seth Gordon, secretary of the American Game Association, representing the hunting sportsmen of America.

The drive for a highly restrictive gun law was led by an intemperate special assistant to Attorney General Cummings, who stated flatly that small arms training for civilians was of small importance and that neither the foot soldier nor the battleship would be of any value in the next war. The outcome of the matter was that Congress adopted the recommendations of the National Rifle Association and the other respected organizations who shared similar views.

The National Firearms Act imposed taxes and registration on fully automatic weapons, sawed-off shotguns, short-barreled rifles, mufflers, and silencers, and required all dealers, importers, and pawn brokers handling this type of fire-

arm to pay an occupational tax. As amended and adopted, the National Firearms Act of 1934 was aimed squarely at the criminal and worked practically no hardship or inconvenience to the law-abiding gun-owning sportsman and citizen. In its final form it was supported enthusiastically by the NRA.

The National Firearms Act, however, was not regarded as adequate by Homer S. Cummings, and he began an immediate campaign to pass more restrictive anti-firearms laws. The character of this campaign was revealed in a statement by one of Cummings' assistants who made known that he intended to offer the Alco Crime Prevention Bill of California as an amendment to the National Firearms Act.

The Alco Bill, named for its author, Director of Prisons Julian H. Alco of California, proposed to outlaw the possession of any weapon "of any description and by whatever name known, which is capable of being concealed upon the person," and provided for indeterminate sentences to all violators. As such it went far beyond the Sullivan Act. Alco's proposal brought him publicity and formed the basic pattern for proposals advanced by the office of Attorney General Cummings.

The NRA met the attack head on. It carried several full-page editorials against the Alco Bill and otherwise supported the thousands of citizens who fought to defeat the bill. It also did some quiet digging into the background of the sponsors. It discovered, among many other damaging factors, that the publicity chairman of Alco's "Crime Prevention Committee" had a police record dating back five years with six arrests on various charges in four years. The NRA then published the record in full in an editorial in the November 1934 issue of *The American Rifleman.* Little was heard from Alco from that time on. His bill received its *coup de grâce* early in 1935 after the convention of the California State Peace Officers Association passed a resolution stating:

> Now therefore be it resolved that we emphatically condemn all efforts to place upon the ballot, or to secure the enactment of the so-called Alco Crime Prevention Law or any other similar drastic anti-firearm laws and denounce such legislation as impractical and un-American, and as an encouragement of, rather than as a means of preventing crimes and criminality, as a positive menace to the safety and defense of the lives and property of law-abiding citizens, and as opposed to every tradition of a hardy and red-blooded, self-reliant, and law-abiding race of Californians and Americans.

The Administration's request for a broader scope in restrictions devoted to unlawful use of firearms led to the adoption in 1938 of the Federal Firearms Act. Its major provisions were to make it a federal offense for anyone who was under indictment or who had been convicted of a felony to transport, ship, receive, or carry firearms or handgun ammunition across interstate or international borders; it made punishable the theft or possession of stolen firearms or ammunition while moving in or part of interstate or foreign commerce; and made it illegal to receive, possess, or dispose of any firearm from which the serial number had been obliterated, removed, or altered.

In keeping with its policy, the NRA supported the enactment of the Federal Firearms Act as vigorously as it had opposed such re-

strictive legislation as the Sullivan Act and the Alco Crime Prevention Bill. The result was sound legislation that worked no hardship on the law-abiding gunowner while providing heavy penalties for the criminal misuse of weapons.

Homer S. Cummings, with apparently little support from President Roosevelt in the White House, still was not satisfied and did all within his power to impose a firearms registration bill; his National Firearms Registration Bill never came to a vote in the Congress.

If President Franklin D. Roosevelt held any ill feelings toward the NRA for its stand against his Attorney General, they did not show in the following letter sent to General Reckord for reading before the annual banquet on February 4, 1938, at the height of the controversy:

> On the occasion of the Annual Dinner of the National Rifle Association, I will be very happy if you will convey my greetings and best wishes for a long life of service for your successful organization.
>
> From a small beginning your Association has grown to large proportions. You are doing what I believe to be a meritorious work, contributing your efforts to carrying on the successful promotion, among the citizens of the Nation, of rifle marksmanship—an accomplishment in which our forefathers so effectively excelled. The growth of your Association is thoroughly consistent with the soundness of the purpose for which it was organized.
>
> Both national and international rifle competitions which you encourage, have served to inject the idea of sport into rifle shooting. I sincerely hope that it may always be kept on this basis, which, while encouraging a free spirit of rivalry also makes an essential contribution to the national defense.

Following passage of the National Firearms Act and the Federal Firearms Act, and reflecting somewhat the increasing effectiveness of the Federal Bureau of Investigation, approximately two decades passed without serious

agitation for further firearms controls, but in 1957 there cropped up a serious weakness in the language of the Federal Firearms Act. Here appeared the innocent-looking sentence, "The Secretary of the Treasury may prescribe such rules and regulations as he deems necessary to carry out the provisions of this chapter [Act]."

This implementation was assumed by the Congress and the public to mean that prescribed rules and regulations would be limited to the intent and purposes of the Act. It was therefore a great shock to find sweeping changes in the Federal Firearms Act published in the Federal Register on May 3, 1957. The proposed changes would have amounted virtually to a federal firearms registration system. Moreover, such regulations would have been imposed by administrative action of the Secretary of the Treasury rather than by Congress. The idea apparently had been conceived by the Chief Counsel of the Senate Judiciary Committee in its investigation of juvenile delinquency. It had been advanced publicly by the Alcohol and Tobacco Tax Division of the Internal Revenue Service, the agency charged with the administration of the Federal Firearms Act. The ATTD claimed as its authority for making the changes that section of the Federal Firearms Act which gave it discretionary powers to "rule and regulate."

Members of the National Rifle Association objected to the proposed changes on the grounds that they would be totally ineffective in reducing the criminal use of firearms, and that they went far beyond the intent of Congress when it had enacted the law. In this the National Rifle Association was joined by a large number of congressmen and senators, many of whom had been instrumental in passing the original law.

Hearings on the proposed changes were held in Washington on August 27 and 29, 1957. The position of the NRA was stated by President Whittington, Frank C. Daniel, Lt. Gen. Floyd A. Parks, and Maj. Gen. Milton A. Reckord (who had helped to draft the original Act), all of whom appeared as witnesses in opposition. A large delegation of congressmen and senators, led by Congressman John D. Dingell of Michigan, strenuously objected to what they considered as usurpation of the powers of Congress, as well as features of the proposals themselves.

As a result of these objections, new regulations, when they were published by the Department of the Treasury on January 18, 1958, contained none of the provisions opposed by members of Congress and the National Rifle Association.

Just as members of Congress and the public had mistakenly placed faith in undeviating, just administration of the Federal Firearms Act, some fair-minded congressmen and others have not detected very dangerous pitfalls in some features of the so-called "Dodd Bills." It is appropriate that NRA President Harlon B. Carter and his predecessors in office have led the fight to keep this firearms legislation free of false concepts.

Loopholes that grant broad discretionary powers to a bureaucratic agency and permit such an arbitrary issuance of regulations as those the ATTD attempted to impose in 1957 have not been forgotten, and their presence in later efforts to frame new firearms laws has been one of the stumbling blocks to reasonable and effective legislation.

The course of the various proposed federal firearms bills since 1963 is difficult to explain but can be easily told. Of the many proposals, the "Dodd Bills" have received the greatest public fanfare. Beginning in 1961, NRA staff members met with the Senate Subcommittee on Juvenile Delinquency chairmanned by Senator Dodd to discuss various legislative drafts concerning firearms.

Within the law-making chambers of our National Capitol matters affecting every person in our fifty states are studied. The seriousness of firearms legislation, its far-reaching effects on the nation, and the constitutional guarantees which relate to it have demanded a close scrutiny of all newly proposed laws. The gun has been the whipping boy for much malicious muckraking and statistical distortion. Knowing this, the majority of our lawmakers have refused to impose gun control laws which are unduly harassing to the law-abiding or based on improper motivation.

Following these conferences, a bill to amend the Federal Firearms Act, known as S-1975, was introduced on August 2, 1963. The NRA supported the features of this proposed law, which had as a primary purpose preventing delivery of handguns to unsupervised juveniles, criminals, narcotics addicts, and adjudicated alcoholics, and prohibited interstate shipment in violation of state or local laws.

In the emotion-charged atmosphere following the death of President Kennedy and the shooting of his assassin, many previously fair-minded and clear-thinking persons lashed out in anti-firearms campaigns as unreasoning as they were intemperate. An immediate object of attack was S-1975 which was amended so that, among other objectionable features, it required what was practically police permission for any law-abiding American citizen to buy a gun that would be purchased outside his own state.

More than three months before the shocking tragedy in Dallas, the NRA had stated its concern about mail-order guns. Noting that a few unscrupulous merchants were creating a situation in need of prompt correction, an editorial in *The American Rifleman* flatly stated, "Steps must be taken to stop the traffic of mail-order guns into unauthorized hands."

At the same time, there was a reminder that in moving against the misuse of firearms due caution should be exercised so that law-abiding citizens would not be severely penalized or deprived of their individual rights.

The principal proponents of the harsh amendments to S-1975 in the Eighty-eighth Congress and subsequent Senate Bills S-14 and S-1592 in the Eighty-ninth Congress chose to ignore such sound advice as that of Senator Magnuson of Washington, who stated, "The solution must not be one conceived in hysteria, born of ignorance, intended to foster complacency and destined to futility. . . . It must to the extent practical prevent the possession and use of arms by the irresponsible but in so doing should not unduly inconvenience or burden the responsible. . . . Any legislation, State or Federal, must consider the constitutional right of our citizens to bear arms. Responsible citizens have the right to possess firearms for purposes of self-protection, security of the nation, hunting, and recognized sporting activities."

Those who have been in the forefront in scoffing at the Second Amendment and have devoted their energies to reckless attacks on the citizens' right to possess arms also have chosen to ignore these significant words of the late President Kennedy: "By calling attention to . . . the right of each citizen to keep and bear arms, our founding fathers recognized the essentially civilian nature of our economy. . . . For that reason I believe the Second Amendment will always be important." If the Second Amendment can be cast aside for the feeble reasons given by the proponents of excessive firearms legislation, how long can other constitutional guarantees we presently enjoy endure?

So it has been that, by repeated excessively harsh proposals, the proponents of firearms legislation have aroused widespread opposition to their unpredictable course.

During this period of legislative deliberations

the American public has been fed a steady diet of sensational publicity by anti-firearms proponents whose pursuit of a theme or a theory has been so inflexible and vitriolic as to confirm that their primary objective is to influence rather than inform. For the most part, efforts have been directed to making the gun, not the user, the villain in the act and to picture a dark side to our firearms history. From these sources you will seldom find mention that guns were the tools with which this nation forged her freedom and with which this freedom has been successfully preserved through succeeding wars. Nor will you learn that firearms are a companion to millions of law-abiding citizens in very healthful recreation. And most certainly you will not be given the easily available statistics that firearms have been a far greater force in keeping the law than in breaking it.

The principal argument used for passage of restrictive firearms legislation is that if guns were removed from the hands of our citizens the war on crime would be more easily won. What are the facts? In the year 1964, for instance, 2,500,000 serious crimes were committed in the United States, and less than 4 per cent involved the use of firearms. Of 184,900 aggravated assaults, only 15 per cent involved the use of firearms. There were more murderers per capita in the period just before the fall of Rome than at any other period in the history of the world, and it is interesting to note that no firearms were available for their gory commission.

The NRA firmly rejects the premise that firearms are a major factor in a rise in crime. Is it the inanimate tool that is responsible for crime or is it persons with distorted, twisted minds? Consider the deaths of the fifty-seven police officers killed in a recent year. We can even look back further than that, and we find that three-fourths of the murderers of police officers for the past five years have had prior records of arrest; one half had prior records of grave assault-type crimes; one-third were on parole or probation when they committed the murder! J. Edgar Hoover, Director of the Federal Bureau of Investigation, recently stated: "Of the fourteen Special Agents killed in gun battles, twelve were slain by criminals who had been previously selected for parole or other types of leniency."

The police strength throughout our country is less than two police employees per 1000 people. Such a figure is possible only because 99 per cent of our people are law-abiding. After a recent Supreme Court decision favoring criminals, the police chief of one of our large cities commented: "If our hands are tied further, citizens will have greater need than ever for armed self-protection."

Certainly law-abiding, God-fearing men and women have a right to protect their loved ones, their homes, and their places of business against the criminal element of our society. And it is this criminal element at which our legislative guns should be aimed, not a scatter-gun shot at every citizen. Self-protection is one of the basic laws of nature. A law-abiding man with a gun is not to be feared by society or by the government. If the government fears the people, then it follows that the people will begin to fear their government.

For a number of years the National Rifle Association has had a deep concern with crime, and has supported many measures to prevent and punish the criminal misuse of firearms. Law and order is one of the major objectives of the NRA, clearly stated in its Bylaws.

In 1965 a major contribution was made toward the common goal of reducing crime by sponsoring an independent Law and Order Committee. While this twenty-man committee has as its chairman a former NRA president, Superior Court Judge Hilliard Comstock of California, and includes several other NRA members, it is composed primarily of unaffiliated, eminent leaders in the fields of law, penology, sociology, the communications media, the military, and other vital segments of our society. This brings to the committee unbiased perspective and great experience in the area of our number one social problem—the maintenance of law and order.

These women are not afraid of guns; they are among the more than a million law-abiding members of their sex who enjoy recreational shooting and for whom a gun in the home provides an extra sense of security.

Barbara Hile

The mission of the committee is broad in scope. Its studies will contemplate the use of firearms in crime; the laws designed to cope with violence; and the history, present character, and varying conditions of violence. In all of this there will be properly fitted the concept of private ownership of firearms. Of special importance will be the committee's recommendations as to how the NRA may make further contributions in support of law and order.

These forward steps demonstrate to the people of the nation that the NRA is proceeding toward proper objectives in a serious and dedicated fashion befitting citizens of good repute.

Guns are not just a part of the man's world. There are approximately a million women who hold hunting licenses; many more enjoy target shooting. There are the interested mothers, wives, and sisters of over twenty million hunters, target shooters, and collectors of antique weapons. Women in the lives of our service men are deeply concerned. A gun in one's home to repel an intruder often gives a sense of security nothing else can provide. We all have a right— even a duty—to look closely at all sides of a matter so vital to us personally and as a nation.

Gertrude Schlernitzauer

The subject of firearms ownership and control involves too many serious factors to sweep it lightly under the rug of ignorance or bias. Everyone is certainly entitled to his own opinions, but nobody has a right to be wrong in his facts and to employ a careless pen or a slanted program in promoting them.

Mindful of the fact that there is room for honest differences of opinion in most problems (as evidenced by 5-to-4 split decisions on important principles in our Supreme Court), the sincerity of opposing views must be accepted if we are to be objective. Everyone knows that the millions of fine citizens who own guns are not a lunatic fringe or trigger-happy morons as suggested by a few writers inclined to muckraking and sensational journalism. And likewise everyone knows that, although disarming the American

Inez Sargent

Pauline Tubb

Gail Liberty

Marianne Jensen

citizen is a primary goal spelled out in the captured Communist document "Rules for Bringing About a Revolution," proponents of restrictive firearms policies are not necessarily communists, pacifists, professional do-gooders, or publicity-seekers.

To get at the truth of some reckless indictments of guns, take a searching look at the statement, "We impose virtually no controls whatever on firearms," which opened a lead story by a former New York Congressman in one of our prominent magazines. For a more informed view, Congressman Cecil R. King of California has observed, "Certainly, the average person on the street has little or no knowledge of the laws that are now in existence with respect to firearms, either at the State or Federal level." This was apparently true of the former New York Congressman who authored the ridiculous statement that there are virtually no firearms controls. In New York State, and especially in New York City where he resides, there are so many restrictive laws regarding the purchase, ownership, and transportation of firearms that it takes a Philadelphia lawyer to figure them out.

In addition to the many state and local laws, the National Firearms Act of 1934, the Federal Firearms Act of 1938, postal laws and regulations, and the Federal Aviation Act of 1958 impose strict controls on fully automatic weapons, sawed-off guns, the movement in interstate or foreign commerce of firearms of all types and handgun ammunition, regulate the transportation of weapons on certain carriers, and provide other far-reaching controls as well as severe penalties for violations.

Actually, we have a very imposing and effective array of firearms laws, a demonstrable fact that must be recognized in any fair appraisal. But this does not mean that our laws are perfect, and new proposals which are sensibly designed to cope with crime should be accorded open-minded consideration. The negative position we are sometimes obliged to take is forced on us by unwarranted, unwise, or discriminatory proposals.

What are the goals? Presumably the proponents of more restrictive firearms legislation seek to reduce our national rates of criminal activity, accidental death, and suicide. It is a little like being against sin; everyone favors the

299

objectives. The big rub comes in the opposing and sometimes irreconcilable views on how the desired goals can be attained. The major debate centers not so much on whether law-abiding citizens may be arbitrarily deprived of their arms, but how far ambitious lawmakers may go in control. The imposition of laws which are excessively restrictive is considered a back-door approach to depriving a citizen of his constitutional rights.

It was George Bernard Shaw who said that our conduct often is influenced not by our experience but by our expectations. Before entering on any adventures in reform it is useful to learn as much as possible about the problem and previous experiences with it. England's experience with excessively restrictive firearms laws may illustrate a point—crimes of violence are up 500 per cent since World War II. Another voice of experience is that of Police Chief Robert V. Murray, of Washington, D. C., who has stated, "It may be argued that any legislation that would reduce the number of pistols in circulation would substantially reduce the number of aggravated assaults. This argument rests on two mistaken premises. First, it assumes that restrictive legislation will prevent criminals from obtaining guns. The fact is that experience has shown that legislation such as the New York Sullivan Law does not reduce the number of pistols in the hands of criminals. Second, the argument assumes that handguns are used in most aggravated assaults, whereas the fact is that pistols are used in only a small percentage of such assaults."

Contrary to statements that the murder rate has gone up alarmingly, the record as provided by the FBI shows that the rate has dropped nearly 40 per cent during the past thirty years. In a recent year, more people were killed by a chance blow from a falling object than by felonious assault involving firearms.

Suicide accounts for the highest number of deaths by firearms, and it is reasonable to as-

sume that a person bent on this course would use other methods if no firearm were available—methods perhaps more gruesome.

Accidents involving firearms are also on the downswing on the record chart. The NRA Hunter Safety and Home Safety programs as well as other NRA training courses share importantly in credit for this improved situation. To keep things in perspective it may be noted that as many people meet accidental death by choking over their food at the dinner table, die by accidental poisoning, or meet their death through involvement with machinery as die in firearms accidents. Over twice as many die from drowning; three times as many die from burns, nine times as many die from falls; and twenty times as many meet accidental death through the most lethal of all, the automobile.

The statistics do not justify the loud outcry for more firearms laws that anti-gun forces have made. History deals with facts, not presumptions. Favorable statistics, however, have not blinded the National Rifle Association to its responsibilities in seeking even better records, nor has the NRA failed to give careful and open-minded study to any reasonable firearms laws projected for the common good. Passing a law does not always bring assurance of improved conditions. The law must be just and it must be so framed as to put its weight on the specific area where improvement is needed. In the case of firearms, this area is *criminal misuse*.

The National Rifle Association has a forthright and uncomplicated policy concerning firearms control legislation. Plainly stated in 1958 and equally applicable today, this policy is as follows:

1. The NRA is opposed to control measures which levy discriminatory or punitive taxes or fees on the purchase, ownership, or use of rifles, shotguns, pistols, and revolvers.

2. The NRA is opposed to proposals to license the possession or purchase of a rifle, shotgun,

300

pistol, or revolver. The inevitable result of such licensing regulation is to vest the arbitrary power to say who may and who may not own a gun in the hands of an appointed or elected official. It is the *illegal use* and not the ownership of a firearm which should be the subject of legislative control.

3. The NRA is opposed to the theory that a target shooter, hunter, or collector, in order to transport a handgun for lawful purposes, should be required to meet the conditions for a permit to carry a weapon concealed on his person.

4. The NRA is opposed to the registration on any level of government of the ownership of rifles, shotguns, pistols, or revolvers for any purpose whatever. Regardless of professed intent, there can be only one outcome of registration, and that is to make possible the seizure of such weapons by political authorities, or by persons seeking to overthrow the government by force. Registration will not keep guns out of the hands of undesirable persons, and few people seriously claim that it will.

5. The NRA is opposed to legislation which denies, or interferes with, individual rights of our citizens or is designed purely for the convenience of law enforcement officers or for the purpose of circumventing due process of law in order to obtain convictions more easily. The desire to see our laws adequately enforced is not justification for any law which can make a prudent, law-abiding citizen an unwitting violator, or which denies the right of self-defense.

When firearms legislation is enacted, it should never exceed any of the following provisions:

1. Legislation designed to prohibit the possession of firearms by persons who have been finally convicted of a crime of violence, fugitives from justice, mental incompetents, drug addicts, and persons while adjudicated an habitual drunkard.

2. Legislation providing severe additional penalties for the use of a dangerous weapon in the commission of a crime.

3. Legislation making the sale of firearms to juveniles subject to parental consent and the use of firearms in public by juveniles subject to adequate supervision.

4. Legislation regulating the carrying of concealed handguns should be reasonable and the requirements for such carrying should be clearly set forth in the law. The conditions having been met, the issuance of a "license to carry" should be mandatory and should license the act of carrying, not the handgun itself.

John M. Schooley, for many years in the U. S. Treasury Department, Manager of Safety and Excise in Denver, Colorado (by law also ex officio sheriff), and a past president of the National Rifle Association, made this public comment on the NRA policy: "There have been and perhaps always will be efforts on the part of uninformed, misguided but sincere people to disarm our citizens in the vain hope criminals will thus be denied the use of firearms in crime. It has been my experience that when these people are presented our point of view in an intelligent and factual manner, most of them quickly realize the wisdom of our firearms legislative policy."

In 1966 the National Rifle Association re-affirmed its general policy and gave positive support to the following: a legislative program that would impose mandatory prison terms for those who commit specified criminal acts while armed with a firearm; an amendment to the Federal Firearms Act making it a federal offense for a federally licensed dealer or manu-facturer to ship a firearm in interstate or foreign commerce in contravention of a state law; an amendment to the National Firearms Act to make subject to that Act the sale or transfer of certain items of military ordnance (such as bazookas, etc.).

Bills to accomplish these desirable steps have been introduced in the United States Senate and in the House of Representatives, and are wholly apart from the changing face of the controversial firearms bill S-1592, long bogged down in committee. They are believed to offer the best chance for quick enactment and effec-tiveness in curbing the *criminal misuse* of fire-arms.

It is the curbing of *criminal misuse* of fire-arms which should be the primary legislative goal. On the side of *lawful use*, our lawmakers should not overlook the national need for ex-tensive marksmanship training. It may be re-called that Chinese children are training with wooden guns, and that Chinese silhouette train-ing targets are made to resemble an American soldier. On the side of *lawful use* it should be recalled that the shooting sports contribute four billion dollars to the national economy, sup-port manufacturing capacities of vital impor-tance to this country in time of war, and pro-vide healthful recreation for millions of our citizens. On the side of *lawful use* it is well to consider these words of the National Police Officers Association: "For every criminal who uses a gun to rob and kill, we have ten times that number of armed citizens who are able to assist the police in capturing these potential killers, because they are armed." And finally on the side of *lawful use* thought should be given to the "silent guns"—those guns currently owned by 40,000,000 of our people which by their very presence constitute a strong deterrent to lawless adventures.

There are many sound reasons based on experience, not on theoretical expectations, why we should look to *people,* not to inanimate wood and metal, for the solution of our crime problems. The way is not through permitting the tentacles of legislative red tape to weaken our defenses, national and personal, or to strangle a precious American heritage.

# The NRA Today

# Its Membership, Its Services, and Its Primary Purposes

## 26

As it approaches the century mark in its history, the National Rifle Association has grown into an organization of approximately three-quarters of a million citizens of the United States. These men and women are pledged that they are not members of any organization which has, as any part of its program, the attempt to overthrow the government of the United States by force—pledged that they have never been convicted of a crime of violence—pledged that, if admitted to membership, they will fulfill the obligations of good citizens and good sportsmen clearly set forth in the Bylaws of the Association.

The NRA has no partisan political leaning. It has no religious bias. It has no racial coloration. It judges Americans according to the decent principles of good conduct and fair play. It is a non-profit, educational organization, supported by the membership fees of public-spirited citizens and clubs. It is not affiliated with any manufacturer of arms or ammunition or with any jobber or dealer who sells firearms and ammunition. It receives no appropriations from Congress. The Association cooperates with all branches of the U. S. Armed Services, federal agencies, state and municipal governments interested in teaching small arms marksmanship to the maximum number of U. S. citizens. During World War II NRA members were responsible for teaching 1,750,000 students the correct use of small arms.

In the past five or six years there has been a tremendous growth in NRA individual memberships, and hundreds of shooting, collecting, and conservation clubs have become affiliated. This spectacular growth has made possible the development of other activities that otherwise might not have been possible for many years. The Association occupied its new headquarters building on Sixteenth Street, N.W., Washington, D. C., in April, 1957. Just four years later, on April 12, 1961, a special meeting of the Board of Directors authorized the con-

struction of the remaining adjacent portion (on the corner of Sixteenth Street and Rhode Island Avenue) which the original plans had projected. The Board of Zoning Adjustments of the District of Columbia finally authorized this construction, after two years of negotiations over zoning regulations, on May 21, 1963. The NRA occupied the new addition late in 1965, thereby greatly increasing the floor space available.

The National Rifle Association today is governed by a Board of Directors consisting of seventy-five prominent citizens who are elected by the Life Members. The Board has general charge of the affairs of the Association and elects the officers and members of the Executive Committee and the Executive Council. Under the Bylaws, it is divided into three Classes of twenty-five, with the term of each Class expiring at the end of three years. Only the Board may amend the Bylaws.

The Executive Committee consists of twenty-two Directors who are authorized to exercise all powers of the Board, except to amend the Bylaws, when the Board is not in session. Twenty of the members are elected by the Board. The executive vice-president and the executive director are members ex officio of both the Executive Committee and the Board of Directors. The secretary is a member ex officio of the Board alone.

Members of the Executive Council are elected for life in recognition of outstanding contributions to the NRA; the Council is advisory to the Executive Committee and the Board of Directors. Customarily, each retiring president of the NRA has been elected to the Executive Council. At the present time, it consists of the twelve surviving past presidents and also Lt. Gen. Julian C. Smith, USMC, and Lt. Gen. Milton A. Reckord, who served so long and ably as executive vice-president.

The NRA program stems largely from the activities of Standing Committees established primarily within the Board of Directors but with some general membership participation. These committees conduct continuing studies of the rules, regulations, and programs pertaining to their respective fields. Each is charged with examining the effectiveness of the organization's activities in its field and with determining ways to promote greater public participation by members and by the public at large. Each also acts as a direct link between the general membership and the Board of Directors, since it must evaluate all suggestions pertaining to its field made by the members. In 1966 there were eight Standing Committees—High Power Rifle, Smallbore Rifle, Pistol and Revolver, Junior and College, Gun Collectors, Hunting and Conservation, Shotgun, and International Shooting. Special committees are appointed as the need may arise.

The members of the Board of Directors represent a broad spectrum of American life and professional interest—business and finance, law and law enforcement, science, the military, education, medicine, communication, conservation, and agriculture. The only common denominator is prominence in their chosen fields and a dedication to the citizen's right to possess firearms for military preparedness, self-protection, and recreation.

The Board elects the president and all other officers of the NRA for terms of one year, but the president may not succeed himself more than once. By custom, the vice-president at the end of his second term usually succeeds to the presidency, and the retiring president becomes a member of the Executive Council.

The executive vice-president is the administrative officer of the National Rifle Association. He is charged with carrying out all policies and programs adopted by the Board and with managing the overall affairs of the Association. The executive director manages the personnel, finances, and business relationships.

The executive vice-president, executive director, secretary, and treasurer stand for re-election every year, but there have been no changes in these posts since 1960. Franklin L. Orth has served as executive vice-president since October 31, 1959. Louis F. Lucas has been treasurer and executive director since these two posts were combined, and an executive of the NRA since 1948. Frank C. Daniel has been on the staff for many years and has served continuously as secretary since 1954.

The staff of the organization is divided today into four major divisions, each supervised by a director immediately responsible to the executive director.

Members of the Editorial and Technical Division test and evaluate new products used in shooting, provide technical advice to members on firearms, handloading, and gunsmithing.

Lt. Gen. Julian C. Smith, USMC, Commanding General of the brave Marine division that stormed ashore and wrested Tarawa from the Japanese in 1943. Member of the NRA Executive Council.

*The American Rifleman*, official journal of the NRA, now has an annual circulation of nearly nine million copies and is recognized as the outstanding magazine on firearms and shooting available anywhere in the world. In 1960, the annual circulation was 4,323,000 copies of a 110-page magazine. Each issue of *The American Rifleman* today contains an average of 124 pages of information for and about shooters. *NRA Tournament News*, also published by the Association, has a substantial circulation.

The Program Division organizes and supervises the competitive shooting programs sponsored by the Association, including the annual NRA Rifle and Pistol Matches at Camp Perry. It is also responsible for the complex tournament program. In 1965, the NRA conducted nearly 3000 tournaments involving high-power and smallbore rifle, pistol, shotgun, and Running Deer, as opposed to 1771 tournaments in 1959. Nearly 150,000 shooters ranging from schoolchildren to police officers and contenders for international shooting honors participated in these tournaments in 1965. The Program Division supervises the marksmanship qualification

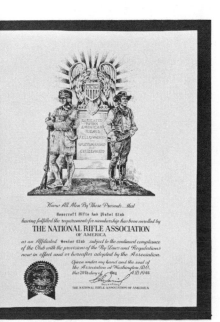

Hundreds of associations of target shooters, hunters, collectors, and others are affiliated in the growing family of the National Rifle Association and are bound by its strict conditions of good citizenship.

Louis F. Lucas, executive director and treasurer, long a very important figure in NRA administrative operations.

Frank C. Daniel, secretary, and able director of a section devoted to legislation, public affairs, hunting, conservation.

program and serves as custodian of the classification records of pistol and rifle target shooters. All tournament shooters are classified in accordance with their demonstrated skill in match shooting. Recording all scores and maintaining the averages for these thousands of shooters is done by the Program Division. This division also supervises all marksmanship training and safety education activities, including the important hunter safety and home safety programs.

The Membership Division handles all promotional work involving the recruitment of new members and the renewal of current memberships and maintains the records of all members. It is the instrument through which the NRA cooperates with the Director of Civilian Marksmanship in determining eligibility for sales of government rifles and other shooting equipment or supplies.

The Business Division handles all sales, purchases, accounting, and shipping and is responsible for maintaining the headquarters building.

In addition to the four major divisions, there is a section devoted to legislation, public affairs, and hunting and game conservation under the

direction of NRA Secretary Frank C. Daniel. Constant vigilance is maintained over legislative proposals affecting guns and shooting and reports are promptly sent to the members affected. This section supervises the NRA Hunter Information Programs and the Hunting Recognition Awards Program. It also compiles the statistics for the Uniform Hunter Casualty Reports.

Since 1948 all the major annual business activity of the NRA has been conducted at a series of meetings held in conjunction with a public exhibit of firearms and shooting equipment. The two exceptions were in 1950, when the outbreak of the Korean War forced their cancellation, and in 1953, when no exhibit was held. Under the present pattern, the Association meets in Washington, D. C., in alternate years and in a city in some other part of the country in every other year.

This gives members across the nation who might otherwise have no direct contact with the officers and staff of the NRA an opportunity to take a personal part in the affairs. Attendance at the annual meetings has increased nearly every year. The largest was the ninety-third

Annual Meetings and Exhibit on April 4-8, 1964, at the Ambassador Hotel in Los Angeles. The official registered attendance was 11,505 members; more than 20,000 members and non-members visited the Exhibit Hall. In 1965, the Washington meetings attracted a total of 16,420 people, the second largest number recorded.

The principal purposes of the annual meetings are to conduct the annual business of the Board of Directors and the current business of the various committees, to inform the members of the activities of the officers and staff during the previous year, and to provide a forum in which the members may express their opinions on what the Association should do in the coming year.

When the NRA was founded in 1871, it had only one major purpose—to develop rifle marksmanship in the National Guard. Its early matches demonstrated the full capabilities of even the relatively crude rifles of the time in the hands of men trained in their use. The poor performance of Regular Army men against the Creedmoor-trained National Guardsmen forced the Army, Navy, and Marine Corps, who until then had no marksmanship training of their own, to adopt training methods and standards developed by the National Rifle Association. Service standards of qualification still follow the NRA pattern.

Ties between the NRA and the Federal Services have been close ever since the turn of the century. In 1903, acting upon the urging of Secretary of War Elihu Root, who was personally convinced of the value of marksmanship training, Congress created the National Board for the Promotion of Rifle Practice. Officers of the National Rifle Association have traditionally served on the Board ever since it was established. When, in 1916, Congress established the post of Director of Civilian Marksmanship it specifically named the National Rifle Association of America as the liaison between the Regular Army and the civilian reserve since no other organization existed to carry out this function.

One of the most important aspects of the NRA program in the realm of national defense has been in training men to carry skill with arms into the Armed Services whenever the need arises. The high school cadet program

William B. Binswanger, Director of the Business Division.

John H. Fauntleroy, Director of the Membership Division.

Exhibits of latest firearms models and accessories along with displays of historic arms such as those shown here have become a feature of the NRA annual meetings.

grew out of a marksmanship program in the public schools of New York City started by Gen. George W. Wingate, one of the founders of the NRA. Since that time the NRA has been publicly recognized and praised for its activities in training young men for possible military service by nearly every President of the United States and by nearly all of its highest-ranking military and naval leaders. This activity, too, has been endorsed and broadened by act of Congress.

On April 15, 1918, Gen. Peyton C. March, Chief of Staff, United States Army, signed orders authorizing the establishment of the Small Arms Firing School at Camp Perry, Ohio, and opened the training to civilians as well as military personnel. In October, 1918, Congress, inspired by the Camp Perry model, created the Infantry School of Arms at Fort Benning, Georgia.

Since that time, the Small Arms Firing School, with courses conducted by experts from the Fort Benning Infantry School of Arms, has been an integral part of the National Matches. It is open to any individual sixteen years of age or older without charge. Rifles, pistols, and ammunition are issued to each student.

Although there are recreational aspects for the civilian participants in the Small Arms Firing School at Camp Perry, the military aspects are paramount. American military strength, decisive in every war in which America has been involved since colonial times, has been based on a civilian reserve rather than on a large standing army. In spite of the awesome weapons at the command of the military today, "old-fashioned" skill with the rifle remains as important today as it was in 1815 at New Orleans or in 1918 at Château-Thierry. At the annual banquet of the National Rifle Association on March 25, 1960, Gen. Lyman L. Lemnitzer, U. S. Army Chief of Staff, stated:

> To prepare ourselves for the variety of wars in which we might engage, we are obliged to maintain a corresponding variety of capabilities in our Nation's military establishment. Each element of this establishment has a vital role to play. We have the capability provided by our nuclear strike forces, which stand ready to deliver retaliatory blows against strategic enemy targets. We have the capability provided by our forces already deployed overseas. . . . We have the capability provided by our Air Force, Navy and Army strategic reserves. . . . In any type of military operations, one thing which has not changed is the importance of the soldier's mastery of his individual weapon—fundamentally the rifle. In fact this importance has increased. . . . I have pointed out that dispersion of units will permit infiltration. Consequently, not only infantrymen but cannoneers, cooks, and clerks must be ready and able to defend themselves from sudden enemy raids. . . . As for the infantryman, himself, the rifle is still his basic weapon.

On the eve of America's expanded involvement in the Vietnam hostilities, these words were prophetic. Relatively recent speakers at the NRA annual banquets have included Gen. David M. Shoup, Commandant of the U. S. Marine Corps; the Hon. Elvis J. Stahr, Jr., Secretary of the Army; the Hon. Fred Korth, Secretary of the Navy; the Hon. Stephen Ailes, Secretary of the Army; Admiral David M. McDonald, Chief of Naval Operations; and Gen. Harold K. Johnson, U. S. Army Chief of Staff. All have endorsed the NRA program and emphasized the importance of civilian marksmanship training in preparation for military service.

308

The NRA's program for training young men who may be subject to military service has been highly praised by military leaders and others in the highest offices of government.

This has not been confined entirely to officials responsible for infantrymen and Marines. The speaker at the banquet in 1959 was Gen. Curtis LeMay, then Vice Chief of Staff, U. S. Air Force, and America's leading exponent of air power. He, too, emphasized the importance of marksmanship training for civilians as a source of potential strength in the defense establishment in the event of war.

Each of the approximately 30,000 graduates of the Small Arms Firing School at Camp Perry since 1953, if not carrying his skill directly into the Armed Services, is capable in time of national emergency of instructing others in the use of military weapons.

Marksmanship qualification courses now available through the NRA include everything from fifteen-foot air rifle courses to the high-power rifle. Since 1926, when the NRA organized its Junior Program, nearly 7,000,000 qualification awards of all types have been issued. Nearly 500,000 qualify every year. In 1965, there were approximately 20,000 certified rifle instructors and 10,000 pistol instructors listed in the files of the NRA. This represents a tenfold increase in both categories since 1960.

In June, 1960, the Committee on Appropriations of the United States Senate stated: "It is the conviction of this committee that the increased emphasis on other phases of national defense should not be permitted to obscure the importance of the vital role that the rifleman will continue to play in future conflicts."

It directed the Department of the Army to study the entire program of the National Board for the Promotion of Rifle Practice with a view toward recognizing and emphasizing marksmanship training among qualified civilians and military personnel. The Army report, approved by the Secretary and forwarded over the signature of the Chief of Staff, included recommendations that the Services make their marksmanship training facilities available to civilians, to the maximum extent possible. It further recommended that the Armed Services train competent civilians and reserve components as instructors and that funds totalling $4 million be made available in the first year and be increased to more than $10 million by 1971.

During a recent period when a few members of Congress have been critical of guns in general, the Director of Civilian Marksmanship in particular, and the National Rifle Association's services in connection with the DCM, rumors were spread that guns and ammunition made available by the U. S. government were being misused. There were wild and unsupported claims that extremist paramilitary organizations were equipping their "private armies" at government expense. Unsupported or not, rumors find their way into the news and sometimes a good juicy rumor heats up the news wires more than plain facts.

As a result of all this political oratory and

309

editorial drum-beating, the independent research firm of Arthur D. Little, Inc., was engaged by the Department of the Army to make a study of the activities and missions of the National Board for the Promotion of Rifle Practice and to review the Army's Civilian Marksmanship Program under the Director of Civilian Marksmanship. The Arthur D. Little Report was released in January, 1966.

This report brought a clear, factual answer to critics of the NBPRP, the DCM, and the NRA. Among its many favorable findings were these:

1. Shooting experience, and particularly marksmanship instruction, with military-type small arms prior to entry into military service contributes significantly to the training of the individual soldier.

2. The marksmanship instruction, supervised practice, safety training, and competitions (including club, interclub, state, regional, and national matches) sponsored and supported by clubs, the NRA, and the DCM are of particular value to the military.

3. The primary contributions that the Civilian Marksmanship Program makes to the military departments in developing competitors for international competitions are many.

4. Law enforcement agencies with organized shooting groups affiliated with the DCM regard the program as "quite important" in supporting their marksmanship training and in enabling their personnel to participate in organized shooting programs.

5. Many DCM-affiliated gun clubs through-

out the country provide NRA-designed "Hunter Safety Programs" to neophyte hunters in an organized effort to reduce shooting accidents among hunters.

6. We consider that the requirement that clubs enrolling with the Director of Civilian Marksmanship be affiliated with the National Rifle Association is quite appropriate. The aims and purposes of the NRA are quite similar and complementary to those of the NBPRP. The network of NRA clubs is the primary vehicle through which the DCM applies its programs and benefits in stimulating shooters and shooting activities. NRA club officers and members provide range facilities, instruction, and manpower on a volunteer basis to carry out the club programs of the DCM. The NRA magazine, *The American Rifleman*, is an excellent vehicle for communicating with individuals interested in various aspects of shooting, including the advantages of affiliating with the DCM. Therefore, it is not only appropriate but essential that the NRA and the NBPRP achieve effective liaison and work closely together. . . . It is quite appropriate that the NRA provides three members to the NBPRP. . . . The NRA is the national sports governing body recognized by the International Shooting Union and thus it has the responsibility for sanctioning all national championships and tournaments for the purpose of selecting representatives on teams for international competitions.

7. Those aspects of the DCM program which relate to the stimulation of broader interest and participation in rifle shooting among the youth of our country should be emphasized more and pursued even more effectively in order to reach a greater percentage of those young men likely to enter military service.

Graduates of the Small Arms Firing School at Camp Perry carry with them not only an educated plan of action but also the potential ability to teach others.

310

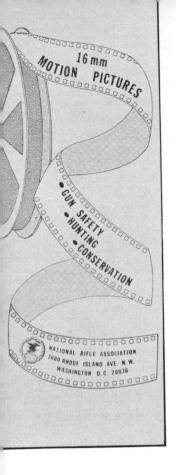

Thus the Arthur D. Little Company, one of the most highly-respected research organizations in the world, reported to our government. They were influenced by nothing but the identifiable facts, which they presented without bias or undue emphasis.

As the NRA was confident it would, this completely impartial and factual report gave strong approval and support for its programs and those of the NBPRP and was an undeniable repudiation of the rumors spread by critics.

In its approach to the problem of the misuse of firearms, the NRA has always taken a positive stand. With the full recognition that the ownership and use of firearms by private citizens will be agreeably accepted by society only so long as guns are used intelligently, the NRA launched its shooting safety program. Since this involves the saving of human life, it has been one of the most rewarding programs of many in which the Association has engaged.

The NRA Hunter Safety Program was designed to give the new hunter information to enable him to prevent accidents while afield. Thirty-seven states and three Canadian provinces now operate firearms safety training programs in cooperation with the NRA. Many make the completion of training in such courses prerequisite to the purchase of first licenses to hunt. Over 3,000,000 individuals have completed this course. Each has received training by qualified NRA instructors in safe gun handling, use, and care.

The results of this program have been rewarding. In New York, where the program began in 1949, the rate of accidents per 100,000 hunters dropped by 35 per cent in the twelve-year period after 1950 in comparison with the previous twelve years. In several states where new hunters had accounted for the majority of accidents, hunters under twenty-one caused fewer accidents as a class than older hunters after the adoption of the NRA program.

In 1963, the NRA adopted its Home Firearms Safety Course, designed primarily to teach those unskilled in the use of firearms to avoid unsafe conditions relating to keeping guns in the home. Thousands of people have completed this course.

One aspect of the NRA program to decrease the criminal use of firearms has been the training of the nation's police in the use of their sidearms. Relations between the NRA and the law enforcement agencies have been close since the 1920s. Law enforcement officers have represented a strong minority on the Board of Directors of the NRA, and several NRA officers, including presidents Schooley and Carter, have been law enforcement officers.

In 1920, the National Rifle Association initiated a survey of all cities of 25,000 or more inhabitants to determine which had training programs for their police officers. Only three replied in the affirmative. As a result of this, the NRA and the National Board for the Promotion of Rifle Practice in 1926 initiated a special Police School as a feature of the Small Arms Firing School at Camp Perry. This included "Hogan's Alley," a mock-up of a "bandit-infested" town with disappearing man-sized targets to familiarize trainees with situations of actual combat. Similar ranges are now standard accessories for training metropolitan police, FBI agents, and military police, and to train infantrymen for street warfare.

In 1930, as an extension of this idea, the NRA established a Police Section in its headquarters staff. By that time, police departments all over the nation were sending teams and selected per-

311

"Hogan's Alley" formerly at Camp Perry, where targets manipulated by an operator appear at doors or windows in a sequence unknown to the shooter, thus providing practice in fast combat-type firing.

sonnel to Camp Perry to avail themselves of the special training and to compete in the National and NRA Matches. By 1936, police officers were dominating most of the handgun events.

The special Police School was discontinued with the outbreak of World War II but reinstated in the Small Arms Firing School as a direct result of the efforts of the NRA in 1956. The NRA provides three or more instructors annually for the Police School.

In 1960, the National Rifle Association further expanded its police program by certifying NRA Police Firearms Instructors assigned to this duty by their supervisors. It devised special training and qualification courses and made available distinctive qualification badges for policemen to wear on their uniforms.

In 1962, the first National Police Pistol Championships were shot at Bloomington, Indiana, over combat-type courses, and have been held annually since that time. In 1961, the NRA tournament program was expanded to include police matches.

Today there are more than 600 police departments affiliated with the National Rifle Association of America, which has certified more than 1000 police firearms instructors. Thousands of police officers are graduates of NRA marksmanship courses. This situation is a far cry from that of 1920, when the NRA survey disclosed that the average police officer of that time was incapable of hitting a man-sized target across a narrow street.

When international shooting competition resumed at the end of World War II, the United States suffered a series of stinging reverses. These were climaxed in the thirty-seventh ISU World Championship Matches in Moscow in 1958, when, out of fourteen matches, the Soviet Union placed first in twelve team matches and took eight individual championships.

There were two major reasons for America's poor showing. One was that the Europeans shot at distances and under rules unfamiliar to American shooters. Members of American shooting teams rarely had an opportunity to practice for more than a few days under these conditions before being pitted against shooters who had often received a year or more of intensive training as teams. After World War II, the Union of Soviet Socialist Republics used the full resources of the government in an effort to demonstrate its claimed superiority of the Communist system over that of the democratic nations of the world. Its shooting teams were superbly organized and intensively trained.

One of the last official acts of Lt. Gen. Floyd L. Parks as executive director of the NRA was to suggest a comparable effort by the United States. The result of his suggestion was the establishment of the Advanced Marksmanship Unit at Fort Benning, Georgia, where American shooters could compete under conditions applying in international competition. The NRA, on its part, began to institute international-type shooting events in its own program. The success of these efforts was eloquently demonstrated in later international matches.

Basic
SHOTGUN
Instruction
INSTRUCTOR'S GUIDE
NATIONAL RIFLE ASSOCIATION          25¢

As it was originally constituted, the National Rifle Association was interested primarily in the military aspects of shooting. After the turn of the century it broadened its outlook to cover purely recreational shooting as well. Under the direction of Gen. James A. Drain it began to concern itself with informal target practice, shotgunning, hunting, and gun collecting. General Reckord and C. B. Lister expanded these horizons still further. They have been broadened even further in recent years to cover all aspects of rifle, shotgun, and pistol shooting, and allied fields.

The NRA, today, is a leading authority on all questions dealing with firearms and their use, handling, and care. Since it has no ties with any commercial manufacturer, its highly trained and superbly equipped technical staff evaluates, tests, and appraises new products with complete objectivity and impartiality. Members are assured that when they send a question to the "Dope Bag," the answer will be as accurate and as complete as possible.

Articles submitted for publication in *The American Rifleman* are judged strongly on their factual content along with good literary quality and interest value. The objective of the editors is to present a complete and well-balanced periodical that will interest and inform both the sandpit plinker and the competitive marksman, the Saturday-morning rabbit hunter and the big-game hunter, the man who wants to know the vintage of his grandfather's squirrel rifle and the collector of old-time handguns. A series of articles under the heading "A Court Case of Consequence" by Judge Bartlett Rummel, former NRA president, has been a popular feature.

Since 1960, the NRA has greatly expanded its activities in fields of less direct but great importance to the shooting public. In addition to the legal aspects of shooting and gun ownership and hunting and range safety, these fields include wildlife conservation and the development and preservation of shooting opportunities.

More than 600 police departments are affiliated with the NRA, and the training is not limited to one sex. Jeanne Bray of the Columbus, Ohio, police.

Modern scientific wildlife management, administered by the Bureau of Sport Fisheries and Wildlife and the various state fish and game agencies, has greatly increased the supply of game in general while increasing the opportunities for sportsmen to enjoy it by developing public hunting grounds and liberalizing hunting seasons where possible.

In furthering the aims of wildlife conservation and management, the NRA has worked closely since 1960 with the International Association of Game, Fish and Conservation Commissioners, the Wildlife Management Institute, the National Wildlife Federation, and the Izaak Walton League of America. To develop this cooperation still further, it created within its Legislative and Public Affairs Division a subdivision of Hunting and Game Conservation. In

William H. Jordan,
Shreveport, La.

Clement L. Theed,
Silver Springs, Fla.

Col. E. F. (Tod) Sloan,
Redwood City, Calif.

Col. John K. Lee, Jr.,
Hyattsville, Md.

Marvin D. Driver,
Allen Park, Mich.

Carefully chosen in respect to practical experience and prominence in endeavors associated with NRA programs, field representatives work closely with members and affiliated clubs in their respective districts; overall efforts are coordinated through the Executive Director.

1961, it initiated as a regular feature of *The American Rifleman* a column of "Game Management Notes," written by Daniel A. Poole, secretary of the Wildlife Management Institute.

This interest has been supplemented by efforts to improve relationships between landowners and sportsmen. To this end in 1961 the NRA developed a Code of Hunting Ethics to which members may subscribe. This code is available in handy card form for presentation to farmers or landowners when asking permission to hunt on their lands.

The Association has also sought to improve standards of sportsmanship by encouraging selective hunting of big game through its Hunting Recognition Awards Program. Originally developed for deer hunters only, this has since been expanded to cover all major North American trophy animals. Boone and Crockett Club standards are used to evaluate candidates for the Silver Bullet Awards, which are offered for outstanding big-game trophies taken by NRA members.

The rapid population growth of the United States, accompanied by urbanization and suburban development, has brought problems not only to the hunter but to the target shooter. Creedmoor, which the NRA built in 1872 in the semiwilderness of western Long Island, was long ago engulfed by the expansion of metropolitan New York City.

Within the past few years, many rural rifle ranges that formerly could accommodate high-power rifle shooting have become hemmed in with apartment buildings, shopping centers, and highways.

To meet this problem, in September, 1957, *The American Rifleman* initiated a new column called "A Place to Shoot" which describes various rifle ranges developed by member clubs or other organizations to make target shooting compatible with growing urbanization. A model indoor pistol and smallbore rifle range was incorporated in the plans for the NRA headquarters building. The NRA also developed plans for all types of range facilities.

At its annual meeting in 1963, the Board of Directors earmarked $100,000 to build a prototype outdoor safety range. In 1964, the Association purchased a tract of ninety-seven acres in Prince Georges County, Maryland, only twenty-five miles from the center of the nation's capital. On this land it is developing a forty-acre shooting area that will accommodate all types of shooting, including high-power rifle, out to 300 meters. Safety walls and baffles eliminate all danger of stray shots and reduce noise to a minimum. As America's open spaces become filled more and more with housing developments and highways, much of the target shooting of the future may be done on ranges following this model.

A few of the many medals and brassards available in the varied NRA fields of interest.

One of the many booklets on range plans and other subjects available from NRA headquarters.

From a handful of New York and New Jersey National Guard officers in 1871, the National Rifle Association of America has evolved into a dynamic organization with a membership rapidly approaching one million. From an interest focused narrowly on the improvement of military marksmanship, it has broadened its horizons to encompass all forms of shooting by law-abiding citizens, from military small-arms training to recreational hunting and target practice. It is deeply interested in the history and evolution of firearms and in many associated subjects in the field of its general mission.

No other organization has done more to train citizens in the basic skills required in time of war or more to school citizens in the safe handling of firearms for peaceful recreation. None has worked harder to improve the proficiency of law enforcement officers in the use of their personal weapons. No organization has defended more staunchly the traditional right of the American citizen to own and use firearms for the defense of his person, home, family, and country or for legitimate recreation. The position of the NRA was expressed eloquently by President Theodore Roosevelt when he declared, "The rifle is the freeman's weapon. The man who uses it well in the chase shows that he can at need use it also at war with human foes."

The primary purposes of the National Rifle Association of America are clearly spelled out in its Constitution and Bylaws. These basic purposes are:

1. To promote social welfare and public safety.

2. To promote law and order.

3. To promote the national defense.

4. To educate and train citizens of good repute in the safe and efficient handling of small arms.

5. To educate and train citizens of good repute in the techniques of design, production, and group instruction.

6. To increase the knowledge of small arms and to promote efficiency in the use of such arms on the part of members of law enforcement agencies, of the Armed Forces, and of citizens who would be subject to service in the event of war.

In order to further these purposes the Association may: conduct research programs; establish and maintain a reference library and museum for its members and the public; publish and distribute text books, manuals, rule books, and other aids to education; grant scholarships, establish training classes, develop and conduct qualification tests and competitions; encourage development of American small arms, ammunition, and accessories; provide and maintain laboratory and testing facilities; encourage the improvement and expansion of target range facilities operated by shooting clubs and by governmental units.

In its near-century of existence, the National Rifle Association of America has accomplished much in each of these fields of endeavor.

# Acknowledgments

The National Rifle Association and the editor express their
great appreciation of the valuable assistance provided by
the following individuals and organizations in assembling
the illustrative material for this book, and for other
helpful contributions:

S. M. Alvis, Howard Bettersworth, Boy Scouts of America,
California State Library, Frederick T. Chapman, The Company
of Military Historians, Tom Ellinwood, James J. Grant (More
Single Shot Rifles), Thomas E. Hall, Rear Admiral John
Harllee, Hercules Powder Company, Iowa City High School,
Frank J. Kahrs, Milton Kaplan, Library of Congress Collections,
Henry N. Marsh, J. W. Marsman, E. S. McCawley, Jr.,
National Rifle Association of Great Britain, National Smallbore
Rifle Association of Great Britain, Association of New Jersey Rifle
and Pistol Clubs, Inc., Olin-Mathieson Chemical Corp. (Win-
chester Division), Allan R. Ottley, Remington Arms Co., Inc.,
William G. Renwick, Ray L. J. Riling, Theodore Roosevelt
Association, Savage Arms Co., Frank M. Sellers, Raymond I.
Smith, Smithsonian Institution, Dr. Walter R. Stokes, Stonehenge
(The Sportsman's Gun and Rifle, Vol. II, 1884), Gerald C.
Stowe, U. S. Army (Photographic Section), West Point
Museum, and to Mrs. Frances Serven for the many hours devoted
to typing, proofreading, crosschecking, and indexing the
manuscript. Rifleman figure on jacket by Don Perceval.